302.23
42

20. JUN. 1997

⊢4 DEC 1997

5031

# POWER
# WITHOUT
# RESPONSIBILITY

# POWER
# WITHOUT
# RESPONSIBILITY

The press and
broadcasting
in Britain

**Fourth Edition**

*James Curran* and *Jean Seaton*

London

First published in 1981 by Fontana
Second edition published in 1985 by Methuen & Co. Ltd
Third edition published in 1988 by
Routledge
11 New Fetter Lane, London EC4P 4EE

Fourth edition published in 1991
Reprinted 1992, 1994, 1995

© 1991 James Curran and Jean Seaton

Printed in Great Britain by
Clays Ltd, St Ives plc

British Library Cataloguing in Publication Data

Curran, James
Power without responsibility: the press and broadcasting
in Britain. —4th. ed.
1. Great Britain. Mass media
I. Title II. Seaton, Jean
302.230941

ISBN 0–415–06450–3

To Albert and Joan Seaton,
Doodles Curran, and the
memory of Geoffrey Curran

# Contents

About the authors    viii
Preface to the fourth edition    ix
Acknowledgements    x
Introduction   *Jean Seaton*    1

**Part I Press history**   *James Curran*    5
1  Whig press history as political mythology    7
2  The struggle for a free press    11
3  The ugly face of reform    25
4  The industrialization of the press    32
5  The era of the press barons    49
6  The press under public regulation    70
7  The press in the age of conglomerates    84

**Part II Broadcasting history**   *Jean Seaton*    129
8  Reith and the denial of politics    131
9  Broadcasting and the blitz    151
10  Social revolution?    178
11  The fall of the BBC    189
12  Class, taste, and profit    203
13  How the audience is made    212
14  The information society: video, cable, and satellite    234

**Part III Theories of the media**    247
15  The sociology of the mass media   *Jean Seaton*    249
16  The liberal theory of press freedom   *James Curran*    277
17  Broadcasting and the theory of public service   *Jean Seaton*    295

**Part IV Politics of the media**    313
18  Contradictions in public policy   *Jean Seaton/James Curran*    315
19  Alternative approaches to media reform   *James Curran*    335

Bibliography    373
Index    409

# *About the authors*

James Curran is Professor of Communications at Goldsmiths' College, University of London. He has written extensively on the mass media and is the editor or joint editor of *Mass Communication and Society; The British Press: A Manifesto; Newspaper History; Culture, Society and the Media; British Cinema History; Media, Culture and Society: A Critical Reader; Bending Reality; The State of the Media;* and *Impacts and Influences: Essays on Media Power in the 20th Century.* He was an academic consultant to the Royal Commission on the Press 1974–7, a weekly columnist for *The Times,* and the founding editor of *New Socialist.*

Jean Seaton is a Senior Lecturer in Sociology at the Polytechnic of the South Bank. She has written on the history and theory of broadcasting, the role of the media during revolutions, in the reporting of atrocities, unemployment, politics, the publicity given to child abuse, and on pornography. She has been a British Academy *Thank Offering to Britain* Research Fellow. She is joint editor, with Ben Pimlott, of *The Media in British Politics,* and is editing a book on *Images of Childhood.*

# *Preface to the fourth edition*

Since the last edition was published, satellite television has been established in Britain, the government has reorganized broadcasting, and national newspapers have rolled off the presses in Fleet Street for the last time. This new edition describes and analyses these changes as well as responding to new developments in the general literature on the media.

Part I on the history of the press has been revised, with chapter 7 on the post-war press being substantially rewritten and extended. Part II on the history of broadcasting has been amended, with chapter 14 on the information society being significantly altered and expanded. Part III, Theories of the media, has been modified; and part IV, The politics of the media, has been reworked to take account of changes in government policy and the public debate about the media. This revision includes a completely rewritten chapter 19 on alternative approaches to media reform. The select bibliography at the end of the book has been pruned and brought up to date.

# Acknowledgements

Although this book is very much a joint effort there has been some division of labour. Thus Jean Seaton has concentrated on broadcasting and the sociology of the mass media (chapters 8–15 and 16), and James Curran on the history and political theory of the press (chapters 1–7, 16). However in some parts of the book it is impossible to say where the work of one author ends and that of the other begins.

We would like to thank the BBC Written Archive Centre for the help of its staff and the use of copyright material, the IBA for information on audiences, and the British Library of Economic and Political Science for permission to quote from the unpublished diary of Hgh Dalton. We are also obliged to J. Walter Thompson Ltd, Leo Burnett Ltd (incorporating the London Press Exchange), the Mirror Group, Associated Newspapers, the Thomson Organization, Express Newspapers, the *Daily Telegraph*, and the *Guardian* for access to company archives and research reports.

We are very grateful to Herminio Martins, Anthony Smith, Colin Seymour-Ure, Malory Wober, Simon Clarke, Simon Frith, Keith McLelland, Nick Hartley, Alan Lovell, and Angela Smith for making many useful comments on draft chapters. James Curran would also like to thank Andrew Goodwin for his invaluable contribution to chapter 6, as well as Angus Douglas and Garry Whannel for skilfully preparing the content analysis summarized in chapter 7, and Brendon Wall and Gill Bucknall for help in compiling Table 3. In addition, he is grateful to Ray Swingler of the Press Council for providing access to the Council's statistical analysis of newspaper circulations before it was published.

We owe a great debt to Mies Rule, Janet Sandell, and Angela Smith for typing successive drafts of this book with their usual speed, accuracy, and good humour.

Jean Seaton would like to thank Annette Zakary, Rebecca Holmes and Amanda Holmes for looking after her sons Daniel and Nathaniel with such affection and thoughtfulness while the second and third editions of this book were being prepared, and finally Claire Bush for her help with baby Seth (and football) while the fourth edition was being finished.

James Curran would like to thank his wife, Margaret Hung, for urging him to write his part of the book and for sustaining him – with her laughter, zaniness, intelligence, and good sense – in the writing of it.

Finally we are especially grateful for the great care with which Ben Pimlott read the manuscript. His detailed criticisms and suggestions immensely improved the final version of the book. We are also particularly indebted to him for giving us the title. Jean Seaton depended on his enthusiasm throughout.

# Introduction

This book is about the press, broadcasting, and politics. It argues that the influence of the media has been immense – on institutions, the conduct of affairs, and the way in which people think and act politically. It also argues that the mass media and mass politics have inspired, reflected, and shaped each other more than has commonly been realized.

The power of the press and broadcasting has often been obscured. Thus, for example, the view that the British Press is one of the great instruments of liberty, an independent fourth estate, the vital defender of public interests, is a central part of our political culture. Yet, as will be shown, this is a very modern theory which has more than an element of special pleading. The theory was produced to justify those who created the press and whose interests it largely served. This does not mean that newspapers, television, and radio have generally been instruments of crude propaganda: rather that the media are political actors in their own right.

It is equally mistaken to believe that the press and broadcasting simply reflect contemporary political forces. In the first place, some groups – stronger, richer, and with better access – are always able to secure more attention than others. Secondly, the media do have some political autonomy. Thus the radical press was relatively strong in 1860, when the labour movement was divided and defeated. Just before the First World War, on the other hand, an increasingly powerful working class had few radical newspapers to support it. In contrast, there have been other times when developments in the media have been more closely related to social moods. During the 1960s a new boldness in television seemed to be connected with a rapid change in public mores. Thus the relationship between the media and society has varied. Indeed this variety is the source of the power which the press and broadcasting may wield. If the media merely mirrored events then they would have little effect on them.

Yet the media are not a force in themselves. Editors and producers – in Britain as elsewhere – are blamed for many things: from race riots to dress fashions, from football hooliganism to the fall of governments. But this scapegoating generally mistakes a catalyst, or even a symptom, for a cause: investing the media with a magical importance they do not possess.

With the extension of the franchise the role of the press changed. Arguably the popular press, together with the mass membership party, helped to produce a predictable electorate. Much more recently television has brought political information to a new section of the population. Yet broadcasting has been obliged to balance political views. It has also developed a style and a rhetoric which are in themselves anti-partisan, and indeed anti-party. As broadcasting became the dominant source of political knowledge, these constraints must have affected popular understanding and involvement in politics.

Now, with the growth of video, cable, and satellite technologies, the conventions of scheduling programmes built up over sixty years are becoming redundant. The capacity of broadcasting to attract a mass, nation-wide audience regularly for any particular programme, or indeed any kind of programme, is fast disappearing. Every previous change in the pattern of communications has had important political consequences. So will this revolution, even though its effects are still a matter for speculation.

The press was the arena of a major political struggle during the nineteenth century. Different classes contended not only for the right to express their own causes and interests but also to suppress other views. The newspapers we have today, and their way of dealing with politics, are a product of that competition. The battle was political. Yet in the end economic pressures were far more effective in limiting the variety of expression than any direct censorship. The market promoted some interests, but at the expense of others.

The control of broadcasting in Britain was not decided by the same kind of political confrontation which had marked the history of newspapers. Although in all countries the state has determined who can broadcast, the conditions of this right have varied enormously. In some liberal democracies broadcasting has been directly controlled, either by government or by a coalition of political parties. In others, private enterprise and the profit motive have been dominating forces. In Britain broadcasting has had some protection from market pressures, and has claimed political independence. These traditions seem likely to alter dramatically under the impact of the new technologies. Increasingly, the markets for the media are international and global: the role of national media is changing.

The first objective of the media has always been to attract an audience. Hence press and broadcasting have sought to provide instantly appreciable material that is loosely described as 'entertainment'. Some people have regarded entertainment as of little social or political importance. Others have accorded it a sinister role: as a device to numb the public into political acquiescence. It is argued here that such views need to be reconsidered.

The assumptions which underlie the conduct of the press and broadcasting also need to be reassessed. Thus it is widely believed that press freedom exists because anyone who does not find his views expressed has the right to start his own newspaper. In practice very few can exercise this right. It might be argued that the same is true of political parties. However, while it may not be practical for an individual or minority group to start a new mass political organization, it is possible to enter and influence existing parties to a far greater extent than is the case with newspapers.

In the same way broadcasting authorities today are less confident than in the past of asserting their omniscient appreciation of the public good. Rather they argue that they attempt to reflect competing interests, interpreting attacks from both left and right as evidence that they are arriving at a proper balance of views. But many of the interests and groups which are now excluded from access to broadcasting fall outside such conventional political definitions. Indeed it will be argued that accuracy, precision, and veracity should not be confused with independence. It is rarely indicated to the public that objectivity is different from the equality of competition between selected opponents.

There is one common view that the role of the media has always been the same. The press and broadcasting have always exaggerated, distorted, and suppressed. Thus, it has been suggested, they have had little overall effect on political life. The trouble with this view, however, is that the role of the press and broadcasting has changed. Arguably the power of the media has increased remarkably in the last forty years. There are fewer alternative sources of information, while the control of the media has become concentrated in fewer hands. At the same time the press

and broadcasting have become less accountable. The public
means of monitoring performance is wholly incapable of coping
with growth and technological change in increasingly complex
industries. This book is, however, based on a ridiculously optimistic
view of the British media. It assumes that it is possible to do
something by government action to make newspapers and broadcasting, not slicker and richer, but better.

Of course, such a notion is well known to be absurd. There are
people (government ministers, for instance) who think that the
worst excesses of the media, as of trades unions, should be
curbed. There are others (shadow ministers, for instance), who look
for a means to correct political bias. There are very few people,
apart from the occasional idealistic journalist, who see a problem
at all. On the one hand, action isn't considered necessary: Britain
may have lost an empire, but many still assume that it has the best
media in the world. On the other, any major interference is seen
as a dangerous infringement of liberty.

This book concludes by suggesting that it is possible to discard
irreverently the conventional wisdom, and start with contrary
assumptions. That a rapidly changing industry needs to be guided.
That something which daily intrudes into our lives in ever more
sophisticated ways needs to be, itself, the subject of continual
public surveillance. That the media interferes with us; therefore
we have a right and a duty to interfere with the media. It is
important that we begin to think more radically about the media,
for the press and broadcasting exercise a massive power, but it is
more than ever a power without responsibility.

# Part I

*Press history*

# 1

# Whig press history as political mythology

The orthodox interpretation of the development of the British press has remained unchanged for over a century. 'The British press', writes David Chaney, 'is generally agreed to have attained its freedom around the middle of the nineteenth century.'[1] This view, first advanced in the pioneering Victorian histories of journalism, has been repeated uncritically ever since in histories of modern Britain and historical studies of the British press.

The winning of press freedom is attributed partly to a heroic struggle against the state. The key events in this struggle are generally said to be the abolition of the Court of Star Chamber in 1641, the ending of press licensing in 1694, Fox's Libel Act, 1792, and the repeal of press taxation – the so-called 'taxes on knowledge' – in the period 1853–61. Only with the last of these reforms, it is claimed, did the press finally become free.

This landmark in the history of Britain is also held to be the product of the capitalist development of the press. Indeed, some researchers place greater emphasis on the market evolution of the press than on its legal emancipation. 'The true censorship', Professor Roach writes of the late Georgian press, 'lay in the fact that the newspaper had not yet reached financial independence, and consequently depended on the administration or the parties.' The growth of newspaper profits, largely from advertising, supposedly rescued the press from economic dependence on the state. This view has been succinctly restated by Ivon Asquith in a scholarly study of the early-nineteenth-century press. 'Since sales were inadequate to cover the costs of producing a paper', he writes,

> it was the growing income from advertising which provided the material base for the change of attitude from subservience to independence. . . . It is perhaps no exaggeration to say that the

growth of advertising revenue was the most important single
factor in enabling the press to emerge as the Fourth Estate of
the realm.

Orthodox histories of the press, with their stress on the free market
and legal emancipation as the foundation of press freedom, provide
a powerful, mythological account with a contemporary moral.
Thus, the legend of the advertiser as the midwife of press freedom
is invoked by journalists on the left as well as on the right to
justify the role of advertising in the press. 'The dangerous dependence of newspapers on advertising', wrote Francis Williams, a
former editor of the Labour *Daily Herald,*

> has often been the theme of newspaper reformers – usually
> from outside its ranks. But the daily press would never have
> come into existence as a force in public and social life if it had
> not been for the need of men of commerce to advertise. Only
> through the growth of advertising did the press achieve
> independence.

Similarly, journalists sometimes cite the historic struggle against
state control of the press as grounds for opposing any legislative
press reform. John Whale concludes, for example, a brief historical
survey of the dismantling of state controls of the press with the
warning that politicians are still seeking 'indirect ways of bringing
state power to bear on unsympathetic journalism'. The principal
way this is being manifested, he cautions, is in proposals to curb
concentration of press ownership.

But while Whig history is invoked to oppose change in the
press, it is summoned as an ally to justify the fundamental
reorganization of broadcasting. For instance, the Peacock Committee – appointed by the Thatcher government to investigate the
funding of the BBC – retold the history of the dismantling of
press censorship[2] as a prelude to arguing for the eventual removal
of all broadcasting 'censorship'. In effect, it deployed a particular
view of newspaper history to press for the reconstruction of
broadcasting along the deregulated, free market lines of print
journalism.

The conventional history of the press thus has an ideological
resonance for our own times. Part of its rhetorical force stems from
the liberating role attributed to the press in the nineteenth century.
According to the New Cambridge Modern History, financially
independent newspapers became 'great organs of the public mind'

which empowered the people and made governments accountable. The emergent, free press is also said to have made a vital contribution to Britain's maturing democracy in the second half of the nineteenth century by becoming more responsible and providing the factual information needed for people to make balanced and informed political judgements. Even a Marxist like Raymond Williams noted with approval that after 1855 'most newspapers were able to drop their frantic pamphleteering',[3] while the radical historian, Alan Lee, portrayed the late Victorian period as a 'golden age' of British journalism.

Agreement among historians is not total. There is a continuing debate about when newspapers became independent of political parties. A number of historians also express misgivings about the growing 'commercialization' of the press, and are sharply critical of the first generation of press lords. But few contest the conventional wisdom, embalmed in a much acclaimed two-volume study by Steven Koss, that there has been 'a transition from official to popular control' of the press during the modern period. Fewer still contest the central thesis of Whig press history that this 'progress of the press' was central to 'the broadening of political liberty'.

What follows is a long overdue attempt to reappraise the standard interpretation of press history.[4] It will indicate the need not merely to re-examine critically the accepted view of the historical emergence of a 'free' press but to stand it on its head. The period around the middle of the nineteenth century, it will be argued, did not inaugurate a new era of press freedom and liberty: it introduced a new system of press censorship more effective than anything that had gone before. Market forces succeeded where legal repression had failed in conscripting the press to the social order.

## Notes

1. References have been kept to a minimum throughout the book but a select bibliography is provided at the end.
2. The Peacock Committee's historical account is extremely simplistic, and ignores the revisionist interpretations advanced by historians of the seventeenth- and eighteenth-century press.
3. R. Williams, *The Long Revolution* (Harmondsworth, Pelican, 1965), p. 218. For a later more critical assessment, see R. Williams, 'The press and popular culture: an historical perspective' in G. Boyce, J.

Curran, and P. Wingate (eds), *Newspaper History* (London, Constable, 1978).

4.  A number of important studies of early-nineteenth-century working-
    class politics – notably by the Thompsons, Hollis, Wiener, and
    Epstein – provide evidence that, by implication at least, casts doubt on
    the conventional Whig thesis of the triumphant rise of a free press in
    mid-Victorian Britain. The wider implications of these studies for re-
    interpreting press history have been buried, however, because their
    focus is on early working-class struggles rather than the long-term
    development of journalism.

# 2

## *The struggle for a free press*

The remarkably resilient Whig interpretation of press history has been sustained by focusing attention upon mainstream commercial newspapers, while ignoring or downplaying the development of the radical press. Only if this selective perspective is maintained does the conventional view of advertising as a midwife of press independence appear plausible.

During the second half of the eighteenth century and in the early nineteenth century, a section of the commercial press became more politically independent largely as a consequence of the growth of advertising. This additional revenue reduced dependence on political subsidies; encouraged papers to reject covert secret service grants (the last English newspaper to receive a clandestine government grant was the *Observer* in 1840); improved the wages and security of employment of journalists so that they became less susceptible to government bribes; and, above all, financed greater expenditure on news-gathering so that newspapers became less reliant on official sources and more reluctant to trade their independence in return for obtaining 'prior intelligence' from the government. This shift was symbolized by *The Times*'s magisterial declaration in 1834 that it would no longer accept early information from government offices since this was inconsistent with 'the pride and independence of our journal' and anyway its 'own information was earlier and surer' (*The Times*, 26 December 1834).

However, the growth of advertising did not transform the commercial press into an 'independent fourth estate'. On the contrary, the development of modern political parties from the 1860s onwards encouraged a closer interpenetration of party politics and commercial journalism. A number of leading proprietors in Victorian and Edwardian Britain were members of parliament,

while some national newspapers were subsidized by party loyalists
or from party funds until well into the twentieth century. This
continuing involvement with government or opposition parties
belied the often repeated claim that the press was an *independent*
check on parliament and the executive: in reality, newspapers
long remained an extension of the party system.[1]

The conventional portrayal of advertising as the midwife of
press independence is also directly contradicted by the emergence
of the radical press as a political force in the late eighteenth
century. As we shall see, early radical papers did not obtain
significant advertising support. Yet they were independent both of
government and of political groupings in parliament. Their rise
plainly demonstrated that newspapers could – and did – become
autonomous from the state through financial support other than
advertising.

Successive governments tried to contain the emergent radical
press through direct legal repression. But although the seditious
and blasphemous libel law was framed in a catch-all form that
made any kind of fundamental criticism of the social order a legal
offence, it was not always easy to enforce. Juries, empowered by
Fox's Libel Act to determine guilt or innocence, were often
reluctant to convict. This was brought home to the authorities by
the sensational acquittals of Eaton, Hardy, and Tooke in the
1790s, Wooler and Hone in 1817, and Cobbett in 1831. The sharp
edge of the law was further blunted in 1843, when Lord Campbell's
Libel Act made the statement of truth in the public interest a
legitimate defence in seditious libel suits.

Even before the 1843 Act was passed, the authorities had come
round reluctantly to the view that libel prosecutions were often
counter-productive. When the editor of *The Republican* was
prosecuted in 1819, the paper's circulation rose by over 50 per
cent. Similarly disillusioning experiences prompted the Attorney
General to conclude in 1843 that 'a libeller thirsted for nothing
more than the valuable advertisement of a public trial in a Court
of Justice'. This disenchantment was reflected in a shift of government policy: there were only 16 prosecutions for seditious and
blasphemous libel in the period 1825–34, compared with 167
prosecutions during the preceding eight years.

Instead the authorities came to rely increasingly on the newspaper stamp duty and taxes on paper and advertisements as a
way of curbing the radical press. The intention of these press
taxes was two-fold: to restrict the readership of newspapers to the

well-to-do by raising cover prices; and to restrict the ownership of newspapers to the propertied class by increasing publishing costs. In this way, control of the press would be in the hands of people who, as Cresset Pelham put it, 'would conduct them in a more respectable manner than was likely to be the result of pauper management'.[2]

The stamp duty was increased by 266 per cent between 1789 and 1815. Publications subject to the stamp duty were redefined in 1819 to include political periodicals. In addition, a security system was introduced which required publishers of weeklies to register their papers and place financial bonds of between £200 and £300 with the authorities. Although the ostensible purpose of this requirement was to guarantee payment of libel fines, its real objective was to force up further the cost of publishing and thus ensure, as Lord Castlereagh explained to the Commons, that 'persons exercising the power of the press should be men of some respectability and property'.[3] Ironically in view of the way in which newspaper costs were to soar subsequently in an unfettered capitalist market, the government was persuaded by the parliamentary opposition that its original intention of insisting on a bond of £500 represented an unacceptable limitation on the freedom to publish.

The government's reliance on taxes and securities as a way of containing the radical press worked for a time. The upsurge of radical journalism that occurred in the wake of the Napoleonic War weakened in the 1820s. But with the revival of radical agitation in the early 1830s, the authorities faced a more formidable challenge – the systematic evasion of the stamp duty by an underground press with a well-organized distribution network and 'victims' fund' for the families of people imprisoned for selling unstamped newspapers.

The government responded initially by seeking to enforce the law more effectively. Printers of unstamped newspapers were rounded up; supplies of paper were intercepted; sellers of underground papers were jailed. At least 1,130 cases of selling unstamped newspapers were prosecuted in London alone during the period 1830–6. But despite these measures, the radical press continued to flourish. 'Prosecutions, fines and imprisonments were alike failures,' the minister in charge of the fight against the unstamped press later recalled.[4] By the summer of 1836 the government was forced to concede defect. The Commons was informed on 20 June that the government 'had resorted to all

means afforded by the existing law for preventing the publication
of unstamped papers', but that 'the existing law was altogether
ineffectual to the purpose of putting an end to the unstamped
papers'.

A crisis had been reached. By 1836 the unstamped press published in London had an aggregate readership of at least 2 million.
Even the government admitted that its circulation exceeded that of
the respectable, stamped press. Indeed the whole system of press
control seemed on the point of final collapse, since leading publishers of stamped papers warned the government that they would
also evade the stamp duty unless more effective steps were taken
to enforce it.

The Whig government responded to the crisis with a well-
planned counter-offensive. New measures were passed which
strengthened the government's search and confiscation powers.
Penalties were also increased for being found in possession of an
unstamped newspaper, and the stamp duty was reduced by 75 per
cent in order to make 'smuggling' less attractive. Thus what has
been seen as a landmark in the advance of press freedom was
manifestly repressive in both intention and effect. As Spring Rice,
the Chancellor of the Exchequer, explained to the Commons, a
strategic concession, combined with increased coercive powers,
was necessary in order to enforce a system that had broken down.
The aim of these new measures, he stated candidly, was to 'put
down the unstamped papers'.[5]

The government's new strategy succeeded in its immediate
objective. 'No unstamped papers can be attempted with success,'
declared Hetherington, a leading radical publisher, shortly after
being released from prison, unless 'some means can be devised
either to print the newspaper without types and presses, or render
the premises . . . inaccessible to armed force'.[6] By 1837 the clandestine radical press had disappeared.

Compliance with the law forced radical newspapers to raise
their prices, even though the stamp duty was much reduced.
Whereas most unstamped papers had sold at 1d in the early
1830s, most of their successors in the 1840s sold at 4d or 5d – a
sum that was well beyond the means of individual working-class
consumers. But the government's aim of destroying the radical
press was nevertheless frustrated by organized consumer resistance. Informal groups of working people pooled their resources
to purchase a radical paper each week. Union branches, clubs,
and political associations financed the collective purchase of

newspapers. Even taverns were threatened with the withdrawal of custom unless they bought radical papers. Partly as a consequence of this concerted resistance, new radical papers emerged which gained even larger circulations than those reached by their best-selling unstamped predecessors selling at a quarter the price.

Admittedly, after 1836, the radical press was not as strong in relation to the respectable press as it had been before. Between 1836 and 1855 there was a substantial growth in the number and circulation of commercial local weekly papers as well as in the readership of religious publications and of family and 'useful knowledge' magazines. But since much of this expansion appears to have taken place amongst the middle and lower-middle classes,[7] it did not greatly diminish the radical press's influence within the working class.

The principal rivals to the radical press within the working class (of whom well over half were literate or semi-literate by the 1830s) were almanacs, printed ballads, gallowsheets, and chapbooks. But radical newspapers far outstripped their rivals as far as the political papers read by the working class were concerned.

Indeed, the radical press was the pacesetter in terms of newspaper circulation throughout much of the period 1815–55. Cobbett's radical *Twopenny Trash* broke all circulation records in 1816–17. This record was probably beaten by the left-wing *Weekly Police Gazette* which, to judge from a government raid on its premises, had a circulation of over 40,000 in 1836 – well over double that of leading conservative weeklies such as the *Sunday Times* and *Bell's Life in London*. In 1838 the militant *Northern Star* gained the largest circulation of any newspaper published in the provinces and, in 1839, the largest national circulation of any paper apart from the liberal radical *Weekly Dispatch*. Its success was followed by the still larger circulation secured by the radical *Reynolds News*, the paper with the second-largest circulation in Britain after the liberal radical *Lloyds Weekly* in the early 1850s. Both publications were the first newspapers to break through the 100,000 circulation barrier in 1856.[8]

Newspaper circulations during the first half of the nineteenth century seem very small by modern standards. But circulation statistics provide a misleading historical index of newspaper consumption, since the average number of readers per copy has declined markedly since the mid-nineteenth century. A copy of a leading radical paper such as the *Northern Star*, selling at 4½d in

1840, cost (if taken as a proportion of the contemporary average male manual worker's wage) the equivalent of well over a pound today. Sharing of high-cost papers, together with the widespread practice of reading papers aloud for the benefit of the semi-literate and illiterate, resulted in a very high number of 'readers' for each newspaper sold. Hollis and Epstein estimate, for instance, that radical papers in the 1830s and 1840s reached upwards of twenty readers per copy. This compares with an average of only two to three readers per copy of contemporary daily papers. Yet even if a cautious estimate of ten readers per copy is taken as the norm for radical papers in the early Victorian period, it still means that leading militant papers such as the *Northern Star* and its successor, *Reynolds News*, each reached at their peak, before the repeal of the stamp duty, half a million readers. This was at a time when the population of England and Wales over the age of 14 was little over 10 million. The emergent radical press was thus a genuinely popular force, reaching a mass public.

## The economic structure of the radical press

The rise of the radical press was a direct consequence of the emergence of a radical trade union and political movement. But its early ascendancy can only be understood in the context of the prevailing economic structure of the press industry. Since this is an important aspect of the central argument that follows, it is worth examining in some detail the finances of the early radical press.

The initial capital required to set up a radical paper in the early part of the nineteenth century was extremely small. Most radical unstamped papers were printed not on a steam press, but on hand presses, which cost as little as £10 to acquire. Metal type was often hired by the hour and print workers paid on a piecework basis.

After 1836 leading stamped radical papers were printed on more sophisticated machinery. The *London Dispatch*, for instance, was printed on a Napier machine, bought with the help of a wealthy well-wisher and the profits from Hetherington's other publications. The *Northern Star* had a steam press specially constructed for it in London. Even so, launch costs were extremely small in comparison with the subsequent period. The *Northern Star*, for instance, was launched in 1837 with a total capital of £690, mostly raised by public subscription.

Financing a paper during its initial establishment period could

often cost more than setting it up. Even so, early trading losses
were minimized by low operating costs. Radical unstamped papers
paid no tax, relied heavily upon news reports filed by their readers
on a voluntary basis, and had small newsprint costs because of
their high readership per copy. Consequently radical unstamped
newspapers needed to attain only a small circulation in order to be
economically viable. For instance the *Poor Man's Guardian,* a
leading newspaper of the early 1830s, broke even as soon as its
circulation reached 2,500.

Even after 1836, when a penny stamp duty had to be paid on
each copy sold, the running costs of the radical press remained
relatively low. The influential *London Dispatch* reported, for
example (17 September 1836), that 'the whole expense allowed
for editing, reporting, reviewing, literary contributions etc., in
fact, the entire cost of what is technically called "making up" the
paper, is only six pounds per week'. In the same issue it reported
that, at its selling price of 3½d, it could break even with a
circulation of 16,000. Similarly the *Northern Star* which, unlike
its predecessors, developed a substantial network of paid correspondents, claimed to be spending little more than £9 10s a week
on its reporting establishment in 1841. Selling at 4½d, it was able
to break even with a weekly circulation of about 6,200. This low
break-even point meant that its run-in costs were very small.
Indeed the *Northern Star* almost certainly moved into profit within
its first month of publication.

Because publishing costs were low the ownership and control
of newspapers could be in the hands of people committed, in the
words of Joshua Hobson, an ex-handloom weaver and publisher
of the *Voice of West Riding*, 'to support the rights and interests of
the order and class to which it is my pride to belong'. Some
newspapers, like the *Voice of the People*, the *Liberator*, and the
*Trades Newspaper*, were owned principally by working men and
trade union organizations. Others were owned by individual proprietors like Cleave, Watson, and Hetherington, many of them
people of humble origins who had risen to prominence through
the working-class movement. While not lacking in ruthlessness or
business acumen, the people they entrusted with the editing of
their newspapers were all former manual workers like William
Hill and Joshua Hobson, or middle-class activists like O'Brien
and Lorymer, whose attitudes had been shaped by long involvement in working-class politics. A substantial section of the
popular newspaper press reaching a working-class audience was

thus controlled by those who were committed to the working-class movement.

This pattern of ownership influenced the way in which journalists working for the radical press perceived their role. Unlike the institutionalized journalists of the later period, they tended to see themselves as activists rather than as professionals. Indeed many of the paid correspondents of the *Poor Man's Guardian*, *Northern Star*, and the early *Reynolds News* were also political organizers for the National Union of the Working Classes or the Chartist Movement. They sought to describe and expose the dynamics of power and inequality rather than to report 'hard news' as a series of disconnected events. They saw themselves as class representatives rather than as disinterested intermediaries and attempted to establish a relationship of real reciprocity with their readers. As the editor of the *Northern Star* wrote in its fifth anniversary issue,

> I have ever sought to make it [the paper] rather a reflex of your minds than a medium through which to exhibit any supposed talent or intelligence of my own. This is precisely my conception of what a people's organ should be.

The second important feature of the economic structure of the radical press in the first half of the nineteenth century was that it was self-sufficient on the proceeds of sales alone. The radical unstamped press carried very little commercial advertising and the stamped radical press fared little better. The *London Dispatch* (17 September 1836) complained bitterly, for instance, of the 'prosecutions, fines and the like et ceteras with which a paper of our principles is sure to be more largely honoured than by the lucrative patronage of advertisers'. The grudge held by the *London Dispatch* and other radical newspapers against advertisers was fully justified. An examination of the official advertisement duty returns reveals a marked disparity in the amount of advertising duty per 1,000 copies (an index of comparison that takes into account differences in circulation) paid by the radical press compared with its more respectable rivals. For example in 1840 two middle-class papers published in Leeds (the *Leeds Mercury* and *Leeds Intelligence*) and the four leading national daily papers (*The Times*, *Morning Post*, *Morning Chronicle*, and *Morning Advertiser*) all paid over fifty times more advertisement duty per 1,000 copies than the radical *Northern Star*, a Leeds-based paper with a national circulation.

A similar pattern emerges in the case of the other leading

radical papers for which returns are available. In 1817, for instance, Cobbett's *Political Register* received only three advertisements: its advertisement duty per 1,000 copies was less than one-hundredth of that of respectable rival periodicals, although this disparity was somewhat reduced by the 1830s. The *London Dispatch* in 1837 was only marginally better off: it paid per 1,000 copies less than one twenty-fifth of the advertisement duty collected from each of its main respectable rivals in London, also with a national circulation.

This lack of support placed radical stamped newspapers at a serious disadvantage. All had less money to spend on editorial development than comparable respectable newspapers enjoying advertising patronage, and some were forced to close with larger circulations than better endowed rivals. This retarded the growth of the radical stamped press at a time when the high price of newspapers, inflated by the stamp duty, was a major deterrent against buying papers amongst the working class.

Yet despite these substantial disadvantages, the absence of advertising did not prevent the radical press from flourishing. While fortunes were not easily made, radical newspapers – both stamped and unstamped – could be highly profitable. Hethering-ton, the publisher of the stamped *London Dispatch*, was reported to be making £1,000 a year from his business in 1837. Similarly the stamped *Northern Star* was estimated to have produced a remarkable profit of £13,000 in 1839 and £6,500 in 1840, which was generated very largely from sales revenue.

This independence from advertising was itself a liberating force. Radical papers were, by the 1830s, increasingly oriented towards a working-class audience, and became more uncompromising in their attacks on capitalism. They were not forced to temper their radicalism or seek a more affluent readership by the need to attract more advertising. Instead they were free to respond to the radicalization of the working-class movement because they relied on their readers rather than advertisers for their economic viability.

## The impact of the radical press

The radical press did not merely reflect the growth of the working-class organizations: it also deepened and extended radical conscious-ness, helping to build support for the working-class movement.

One of the most important, and least remarked, aspects of the development of the radical press in the first half of the nineteenth century was that its leading publications developed a nationwide circulation. Even as early as the second decade, leading radical papers like the *Twopenny Trash*, *Political Register*, and *Republican* were read as far afield as Yorkshire, Lancashire, the Midlands, and East Anglia, as well as in the south of England. By the early 1830s the principal circulation newspapers like the *Weekly Police Gazette*, the *Poor Man's Guardian*, and *Dispatch* had a distribution network extending on a north-south axis from Glasgow to Land's End, and on an east-west axis form Carmarthen to Norwich. Part of the impact of the radical press stemmed from this central fact – the extent of its geographical distribution.

The radical press was effective in reinforcing a growing consciousness of class and in unifying disparate elements of the working community, partly because its leading publications provided national coverage and reached a national working-class audience. It helped to extend the often highly exclusive occupational solidarity of 'the new unionism' to other sectors of the labour community by demonstrating the common predicament of unionists in different trades throughout the country. Workers attempting to set up an extra-legal union read in the radical press in 1833–4, for instance, of similar struggles by glove workers in Yeovil, cabinet-makers and joiners in Glasgow and Carlisle, shoe-makers and smiths in Northampton, and bricklayers and masons in London, as well as of working-class struggles in Belgium and Germany. Similarly the radical press helped to reduce geographical isolation by showing that local agitation – whether against Poor Law Commissioners, new machinery, long working hours, or wage cutting – conformed to a common pattern throughout the country. The radical press further expanded its readers' field of social vision by publishing, particularly in the later phase from the 1830s onwards, news that none of the respectable papers carried, and by interpreting this news within a radical framework of analysis. It was, in the words of the Chartist leader, Feargus O'Connor, 'the link that binds the industrious classes together'.[9]

The radical press also helped to promote working-class organizations. Movements ranging from early trade unions to political organizations, like the National Union of the Working Classes and the Chartist Movement, partly depended for their success on the publicity they obtained from the radical press. O'Connor recalled that before the emergence of Chartist newspapers, 'I found that the press was entirely mute, while I was working myself to death, and that a meeting in one town did nothing for another.' Press publicity stimulated people to attend meetings and to become involved in political and industrial organizations; it also brought the activist vanguard of the working-class movement into national prominence helping, for example, to turn farm workers victimized for joining a trade union in the remote village of Tolpuddle into national working-class heroes. No less important, it helped to sustain the morale of activists in the working-class movement confronted by what must have seemed, at times, insuperable odds. Without the *Northern Star*, declared one speaker at a local Chartist meeting, 'their own sounds might echo through the wilderness'.[10]

Above all, the radical press contributed to a major political shift within a section of the working class. We have become so accustomed to the individualized pattern of newspaper consumption amidst a steady flow of information from a variety of media that it is difficult to understand the political significance of newspapers in the early nineteenth century. Newspapers were often the only readily available source of information about what was happening outside the local community and, in some cases, generated passionate loyalty amongst their readers. Fielden recalls, for instance, 'on the day the newspaper, the *Northern Star*, O'Connor's paper, was due, the people used to line the roadside waiting for its arrival, which was paramount to everything else for the time being'. The impact of the radical press was further reinforced by the discussions that followed the reading aloud of articles from newspapers in taverns, workshops, homes, and public meetings, vividly described in numerous memoirs and reminiscences.[11] This social pattern of consumption (which continued on a diminished scale late into the nineteenth century) resulted in political newspapers having a much greater agitational effect than those of today.

The first wave of radical papers from the 1790s through to the late 1820s played an important part in the psychological reorientation that preceded the political mobilization of a section of the working class. They raised expectations both by invoking a mythical past in which plenty and natural justice had prevailed, and by proclaiming the possibility of a future in which poverty could be relieved through political means. It was this raising of hopes, combined with a direct assault on the Anglican 'morality' which sanctioned the social order, that most alarmed parliamentarians at the time. As Dr Philimore, MP, warned the

Commons following official reports that servants and common soldiers had been seen reading radical newspapers,

> Those infamous publications ... inflame [working people's] passions and awaken their selfishness, contrasting their present conditions with what they contend to be their future condition – a condition incompatible with human nature, and with those immutable laws which Providence has established for the regulation of civil society.[12]

The radical press not only helped to erode political passivity, based on fatalistic acceptance of the social system as 'natural' and 'providential', but also began to dispel the collective lack of confidence that had inhibited working-class resistance. The least valued section of the community was able to obtain a new understanding of its role in society through its own press. 'The real strength and all the resources of the country,' characteristically proclaimed Cobbett's *Political Register,* for instance, 'ever have sprung from the *labour* of its people.' This novel view of the world, popularized through the more radical journals, provided a means of reordering the entire ranking of status and moral worth in society. The highest in the land were degraded to the lowest place in society as unproductive parasites: working people, in contrast, were elevated to the top as the productive and useful section of the community. The early militant press thus fostered an alternative value system that symbolically turned the world upside down. It also repeatedly emphasized the potential power of working people to effect social change through the force of 'combination' and organized action.

The radical press also played a part in radicalizing the emergent working-class movement by developing a more sophisticated political analysis. The first generation of radical papers that developed during the Napoleonic War was trapped inside the political and social categories of the eighteenth-century liberal attack on the aristocratic constitution. Conflict was generally portrayed in political terms as a struggle between the aristocracy and the 'productive classes' (usually defined to include working capitalists as well as the working classes); criticism was mainly focused upon corruption in high places and repressive indirect taxation that allegedly impoverished the productive community. The main thrust of this early radical criticism was thus largely in terms defined by middle-class critics that would leave the reward structure of society fundamentally unchanged.

By the 1830s the more militant papers had shifted their focus of attack from 'old corruption' to the economic process which enabled the capitalist class to appropriate in profits the wealth created by labour. Conflict was redefined as a class struggle between labour and capital, between the working classes and a coalition of aristocrats, 'millocrats', and 'shopocrats'. This more militant analysis signposted the way forward towards a far-reaching programme of reconstruction in which, in the words of the *Poor Man's Guardian* (19 October 1833), workers will 'be at the top instead of at the bottom of society – or rather that there should be no bottom or top at all'.

This new analysis was often conflated with the old liberal analysis in an uncertain synthesis. There was, moreover, a basic continuity in the perspectives offered by the less militant wing of the radical press, which grew in influence during the 1840s. But such continuity should come as no surprise. It was only natural that the political complexion of the broad left press should reflect the ebb and flow of militancy within the radical movement. Nor is it at all surprising that traditional political beliefs should have persisted over a time-span as brief as twenty-five years. But so long as the activist working class controlled its own popular press, it collectively possessed the means to arrive at a more radical understanding of society. It also had an institutional resource for defining, expressing, and maintaining a radical public opinion different from that proclaimed by the capitalist press, as well as a defence against the ideological assault mounted on the working class through schools, mechanics' institutes, and useful knowledge magazines.

The militant press sustained a radical sub-culture, which represented a potential threat to the social order. Indeed in 1842, a General Strike was called to secure universal suffrage through the force of industrial action. It received extensive support in industrial Lancashire, much of Yorkshire, and parts of the Midlands. While the strike was crushed, and some 1,500 labour leaders were imprisoned, it was a sign of an increasingly unsettled society in which the radical press had become a destabilizing element.

In short, the control system administered through the state had failed. Neither prosecutions for seditious libel nor a tax system designed to ration newspapers had succeeded in preventing the rise of the radical press. As we shall see, this prompted thoughtful parliamentarians to consider whether there might be a better way of containing insurgent journalism.

## Notes

1. In the last fifteen years, five researchers – George Boyce, Alan Lee, Stephen Koss, Colin Seymour-Ure, and Lucy Brown – have documented the press's continuing involvement in party politics long after the press is supposed to have blossomed as an 'independent fourth estate'. Their studies have thus modified one aspect of the traditional Whig interpretation of press history. For more about this, see chapter 5.
2. Pelham, *Parliamentary Debates*, 11 (1832), cols 491–2.
3. Castlereagh, *Parliamentary Debates,* 91 (1819), cols 1,177 ff.
4. Spring Rice, *Parliamentary Debates*, 138 (1855), col. 966.
5. Spring Rice, *Parliamentary Debates*, 34 (1836), cols 627–34; 37 (1837), col. 1,165.
6. *London Dispatch* (17 September 1836).
7. Report of the Select Committee on Newspaper Stamps (SCNS), *Parliamentary Papers*, 17 (1851); Milner-Gibson, *Parliamentary Debates*, 135 (1853), col. 1,136, amongst others.
8. P. Hollis, *The Pauper Press* (London, Oxford University Press, 1970), p. 95; *Parliamentary Debates*, 34 (1836), col. 627; SCNS Appendix 4; V. Berridge, 'Popular Sunday papers and mid-Victorian society' in G. Boyce, J. Curran, and P. Wingate (eds), *Newspaper History* (London, Constable, 1978), p. 249.
9. *Northern Star* (16 January 1841).
10. *Northern Star* (26 August 1848).
11. For instance W. E. Adams, *Memoirs of a Social Atom*, vol. 1 (London, Hutchinson, 1903), pp. 164–6; interview with Wesley Perrins, *Bulletin of the Society for the Study of Labour History* (1970), pp. 16–24.
12. Dr Philimore, *Parliamentary Debates*, 91 (1819), col. 1,363.

# 3

## *The ugly face of reform*

The parliamentary campaign against 'the taxes on knowledge' is generally portrayed as a triumphant campaign for a free press, sustained by an amalgam of special interests but motivated largely by libertarian ideals in opposition to the authoritarian legacy of the past.[1] The only discordant note in this inspiring account comes from the parliamentary campaigners celebrated in this historical legend. Their aims and, indeed, their public utterances are difficult to reconcile with the historic role assigned to them in liberal ideology.

Widespread evasion of the stamp duty in the early 1830s caused press regulation to become a major political issue. Traditionalists argued that the government should enforce the stamp duty with tougher measures, while a relatively small group of reformers in parliament argued that the stamp duty had become unenforceable in the face of mass resistance and should be repealed. The two sides to the debate did not disagree over objectives so much as over tactics. As the Lord Chancellor succinctly put it in 1834,

the only question to answer, and the only problem to solve, is how they [the people] shall read in the best manner; how they shall be instructed politically, and have political habits formed the most safe for the constitution of the country.

Traditionalists alleged that abolition of the stamp duty would result in the country being flooded with 'atrocious publications'. Reformers countered by arguing that the stamp duty merely suppressed 'the cheap reply' to seditious publications from responsible quarters. Radical publishers were not being stopped by inefficient controls. Instead they were being given a clear field in which to indoctrinate the people with 'the most pernicious doctrines' without encountering any competition.[2]

Underlying this difference over tactics were divergent approaches to social control. Supporters of press regulation tended to favour coercion. Reformers, on the other hand, generally stressed the importance of engineering social consent. As Bulwer Lytton argued when proposing the repeal of the stamp duty in 1832:

> At this moment when throughout so many nations we see the people at war with their institutions, the world presents to us two great, may they be impressive examples. In Denmark, a despotism without discontent – in America, a republic without change. The cause is the same in both: in both the people are universally educated.

The parliamentary repeal lobby argued that the lifting of the stamp duty would encourage men of capital to invest in an expanding market and consequently enrol 'more temperate and disinterested friends of the people who would lend themselves to their real instruction'. In particular, many of the parliamentary campaigners of the 1830s believed that cheap newspapers, owned by capitalists, would become an educational weapon in the fight against trade unionism. Francis Place, the organizing secretary of the repeal campaign, even told a parliamentary Select Committee in 1832 that 'there would not have been a single trades union either in England or Scotland' if the stamp duty had been repealed some years earlier. Similarly Roebuck informed the Commons that if the stamp duty had been lifted the agricultural workers at Tolpuddle would probably not have been so ignorant as to have joined a trade union. Another leading campaigner, Grote, was even more sanguine about the benefits of an expanded, capitalist press: 'a great deal of the bad feeling that was at present abroad amongst the labouring classes on the subject of wages' was due, he believed, to 'the want of proper instruction and correct information as to their real interests' caused by taxes on the press.[3]

What these parliamentary campaigners for a 'free press' emphasized was not libertarian principle but the need for a more positive approach to political indoctrination. Their speeches occasionally betrayed anxiety, however, that the time might not be right to lift controls on the press. It was this ambivalence which perhaps explains why so few amongst the repeal lobby of MPs voted consistently against the government's counter-offensive in 1836 designed, as we have seen, to restore the stamp duty and destroy the radical press. In the revealing words of Collet, who was later to co-ordinate the campaign for a free press in

Westminster, the government's attack on radical journalism was 'not a liberal, but it was in some respects, a statesman-like measure'.[4]

## The new campaign

A new parliamentary lobby against 'the taxes on knowledge' was organized in 1848. Although it posed as a broadly based organization, it had a narrow social base. As Cobden confided privately, 'Exclusively almost, we comprise steady, sober middle-class reformers.' The driving force behind the campaign was a group of liberal industrialist MPs who saw in the repeal of press taxation a means of propagating the principles of free trade and competitive capitalism. In particular, they hoped that a reduction of newspaper prices, following the abolition of press taxes, would assist the growth of the local commercial press with which many of them were closely connected and undermine the dominant position of the 'unreliable' *Times* by exposing it to increased competition.

They skilfully involved a variety of different interest groups in the campaign – all of whom had something to gain from the expansion of a cheap press – such as temperance campaigners, adult educationalists, publishers (though these were deeply divided over the stamp duty), and proselytizing politicians of varying persuasions. The differences between them merely reflected, for the most part, competition between rival élites for the attention and support of the subordinate classes. However, the common concern of most leading supporters of the campaign was to secure the loyalty of the working classes to the social order through the expansion of the capitalist press. 'The larger we open the field of general instruction,' declared Palmerston when speaking for the repeal of the stamp duty in the Commons, 'the firmer the foundations on which the order, the loyalty and good conduct of the lower classes will rest.' Repeal the taxes on knowledge, proclaimed the Irish politician, Maguire, and 'You render the people better citizens, more obedient to the laws, more faithful and loyal subjects, and more determined to stand up for the honour of the country.' 'The freedom of the press', argued Gladstone, 'was not merely to be permitted and tolerated, but to be highly prized, for it tended to bring closer together all the national interests and preserve the institutions of the country.' The new market-based press, they were agreed, would be an effective instrument of social control.[5]

But while the fundamental objectives of the campaign against press taxes were the same as before, its rhetoric was modified. Whig history was invoked more often to stigmatize supporters of press taxes as enemies of liberty and the heirs of court censorship of the press. Opposition to press taxation was more frequently voiced in the form of abstract and elevated principle. Freedom of expression should not be taxed; truth would confound error in open debate; good publications would drive out bad ones in fair competition; and even that truth would emerge only through the interplay of the free market-place of ideas.

Reformers' apposition of libertarian and authoritarian arguments may seem a little incongruous to contemporary ears. But most respectable campaigners against the 'taxes on knowledge' appear not to have perceived any tension to exist between the concepts of press freedom and social control. As Alexander Andrews, editor of the first journalists' trade journal, eloquently argued, for instance, the great mission of a free press was to 'educate and enlighten those classes whose political knowledge has been hitherto so little, and by consequence so dangerous'. This theme of political indoctrination fused naturally and unselfconsciously with that of liberty. 'The list of our public journals,' Andrews continued, 'is a proud and noble list – the roll call of an army of liberty, with a rallying point in every town. It is a police of safety, and a sentinel of public morals.'[6] The very facility with which these dissonant themes could be conflated reveals the ideological universe within which the press freedom campaign was constructed. A tacit model of society which admitted no conflict of class interest, only a conflict between ignorance and enlightenment and between the individual and the state, provided the mental framework in which a free press could be perceived as both a watch-dog of government and guard-dog of the people.

However, commitment to the principle of free competition was not entirely disinterested. The arguments for a free market press were part of a wider set of arguments that had been deployed in middle-class-dominated campaigns against the aristocratic state across a broad front. Open competition in the free market-place of talent had become the rallying cry behind the campaigns to reform the armed forces, the civil service, and the universities during the 1850s, which opened up new avenues of influential and well-remunerated employment to the professional middle class. The material blessings of competition in the free market had also been extensively invoked in the attacks on the Corn Law and protectionism during the 1840s and 1850s. In the context of the press, enthusiasm for reform reflected a growing confidence amongst middle-class reformers that their views would prevail at a time when their intellectual ascendancy seemed increasingly assured.

The key members of the press freedom campaign were also under no illusion that a free market would be neutral. More sophisticated than their predecessors in the 1830s, they had a better understanding of how the press industry worked. The repeal of press taxes, declared Milner-Gibson, president of the Association for the Promotion of the Repeal of the Taxes on Knowledge (APRTK), would create 'a cheap press in the hands of men of good moral character, of respectability, and of capital'. Aware of the rise of capital and operating costs in popular newspaper publishing in the USA, he believed that free market processes would favour entrepreneurs with large financial resources. Free trade, he stressed, in common with other leading campaigners, would 'give to men of capital and respectability the power of gaining access by newspapers, by faithful record of the facts, to the minds of the working classes'. The free market, argued Sir George Lewis, the Liberal Chancellor of the Exchequer, would promote papers 'enjoying the preference of the advertising public'. Furthermore, reformers argued, responsible control over a cheap press would educate public demand. As one campaigner put it, 'The appetite grows by what it feeds on.'[7]

Most reformers also assumed that journalists would be unresponsive to radical ideas because of their background and social position. The establishment of a cheap press, explained Hickson, a leading campaigner, would create a new hierarchical system of communication in which journalists 'two or three degrees' above the labouring classes would enlighten them. To Gladstone, the principal attraction of repeal was that it would lead to more men of 'quality' working in the press, and consequently educating the people. 'A perfectly free press', wryly commented the journalist, J. F. Stephen, 'is one of the greatest safeguards of peace and order' since successful journalists belong to 'the comfortable part of society' and will 'err rather on the side of making too much of their (comfortable) interests than on that of neglecting them'.[8]

Reinforcing this commitment to creating a cheap, unrestricted press was a growing conviction that it was now safe to lift controls. The radical working-class movement was on the retreat in the 1850s. There was, proclaimed reformers, 'a great increase of intelligence among the people'.[9] Even those who were uncertain whether the working class would 'become the glory, or might prove greatly dangerous, to the peace of the country', agreed that it was a good time to attempt an experiment. Significantly only those who were convinced that the lower classes were wedded to radical prejudices (and this group included not only entrenched traditionalists but also some distinguished liberals committed to free market competition in other spheres)[10] remained resolutely opposed to the repeal of the stamp duty.

The campaign against press taxes was conducted with remarkable skill and tenacity. Reformers packed the Parliamentary Select Committee on the Stamp Duty and largely determined the contents of its report. They attacked poorly briefed ministers and won the support of officials in the Board of Inland Revenue. They harassed the government through the law courts, exposed the inconsistencies in the way the stamp duty was enforced, organized public meetings, petitions, and deputations, and attacked press taxes in sympathetic newspapers. Their political virtuosity was finally rewarded with the abolition of the advertisement duty in 1853, the stamp duty in 1855, the paper duty in 1861, and the security system in 1869.

But the parliamentary campaign for a free press was never inspired by a modern libertarian commitment to diversity of expression. Indeed the ruthless repression of the unstamped press in the mid-1830s had much the same objective as the campaign which set the press 'free' twenty years later: the subordination of the press to the social order. All that had changed was a growing commitment to positive indoctrination of the lower orders through a cheap press, and a growing conviction that free trade and normative controls were a morally preferable and more efficient control system than direct controls administered by the state. Underlying this shift was the growing power and confidence of the Victorian middle class, which dominated the parliamentary campaign for repeal of press taxes and recognized in the expanding press a powerful agency for the advancement of their interests.

The confidence of reformers in the 'free' market-place of opinion proved to be justified. The radical press was eclipsed in the period after the repeal of press taxes. Why this happened has never been adequately explained.

## Notes

1. For instance G. A. Cranfield, *The Press and Society* (Harlow, Longman, 1978), p. 205. This view is contested in relation to the 1830s by P. Hollis, *The Pauper Press* (London, Oxford University Press, 1970), and by J. Wiener, *The War of the Unstamped* (New York, Cornell University Press, 1969).

2. *Parliamentary Debates*, 13 (1832), cols 619–48; 23 (1834), cols 1,193–1,222; 30 (1835), cols 835–62; 34 (1836), cols 627 ff.; 35 (1836), cols 566 ff., 46 (1837), cols 1,164–84. In actual fact the radical unstamped press did not have a 'clear field'. The authorities harassed radical unstamped papers, while regularly turning a blind eye to 'moderate' unstamped papers in the early 1830s.

3. Place, Select Committee on Drunkenness, *Parliamentary Papers*, 8 (1834), question 2,054; Roebuck, *Parliamentary Debates*, 23 (1834) cols 1,208–9; Grote, ibid., col. 1,221.

4. C. D. Collet, *History of the Taxes on Knowledge: Their Origin and Repeal*, vol. 1 (London, T. Fisher Unwin, 1899).

5. Palmerston, *Parliamentary Debates*, 127 (1854), col. 459; Maguire, *Parliamentary Debates*, 157 (1860), col. 383; Gladstone, cit. J. Grant, *The Newspaper Press: Its Origins, Progress and Present Position* (London, Tinsley Brothers, 1871–2).

6. A. Andrews, *The History of British Journalism to 1855* (London, Richard Bentley, 1859), ii, p. 347.

7. Milner-Gibson, *Parliamentary Debates*, 137 (1855), col. 434, and *Parliamentary Debates*, 110 (1850), col. 378; Lewis, *Parliamentary Debates*, 137 (1855), col. 786; Whitty, Report of the Select Committee on Newspaper Stamps (SCNS), *Parliamentary Papers*, 17 (1851), para. 600.

8. Hickson, SCNS (1851), para. 3, 169; Gladstone, *Parliamentary Debates*, 137 (1855), col. 794: J. F. Stephen, 'Journalism', *Cornhill Magazine*, 6 (1862).

9. Bulwer Lytton, *Parliamentary Debates*, 137 (1855), col. 1,118; Ingram, *Parliamentary Debates*, 151 (1858), col. 112; Digby Seymour, *Parliamentary Debates*, 125 (1853), col. 1,166.

10. For instance J. R. McCulloch, *Dictionary of Commerce and Commercial Navigation* (London, Longman, Brown, & Green, 1854), p. 893.

# 4

## The industrialization of the press

During the half century following the repeal of the 'taxes on knowledge', a number of radical newspapers closed down or were eventually incorporated, like the *Reynolds News*, into the mainstream of popular Liberal journalism. Militant journalism survived only in the etiolated form of small circulation national periodicals and struggling local weeklies. Yet this decline occurred during a period of rapid press expansion, when local daily papers were established in all the major urban centres of Britain and a new generation of predominantly right-wing national newspapers came into being. These included newspapers such as the *People* (1881), *Daily Mail* (1896), *Daily Express* (1900), and *Daily Mirror* (1903), which have played a prominent role in British journalism ever since.

Most historians, on the left as well as the right, attribute the decline of radical journalism to a change in the climate of public opinion. The collapse of Chartism in the early 1850s produced a wave of disillusion. Many radical activists were absorbed into the Liberal Party, particularly after the upper strata of the working class gained the vote in 1867. Trade unions also became more inward looking, seeking to improve wages and working conditions rather than to change the structure of society. These changes were reinforced by the winning of significant social reforms and, above all, by the relative success of the British economy: most workers in employment became substantially better off during the second half of the nineteenth century. Intensive proselytization of the working class through schools, churches, youth clubs, and other socializing agencies like the Volunteer Force also contributed to the spread of anti-socialist views.

These developments diminished the potential market for radical journalism. They also had another consequence which has tended to be overlooked. The reduction of support for the left made it more difficult to raise money within the working-class movement for new publishing ventures. As the TUC Congress debates in the early part of the twentieth century make clear, many Liberal and Lib-Lab trade unionists were reluctant to invest their members' money in setting up new socialist publications because they had become reconciled to the commercial press.

However, this *'zeitgeist'* interpretation provides an insufficient explanation for the fall of the radical press. It is based on the simplistic assumption that newspapers reflect popular attitudes because they are forced to respond to public demand in order to stay in business in a competitive marketplace.

In fact the evidence clearly shows that there was no close correspondence between the climate of opinion in the country and the political character of the press. What may be broadly defined as the radical press was still a powerful force in popular journalism in 1860 when the working-class movement was divided and defeated. In sharp contrast, the radical press was dwarfed by its rivals fifty years later, when the radical movement was gathering momentum.[1] The steady growth of general trade unionism, the radicalization of skilled workers, the spread of socialist and Labourist ideas, and the revival of industrial militancy did not give rise to an efflorescence of radical journalism in the decade before the First World War, although it produced a few notable publications. The absence of a close correlation between press and public opinion is further underlined by voting figures. In the 1918 general election, for instance, the Labour Party gained 22 per cent of the vote but did not obtain the unreserved support of a single national daily or Sunday newspaper.

Lucy Brown has recently suggested a supplementary explanation for the decline of 'critical vigour' in the Victorian press. She shows that the political élite devoted more time and skill to cultivating the press, and became increasingly dominant as sources and definers of news. But while this helps to explain the rightward drift of part of the commercial press, it still does not account for the eclipse of radical journalism. The militant press's adversarial style effectively inoculated it against the gentler arts of press management described by Brown. Its weakness was more fundamental: its share of circulation steadily declined during the later Victorian period.

Virginia Berridge has advanced a more compelling, if incomplete, explanation of the decline of committed journalism. This was due, she argues, to the 'commercialization' of the popular press. New popular papers came into being which were primarily business ventures, relying on sensationalist manipulation of popular sentiment rather than what she calls the 'genuine arousal' of militant journalism. In other words, they concentrated on entertainment rather then taxing political analysis, and consequently secured a much larger audience than politically committed papers.

Berridge's pioneering analysis focuses attention upon a significant change within part of the radical press. Its circulation during the 1840s was swollen by the emergence of the *News of the World* and *Lloyds Weekly*, both commercial papers whose radicalism was the product more of commercial expediency than of political commitment. As the *News of the World* frankly stated in its first issue (1 October 1843), 'It is only by a very extensive circulation that the proprietors can be compensated for the outlay of a large capital in this novel and original undertaking.' Although the same issue contained an impassioned attack upon conditions in some poor-houses, where inmates were forced to wear prison clothes, the paper also made clear that its general orientation was to please as many people as possible by serving 'the general utility of all classes'. This led to the adoption of consensual views and the growth of entertainment at the expense of political news. Yet, not very surprisingly, Sunday papers in the *News of the World* mould, with a professionally processed combination of news, sport, human interest stories, and political commentary, proved more appealing than the didactic journals that were the principal organs of the left in late Victorian Britain.

This explanation is persuasive as far as it goes. But it glosses over one striking feature of the development of the radical press. During the first half of the nineteenth century left-wing papers evolved from being journals of opinion, based on a quarto format, into broadsheet newspapers carrying news as well as commentary. This change was particularly marked during the 1830s, and was accompanied by a significant broadening of news content. Some of these radical papers began to develop a wide audience appeal by drawing upon the popular street literature tradition of chapbooks, broadsheets, gallowsheets, and almanacs. Indeed Cleave's *Weekly Police Gazette,* the *London Dispatch*, and the early militant *Reynolds News* were important partly because they started to rework this popular tradition in ways that projected a radical ideology through human interest news and entertainment as well as through political coverage.

Why, then, did the committed radical press increasingly retreat in the second half of the nineteenth century into the ghetto of narrowly politicized journalism? Why did it leave the field of popular news coverage and entertainment to the commercial press? Thus the question that needs to be asked is not why Victorian working people should have preferred the *News of the World* to rather arid socialist journals such as *Justice* and *Commonweal*, but why the radical press should have failed to live up to its early promise (or, in Berridge's terms, to its early indications of superficiality).

Her analysis is an historical version of a standard critique of mass culture. This assumes that material commercially processed as a commodity for the mass market is inevitably 'debased' because it relies on the manipulation of public tastes and attitudes for profit. This is based on assumptions that are open to question. In the context of Victorian Britain, it also obscures under the general heading of 'commercialization' the complex system of controls institutionalized by the industrialization of the Victorian press.

## The freedom of capital

One of the central objectives of state economic controls on the press – to exclude pauper management – was attained only by its repeal. The lifting of press taxes resulted in cheaper newspapers and an enormous expansion of market demand, and this led in turn to the development of expensive new print technology. Rotary presses, fed by hand, were introduced in the 1860s and 1870s and were gradually replaced by web rotary machines of increasing size and sophistication in late Victorian and Edwardian England. 'Craft' composing was mechanized by Hattersley's machine in the 1860s, and this was later replaced by the linotype machine in the 1880s and 1890s. Numerous innovations were also made in graphic reproduction. These developments led to a sharp rise in fixed capital costs. Northcliffe estimated half a million pounds as 'the initial cost of machinery, buildings, ink factories and the like, and this was altogether apart from the capital required for daily working expenses' in setting up the *Daily Mail* in 1896 – although this figure almost certainly included the cost of establishing the paper as a property around which other publications were grouped.[2]

This enormous increase in capital investment made it much more difficult for people with limited funds to break into mass publishing. It also gave considerable economic advantages to newspaper groups which printed more than one paper at the same plant. The profits from the vertical integration of publishing – Edward Lloyd led the way in the 1870s and 1880s by establishing paper mills and growing esparto grass as raw material for paper – were also reinvested in the development of newspaper enterprises. Nevertheless, the rising fixed capital costs of newspaper publishing did not constitute an insuperable obstacle to the launch of new publications with limited capital resources even in the national market. Newspapers like the *Daily Herald*, launched in 1912, could be started with only limited capital by being printed on a contract basis by an independent printer.

A more important financial consequence of the repeal of press taxes was to force up the running costs of newspaper publishing. National newspapers became substantial enterprises with large staffs and long print runs. They also cut their cover prices. The combination of rising expenditure and lower cover prices forced up the circulation level that newspapers had to achieve in order to be profitable. This raised, in turn, the run-in costs of new papers before they built their circulations to break-even point. New newspapers could be launched with limited funds and derelict newspapers could be bought relatively cheaply. It was increasingly the establishment of newspapers that required large capital resources.

Thus in 1855 Disraeli was advised by D. C. Coulton that a capital of about £20,000 was needed to start a London daily paper. In 1867 W. H. Smith estimated that about £50,000 was needed to fund a new London morning paper. By the 1870s Edward Lloyd needed to spend £150,000 to establish the *Daily Chronicle* (after buying it for £30,000). During the period 1906–8 Thomasson spent about £300,000 attempting to establish the liberal daily, *Tribune*. By the 1920s, however, Lord Cowdray spent about £750,000 attempting to convert the *Westminster Gazette* into a quality daily. Even more was spent on developing mass-circulation papers during the same period.

Indeed the full extent of the material transformation of the press is perhaps most clearly revealed by comparing the launch and establishment costs of newspapers before and after the industrialization of the press. As we have seen, the total cost of establishing the *Northern Star*, a national weekly newspaper, on a profitable basis in 1837 was little more than £690. It was able to break even with a circulation of about 6,200 copies, which was probably achieved within the first month. In contrast the *Sunday*

*Express*, launched in 1918, had over £2 million spent on it before it broke even, with a circulation of well over 250,000. Thus while a public subscription in northern towns was sufficient to launch a national weekly in the 1830s, it required the resources of an international conglomerate controlled by Beaverbrook to do the same thing nearly a century later.[3]

These statistics illustrate the privileged position of capital in the creation of the modern press. Even when the costs of launching and establishing a popular paper were relatively low in the 1850s and 1860s, they still exceeded the resources readily available to the working class. The *Beehive*, for instance, was started in 1862 with a capital of less than £250 raised by trade union organizations and a well-to-do sympathizer. Its inadequate funding crippled it. Although it set out to be a paper with a broad audience appeal, it lacked the finances to be anything other than a weekly journal of opinion. Despite a small amount of additional capital put up by unions and other contributors, it was also forced to sell at double the price of the large-circulation weeklies it had been intended to compete against. In effect, its under-capitalization condemned it to the margins of national publishing as a specialist, if influential, weekly paper.

As the resources of organized labour increased, so did the costs of establishing a national paper. It was not until 1912 that papers financed and controlled from within the working class made their first appearance in national daily journalism – long after most national daily papers had become well established. The brief career of the *Daily Citizen*, and the early history of the *Daily Herald*, illustrate the economic obstacles to setting up papers under working-class control. The *Daily Citizen*, launched in 1912 with a capital of only £30,000 (subscribed mainly by trade unions), reached a circulation of 250,000 at its peak within two years and was only 50,000 short of overhauling the *Daily Express*. But although the *Daily Citizen* almost certainly acquired more working-class readers than any other daily, it still closed three years after its launch.

The more left-wing *Daily Herald*, started with only £300 and sustained by public donations, lurched from one crisis to another despite reaching a circulation of over 250,000 at its meridian before 1914. On one occasion it came out in pages of different sizes and shapes because someone 'found' old discarded paper supplies when the *Daily Herald* could no longer afford to pay for new paper. On other occasions it bought small quantities of paper under fictitious names from suppliers all over the country; the directors of the *Daily Herald* eventually threatened to organize industrial action against paper manufacturers, a stratagem that secured paper supplies without a guarantee. While the *Daily Citizen* closed, the *Daily Herald* survived by switching from being a daily to becoming a weekly during the period 1914–19. Lack of sufficient capital prevented its continuation in any other form.

The rise in publishing costs helps to explain why the committed left press in the late nineteenth century existed only as under-capitalized, low-budget, high-price specialist periodicals and as local community papers, an important but as yet relatively un-documented aspect of the residual survival of the radical press. The operation of the free market had raised the cost of press ownership beyond the readily available resources of the working class.

Market forces thus accomplished more than the most repressive measures of an aristocratic state. The security system introduced in 1819 to ensure that the press was controlled by 'men of some respectability and capital' had fixed the financial qualifications of press ownership at a mere £200–300. This financial hurdle was raised a hundredfold in the period celebrated for the rise of a free press.[4]

But although the heavy capitalization of the British press was an important factor inhibiting the launch of new radical papers, it still does not explain the ideological absorption of radical papers already in existence before the repeal of the press taxes. Nor does it fully explain why small-circulation radical papers could not develop into profitable mass-circulation papers and accumulate enough capital, through retained profits, to finance new publica-tions. For an answer to these questions we need to look elsewhere.

### The new licensing system: advertising

The crucial element of the new control system was the strategic role acquired by advertisers after the repeal of the advertisement duty in 1853. Before then, the advertisement tax had made certain forms of advertising uneconomic. As John Cassell, the publisher of popular useful knowledge publications, argued before the Parlia-mentary Select Committee on Newspaper Stamps, 'It [the advertise-ment duty] entirely prevents a certain class of advertisements from appearing: it is only such as costly books and property sales by auction that really afford an opportunity of advertising and for paying the duty.'

Cassell exaggerated the impact of the advertisement duty for political reasons. The growth of trade, and the halving of the advertisement duty in 1833, had led to a substantial increase in press advertising in the 1830s and 1840s. Even before that, most commercial newspapers – but not the radical press – had been reliant on advertising. But it was only with the abolition of the advertisement duty in 1853 that popular press advertising came fully into its own. Between 1854 and 1858, for instance, *Reynolds News* increased its advertising volume by over 50 per cent. This surge in advertising expenditure, combined with the repeal of the stamp and paper duties, transformed the economic structure of the popular press. The modal price of popular papers was halved in the 1850s and halved again in the 1860s. At the new prevailing price structure, nearly all newspapers – including those with very large circulations like *Reynolds News* – depended on advertising for their profits since their net cover prices no longer met their costs. Advertisers thus acquired a *de facto* licensing authority since, without their support, newspapers ceased to be economically viable.

Rising circulations, falling print unit costs and, between 1875 and 1895, the sharp fall in the price of newsprint did not diminish the central role of advertising in the press. Advertising expenditure steadily increased in the Victorian and Edwardian period, rising to an estimated £20 million in 1907. This financed bigger papers, more staff, and the introduction of sale-or-return arrangements with distributors. It also helped to underwrite a further halving of the price of most popular papers to ½d in the late Victorian period.

The political implications of newspapers' economic dependence on advertising have been ignored largely because it is assumed that advertisers bought space in newspapers on the basis of market rather than political criteria. But political considerations played a significant part in some advertisers' calculations during the Victorian period. In 1856 the principal advertising handbook detailed the political views of most London and local newspapers with the proud boast that 'Till this Directory was published, the advertiser had no means of accurately determining which journal *might be best adapted to his views*, and most likely to forward his interests'[5](emphasis added). Even non-socialist newspapers found that controversial editorial policies led to the loss of commercial advertising. The *Pall Mall Gazette*'s advertising revenue dropped sharply in response to its 'Maiden Tribute' crusade in 1885 in which the editor 'procured' a 15-year-old girl as part of his paper's campaign to raise the legal age of consent. The *Daily*

*News* was boycotted by some advertisers in 1886 when it campaigned for Home Rule. Government advertising long continued to be allocated on a partisan basis. As late as 1893 the incoming Home Secretary, Herbert Asquith, was told that generally 'it is the custom to transfer advertisements according to the politics of governments'.

Political prejudice in advertising selection almost certainly declined during the latter part of the nineteenth and early twentieth centuries. The rise of advertising agencies, the emergence of major, national advertisers, and the increasing availability of circulation statistics encouraged the adoption of a more professional approach. Even so, the frequent remonstrations against 'mixing business and politics' in advertising manuals published between 1850 and 1930 suggest that political prejudice continued to influence some advertisers.

But even when political partisanship played no part in advertising selection, left-wing publications still faced discrimination on commercial grounds. As the head of a well-known advertising agency wrote in 1856, 'Some of the most widely circulated journals in the Empire are the worst possible to advertise in. Their readers are not purchasers, and any money thrown upon them is so much thrown away.' Newspapers read by the well-to-do were assessed differently. 'Character is of more importance than number,' advised an advertising handbook in 1851, adding that 'a journal that circulates a thousand among the upper or middle classes is a better medium than would be one circulating a hundred thousand among the lower classes.' Similar, though usually less extreme, advice continued to be given for a long time. For example Sir Charles Higham, the head of a large advertising agency, wrote in 1925, 'A very limited circulation, but entirely among the wealthy . . . may be more valuable than if the circulation were quadrupled.'[6]

Many advertisers also made a key distinction between the skilled and poor working class. Indeed the latter were often excluded from the early market research surveys in the 1920s on the grounds that they were not worth bothering about. Once newspapers became identified with the poor, they found it difficult to attract advertising. As an advertising handbook cautioned in 1921, 'You cannot afford to place your advertisements in a paper which is read by the down-at-heels who buy it to see the "Situations Vacant" column.'[7]

This combination of economic and political discrimination by advertisers crucially influenced the development of left-wing journalism. In the first place, it exerted pressure on the radical press to move up-market in order to survive. A number of radical newspapers redefined their target audience, and moderated their radicalism, in an attempt to attract the more affluent readers that advertisers wanted to reach.

This process is well illustrated by the career of *Reynolds News*. It was founded in 1850 by George Reynolds, a member of the left-wing faction of the Chartist National Executive. Reynolds had urged a 'physical force' strategy in 1848 and opposed middle-class collaboration in the early 1850s. His paper was initially in the *Northern Star* tradition of class-conscious radicalism, and had close links with the working-class movement.

Yet despite its radical origins, *Reynolds News* changed under the impact of the new economic imperatives of newspaper publishing. The fact that it never provided, even at the outset, a consistent theoretical perspective doubtless made it vulnerable to ideological incorporation. Inevitably it was influenced by the decline of radicalism in the country during the 1850s and early 1860s. But an important factor in its absorption was the need to attract advertising revenue. The change was symbolized by the inclusion of regular features on friendly societies in the year after the repeal of the advertisement duty, as a ploy to attract advertising. Thus enterprises which had been regularly attacked in militant newspapers as 'a hoax' to persuade working-class people to identify with capitalism became a much-needed source of revenue for *Reynolds News*.

The paper continued to take a radical stand on most major events of the day, but it increasingly expressed the individualistic values of the more affluent readers it needed to attract. It adopted many of the tenets of political economy that it had so virulently attacked during the 1850s, even to the extent of accepting the palliatives of 'prudent marriage' (i.e. sexual restraint) and emigration as solutions to unemployment. It also concentrated on the common denominators of radicalism that united the lower-middle and working classes – attacks on the 'vices' of the aristocracy, privilege, corruption in high places, the monarchy, placemen, and the Church. Attacks on industrial capital were modulated to attacks on monopoly and speculators, while criticism of shopkeepers as the exploitive agents of capital gave way to articles that celebrated the expansion of the Victorian economy. *Reynolds News* became a populist paper catering for the coalition of lower middle-class and working-class readers necessary for its survival, with occasional bursts of radicalism as a reminder of its past. Acquired by the Dicks family in 1879 and later by J. H. Dalziel, it gradually evolved into a conventional Liberal paper.

Reynolds was accused of commercial opportunism by contemporary critics (including Karl Marx). Yet it is difficult to see what else he could have done if the paper was to survive the transition to an advertising-based system. Even the radical *People's Paper* boasted in 1857 of its appeal to 'high paid trades and shop-keepers' in its promotion to advertisers. Failing to attract affluent readers in sufficient numbers, the *People's Paper* was forced to close down with a circulation far larger than middle-class weeklies like the *Spectator* and *John Bull*.

Radical newspapers could survive in the new economic environment only if they moved up-market to attract an audience desired by advertisers or remained in a small working-class ghetto, with manageable losses that could be met from donations. Once they moved out of that ghetto and sought a large working-class audience, they courted disaster. If they sold at the competitive prices charged by their rivals, they made a loss on each copy sold due to lack of advertising. If they increased their sales, they merely incurred greater losses and moved more heavily into dept.

This fate befell the London *Evening Echo*, which was taken over by wealthy radicals in 1901 and relaunched as a socialist paper. A special number was issued, firmly committing the paper to 'the interests of labour as against the tyranny of organized capital'. In the period 1902–4 its circulation rose by a phenomenal 60 per cent, leading to its abrupt closure in 1905. The growth of advertising had failed to keep pace with the growth of circulation, making the continuance of the paper impossible.[8]

The same thing almost happened to the *Daily Herald* when it was relaunched as a daily in 1919. It spent £10,000 on promotion – a small amount by comparison with its main rivals, but sufficient to ensure that it sharply increased its circulation. 'Our success in circulation', recalled George Lansbury, 'was our undoing. The more copies we sold, the more money we lost.' The situation became increasingly desperate when, partly aided by the unexpected publicity of attacks on the *Daily Herald* by leading members of the government alleging that it was financed from Moscow, the *Daily Herald*'s circulation continued to rise in 1920. 'Every copy we sold was sold at a loss,' mourned Lansbury. 'The rise in circulation, following the government's attacks, brought us nearer and nearer to disaster.'[9] The money raised from whist drives, dances, draws, and collections was not enough to offset the shortfall of advertising. Even the expedient of doubling the paper's price in 1920 did not compensate for lack of advertising. Money from the miners and the railwaymen stopped the paper from closing. But the only way the paper could be saved, in the long term, was by being taken over as the official organ of the Labour Party and TUC in 1922. A paper that had been a freewheeling vehicle of the left, an important channel for the dissemination of syndicalist ideas in the early part of the twentieth century, became the official mouthpiece of the moderate leadership of the labour movement. Lack of advertising forced it to become subservient to a new form of control.

In short, one of four things happened to national radical papers that failed to meet the requirements of advertisers. They either closed down; accommodated to advertising pressure by moving up-market; stayed in a small audience ghetto with manageable losses; or accepted an alternative source of institutional patronage.

Yet publications which conformed to the marketing require-ments of advertisers obtained what were, in effect, large external subsidies which they could spend on increased editorial outlay and promotion in order to attract new readers. Rising advertising expenditure also provided a powerful inducement to entrepreneurs to launch publications directed at markets that advertisers par-ticularly wanted to reach. Between 1866 and 1896 the number of magazines increased from an estimated 557 to 2,097, many of which were trade, technical, and professional journals aimed at specialized groups attractive to advertisers. The number of local dailies grew from only 2 in 1850 to 196 in 1900, falling to 169 by 1920 due mainly to the casualties caused by intense competition. There was also a substantial expansion in the number of local weekly papers from fewer than 400 in 1856 to an estimated 2,072 in 1900, declining to an estimated 1,700 by 1921. Above all, there was a substantial increase in the number of national daily and Sunday papers, mostly founded between 1880 and 1918, which catered either for mass, middle-market audiences or small élite audiences.[10]

This growth in the number of publications was accompanied by an enormous expansion in newspaper consumption. Annual newspaper sales rose from 85 million in 1851 to 5,604 million in 1920. Only part of this increase was due to rapid population growth: the number of newspapers purchased *per capita* over the age of 14 rose from 6 copies in 1850 to 182 copies in 1920. Even allowing for a reduction in the number of readers per copy, due to a marked decline in the collective purchase and reading aloud of newspapers, this still constitutes a remarkable increase in the audience reached by the press. Sunday and local daily papers achieved aggregate circulations of 13.5 million and 9.2 million respectively by 1920. In contrast the national daily press with a predominantly middle-class public had a circulation of only 5.4 million in 1920, while the local weekly press (which was particularly strong in rural areas) had a 9.2 million circulation.[11]

This growth was not simply the consequence of the sharp reduction in newspaper prices. Adult literacy (as measured very imperfectly by the ability to sign one's name) rose from 69 per cent in 1850 to 97 per cent in 1900. The normal number of hours worked in many industries fell from 60 hours a week to 54 hours or less between 1850 and 1890, and average real wages rose by an estimated 84 per cent between 1850 and 1900. These social changes provided the essential background for the expansion of the capitalist press with important consequences for the political development of modern Britain.

## Impact of the industrialized press

Traditional educationalists at the turn of the nineteenth century like Hannah More had taught working-class children to read but not to write. The intention had been to endow the working class with the ability to read what was good for them but to prevent them from writing anything that might be harmful to the social order. Something approaching this division between consumption and production was institutionalized through the industrialization of the press.

Many of the new local dailies were started or bought by leading local industrialists. Both the *Northern Daily Express* and the *Northern Leader* were bought by colliery owners; the *South Shields Gazette* was acquired by Stevenson, a member of a local chemical manufacturing family; the *Bolton Evening News* belonged to local industrialists, the Tillotsons; the *Yorkshire Post*'s principal shareholder was the Leeds banker, Beckett-Denison; the *Ipswich Express* was owned by Colman, the mustard manufacturer, and so on. These papers offered a very different view of the world from that of the early radical press they supplanted. Papers like the *Northern Star* had amplified class conflicts in the local community ('to talk of reconciliation between the middle and working classes

in Leicester will, henceforth, be a farce'[12] was a typical lead-in to one
of its news reports). In contrast the new local commercial press
tended to block out conflict, minimize differences, and encourage
positive identification with the local community and its middle-class
leadership. Characteristic of this style of consensual journalism was
a report in the Leeds Mercury (printed in the same city as the
*Northern Star*) of a local dignitary addressing the annual public
soirée of the Leeds Mechanics Institute on the subject of 'these
popular institutions, sustained by the united efforts of all classes . . .
thereby to promote the virtue, happiness and peace of the
community'.[13]

The early militant press had fuelled suspicion of middle-class
reformists with a barrage of criticism against 'sham-radical
humbugs' and 'the merciful middle-class converts to half Chartism
at half past the eleventh hour'.[14] In contrast the new local daily
press encouraged its readers to identify with the political parties
controlled by the ruling class. Ten of the new local dailies that
emerged between 1855 and 1860 were affiliated to the Liberal
Party; eighteen created between 1860 and 1870 were affiliated to
the Tory or Liberal Party, and forty-one of the local dailies
created in the following decade were similarly linked to the two
great parties. The new party press played a central role in
transforming what had been essentially aristocratic factions in
parliament into mass political movements by mobilizing popular
support behind them. It thus reinforced the division of the working-
class movement through its absorption into rival parliamentary
parties.

The new liberal press diluted the ideology of the early militant
press to such an extent that it acquired a new, therapeutic meaning
for the functioning of the social system. The co-operative ethos
that would inform the new social order, proclaimed by some
militant papers, became transmuted into the spirit of partnership
between masters and men that would make the British economy
prosper. The early radical stress on moral regeneration through
social reconstruction became a celebration of moral improvement
through the spread of middle-class enlightenment. And the value
formally attached to self-education as a means of ideological
resistance to class domination gave way to a stress on the
undifferentiated acquisition of 'knowledge' as the route to individual self-advancement and economic progress. Admittedly these
transformations drew upon a radical tradition that contained
contradictory elements within it. But by emphasizing the liberal

rather than more radical lineaments of this tradition, the new press contributed to the disorganization of the working-class movement.

There were important differences between individual newspapers, particularly in relation to their coverage of trade unions. But notwithstanding these differences, all national newspapers launched between 1855 and 1910, and the overwhelming majority of new local daily papers, encouraged positive identification with the social system. The shift in the press that this represented is perhaps best illustrated by the way in which Queen Victoria was portrayed. Most radical papers in the period 1837–55 were aggressively republican: the Queen was vilified as politically partisan and reactionary, the head of a system of organized corruption, the mother of a brood of royal cadgers, and the friend and relative of European tyrants. In contrast the new press portrayed the Queen particularly from the mid-1870s onwards as a dutiful and benign matriarch, who symbolized in an almost talismanic way the moral and material progress of her reign. Projecting her as a living embodiment of national unity, they also played a key role in converting the jubilee celebrations of 1887 and 1897 into popular, mobilizing rites of national communion.

Above all, the new popular press fostered the wave of imperialism that swept through all levels of society. It tended to portray Britain's colonial role as a civilizing mission to the heathen, underdeveloped world, and as an extended adventure story in which military triumphs were achieved through individual acts of courage rather then through superior technology. Common to both themes was pride in Britain's ascendancy: as the *Daily Mail* (23 June 1897), the most popular daily of late Victorian Britain, enthused:

> We send out a boy here and a boy there, and the boy takes hold of the savages of the part he comes to and teaches them to march and shoot as he tells them, to obey him and believe in him and die for him and the Queen. A plain, stupid, uninspired people they call us, and yet we are doing this with every kind of savage man there is.

This celebration of Britain's dominion sometimes struck a more atavistic note as in this report of the 1898 Sudan expedition in the *Westminster Gazette*:

> A large number of the Tommies had never been under fire before . . . and there was a curious look of suppressed excite-

ment in some of the faces. ... Now and then I caught in a man's eye the curious gleam which, despite all the veneer of civilization, still holds its own in man's nature, whether he is killing rats with a terrier, rejoicing in a prize fight, playing a salmon or potting Dervishes. It was a fine day and we were out to kill something. Call it what you like, the experience is a big factor in the joy of living.

The paper which celebrated 'potting Dervishes' was, in terms of the political spectrum represented by the contemporary national press, on 'the left'. It was, for example, one of the few liberal papers not to join the press campaign for vengeance during the Boer War. However, it joined all other daily papers of note in providing uncritical, Hun-hating support for Britain's involvement in the First World War.

## Conclusion

In short, the radical press was decisively defeated after the abolition of the 'taxes on knowledge'. But its defeat cannot be attributed solely to the changed climate of opinion, following the collapse of the Chartist Movement. The '*zeitgeist*' or 'sovereign consumer' theories of the press and social change fail to account for why the press, taken as a whole, moved further to the right than public opinion; nor does it explain why the subsequent revival of the radical movement did not give rise to a stronger revival of radical journalism. Both the extent and permanence of the eclipse of the radical press as the dominant force in national popular journalism was due to structural changes in the press industry. The industrialization of the press, with its accompanying rise in publishing costs, led to a progressive transfer of ownership and control of the popular press from the working class to wealthy businessmen, while dependence on advertising encouraged the absorption or elimination of the early radical press and stunted its subsequent development before the First World War.

## Notes

1. For the relative weakness of the radical press in 1910, see A. J. Lee, 'The radical press' in A. Morris (ed.), *Edwardian Radicalism 1900–1914* (London, Routledge & Kegan Paul, 1974).
2. R. Pound and G. Harmsworth, *Northcliffe* (London, Cassell, 1959), p. 206.

3. A. J. P. Taylor, *Beaverbrook* (London, Hamish Hamilton, 1972), p. 175.

4. The costs of market entry for mass publishing were particularly high in Britain due to the dominant role of the national press. This partly explains why the radical press in Britain was much weaker than in some other European countries, where the press remained decentralized and entry costs were lower.

5. *Mitchell's Newspaper Press Directory* (Mitchell, 1856). It should be noted, however, that Mitchell himself cautioned advertisers against political bias.

6. *Mitchell's Newspaper Press Directory* (Mitchell, 1856); Anon., *Guide to Advertisers* (1851); C. Higham, *Advertising* (London, Williams & Norgate, 1925), p. 166.

7. C. Freer, *The Inner Side of Advertising: A Practical Hand-book for Advertisers* (London, Library Press, 1921), p. 203.

8. F. W. Pethick-Lawrence, *Fate Has Been Kind* (London, Hutchinson, 1943), pp. 65 ff.

9. G. Lansbury, *The Miracle of Fleet Street* (London, Victoria House, 1925), pp. 160 ff.

10. The figures for regional dailies relate to Britain and for other categories of publications to the UK, as reported in *Mitchell's Newspaper Press Directory*.

11. N. Kaldor and R. Silverman, *A Statistical Analysis of Advertising Expenditure and of the Revenue of the Press* (Cambridge, Cambridge University Press, 1948), p. 84.

12. *Northern Star*, 7 May 1842.

13. *Leeds Mercury*, 14 June 1851.

14. *Northern Star*, 26 February and 11 June 1842.

# 5

# The era of the press barons

The era of the press barons is often seen as a maverick interlude in the development of the press when newspapers became subject to the whims and caprices of their owners. According to this view, the press barons built vast press empires and ruled them like personal fiefdoms. In the hands of men like Beaverbrook and Rothermere, newspapers became mere 'engines of propaganda' manipulated in order to further their political ambitions. As Baldwin said in a memorable sentence (suggested to him by his cousin, Rudyard Kipling), 'What proprietorship of these papers is aiming at is power, and power without responsibility – the prerogative of the harlot throughout the ages.'

The despotic rule of the press barons is usually compared unfavourably with a preceding 'golden age' when proprietors played an inactive role and 'sovereign' editors conducted their papers in a responsible manner. In some accounts, too, the era of Northcliffe and Rothermere is contrasted with the period after the Second World War when journalists became more educated, independent, and professional. The press barons have thus become favourite bogeymen: their indictment has become a way of celebrating the editorial integrity of newspapers, past and present.

But in reality the reign of the press barons did not constitute an exceptional pathology in the evolution of the press, but merely a continuation of tendencies already present before. Indeed in so far as the barons can be said to be innovators, it is not for the reasons that are generally given. They did not break with tradition by using their papers for political propaganda; their distinctive contribution was rather that they downgraded propaganda in favour of entertainment. Nor did they subvert the role of the press as a fourth estate: on the contrary it was they who detached the commercial press from the political parties and, consequently, from government. What actually happened is, in some ways, the exact opposite of the myth.

## The creation of press empires

The press chains created by the press barons in the late nineteenth and early twentieth centuries were not a new phenomenon. Multiple ownership of weekly newspapers had developed as early as the eighteenth century largely because it enabled costs to be reduced through shared services. Local daily chains had also emerged shortly after the local daily press was established. By 1884, for instance, a syndicate headed by the Scots-American steel magnate, Carnegie, controlled eight dailies and ten weeklies. During the same period major groups were also being formed in London, most notably by Edward Lloyd who controlled two mass-circulation papers – *Lloyds Weekly* and the *Daily Chronicle* – along with other publications.

Although some of the papers controlled by the press barons also gained a dominant market position, this, too, had been a traditional feature of the development of the press. Papers which secured an initial circulation lead over their rivals generally enjoyed lower unit costs (due to their ability to spread the high costs of the 'first copy' over a larger print run), as well as more sales and advertising revenue. This helped them to increase their circulation lead by spending more on editorial outlay, promotion, and, sometimes, price-cutting.

The press barons' empires were also swollen by the rapid growth of circulation that took place during their lifetimes. But a sustained increase of demand for newspapers had characterized the development of the press ever since the eighteenth century and had been particularly pronounced, as we have seen, in the period after the repeal of press taxes.

These three traditional features of the press – chain ownership, an expanding market, and a tendency for a few papers to become dominant – merely became more accentuated under the press barons. Between 1890 and 1920 there was a rapid acceleration of newspaper chains incorporating national as well as local papers. By 1921 Lord Northcliffe controlled *The Times*, the *Daily Mail*, the *Weekly* (later *Sunday*) *Dispatch*, and the *London Evening News*; his brother, Lord Rothermere, controlled the *Daily Mirror*, the *Sunday Pictorial*, the *Daily Record*, the *Glasgow Evening News*, and the *Sunday Mail*. Jointly they owned the large magazine group Amalgamated Press and their brother, Sir Lester Harmsworth, had a chain of newspapers in the south-west of England. Together they owned newspapers with an aggregate circulation of over 6 million – probably the press grouping with the largest sale in the western world at the time.[1] In addition the Hulton chain controlled three Sunday and four daily papers and the Pearson chain included nine daily and twenty-one local weekly papers.

Between the wars, concentration of press ownership entered a new phase, with the spectacular consolidation of the regional chains. The percentage of provincial evening titles controlled by the big five chains rose from 8 to 40 per cent between 1921 and 1939; their ownership of the provincial morning titles also increased, from 12 to 44 per cent during the same period. The power of the chains was further extended by the elimination of local competition. Between 1921 and 1937, the number of towns with a choice of evening paper fell from twenty-four to ten, while towns with a choice of local morning paper declined from fifteen to seven.

The principal pacesetters in the expansion of the regional chains were the Berry brothers, Lords Camrose and Kemsley. Their group grew from four daily and Sunday papers in 1921 to twenty daily and Sunday papers in 1939. This was achieved only after a long-drawn-out and costly 'war' with Lord Rothermere, which was eventually resolved in a series of local treaties in which the three lords divided up different parts of the country between them.

During the inter-war period there was also an enormous increase in the sales of national dailies which overtook for the first time that of local dailies. Between 1920 and 1939 the combined circulation of the national daily press rose from 5.4 million to 10.6 million, while that of the local daily and weekly press remained relatively static. This major expansion of the London-based press meant that some proprietors commanded very large audiences, even when they owned relatively few papers. This was particularly true of Lord Beaverbrook whose small empire of only four papers included one market leader which pushed up the total circulation under his control to 4.1 million by 1937.

These changes in the ownership and readership of the press meant that, after the death of Lord Northcliffe in 1922, four men – Lords Beaverbrook, Rothermere, Camrose, and Kemsley – established a dominant position during the inter-war period. In

1937, for instance, they owned nearly one in every two national and local daily papers sold in Britain, as well as one in every three Sunday papers that were sold. The combined circulation of all their newspapers amounted to over 13 million.

However, there was a shift away from proprietorial domination of the press during the later part of the inter-war period. In 1937 the three leading Sunday papers' owners (Kemsley, Beaverbrook, and Camrose) controlled 59 per cent of national Sunday newspaper circulation – significantly less then the 69 per cent share of national Sunday circulation controlled by three relatively obscure proprietors (Dalziel, Riddell, and Lloyd) in 1910. Similarly in 1937 Rothermere, Beaverbrook, and Cadbury controlled 50 per cent of national daily circulation – again, much less than the 67 per cent share controlled by Pearson, Cadbury, and Northcliffe in 1910.

Underlying this shift was a decline in individual proprietorship and a successful assault on the major press groups. There was a revival of corporate press ownership during the inter-war period with the relaunch of the *Daily Herald*, the acquisition of *Reynolds News* by the Co-operative Movement, and the launch of the *Daily Worker* in 1930. The rise in publishing costs also resulted in a dispersal of newspaper ownership through the sale of shares so that three important papers – the *Daily Mirror*, *Sunday Pictorial*, and the *People* – ceased to have a dominant shareholder. The press magnates' hegemony over the press was, in fact, waning during the period celebrated for their ascendancy.

## Press barons and proprietorial control

Not all proprietors attempted to use their papers for political purposes. For instance Astor, joint owner of *The Times* after 1922, was teased by his friends for not reading his own paper. Indeed even proprietors like Northcliffe, Rothermere, Beaverbrook, and Kemsley, who saw their papers as an extension of their own political views, did not exercise a uniform degree of control over all their papers.

Thus in the late 1930s Beaverbrook deluged the *Daily Express* with instructions to support appeasement ('No War Talk. NO WAR TALK', read one telegram of that period), but did not seem to mind that its sister papers, the *Sunday Express*, adopted a traditional patriotic hostility towards Germany, or that another of his papers, the *Evening Standard*, under the socialist editor Percy

Cudlipp, urged a popular front against fascism. Similarly Northcliffe was mainly concerned in his later years with the *Daily Mail*, a preoccupation that his brother Rothermere later shared.

The two archetypal press barons, Northcliffe and Beaverbrook, had very different personal styles. While Northcliffe was notorious for personally harassing his staff, Beaverbrook's remoteness was legendary. In *Scoop*, Evelyn Waugh satirized a visit to him:

> The carpets were thicker [as one approached Lord Copper's private office], the lights softer, the expressions of the inhabitants more careworn. The typewriters were of a special kind: their keys made no more sound than the drumming of a bishop's finger-tips on an upholstered prie-dieu. The telephone buzzers were muffled and purred like warm cats. The personal private secretaries padded through the ante-chambers and led them nearer and nearer to the presence.

Yet despite their differences of personality, both men exercised detailed control over their favourite papers through a constant barrage of instructions. Beaverbrook sent 147 separate instructions to the *Express* in one day. Northcliffe would sometimes phone his staff at 6 in the morning: 'Wake up! Have you seen the papers yet?' he would demand. One editor, who replied that you could not get the *Mail* in Northlake at 6 am, was woken up at 5 the next morning by a pantechnicon backing into his garden, delivering a copy.

The press barons maintained their personal domination with extreme ruthlessness. Northcliffe, in particular, had a brisk way of dismissing employees. 'Who is that?' Northcliffe said on the phone. 'Editor, *Weekly Dispatch*, Chief,' came the reply. 'You were the editor,' responded Northcliffe. When a luckless sub-editor filled a lull in conversation over lunch with the information that he had been shipwrecked three times, Northcliffe abruptly said, 'Four times'. Beaverbrook also had a fearsome reputation. 'Fleet Street', recalled one of his employees, 'was strewn with the corpses of *Express* editors.'[2]

The barons combined terror with generosity. Journalists' memoirs and official histories are full of anecdotes about the sudden gifts, holidays, and salary rises which were showered on staff. As a genre these stories could be called 'Courageous underling gets his reward'. They usually take the form of the plucky journalist standing up for himself (or, more rarely, for what he believes) in the face of the baron's fury. They are clearly intended to enhance both the baron, who is revealed as discriminating and fundamentally right-minded in his judgements, and the journalist, whose independence is demonstrated by his courage. But what they actually reveal is an almost continuous process of humiliation. Bernard Falk, usually rewarded with a cigar when he took down Northcliffe's dictated social column for the *Mail*, was once allowed to choose the one he wanted. 'What!' said Northcliffe, 'You have the nerve to pick on those cigars! Don't you know, young man, that they cost 3/6 each?' 'Yes,' said the intrepid reporter, 'but they're worth every penny.' Another editor who dared to disagree with Northcliffe recorded gratefully the telegram he received: 'My dear Blackwood, you are grossly impertinent to your affectionate Chief.'

Losing a battle with a baron hardly made such a good story. Buckle, the editor of *The Times* (whose editorial independence Northcliffe had promised to uphold), was eased out of the editorship when he failed to adapt to the political views and managerial strategy of the Chief. Lewis Macleod, literary editor of the *Mail*, received a communique from Northcliffe: 'This is the last occasion on which I can tolerate Macleod's gross neglect and carelessness. He will read this message out to the editorial conference on Monday.' When Northcliffe was angered by what he thought were defects on the *Daily Mail*'s picture page, he lined up all involved in its production and put the tallest man in charge. Feeling dissatisfied with the *Mail*'s advertising department, he appointed the commissionaire to vet advertisements. Beaverbrook was also unpredictable though not on the scale of Northcliffe.[3] Yet behind both men's seemingly random acts of ferocity and generosity, there was a consistent purpose. Beaverbrook ensured that many of his best journalists wrote under pseudonyms so that, if they left the *Express*, they could not take the goodwill of their copy with them.

Northcliffe and Beaverbrook shaped the entire content of their favourite papers, including their layout. Thus Northcliffe raged at an employee at *The Times*, 'What have you done with the moon? I said the moon – the *Moon*. Someone has moved the moon! . . . Well, if it's moved again, whoever does it is fired!' (The position of the weather report had been changed.) Beaverbrook and Northcliffe constantly pestered journalists about the language and phrasing of their reports. 'To Eastbourne's balding, myopic, Edinburgh-trained physiotherapist, William John Snooks, 53, came the news that . . .' parodied Tom Driberg, a former *Express* journalist, in the approved Beaverbrook style. Both press barons also interfered in the choice of pictures. 'Alfonso' (the King of Spain), complained Northcliffe, 'is always smiling. This smile is not news. If you get a picture of Alfonso weeping, *that* would be news!'

The barons' personal foibles influenced the selection of news stories, thereby helping to form what are now the news values of the national press. Northcliffe had a lifelong obsession with torture and death: he even kept an aquarium containing a goldfish and a pike, with a dividing partition, which he would lift up when he was in need of diversion. His obsession was reflected in his first magazine, *Answers*, which dealt with such enquiries as, 'How long is a severed head conscious after decapitation?' The first feature article Northcliffe wrote for his first evening newspaper described the day he spent with a condemned murderer in Chelmsford jail. He later briefed *Daily Mail* staff to find 'one murder a day'. Similarly Beaverbrook, a hypochondriac, told the editor of the *Daily Express* that 'The public like to know . . . what diseases men die of – and women too.'

Proprietors' perceptions of their readers set the tone of their papers. The *Daily Express* aimed, in Beaverbrook's words, at 'the character and temperament which was bent on moving upwards and outward', reflecting Beaverbrook's own New World ethic, with its celebration of the self-made. The *Daily Mail*, on the other hand, projected a more static, hierarchical world in keeping with Northcliffe's more traditional brand of conservatism and catered, as Northcliffe patronizingly put it, for 'people who would like to think they earned £1,000 a year'.

The proprietorial control exercised by the press magnates did not represent, however, a decisive break with the past. Indeed Lucy Brown's recent revisionist account of the Victorian commercial press even argues that 'what is an important and unvarying generalization is that the sovereign powers of decision were exercised by the proprietors and not by the editors'. Many of the Victorian editors celebrated for their independence, such as C. P. Scott of the *Manchester Guardian* (1877–1929), were either the owners of the papers they edited or members of the proprietorial family. Other leading editors prove, on close examination, to have been less autonomous than has usually been claimed. Even Delane of *The Times*, often seen as a model of the sovereign editor, was repeatedly excluded from key planning decisions affecting the development of his paper. Indeed he was so convinced that he was going to be sacked, at one stage, that he started 'taking dinners' in order to be eligible to practise as a barrister. Others were less fortunate: Cook, Gardiner, Massingham, Greenwood, Annand, Watson, and Donald were only some of the distinguished editors who were compelled to resign between 1880 and 1918 as a result of political disagreements with their proprietors.

The tradition of editorial sovereignty which the press magnates allegedly destroyed was, to a large extent, a myth. It has been inspired by journalists like Sir Robert Ensor and Michael Foot to legitimize the political argument that editors rather than proprietors should be in charge of newspapers' editorial columns. Only in a very limited sense can the proprietorial style of the press barons be said to differ from that of their predecessors, most of whom were also involved in the editorial side of their papers. The press barons, by contrast, exercised personal control over all aspects of their newspapers on an almost daily basis. They were business managers as much as editors-in-chief. Yet even this difference should not be overstated since some of the Victorian pioneers of 'popular' journalism, notably Edward Lawson of the *Daily Telegraph* and Edward Lloyd, were also active business as well as editorial managers of their papers.

## Profits and politics

The press barons have been portrayed by historians primarily as journalist-politicians – a view of themselves which they publicly cultivated. Beaverbrook, for instance, told the first Royal Commission on the Press that he ran the *Daily Express* 'merely for the purpose of making propaganda and with no other motive'. Yet this simple image has tended to obscure another, more important aspect of their dominion over the press.

The press barons were forced by economic pressures to seek increasingly large circulations. Intense competition resulted in rising levels of paging, bigger editorial staffs, and, above all, massive promotion. Northcliffe and Rothermere led the way by spending, up to 1928, approximately £1 million on the *Daily Mail*'s readers' insurance scheme in order to attract more readers. Rival press magnates fought back with competitions offering lavish prizes and their own readers' insurance schemes. After a legal judgement in 1928 outlawed newspaper competitions as lotteries, promotion shifted towards free gifts. Teams of canvassers moved through the countryside offering surprised housewives anything from cameras and wristwatches to silk stockings and tea-kettles, in return for taking out a newspaper subscription. The promotion

for the *Daily Herald* alone is estimated to have amounted to £1
per new reader between 1930 and 1932. Even in 1937, when the
'circulation war' had abated, a typical national daily newspaper
employed five times as many canvassers as editorial staff.[4] The
effect of this heavy promotion and rising editorial outlay was to
force up costs and, therefore, the circulations that popular newspapers needed to achieve in order to stay profitable.

Publishers were consequently under increasing pressure to give
more space to material with a universal appeal to less
differentiated audiences. The editorial implications of this were
spelt out in market research, which most leading publishers
commissioned during the 1930s, into what people read in newspapers. A major survey, based on a national quota sample of over
20,000 people and commissioned by the *News Chronicle* in 1933,
revealed, for instance, that the most-read news in popular daily
papers were stories about accidents, crime, divorce, and human
interest. They had a near-universal appeal. In contrast most
categories of public affairs news had only an average or below-
average readership rating. This was because, although some
aspects of public affairs had an above-average readership among
men and people over the age of 35, they had a weak appeal among
women and the young. Public affairs content was thus, in marketing
terms, a commodity with a sectional appeal. It lacked, moreover,
the passionate following amongst a large minority commanded by
sport, and it also lacked the appeal to advertisers possessed by
some minority consumer features.

Pressure to maximize audiences consequently resulted in the
progressive downgrading of political coverage. By 1936 six out of
a sample of seven papers devoted more space to human interest
content than to public affairs – indeed, in some cases three or four
times as much.[5] The one exception was the *Daily Herald*, which
allocated 33 per cent of its editorial content to public affairs –
substantially more even than the *Daily Telegraph*. The *Daily
Herald*'s commitment to political coverage reflected the concerns
of its TUC-nominated directors. For the press barons, profits
mattered more than politics.

This shift away from the traditional concept of a *news*paper to
a magazine miscellany was part of a long-term trend dating back
to the mid-nineteenth century. It accelerated, however, during the
inter-war period. Thus between 1927 and 1937 the *Daily Mail*'s
sports coverage rose from 27 to 36 per cent of its total news,
while home political, social, and economic news fell from 10 to 6
per cent of total news content.[6]

The quality press remained more faithful to the traditional concept of the newspaper, despite the fact that market research showed that the most-read news items in quality dailies were very similar to those in popular papers.[7] However, quality newspapers were protected from the economic pressure to build large circulations because over two-thirds of their revenue came from advertising secured by reaching small, élite audiences. Advertising thus discouraged quality papers from adopting popular editorial strategies by making it financially disadvantageous for them to dilute the class composition of their readership.

## The rise of the 'fourth estate'

The press barons are usually accused of using their papers as instruments of political power. But they were hardly unique in this. What made the press magnates different is that they sought to use their papers, not as levers of power within the political parties, but as instruments of power against the political parties. The basis of the Establishment's objection to men like Rothermere and Beaverbrook was not that they were politically ambitious, but that they were politically independent.

In the early twentieth century the majority of London-based daily papers were owned by wealthy individuals, families, or syndicates closely linked to a political party. Between 1911 and 1915, for instance, funds from the Unionist Central Office were secretly paid through respectable nominees to the *Standard*, *Globe*, *Observer*, and *Pall Mall Gazette*. A wealthy Conservative syndicate, headed by the Duke of Northumberland, bought the Tory *Morning Post* in 1924. Similarly Lloyd George engineered the purchase of the *Daily News* in 1901 by the Cadbury family in the Liberal interest, and arranged the purchase of the *Daily Chronicle* in 1918 through a syndicate headed by Dalziel with money accumulated through the sale of honours and laundered through the Lloyd George Fund.

This pattern of political control was undermined by the growth of advertising expenditure (mostly on the press) which nearly trebled from £20 million in 1907 to £59 million in 1938. This funded an escalating rise in editorial and promotional spending, and increasingly made papers too expensive for political parties and their supporters to sustain. Pearson refused to dig deeper into his pocket to keep the *Westminster Gazette* going in the Liberal interest after 1928; Lloyd George and his associates were forced to sell the *Daily Chronicle* in 1928 to the Inveresk chain; the TUC gave up financial control of the *Daily Herald* to the Odhams Group in 1929; no Tory syndicate could be found to prevent the *Daily Graphic* closing in 1926 or the *Morning Post* disappearing in 1937.

The enormous expansion of advertising weaned the national press from dependence on the political parties. Although most major press barons were Tories, they were first and foremost newspapermen. With the exception of papers controlled by Beaverbrook in his early days, all their publications were subsidized solely by advertising, and consequently were free to operate entirely independently of political patronage. An independent 'fourth estate', prematurely announced in the mid-nineteenth century, came much closer to reality during the inter-war period, under the aegis of the press barons.

Beaverbrook and Northcliffe played an important part in the political revolt that unseated Asquith as premier in 1916, and established Lloyd George in his place. The press barons played a more unconventional role after the war by directly confronting the political parties. Between 1919 and 1922 Rothermere, aided by Northcliffe, unleashed a violent propaganda campaign against 'squandermania', urging extensive cuts in public spending, the abandonment of wartime planning controls, and the sale of publicly owned enterprises. When the Coalition government partially rejected these policies, Rothermere appealed directly to the country by backing the Anti-Waste League in parliamentary by-elections in 1921. Three Anti-Waste League candidates succeeded in winning at Dover, Westminster St George's, and Hertford. Although these victories were not matched by by-election gains elsewhere, Rothermere had demonstrated the strength of grass-roots Conservative opposition to government policies. Partly in response to this pressure, the Ministries of Shipping, Munitions, and Food were abolished, a wide range of public controls was lifted, and publicly owned factories and shipyards were sold to private enterprise.

The Anti-Waste Campaign petered out with the break-up of the Coalition government in 1922, and its replacement by a Conservative administration backed by the press barons. But Beaverbrook and Rothermere later became persuaded that Britain's economic problems could be solved by converting the Empire into a free trade zone protected by a high tariff wall. Unable to convince the Conservative Party leadership, they again made an independent foray into politics by backing the United Empire Party (UEP) and campaigning in October 1930 for its by-election candidate, Vice-Admiral Turner, in the safe Tory seat of Paddington. The UEP candidate won unexpectedly, and this was followed by another by-election upset at East Islington where Labour won and the official Conservative candidate was beaten by the UEP into third place. This precipitated a revolt within the Conservative Party. Sir Robert Topping, the chief Conservative agent, wrote a memorandum saying that the party leader, Stanley Baldwin must go, which was subsequently endorsed by most leading Conservatives consulted by Neville Chamberlain, the party chairman. Baldwin, for a time, agreed to go quietly, telling the chairman bitterly that 'the sooner, the better' suited him.

Stanley Baldwin decided in the end to stay and fight, staking his political career on the outcome of the parliamentary by-election at Westminster St George's. Mounting a brilliant political campaign in which he shifted attention from Empire free trade to the unaccountable power of the press barons, he helped the official Conservative candidate, Duff Cooper, to win the by-election with a comfortable majority. Thereafter Baldwin's personal position was safe, though he was sufficiently shaken to make what was, in effect, a peace treaty with Beaverbrook shortly after the by-election.

The impetus behind the Empire free trade campaign was broken by the 1931 crisis, the collapse of the Labour government, and the landslide election victory won by the Coalition administration headed by Ramsay MacDonald. It was also weakened by lack of enthusiasm in the Dominions for the press barons' grand design. Nevertheless, Beaverbrook and Rothermere succeeded in strengthening the imperialist wing within the Conservative Party and some imperial preference policies were implemented during the 1930s. This was more than Joseph Chamberlain, the great apostle of Empire free trade, achieved during the nineteenth century despite his explosive impact on late Victorian politics.

Rothermere subsequently came out in support of the British Union of Fascists (BUF) in 1934. His papers pumped out stirring calls like 'Give the Blackshirts a Helping Hand' (*Daily Mirror*, 22 January 1934) and 'Hurrah for the Blackshirts' (*Daily Mail*, 15 January 1934). The *Evening News*, under his control, even ran a competition for the best letter on the theme of 'Why I like the Blackshirts'. This support from a mass-circulation press thrust a relatively obscure organization into the limelight and contributed to an increase in its membership. But Rothermere withdrew his support after little more than five months, thereby helping to deny the BUF the legitimacy which it needed in order to attract substantial right-wing 'respectable' support.

## The press barons and the social order

Some historians have interpreted the relative failure of the press barons to persuade people to vote for the new political parties and causes they championed as evidence that they exercised no significant political power. Thus A. J. P. Taylor writes, 'Though people bought Northcliffe's papers for their news, they were no more impressed by his political sense than that of any other successful businessman.' But to define the impact of the press barons in terms appropriate to pressure groups is to misunderstand the nature of their influence. Their main significance lay in the way in which their papers provided cumulative support for conservative values and reinforced opposition, particularly among the middle class, to progressive change.

The papers controlled by the press barons conjured up imaginary folk devils that served to strengthen commitment to dominant political norms and to unite the centre and the right against a common enemy. The most prominent of these public enemies were British Marxists controlled from Moscow. The first ineffectual Labour coalition administration formed in 1924 was branded as a Marxist-dominated regime by the press barons' papers, even though it showed little signs of pursuing radical policies during its short period in office. In the subsequent general election campaign, the 'red peril' campaign reached new heights. 'Civil War plot by Socialists' Masters,' screamed the *Daily Mail*'s (25 October 1924) front page banner headline, heading a report of a letter supposedly sent by Zinoviev (president of the Third Communist International in Moscow) to the British Communist Party. Although the letter was patently a forgery, it was given massive, largely uncritical publicity by all the press barons' papers, and was shamelessly exploited to define the choice before the electorate as a simple one between moderates and Marxists, British civilization or alien domination. 'Vote British, not Bolshie,' urged the *Daily Mirror* (29 October) in its front page headline. Underneath it printed the simple question in heavy type, 'Do You Wish to Vote for the Leaders of Law, Order, Peace and Prosperity?' (with reassuring pictures of Lloyd George, Baldwin, Asquith, and Austen Chamberlain), 'or to Vote for the Overthrow of Society and Pave the Way to Bolshevism?' (with sinister pictures of Russian leaders).

It is doubtful whether such crude propaganda deterred many would-be Labour voters – not least because the majority of working people did not read a daily paper in 1924 (unlike ten years later). Although the Labour Party lost forty seats, its share of the vote increased by 3.2 per cent largely because it fielded sixty-four more candidates. But the effect of the sustained red scare in the press was to polarize the election between left and right. The centre vote collapsed, with the Liberal Party being reduced from 158 to 40 seats. The hysteria whipped up by the press also contributed to a massive increase in turn-out, which rose by over 2 million compared with the previous general election held less than a year before. The combined effect of Liberal defections and reduced abstentions inflated the Conservative vote and resulted in a landslide Tory victory.

The press also tended to select and interpret the news within a dominant framework. Most national newspapers, for instance, portrayed the 1926 General Strike as a conflict between a minority and the majority. By framing the dispute in this way, they detached strikers from their class base and obscured the true nature of the conflict. The minority–majority paradigm also offered an explanation of the strike: it was the work of communist militants opposed to the democratically elected government and the rule of the majority. 'The defeat of the General Strike', declared the *Daily Mail* (14 May 1926), 'will end the danger of communist tyranny in Europe.' The portrayal of strikers as a threatening minority also served to legitimate political retribution as a collective act of self-defence. 'Trade unionists in this country', declared the *Observer* (16 May 1926), 'are and always will be a minority, and if they seriously try to break the majority, they make it quite certain that the majority, if further provoked, will break them.' A similarly persuasive and traditionalist framework was deployed in explaining the recession. It was widely portrayed as a 'natural catastrophe', comparable to a hurricane or flood. In this way, the appropriate response was defined as national unity in the face of a common calamity rather than radical new policies.

The press controlled by the barons helped to sustain the dominant culture by stigmatizing radical opponents of the political order. The communist-dominated Unemployed Workers' Movement, for instance, received hostile coverage when it organized marches of unemployed workers from Scotland, Wales, and the north of England all converging on London early in 1929. The *Daily Mail* (24 February 1929) called it 'a weary tramp to advertise Reds', while *The Times* (11 January 1929) called it 'heartless, cruel and unnecessary'. In common with most other papers, they deflected attention from the issue of unemployment by defining the protest mainly in terms of the threat it posed to law and order. Significantly the press provided much more sympathetic coverage of the 1936 Jarrow March, which had the support of both Conservative and Labour councillors and a much more limited political goal. The press thus helped to police the boundaries of legitimate dissent.

The central core of the conservatism expressed by papers under the barons' control was a deep and emotional attachment to Britain and her Empire. This intense patriotism sometimes shaded off into open racism and, particularly in the case of the papers controlled by Rothermere, aggressive anti-semitism. The *Daily Mail* (10 July 1933) explained, for instance, the background to Hitler's rise in this way:

> The German nation was rapidly falling under the control of its alien elements. In the last days of the pre-Hitler regime there were twenty times as many Jewish government officials in Germany as had existed before the war. Israelites of international attachments were insinuating themselves into key positions in the German administrative machine.

Such interpretations of the rise of fascism in Europe served to reinforce popular anti-semitism in Britain and contributed to the maintenance of Britain's restrictive immigration policy which prevented some German Jews from finding refuge in Britain.

## Modification of economic controls

Although the press became more independent of political parties and of government, it operated within an economic framework which limited the range of voices that could be heard. The rise in publishing costs during the inter-war period, largely funded by advertising, sealed off entry into the national newspaper market. With one exception, no new national daily or Sunday newspaper was successfully established between 1919 and 1939, largely because of the prohibitive cost of establishing new papers. The one exception – the Communist *Sunday Worker*, launched in 1925 and converted into the *Daily Worker* in 1930 – was boycotted by distributors, and was so under-financed that it existed only on the margins of publishing with a circulation of well under 100,000.

The easiest way to break into national newspaper publishing

was to buy an established newspaper. But even this still required massive expenditure to develop and promote the title that had been acquired. The level of investment needed was beyond the readily available resources of the Co-op when it took over *Reynolds News*. Indeed the triumphant rise of the *Daily Herald* would never have happened on such a spectacular scale if Odhams had not acquired a 51 per cent interest in the paper in 1929 and spent £3 million on its relaunch. Carrying twice as many pages as before, equipped with a northern as well as a London printing plant, and very heavily promoted, the *Daily Herald* increased its circulation from a little over 300,000 in 1929 to 2 million in 1933. Without this backing by one of the country's largest publishing conglomerates (based on a serious commercial miscalculation since, though the *Daily Herald* was a popular success, it was a financial failure), even Labour's official voice would have been muzzled by the capital requirements of mass publishing.

The persistence of advertising discrimination against left publications acted as a further brake upon their development. *Reynolds News*, for instance, received only 0.82d per copy in gross advertising revenue in 1936, less than half that obtained by the *Sunday Express* (1.9d per copy) and less than one-eighth of that bestowed on the *Sunday Times* (6.4d per copy).[8] Left publications were also forced to close down with circulations far higher than those of their respectable rivals. Thus the *Clarion* closed in 1933 with a circulation of over 80,000 copies – more than four times that of the *Spectator* and ten times that of the *Economist*. Even massive circulations were not enough to attract some mass-market advertisers. In 1936 the *Daily Herald* obtained less than half the gross advertising revenue per copy of the smaller-circulation *Daily Mail*.

But advertising hostility to the radical press was not as great during the inter-war period as it had been before. The standard advertising textbook of the 1930s advised that 'The first test that must always be applied to a press advertising medium is the cost of placing an advertisement of a given size before a given number of suitable readers.' While this precept was not new, the ability to put it into effect was. Circulation figures became more reliable during the 1920s and this trend was consolidated by the establishment of the Audit Bureau of Circulation in 1931. Survey research into the size and social composition of newspaper readership was introduced on a commercial basis in 1924 and obtained official endorsement from the advertising industry in 1930.

The provision of reliable statistical data encouraged a more impersonal approach to advertising selection, based on quantifiable cost criteria, in which political value-judgements played a less important part. Readership research also caused advertisers to reassess stereotyped images of the readers of left publications as being 'down at heel'. For instance the 1934 official readership survey showed that the *Daily Herald* was read by more middle-class people than *The Times* (even though the *Herald*'s readership was predominantly working class).

The development of market research in the 1920s also helped radical publications by underlining the importance of the working-class market. Typical of the shift of orientation among many advertisers during this period was Sun-Maid Raisins, which changed its advertising from high-class women's magazines to mass market media in 1929 because research 'shows that 91.2 per cent of the families of Great Britain have incomes of under £400'.[9] The adoption of more sophisticated methods of analysis reinforced this more positive valorization of the working-class market. 'Inequalities of consumption', concluded the principal marketing manual of the mid-1930s, 'are less than inequalities of income, and inequalities of income are less than inequalities of wealth.'[10] A similar message was put rather less abstractly in the trade promotion of Odhams, the publisher of the *Daily Herald, John Bull*, and other working-class publications. As one of their advertisements proclaimed, 'If the housewives who read *John Bull* put their purses together next year, they could buy the Giaconda diamond or Da Vinci's "Mona Lisa" hundreds of times over, then they could spend the change on the richest treasures of Bond Street or the Rue de la Paix.'

Selling the working class to advertisers was made easier by the growth of working-class purchasing power, and the related growth of large-scale production of mass market goods. *Per capita* annual consumer expenditure at constant (1913) prices rose from £42 in 1921 to £54 in 1938, a large increase that reflected the rise of real wages among working people in employment during the Depression. This contributed to an enormous increase in the purchase of branded products like cosmetics, medicines, bicycles, and electrical appliances.

These cumulative changes were of crucial importance in enabling the *Daily Herald* to gain in influence and circulation. Although it obtained only a fraction of the advertising revenue per copy of its main rivals, it was still able to pick up over £1.5 million in gross advertising receipts by 1936. Without this backing, the *Daily Herald* would have been forced to double its price and so lose circulation. Even this might not have been enough to cover the losses incurred by its very heavy promotion and expanding circulation. Indeed despite its increased advertising, the *Daily Herald* was still trading at a loss when it became the western world's largest circulation newspaper in 1933.

Changes in the orientation of advertisers contributed to another important development in the press – the relaunch of the *Daily Mirror* and *Sunday Pictorial*. In the early 1930s the *Daily Mirror* seemed to be a dying paper. Although it had a disproportionately middle-class readership, it was denied the usual benefits of reaching an affluent audience because most advertisers then subscribed to the mistaken view that tabloid papers were read only sketchily. In addition, its circulation was declining by about 70,000 a year and had dropped below 800,000 by 1933. In anticipation of its closing, the *Daily Mirror* was deserted by its principal owner, Rothermere.

Rothermere's disengagement enabled the paper to change direction. Bartholomew was created editorial director in 1933, and the paper was skilfully steered towards a gap in the market. Advertisers' traditional orientation towards middle- and lower-middle-class readers had encouraged the lower end of the market to be neglected. However, the shift in the outlook of many advertisers indicated that a paper which recruited new working-class readers would get advertising support. The inspiration behind the paper's relaunch was essentially a marketing one, and this was reflected in the close involvement of a leading advertising agency, J. Walter Thompson (JWT), in every stage of the paper's rebirth. JWT carried out market research into readers' preferences, advised on layout, relinquished members of its staff to become key members of the new *Mirror* team, and, above all, urged it clients to back the new venture with advertising.

A change in market direction for the *Daily Mirror* required a corresponding shift in the paper's politics. As Cecil King, the paper's advertising director put it,

> Our best hope was, therefore, to appeal to young, working-class men and women. . . . If this was the aim, the politics had to be made to match. In the depression of the thirties, there was no future in preaching right-wing politics to young people in the lowest income bracket.

The political shift of the *Daily Mirror* was nevertheless cautious.

It backed Baldwin as Prime Minister in the 1935 general election, gradually adopted an anti-appeasement policy, but drew back from anything as extreme as support for the Labour Party. It also developed an ambiguous social identity that mirrored its political uncertainty, combining traditional features about debutante balls with racy articles aimed at young working people.

Although commercial pressures encouraged an editorial adjustment, they actively discouraged the *Daily Mirror* from moving too far down-market or editorially too far to the left. The *Mirror's* management became nervous about alienating its traditional, predominantly Conservative, and disproportionately middle-class readership. They also became even more apprehensive about the paper becoming stereotyped as a working-class tabloid at a time when working-class audiences generated much less advertising than middle-class audiences. Indeed the *Daily Mirror* even undertook a promotion campaign in the advertising trade press boasting of its upper-class, 'A' readership (the top 5 per cent of the country). 'Only one of the six popular national papers', the *Daily Mirror* declared in 1938, 'can claim more "A" class readers.'

The really important change in the *Daily Mirror*, however, was not its flirtation with reformist politics, but its relegation of politics in favour of material with a wider appeal to women and young readers. Between 1927 and 1937 the *Daily Mirror* cut by half the proportion of its news devoted to political, social, economic, and industrial issues.[11] The shift meant that, in 1936, the *Daily Mirror's* coverage of domestic public affairs was less than half that of its sports coverage, and little over one-third of its coverage of crime, sex, and other human interest content. Even more striking, its analysis of public affairs, whether in the form of editorials or feature articles, accounted for a mere 2 per cent of its editorial content.[12] The *Daily Mirror's* relaunch constituted a key moment in the incorporation of the press by the entertainment industry.

The relaunch of the *Daily Mirror* was extremely successful. Its circulation rose to 1.5 million by 1939 and, after an initial period of difficulty, its advertising revenue also increased substantially. The *Mirror's* success prompted a similar marketing operation on its sister paper, the *Sunday Pictorial*, in 1937, under the aegis of Cecil King and Hugh Cudlipp. The *Sunday Pictorial* also moved away from right-wing politics and a middle-class social identity without becoming left wing or working class. 'Our "A" class readership', the *Sunday Pictorial* reassured advertisers, 'is greater than that of any other Sunday paper.'

Advertising patronage still inhibited the development of radical journalism. Yet the rise of working-class living standards, and changes in the way in which advertisers selected media, had encouraged a move away from right-wing politics by part of the popular press. The foundation had been laid for the development of a powerful social democratic press that would press for reform in the different social and economic context of the Second World War.

## Notes

1. Circulation figures for the inter-war period are not entirely reliable. The principal sources for circulations used in this chapter have been T. B. Browne's annual *Advertisers' ABC*; Royal Commission on the Press 1947–9 Report (London, HMSO, 1949); N. Kaldor and R. Silverman, *A Statistical Analysis of Advertising Expenditure and of the Revenue of the Press* (Cambridge, Cambridge University Press, 1948); W. Belson, *The British Press* (London, London Press Exchange Ltd, 1959); the Audit Bureau of Circulations; and individual publishers.
2. In fact most of Beaverbrook's senior editors kept their jobs for exceptionally long periods of time, though this was less true of his more junior employees.
3. Northcliffe's unpredictability increased to the point of insanity, possibly induced by syphilis.
4. *Report on the British Press* (London, Political & Economic Planning, 1938), p. 132.
5. The relative proportion of space devoted to different categories of article is what is significant in discussing the evolution of the newspaper as a genre rather than absolute changes, which will vary according to the volume of paging. For a different view, see Ralph Negrine, *Politics and the Mass Media in Britain* (London, Routledge, 1989), pp. 84–8. Our content analysis was based on a sample of twelve issues of each daily, and six issues of each Sunday paper in 1936. Public affairs is defined as political, social, economic, industrial, scientific and medical affairs. For a summary of the results, see chapter 7.
6. *Royal Commission on the Press 1947–9 Report*, Appendix 7, p. 250.
7. *A Survey of Reader Interest* (*News Chronicle*, 1934).
8. 'A statistical survey of press advertising during 1936' (London Press Exchange Ltd records). The figures exclude certain forms of classified advertising.

9. 'The Sun-Maid plan 1929–30' (J. Walter Thompson Ltd records).
10. G. Harrison and F. C. Mitchell, *The Home Market: A Handbook of Statistics* (London, Allen & Unwin, 1936), p. 6.
11. *Royal Commission on the Press 1947–9 Report*, Appendix 7, pp. 257–8.
12. See note 5. This represented a reduction in real terms during the period 1927–37, notwithstanding the increase in the size of the *Daily Mirror* and the rise in the proportion of its editorial content devoted to news.

# 6

# The press under public regulation

Nostalgia has encouraged the belief that the British people closed ranks with bulldog determination under the unchallenged leadership of Churchill during the Second World War. This mythical view obscures the political and social crisis of the early war years, which led to a major confrontation between the government and the left press.

Many senior politicians and officials doubted the commitment of the British people to winning the war. A significantly named Home Morale Emergency Committee of the Ministry of Information reported in June 1940 on 'fear, confusion, suspicion, class feeling and defeatism'. Even the ministry's parliamentary secretary, Harold Nicolson, confided in his diary during this period, 'It will now be almost impossible to beat the Germans.'[1] For at least the first two and a half years of the war, the relationship between the authorities and the press was dominated by an excessive and probably misplaced concern about the state of public morale.

This anxiety was combined with growing concern amongst conservative politicians and civil servants about the growth of radicalism in Britain. In February 1942 the ministry's Home Intelligence Division reported a wave of admiration for Soviet Russia and a growing suspicion amongst sections of the working class that financial vested interests were hampering the war effort. A month later the ministry commented on what was to become a familiar theme – the flowering of 'home-made Socialism' of which important elements were 'a revulsion against "vested interests", "privilege", and what is referred to as "the old gang"' and 'a general agreement that things were going to be different after the war'.[2] In these circumstances, left-wing criticism in the press took on an added meaning. Not only did it seem, in the eyes of some, to be undermining military discipline and impeding efficient production, but also it was adding to political divisions at home when the nation desperately needed to be united against the common enemy. Indeed the maintenance of public morale came close to being equated by some ministers and officials with suppressing radical criticism of any kind.

Yet a succession of military defeats provoked mounting attacks on 'the old gang'. In 1940 Neville Chamberlain was forced to resign as Prime Minister. The new Coalition government under Churchill also came under growing attack as the military situation deteriorated. A cumulative political crisis developed which was only partially defused by changes in the Cabinet and leadership of the armed forces in 1940, 1941, and 1942. Press censorship thus became part of a beleaguered administration's battle for survival.

The circumstances of the Second World War also called for special measures. The strategic objective of the blitz was not only to impede war production but also to destroy the ability and will of the civilian population to service the war effort. This inevitably made regulation of the press an even more sensitive issue than it had been during the First World War.

## Censorship and resistance

Amid mounting fears of invasion in the summer of 1940, the government issued regulations which gave the Home Secretary sweeping powers to control the press. The most important of these was Regulation 2D which gave the Home Secretary the personal power to ban any publication which published material 'calculated to foment opposition to the prosecution to a successful issue of any war in which His Majesty is engaged'. The regulation also denied the offending publication any automatic right of appeal or recourse to the law courts. As one angry MP declared, 'Its effect will be to put the Ministry of Home Security in a position by no means inferior, as regards the scope of its powers over newspapers, to that occupied by the distinguished Dr Goebbels in Germany.'[3]

A major campaign was organized against these new measures. Leading members of the old political establishment, including Lloyd George, were mobilized, and much of the press joined in the protest. Concerted opposition was mounted in the Commons with the result that the government secured ratification of the regulations by only thirty-eight votes – the smallest majority on any issue gained by the new government. This opposition was important because it secured two vital concessions that limited the way in which the regulations were subsequently implemented. First, Sir John Anderson, the Home Secretary, gave an undertaking that no amendments would be made to the regulations without parliamentary consultation. Cabinet memoranda show that three months later this pledge was effective in blocking moves to ban publications which were deemed to 'disrupt the unity of effort' in the country.[4] Secondly, Sir John Anderson indicated in the Commons that the regulations would apply only to papers opposed to the continuance of the war. When government ministers later wanted to close down a pro-war paper, they felt it necessary to re-interpret the scope and purpose of the regulations. This created a delay which enabled effective opposition to be organized.

## Silencing the Communist press

Following a unanimous Cabinet decision, the Communist *Daily Worker* and the *Week* were closed on 21 January 1941. The *Daily Worker* had modified its anti-fascist editorial policy, following the signing of the Nazi-Soviet pact in 1939, and attacked the war as a struggle between imperialist powers. The ostensible ground for banning the two papers was that they were impeding the war effort by setting people against the war. This was not borne out by research undertaken by the Ministry of Information, which indicated that both publications had little influence on public attitudes. The *Daily Worker* accounted for less than 1 per cent of total national daily circulation, while the *Week* had an even smaller audience.

But if the two papers did not damage public morale, they clearly damaged the morale of the Cabinet. The *Daily Worker* campaigned on a number of sensitive issues – notably the in-adequacy of deep shelters and civil defence preparations – which the Cabinet was not in a position to remedy in the short term. The *Daily Worker* also published vituperative personal attacks on ministers – including a cartoon portraying Bevin, the Minister of Production, as being in the pay of capitalist bosses – which caused deep personal offence.

The ban on the two papers was also part of a wider government campaign against Communism in Britain which was being organized by the interdepartmental Committee on Communist Activities, including representatives from the Foreign Office and MI5, strongly supported by leading right-wing ministers. That the ban

was motivated, in part, by political prejudice – and not simply by
a concern about the papers' impact on public morale – is underlined by the unwillingness of the authorities to allow the *Daily
Worker* to start publication again when the British Communist
Party came round to full-hearted support of the war.

The government chose to close down the two Communist papers
by ministerial decree rather than by prosecuting them through the
law courts. Summary execution was preferred, partly because the
government feared that it might lose the case and partly because,
as a private memorandum from the Home Secretary explained, a
law suit would provide the *Worker* with 'a good opportunity for
propaganda against what it would describe as the government's
effort to "gag" the press.'[5] Although the government's actions
clearly amounted to an attack on press freedom, the self-
appointed watchdogs against the abuse of executive power were
mostly silent or approving. When the Home Secretary informed
the Newspaper Proprietors Association of the ban, only one person
objected. In parliament the more successful of the two motions
opposing the government's actions attracted only eleven votes.

## Harassment of the left press

The assault on the Communist press was part of a wider move to
curb criticism from left papers. The *Daily Herald*, which had been
outspokenly critical during the early stages of the war, moderated
its tone when the Labour Party joined the coalition. Pressure was
brought to bear upon the paper through its TUC-nominated
directors. Appeals to loyalty also helped to subdue criticism of
the government in *Reynolds News*, the paper of the Co-operative
Movement. But the *Daily Mirror* and *Sunday Pictorial*, which
moved sharply to the left during the war, were much more
difficult to deal with. They were not controlled by the labour
movement, nor were they answerable to a dominant shareholder
(as the Cabinet discovered after a secret investigation into the
shareholders of the two papers).

At first pressure was exerted informally through a series of
meetings between senior members of the government and directors
of the two papers. When this failed, Churchill urged a more direct
approach. Both papers, he argued in a Cabinet meeting on 7
October 1940, published articles that were subversive. He went
on to suggest that a conspiracy lay behind this criticism. 'There
was far more behind these articles', Churchill warned, 'than

disgruntlement or frayed nerves. They stood for something most dangerous and sinister, namely an attempt to bring about a situation in which the country would be ready for a surrender peace.'[6]

The new Home Secretary, Herbert Morrison, asked for time to consider the issue. The next day he circulated a sharply worded memorandum to his Cabinet colleagues in which he suggested that 'There is much in the papers (*Daily Mirror* and *Sunday Pictorial*) which is calculated to promote a war spirit. They seem to be clearly anxious for the defeat of Hitlerism.' After arguing that government action would be counterproductive, he declared, 'It is a tradition of the British people that they still remain obedient to the constituted authorities while retaining their liberty to ridicule and denounce the individuals who are actually in authority.'[7]

An unlikely struggle developed in which Morrison, the archetypal machine politician, vigorously defended press freedom against Churchill, a former journalist famous for his eloquent speeches in defence of liberty. In the next Cabinet meeting, Churchill accused the *Daily Mirror* and *Sunday Pictorial* of 'trying to rock the boat' and demanded 'firm action to deal with this menace'. He was strongly supported by, among others, Sir John Anderson who was in favour of issuing a warning to the two papers and then closing them down if they did not change their attitude. Morrison opposed this, arguing that such action would divide the Commons on party lines and amount to 'interference with the liberty of the press'.

In the end the Cabinet agreed, at Beaverbrook's suggestion, to exert pressure on the two papers through the Newspaper Proprietors Association (NPA). A meeting was arranged between Beaverbrook and Attlee, representing the government, and the NPA. The proprietors were warned that compulsory censorship might be introduced if the *Daily Mirror* and *Sunday Pictorial* were not more restrained. The proprietors protested strongly against compulsory censorship at the meeting, but they subsequently urged the senior management of the *Daily Mirror* and *Sunday Pictorial* to exert a moderating influence on their staff. The effect of this intervention was limited. 'We shall pipe down for a few weeks,' Cecil King, a director of both papers, commented in his diary.

Churchill's allegations that the two papers were motivated by a desire to secure 'a surrender peace' was unjustified. Both papers were totally committed to winning the war. Indeed they had opposed appeasement with Germany before anti-appeasement had become government policy: they had also backed Churchill for the leadership on the grounds that he would push for a more vigorous prosecution of the war. The tone of the *Mirror* was every bit as belligerent as that of Churchill himself: 'We appeal to every worker and every employer to play the man . . . stick to your job unless it is foolhardy to do so' (30 September 1940). The *Sunday Pictorial* was no different. Pillorying Lloyd George as 'the Marshal of the weak and the terrorized' when he proposed a negotiated settlement, it had even less time for pacifists. 'Put the lot behind barbed wire,' it urged.

The real reason for the attack on the two papers was that they had become increasingly critical of the government. The *Sunday Pictorial* (29 September) called the reverse at Dakar 'another blunder' while the *Daily Mirror* referred pointedly to 'futile dashes at remote strategic points'. Both papers began also to urge social reform at home. But they left no doubt in the mind of their readers that victory against Hilter was what mattered most. 'However bad the "pluto-democratic" world may be', declared a *Daily Mirror* columnist, 'it is at least better than the depravity that would suppress all independent action and thought under the devilish way of life commended by Nazi fanatics.'

Clashes between the government and the *Mirror* and *Pictorial* recurred throughout 1941 and early 1942, largely because both sides had irreconcilable views about what constituted the national interest.[8] Leading Conservative ministers believed that criticism of officers in the *Daily Mirror* – including a reference to 'brass-buttoned boneheads, socially prejudiced, arrogant and fussy' – served to undermine the respect for rank that was the basis of good discipline in the army. They also felt that the *Daily Mirror*'s calls for post-war reconstruction were needlessly introducing political controversy and dividing the nation at a time of national emergency. The *Daily Mirror*, with an average circulation of 1,900,000, had become in their view a serious obstacle to winning the war.

*Daily Mirror* journalists, on the other hand, saw themselves as contributing to the war effort. They argued that Britain, in its hour of need, could not afford the incompetence that arose from snobbery and privilege: responsible jobs should go to those selected on the basis of ability rather than of birth. And plans for a new deal after the war were not divisive in a society already divided by class inequalities: on the contrary a programme for 'winning the peace'

would help win the war by motivating people to contribute even
more to the war effort.

These differences flared up into a full-scale confrontation in
March 1942. The occasion, though not the cause, of the confrontation was a cartoon published in the *Daily Mirror* by Zec which
showed a torpedoed sailor adrift on a raft in the open sea with the
caption: 'The price of petrol has been increased by one penny –
official.' This was interpreted by Churchill and many of his
Cabinet colleagues to be an unprincipled attack upon the government for sanctioning oil company profiteering at the expense of
people's lives. Its real intention was quite different: Zec meant it
as an attack upon the needless waste of petrol by dramatizing the
human sacrifice involved in shipping oil to Britain. This was how
it was understood by most people, according to a Home Intelligence
Report, as well as by most MPs who commented on it in a
subsequent Commons debate.[9]

The misconceptions about the Zec cartoon were symptomatic of
the demoralization within the Cabinet. In the three months preceding the confrontation with the *Daily Mirror*, the allies had
suffered defeats at Guam, Wake, Hong Kong, Manila, the Dutch
East Indies, Rangoon, Benghazi, and Singapore. In the embattled
atmosphere of Cabinet discussions, the press came to be blamed
by ministers on the left as well as the right for some of the things
that were going wrong. Bevin, the Labour Minister, demanded in
a highly emotional state, 'how was he to "press" people almost
into the Merchant Navy if they were then to see the suggestion (in
the Zec cartoon) that they were being "pressed" in order to put
the price of petrol up for the owners?' The *Daily Mirror*'s staff
had become scapegoats for failure. 'We will flatten them,' Churchill
told his Information Minister, Brendan Bracken.[10]

The assault on the *Daily Mirror* was, however, part of a more
general struggle for political survival. A *Daily Mirror* editorial on
16 February 1942 came very close to demanding a new administration in a sweeping indictment:

> The assumption that whatever blunders are committed, and
> whatever faults are plainly visible in organization, we must still
> go on applauding men who muddle our lives away, is a travesty
> of history and a rhetorical defiance of all the bitter lessons of
> past wars.

Many politicians thought that the government would be forced to
resign between the winter of 1941 and the summer of 1942.

Churchill himself believed that he might be ousted. 'My diary for 1942', writes a member of Churchill's personal entourage, 'has the same backcloth to every scene: Winston's conviction that his life as Prime Minister could be saved only by victory in the field.' Even the general public, previously more loyal to the premier and his administration than the political élite, showed signs of turning against Churchill.[11]

The attack on the *Daily Mirror* was thus a pre-emptive strike against the government's principal critic. Its purpose, as discussion amongst Cabinet ministers made clear, was not only to silence the *Daily Mirror* but also to intimidate the rest of the press into adopting a less critical stance. Churchill demanded the immediate closure of the *Daily Mirror* in a full Cabinet meeting on 9 March 1942. The matter was referred to a Special Committee under the chairmanship of Sir John Anderson. The committee was advised by the law officers (rather surprisingly in view of the terms in which censorship regulations had been introduced) that it was legal to close down the *Daily Mirror* because, although it supported the war, it impeded its 'successful prosecution'. Indeed the Lord Chancellor urged immediate suspension of the paper since the experience of the last war suggested that quick, decisive action would be effective. 'When the then Home Secretary quite illegally suppressed the *Globe* newspaper,' he recalled, '. . . there was a row in the House in one debate in which the government received overwhelming support, and nothing was ever heard of the *Globe* newspaper again.'[12]

The committee did not, however, endorse the proposal to close the *Mirror* although it suggested that 'it would be helpful if an example could be made' to curb press criticism. Those opposed to an immediate ban stressed that 'It was clear from the debates in parliament at the time when Regulation 2D had been enacted that it would be used to deal with Communist, Fascist or Pacifist Anti-War agitators' – but not, they pointed out, 'for the purposes now suggested'. There had to be a public redefinition of the government's censorship powers before anything could be done.[13]

At this stage a near consensus had been reached in favour of banning the *Daily Mirror*. The hawks, who wanted immediate suspension, had been strengthened by the recruitment of Bevin, the only trade union leader in the Cabinet. The opposition of the doves, on the other hand, had weakened. They stood out for giving the *Daily Mirror* one last chance in which to reform itself, while at the same time seemingly consenting to the paper's suppression if it did not 'improve'. Even Morrison, the principal dove and the minister who would be responsible for carrying out Cabinet policy, apparently agreed that if the *Daily Mirror* people 'did not amend I would suppress them'.[14]

Morrison announced that Defence Regulation 2D empowered the government to ban pro-war papers which undermined the war effort, even if the offence was not intentional but merely arose from a 'reckless and unpatriotic indifference'. He added that the *Daily Mirror* would be banned without further notice unless 'those concerned recognized their public responsibilities'. The same warning was given personally to the *Daily Mirror*'s senior management, and a report of the meeting released to the press.

Most members of the government clearly did not anticipate the storm of protest that followed. A large group of MPs demanded a special debate in the Commons. In a packed House a Liberal MP, Wilfred Roberts, aptly quoted an article published in the USA by the Minister of Information, Brendan Bracken. In this Bracken had argued that 'the savage censorship imposed on the French press played no small part in the fall of France. It encouraged defeatism, and bred complacency. A blindfolded democracy is more likely to fall than to fight.' A Labour MP, Frederick Bellenger, then cited an article written by Herbert Morrison during the First World War in which he had urged all soldiers not to fight 'your German brother' in an imperialist struggle. Morrison was pointedly asked why he was not now extending the same freedom of expression to others.

As the debate progressed, it became clear that it was the government rather than the *Daily Mirror* which was on trial. While loyal Conservative MPs rallied to Morrison's defence, the great majority of Labour and Liberal MPs were opposed. The Coalition administration was confronted, as Morrison had feared, with an issue that divided the Commons along party political lines.

Newspaper proprietors and editors were also not as compliant as they had been over the closure of the *Daily Worker*. While many Sunday and local papers supported the government, the majority of national daily papers sided with the *Mirror*. It thus became clear that closing down the *Daily Mirror* would lead to a major confrontation with a powerful section of the press.

The strength of opposition was such that the *Daily Mirror* was never really in any danger of being closed down after March 1942. Thereafter official displeasure took the form of harassment, such as Churchill's personal request that Cecil King be conscripted into the armed forces.[15] The victory was not, however, entirely one-sided. The *Daily Mirror*'s outspoken radicalism became more subdued and the paper's most controversial column-ist, Cassandra (Connor), decided it was time to join the army.

The defence of the *Daily Mirror* overlapped with a major campaign to lift the ban on the *Daily Worker*. Mass rallies were organized in Trafalgar Square and in London's Central Hall. The Labour Party Annual Conference voted down its national execu-tive's recommendation by backing the ending of the ban. The Co-operative Congress and the Scottish TUC followed suit. In the face of this escalating pressure from the organized working class, the government relented. The ban on the *Daily Worker* was lifted on 26 August 1942 – more than a year after the USSR had become one of Britain's closest allies.

## The defeat of censorship

The *Daily Mirror* and *Daily Worker* campaigns were part of a wider victory against the abuse of censorship powers. The notorious Regulation 2D was never again used after 1942. All proposals for compulsory censorship of the press were rejected. An ingenious scheme for bringing pressure to bear on newspapers by allocating rationed newsprint to publications solely according to their contri-bution to the war effort was also turned down.

Admittedly, the government drew back from taking full ad-vantage of its censorship powers partly because the press proved, on the whole, to be co-operative. The Chairman of the Newspaper Emergency Council, for instance, wrote to the Ministry of Information in 1939 that 'Our respective tasks and duties are complementary.'[16] Some editors even took the Ministry of Informa-tion to task for being too permissive in its advisory guidelines about what should not be published. The press, including critical and independent-minded papers like the *Daily Mirror*, consciously sought to bolster public morale at the expense of objective report-ing. Coercive censorship was made, to some extent, unnecessary by self-censorship.

The authorities were also restrained from exercising greater control over the press through purely pragmatic considerations. Military censorship of dispatches sent by war correspondents accompanying the armed forces provided a discreet means of regulating uncomfortable news. A number of senior Ministry of Information officials also became convinced that compulsory censorship was unnecessary, once they came round to the view that public morale was holding up. Some also felt that the credibility of a largely co-operative press would be undermined if it was seen to be directly controlled by the government. These arguments from the Ministry of Information helped to deflect more authoritarian attempts to censor newspapers. When the military situation improved after the summer of 1942, and the position of Churchill's administration became secure, ministers also became notably less sensitive to criticism.

But widespread commitment to the ideal of a free press also played an important part in stopping illiberal politicians like Churchill and Anderson from taking control of the press. Press freedom was one of the symbols of democracy that Britain was defending against Nazi Germany. This became a rallying slogan for anti-censorship campaigns which the government could not afford to ignore. When a senior official in the Ministry of Information wrote that 'It would be improper to propose in this country either a moral or a political censorship of opinion, for that would be contrary to the last 300 years of English history,' he added a significant postscript: 'It would also be perilous in view of the recent events surrounding the *Daily Mirror* and *Daily Worker* and the parliamentary and public attention that has been paid to them.'[17] In resisting the abuse of arbitrary censorship powers, relatively obscure politicians like Bellenger and Roberts, along with a large number of now-forgotten labour movement activists, kept alive the tradition of an independent press. The political processes of a democratic society saved government from itself.

## Freedom from commercial controls

Ironically it was partly the government's economic intervention in the press industry that caused leading politicians to be subject to such unwelcome scrutiny by left-wing newspapers. Newsprint was rationed, on a statutory basis, from 1940 in order to husband a scarce resource and ensure its equitable distribution. An unintended effect of this control was to liberate the press from some of the economic pressures that had previously inhibited the development of radical journalism.

Newspaper managements voluntarily curtailed the amount of advertising they took because newsprint rationing reduced papers to less than one-third of their pre-war size. This self-imposed rationing was formalized in 1942 by new regulations which restricted the proportion of newspaper space which could be allocated to advertising. As a consequence, the money that people paid for their papers once again made a substantial contribution to the finances of the press. London-based dailies, for instance, derived 69 per cent of their revenue from sales in 1943, compared with only 30 per cent in 1938.

Newsprint rationing also redistributed advertising expenditure. Newspapers which had difficulty attracting advertising before the war found agencies begging them to take their orders due to the general shortage of advertising space. This meant that radical editorial policies and low-paid readerships no longer carried a financial penalty.

These changes did not in themselves account for the sharp move to the left made by some papers during the war. The experience of the war changed the outlook of journalists and expanded the demand for radical journalism. As A. C. H. Smith has shown, a radicalizing rapport developed between the *Daily Mirror* and its audience. Readers' letters and documentary-style reporting influenced the tone and orientation of the paper, helping it to acquire a distinctively working-class voice. But while economic controls did not cause the wartime transformation of the *Daily Mirror* and *Sunday Pictorial*, they provided the economic environment that made the shift possible.

Economic pressures had restrained both papers from moving further to the left in the late 1930s. But the wartime liberation from advertisers meant that they could aim solely at a working-class readership. They could also develop clear political identities in keeping with their more homogeneous audiences. Survey research shows that the *Sunday Pictorial* entered the war with a disproportionately middle-class readership and re-emerged after the war with a mainly working-class one. Similarly the *Daily Mirror* had the most cross-sectional readership of all national dailies in 1939, but its readers were solidly proletarian by 1947. The readership of both papers was also overwhelmingly Labour immediately after the war.

Newsprint rationing also reduced the polarization between quality and popular papers. Popular papers were no longer under intense pressure to seek ever larger audiences because circulation levels were 'pegged' during much of the war. By reducing costs and redistributing advertising, newsprint controls also increased the profitability of many newspapers. These changes coincided with a new interest not only in war news, but also in public affairs in general. As a consequence the proportion of space devoted to public affairs doubled in all wartime popular national dailies, save in the already politicized *Daily Herald*.

Wartime controls thus contributed to the development of a radical and less entertainment-oriented press. The aggregate circulation of the *Daily Mirror* and *Sunday Pictorial*, combined with that of the *Daily Herald*, *Reynolds News*, and *Daily Worker*, amounted to nearly 9 million copies in 1945. This formidable grouping of papers was supplemented by the progressive *Picture Post*, an illustrated weekly with a readership (as distinct from circulation) of well over 4 million people. Not since the mid-Victorian period had the left been so well represented within the press.

These publications provided a strong impetus behind social democratic change in wartime Britain. This can be illustrated by the reception given to the Beveridge Report, published in 1942, which provided the basis of many of the reforms later implemented by the Attlee government. The report was hailed by the left press with banner headlines, congratulatory editorials, and detailed summaries of its recommendations. It 'will so much break the old order', proclaimed the *Sunday Pictorial* (6 December 1942), 'that it will rank as little short of a Magna Carta for the toiling masses in Britain'. According to the *Daily Herald* (2 December 1942) the report was a 'massive achievement'. The *Daily Mirror* (2 December 1942) was scarcely less lyrical. Anticipating counter-arguments, it also published a sober article by Beveridge entitled, 'Britain Can Afford It'. The report also received sympathetic coverage from liberal papers such as the *News Chronicle* and *Manchester Guardian*, and even from the Conservative *Daily Mail*. As Cecil King noted at the time, 'The volume of press support is so great that it seems to be assumed in the House that it will be politically impossible to drop the Report.'

What might have been a relatively obscure official document which the Tory Minister of Information had initially wanted to be published quietly, was transformed with the help of press publicity into a cornerstone of the new consensus. Indeed a British Institute of Public Opinion survey in 1943 found that no fewer than 86 per cent of people wanted the Beveridge Report to be adopted. Radical newspapers were thus helping to lay the foundation for Labour's 1945 landslide victory more than two years before Labour's election campaign even began.

In short, public regulation during the Second World War helped rather than hindered the growth of radical journalism. Government attempts to silence the radical press were largely defeated, while official economic controls had the effect of making the press more responsive to changes in the public mood. State intervention proved to be, on balance, a liberating rather than a repressive influence.

## Notes

1. Ministry of Information (INF) 1/250, Report to Policy Committee (June 1940); H. Nicolson, *Diaries and Letters 1930–45* (London, Collins, 1967), p. 96
2. INF 1/292, Home Intelligence Weekly Report 73 (16–23 March 1942), Appendix.
3. *Parliamentary Debates*, 363 (1940), col. 1,307.
4. CAB 66/12, WP 402 (40) (8 October 1940).
5. CAB 66/14 (23 December 1940).
6. CAB 65/9, WM 267 (40) (7 October 1940).
7. CAB 66/12, WP 402 (40) (8 October 1940).
8. See, for instance, W. Armstrong (ed.), C. King, *With Malice Toward None* (London, Sidgwick & Jackson, 1970), pp. 94–9 and 103–7.
9. H. Cudlipp, *Walking on the Water* (London, Bodley Head, 1976), pp. 134–6; INF 1/282 Home Intelligence Weekly Report 78 (23–30 March 1942); *Parliamentary Debates* 378 (1942), cols 2,233–308.
10. Simon, CAB 66/23, WP 124 (42) (17 March 1942); Bevin and Churchill cited in A. J. P. Taylor (ed.), *Off the Record: W. P. Crozier, Political Interviews 1933–43* (London, Hutchinson, 1973), pp. 311 and 325.
11. Eden cited in J. Harvey (ed.), *The War Diaries of Oliver Harvey 1941–5* (London, Collins, 1978), p. 94; Churchill cited in Lord Moran, *Winston Churchill* (London, Sphere, 1968); INF 1/292 Home Intelligence Weekly Report 72 (February 1942).
12. In fact the *Globe* was suspended only briefly.
13. CAB 65/25, WM 35 (42) (18 March 1942).
14. A. J. P. Taylor (ed.), *Off the Record: W. P. Crozier, Political Interviews 1933–43* (London, Hutchinson, 1973), p. 325.
15. Cecil King was medically unfit for the armed forces. This was the reason why he had not joined up in the first place.
16. INF 1/187, Letter to Censorship Bureau (10 September 1939).
17. INF 1/238, Memorandum from R. H. Parker (15 April 1942).

# 7

# The press in the age of conglomerates

The leading historian of the British press, Stephen Koss, portrays the post-war period as the apotheosis of political journalism. 'By 1947', writes Koss, 'the party attachments of papers – as they had been understood to operate over the preceding hundred years – were effectively abandoned.' The press became fully independent of political parties and hence government, thus completing 'the halting transition from official to popular control'.[1]

This supposedly resulted in a marked improvement in the quality of political reporting and analysis. According to Koss,

> newspapers grew steadily more catholic and less partisan in their ordinary news coverage. When confronted by a general election, they usually expressed a party preference, but always with at least a gesture of pragmatism and often for a different party from the one they had previously endorsed.

This more open-minded style of journalism is attributed by Koss to the emergence of a new type of proprietor who was 'a business-man first and foremost', oriented towards what sold rather than what furthered a party interest or ideological viewpoint. The man who 'personified' this pragmatic, undoctrinaire approach, in Koss's judgement, is Rupert Murdoch, whose 'papers, both in Britain and elsewhere, lurched from one party persuasion to another for reasons that were seldom articulated and manifestly more commercial than ideological'.

This analysis is broadly echoed by many other accounts of the post-war press. Their common theme is that newspapers were emancipated not only from party tutelage but also from the personal dominion of press magnates. According to John Whale, for instance, 'the newspaper's staff is left to get on with the job' in the modern press because many of the new proprietors 'have global problems of trade and investment to occupy their minds'. Like Koss, he sees control of the contemporary press as residing increasingly in the market-place.

Like all persuasive mythologies, these portrayals connect with an element of truth. But their overall assessment is misleading because they inflate short-lived trends into permanent transformations, and ignore developments which run counter to their conclusions. The post-war press was not transformed, in reality, by the arrival of 'market democracy'.

## The re-emergence of interventionist proprietors

During the immediate post-war period a substantial section of the press remained subject to the personal control of aggressively interventionist proprietors: the second Viscount Rothermere, Beaverbrook, Camrose, Kemsley, and, after 1948, David Astor. The Labour movement papers, the *Daily Herald* and *Reynolds News,* were also tethered to the editorial line laid down by their political masters.

However, this hierarchical pattern of control gave way to a greater delegation of editorial authority in the regional press and in a growing section of the national press. The person who typified this change was Lord Thomson, who acquired the Kemsley empire in 1959 and *The Times* in 1967. Within the framework of an agreed budget, his editors enjoyed a high degree of autonomy. Publicly he declared, 'I do not believe that a newspaper can be run properly unless its editorial columns are run freely and independently by a highly skilled and dedicated professional journalist.' His British editors have broadly corroborated this statement. Harold Evans, for instance, could recollect only one occasion in his fourteen years as editor of the *Sunday Times* when he received political guidance from Lord Thomson: the proprietor, he was told in 1974, would be unhappy if the *Sunday Times* supported the Labour Party in the forthcoming general election.

Fleet Street became less hierarchical in the 1960s and early 1970s. The *Daily Herald* was freed from following the Labour Party line; Sir Max Aitken proved to be less dictatorial than his father, Lord Beaverbrook; Astor's proprietor-editor regime at the *Observer* came to an end; and, perhaps, most important of all, Cecil King was ousted in 1968 after authorizing a front-page article in the *Daily Mirror* calling for the removal of the Prime Minister and the establishment of a national government without discussing the matter with the paper's editor. King's lordly action was in the seigneurial tradition of his uncle, Lord Northcliffe: his dismissal by his fellow directors in response to what they called his 'increasing preoccupation with politics' seemed, at the time, to signify the end of an era.

These changes in the control of the press coincided with the rise of specialist correspondents. Their number increased and they acquired a greater degree of autonomy than general reporters. As Jeremy Tunstall's research in the late 1960s showed, specialist correspondents tended to hunt in packs and to regularly exchange information and ideas with each other. This fostered the development of a group consensus and encouraged journalists to resist pressure from their news desks.

The devolution of authority within newspaper organizations, at a time of broad political consensus, encouraged a more bipartisan approach to political reporting and commentary. This was reflected, for instance, in the growing number of newspapers which invited politicians to write articles opposing the editorial line of their leaders during general election campaigns. But although the interventionist tradition of proprietorship waned during the 1960s, it did not disappear. This was highlighted by a private management inquiry commissioned by publishers, which concluded in 1966:

> When all allowances have been made for variations within the industry, its most striking feature, and possibly its greatest problem, is its dominance by a small number of highly individualistic proprietors with their own personal interests and philosophy of management.

This was clearly a reference to the proprietorial regimes at the *Telegraph*, *Express*, and *Mail* groups.

The extent to which political partisanship declined during the post-war period has also been overstated. Thus Stephen Koss's sweeping claim that national newspapers 'often' supported 'a different party from one they had previously endorsed' proves, on close inspection, to be inaccurate. The *Daily Express*, *Daily Mail*, *Daily Mirror*, *Daily Telegraph*, *Daily Sketch*, *Daily Herald*, and *News Chronicle* each backed with unwavering loyalty the same political party in post-war general elections.[2] Only *The Times* (before 1983) and the *Guardian* approximate to Koss's mythical norm.

Moreover, national newspapers became markedly more partisan from 1974 onwards. This was partly in response to the growing polarization of British politics. But it also reflected the cumulative impact of a new generation of partisan, interventionist proprietors. The extent of their editorial involvement has perhaps been exaggerated by the recent spate of journalists' memoirs and reminiscences which have tended to focus on untypical periods of conflict between proprietors and editors caused by changes of ownership and editorial strategy. But they leave no doubt that Koss's portrayal of Murdoch and other contemporary proprietors as market-led pragmatists is deeply misleading.

Indeed Koss's claim that the political orientation of Murdoch's papers fluctuated in response to the shifting currents of public opinion could not be further from the truth. Murdoch's British papers moved to the right because he became increasingly right wing. Moreover these changes were imposed by Murdoch regardless of the views of his readers. The *Sun* switched from Labour to Conservative in the February 1974 general election despite the fact that over half of its readers were Labour supporters. After 1975 it developed into a partisan Thatcherite paper *in opposition* to the opinions of its readers (only 40 per cent of whom supported the Conservatives in the 1987 general election).[3] Similarly, *The Times* and the *Sunday Times* became under his control Thatcherite papers at a time when political partisanship was weakening and the political centre was gaining in support. Only *Today,* acquired by Murdoch in July 1987, exhibited some independence by developing a 'green' tinge, although it has since drifted more towards the right.

Murdoch also imposed an editorial reorientation of his papers in Britain through a personalized style of management reminiscent of the earlier press barons. 'I did not come all this way', he declared at the *News of the World*, 'not to interfere.' Stafford Summerfield, its long-serving editor, found to his dismay that the new proprietor 'wanted to read proofs, write a leader if he felt like it, change the paper about and give instructions to his staff'. A series of clashes with Murdoch, partly over the issue of whether the editor should be accountable to the paper's board or to Murdoch personally, hastened Summerfield's departure.

A subsequent editor of the *News of the World,* Barry Askew, also records Murdoch's extensive editorial interventions when he was in London. 'He would come into the office', Askew recalls, 'and literally rewrite leaders which were not supporting the hard Thatcherite line.' Askew, who was not a Thatcherite enthusiast, lasted only nine months.

Murdoch reconstructed the *Sun* by working closely with a talented but compliant editor, Sir Larry Lamb, whom he had handpicked for the job. But he adopted a more circumspect approach towards *The Times* and *Sunday Times*. During his bid for Times Newspapers in 1981, he was asked whether he would change their character. 'Oh no, no, I would not dream of changing them at all,' he had replied. But to assuage sceptical critics, Articles of Association and independent directors were none the less imposed at Times Newspapers with the intention of preserving their editorial independence.

Although Murdoch never issued a direct editorial instruction to the editor of the *Sunday Times,* Frank Giles, he made his views forcibly known. 'Murdoch, the paper spread out before him', Giles recollects, 'would jab his fingers at some article or contribution and snarl, "what do you want to print rubbish like that for?" or pointing to the by-line of a correspondent, assert that "That man's a Commie".' Further pressure was funnelled through Gerald Long, the new managing director appointed by Murdoch, prompting the editor to establish a dossier called the 'Long Insult File'. Undermined by a series of calculated humiliations (on one occasion, Murdoch entertained guests by firing an imaginary pistol at his editor's back), Frank Giles retired early. His replacement was a more reliably Conservative journalist, Andrew Neil, who moved the paper further to the right.

The editor of *The Times,* Harold Evans, recalls similar pressure from his proprietor. Murdoch 'creates an aura', recollects Evans.

> The aura he created in 1981–2 was one of bleak hostility to Edward Heath and the Tory rebels, and contempt for the Social Democrats. He did this by persistent derision of them at our press meetings and on the telephone, by sending me articles marked worth reading which espoused right-wing views, by jabbing a finger at headlines which he thought could have been more supportive of Mrs. Thatcher – 'You're always getting at her' – and through the agency of his managing director, Long.

The latter bombarded him with memos containing reprimands such as 'the Chancellor of the Exchequer says the recession has ended. Why are you having the effrontery in *The Times* to say that it is not?'

Murdoch sought to exercise control indirectly at *The Times* by declining to fix an editorial budget. Consequently, Evans was compelled to seek permission for editorial decisions involving significant extra spending. As relationships soured due to the centrist political orientation of the paper, and its slow growth of circulation against a background of heavy losses, Murdoch actively fomented opposition among a group of journalists personally hostile to the editor. In an atmosphere thick with intrigue, in which Evans's personal aide was secretly reporting to the opposition group, Evans resigned in 1983 rather than 'be subjected to a thousand humiliations, challenged on every paperclip'. He was replaced by two editors each more right-wing than the last. However, Simon Jenkins was installed as editor in 1990, and steered the paper in a less partisan direction in order to staunch the loss of readers to the *Independent*.

Another active interventionist, Victor (later Lord) Matthews, became head of the Express group between 1977 and 1985. 'By and large editors will have complete freedom,' he promised, 'as long as they agree with the policy I have laid down.' During his first flush of enthusiasm as proprietor, he forced his editors to endure lengthy discourses of homespun political philosophy, which then had to be recreated as editorials. Only the most outrageous *ex cathedra* judgements seem to have been resisted. 'I had to plead against the *Evening Standard*', remembers Simon Jenkins, its former editor, 'being expected to call for a nuclear first strike on Moscow, to rid the world of communism, just like that.' Lord Matthews' staff were also a little taken aback by his novel sense of news values. 'I would find myself in a dilemma', he publicly declared, 'about whether to report a British Watergate affair because of the national harm. I believe in batting for Britain.'

But what perhaps most clearly reveals how little Matthews conformed to Koss's idealized view of the new generation of proprietors was Matthew's troubled relationship with his new paper, the *Daily Star*, launched in 1978. Ironically it owed its existence to commercial considerations since it was conceived primarily as a way of making better use of under-employed printing plant and staff. Matthews was persuaded initially that it had to be relatively radical since it was aimed at a 'down-market', mostly Labour-voting audience. But when the *Daily Star*'s editor, Peter Grimsditch, argued that the paper should actually support the Labour Party in the 1979 general election, Matthews vetoed this on explicitly political grounds. Even after the election, he responded to the paper more as a partisan reader than as a market-oriented publisher. For example on reading the proofs of a *Daily Star* leader critical of the Thatcher government's first budget, he angrily phoned the editor, 'There aren't any poor. You can take my word for it. There are no poor in this country.' The leader was duly modified to accommodate this insight.

In the end, Grimsditch was sacked and the paper became another Tory tabloid. It vigorously supported the Conservative Party in the 1983 election, even though only 21 per cent of its readers voted for Mrs Thatcher. Even when Lord Matthews was ousted by Lord Stevens in a corporate take-over, the *Star* continued to be a right-wing paper that reflected the Conservative views of its new proprietor rather than the predominantly centre-left views of its readership. As Lord Stevens explained, 'I would not be happy to be associated with a left-wing paper. I suppose the papers [in the Express Group] echo my political views. . . . I do interfere and say enough is enough.'

The third dominant personality to emerge in the national press was Robert Maxwell, a former right-wing Labour MP who acquired the Mirror Group in 1984. He brought to an end the relatively autonomous regime that had existed when the group was owned by Reed International during the 1970s and early 1980s. In the early days of his proprietorship, he was in the office almost every night phoning, according to Alastair Hetherington, as often as six times in the evening to staff who were working on political reports. 'I certainly have a major say', he declared recently, 'in the political line of the paper [*Daily Mirror*].' Running newspapers, he declared on another occasion, 'gives me the power to raise issues effectively. In simple terms, it's a megaphone.'

Although the current controllers of the three largest press empires in Britain (Murdoch, Maxwell, and Stevens) are all interventionists, proprietorial control has not been reasserted uniformly throughout the national press. The third Viscount Rothermere, controller of Associated Newspapers, lives mostly in France and allows his editors considerable leeway, although he claims to map 'the overall strategy my papers will take'. The right-wing Canadian businessman, Conrad Black, who acquired the Telegraph Group in 1985, initially adopted the strategy of choosing senior executives 'in general sympathy ideologically and philosophically' with his views, and allowed them a relatively free hand. But in 1989 he established a base in England, complained publicly about what he called the *Daily Telegraph* editor's 'flirtation with incorrect thinking about Ulster and about South Africa', and asserted more direct control over his British newspaper group. Tiny Rowland, who gained control of the *Observer* in 1981, has never fully dominated the paper. But this was not, as we shall see, from personal choice.

## Concentration of media ownership

The revival of personal proprietorship has coincided with the growth of press concentration. Between 1947 and 1988, the three leading press groups increased by over a third their share of the total daily and Sunday paper market. This resulted in Murdoch, Maxwell, and Stevens controlling in 1988 57 per cent of *total* daily and Sunday circulation and, due to their dominant position in Fleet Street, three out of four *national* newspapers sold in Britain.

This dramatic development was the product principally of newspaper acquisitions by the leading press chains. For a time in the late 1960s and early 1970s, it looked as if the rise of Murdoch

Table 1 *Concentration of ownership of daily and Sunday newspapers, 1947–88*

| | The three leading corporations' shares of: | | | | |
| | Total daily and Sunday paper circulation | Total daily paper circulation | Total Sunday paper circulation | National daily circulation | National Sunday circulation |
| --- | --- | --- | --- | --- | --- |
| | % | % | % | % | % |
| 1947 | 42 | 42 | 66 | 62 | 60 |
| 1961 | 65 | 67 | 84 | 89 | 84 |
| 1976 | 53 | 49 | 80 | 72 | 86 |
| 1988 | 57 | 55 | 73 | 73 | 81 |

*Sources*: derived from *Royal Commission on the Press 1947–9 Report* (1949), Appendices 3 and 5; *Royal Commission on the Press 1961–2 Report* (1962), Appendices 2, 3, and 4; *Royal Commission on the Press 1974–7 Final Report* (1977), Annex 3; *Annual Report of the Press Council 1989* (1990), Table 4.

*Note*: The three leading publishing corporations have been defined in terms of their market share of *each* of the categories of publication listed in this table. Total daily and Sunday paper circulation has been calculated by multiplying daily paper circulation six times to obtain a weekly circulation of daily and Sunday papers. This gives lower but more adequate figures than those calculated by the Press Council, which treat Sunday and daily circulation as equivalent and merely add the two together.

would cause the trend towards oligopoly to be reversed. But in
the event the consolidation of his empire increased centralized control of the press. The subsequent introduction of new print technology did not have the salutary consequences that were predicted.
Between 1985 and 1988, the big three publishers' proportion of total
daily and Sunday paper circulation declined by only one percentage
point.

The leading publishers of regional newspapers also consolidated
their position (see Table 2). Their biggest gains were registered in
the local weekly press, where the leading five publishers more
than trebled their market share between 1947 and 1988. In a
growing number of sub-regions extensive monopolies were also
created in which all or nearly all paid-for papers were owned by
the same group.

Table 2 *Concentration of ownership in the provincial press, 1947–88*

| | The five leading chains' share of: | | | |
| | Regional evening newspaper circulation | Regional morning newspaper circulation | Local weekly circulation | Local weekly freesheet circulation |
|---|---|---|---|---|
| | % | % | % | % |
| 1947 | 44 | 65 | 8 | – |
| 1961 | 53 | 70 | 13 | – |
| 1976 | 58 | 69 | 25 | NA |
| 1988 | 54 | 73 | 27 | 38 |

*Sources*: derived from *Royal Commission on the Press 1947–9 Report*
(1949), Appendices 4 and 5; *Royal Commission on the Press 1961–2
Report* (1962), Appendices 2, 3, and 4; *Royal Commission on the
Press 1974–7 Final Report* (1977), Annex 3; and N. Hartley, P. Gudgeon,
and R. Crafts, *Concentration of Ownership in the Provincial Press*
(Royal Commission on the Press 1974–7, Research Series 5); *Annual
Report of the Press Council 1989* (1990), Tables 4 and 5 and D1 and
D2.
*Note*: The five leading chains are not all the same in each category of
publication.

Although local freesheets mushroomed in the 1970s and 1980s,
they have also come to be organized into chains. The five principal,
freesheet groups – all of them major publishers of paid-for newspapers – accounted for over one-third of the weekly freesheet
market by 1988.

The development of press concentration was part of a more general trend towards increasingly centralized control over the leisure industries. The top five companies in each media sector controlled in the mid-1980s an estimated 40 per cent of book sales, 45 per cent of ITV transmissions, between half and two-thirds of video rentals, record, cassette, and compact disc sales, and over three-quarters of daily and Sunday paper sales (see Table 3). Many of these companies were linked to each other through cross-ownership. For example, Pearson controlled in 1989 not only Westminster Press, one of the largest regional press groups in Britain, but also the major book publishers, Penguin, in addition to a 20 per cent stake in the ITV major, Yorkshire TV. Murdoch, in turn, was the second largest shareholder in the Pearson Group and a partner in the merged satellite TV service, British Sky Broadcasting.

This move towards growing concentration of media power was part of a worldwide trend. Indeed, British newspapers and other media interests were, in many cases, merely the northern outposts of global media empires. Thus Murdoch's five British national papers are part of his chain of newspapers extending on a north–south axis from London to Adelaide, and on an east–west axis from Budapest to Boston. These are merely a subsidiary of a much

Table 3   *Concentration of media ownership*

*Market share of top five companies in selected media sectors*

|  | % |
| --- | --- |
| ITV programmes (transmissions) | 45.5 |
| National dailies (circulation) | 95 |
| National Sundays (circulation) | 92 |
| National and regional dailies (circulation) | 75 |
| National and regional Sundays (circulation) | 91 |
| Books (sales) | 40 |
| Single records (sales) | 58 |
| LPs, cassettes, and compact discs | 60 |
| Video rentals | 66 |

*Sources: IBA Annual Report and Accounts (1985–6); 32nd Annual Report of the Press Council 1985 (1986); Jordans' Review of Marketing and Publishing Data (1984); British Phonograph Yearbook (1986); British Videogram Association (Gallup, 1986).*

bigger media empire including an American movie major
(Twentieth Century Fox), a US TV network (Fox TV), European
satellite TV (B Sky B), major book publishers in the UK
(Harper Collins) and the US (Harper & Row), and a mass circulation magazine group in the US (Triangle), among other media
interests. The *Telegraph*, the *Sunday Telegraph*, and the Thomson
regional press group in Britain are fiefdoms controlled by two
Canadian-based media empires. The Mirror Group in Britain is
part of a much larger communications group, including French TV
(TF–1), satellite TV (MTV), book publishing in the UK (Pergamon)
and US (Macmillan), dominated by Maxwell (see Table 4).

These communications conglomerates are now growing at an
accelerating rate, assisted by three developments: the rise of
satellite and cable television, the privatization of broadcasting,
and the loosening of media cross-ownership rules (by some social
democratic as well as right-wing governments). Increasingly, the
magnates dominating the British media are, in Bagdikian's
phrase, 'lords of the global village'.

## Conglomerates, profits, and politics

The other key related change in the post-war press was its integration into the core sectors of financial and industrial capital (see
Table 4). Between 1969 and 1986 nine multinational conglomerates bought over 200 newspapers and magazines with a
total circulation of 46 million at the time of purchase (excluding
publications resold to each other). Some of these (Atlantic Richfield, Lonrho, Trafalgar House, Reed, Hollinger) were primarily
engaged in activities outside publishing and their involvement in
Fleet Street was sometimes shortlived. Others (the conglomerates
controlled by Murdoch, Maxwell, the Cowdrays, and Stevens)
were originally printing or publishing companies which expanded
into other areas like banking and transport. There is now no
popular national newspaper in Britain which does not have, or is
not controlled by, a major interest outside the media.[4] All the
major regional press groups are linked through cross-ownership to
interests outside publishing.

This integration of the press into finance and industry created
conflicts of interest. It gave rise to no-go areas where newspapers
were sometimes reluctant to investigate for fear of stepping on
corporate toes. As *The Times*, then owned by the Thomson
Organization, candidly told the last Royal Commission on the

Table 4  *The conglomeration of the British press*[a]

| | *Main British press interests* | *Selected other media interests* | *Selected non-media interests* |
|---|---|---|---|
| Pergamon Holding Foundation (Maxwell) | *Daily Mirror*<br>*Sunday Mirror*<br>*Sunday People*<br>*Daily Record*<br>*Sunday Mail*<br>(Total newspaper circulation 10.5 million) | British Cable Services<br>TF–1 TV (France)<br>Merril Publishing (USA)<br>Pergamon Press<br>Macmillan (USA)<br>Magyar Hirlop (Hungary) | E.J.Arnold (furniture)<br>Hollis Plastics<br>Paulton Investments<br>Jet Ferry International (Panama)<br>Milthorp Machinery (Australia) |
| News Corporation (Murdoch) | *Sun*<br>*News of the World*<br>*The Times*<br>*Sunday Times*<br>*Today*<br>(Total newspaper circulation 11.9 million) | B Sky B<br>Harper Collins (Fontana)<br>Channel Ten (Sydney)<br>Herald and Weekly Times Group (Australia)<br>Fox TV (USA)<br>Harper & Row (USA) | Ansett Transport (Australia)<br>Santos (Natural gas – Australia)<br>News-Eagle (Offshore oil – Australia)<br>Snodland Fibres<br>Whitefriars Investment |

| | Main British press interests | Selected other media interests | Selected non-media interests |
|---|---|---|---|
| United Newspapers (Stevens) | *Daily Express*<br>*Sunday Express*<br>*Daily Star*<br>United Provincial Newspapers<br>United Magazines<br>Morgan-Grampian Magazines<br>(Total newspaper circulation: 5.6 million) | TV-am<br>Asian Business Press (Singapore)<br>Specialist Publications (Hong Kong)<br>Capital Radio<br>Inter Media Group (USA) | JBS Properties<br>M G Insurance<br>Moncroft Finance<br>PRN Holdings (USA)<br>David McKay Inc. (USA) |
| Reed Group[b] | IPC Magazines<br>IPC Business Press<br>Reed Regional Publishing<br>(Total newspaper circulation: 0.5 million) | Butterworth<br>IPC Business Press (USA)<br>Trade News Asia (Singapore)<br>Européenne de Publications SA (France) | Reed Finance (South Africa)<br>Reed Canadian Holdings<br>WPM Finance (Bermuda) |
| Associated Newspapers (Rothermere) | *Daily Mail*<br>*Mail on Sunday*<br>*Weekend*<br>Northcliffe Newspapers<br>(Total newspaper circulation: 5.3 million) | London Broadcasting Company<br>Herald-Sun TV (Australia)<br>Esquire Magazine Group (USA) | Bouverie Investments (Canada)<br>Consolidated-Bathurst (Canada)<br>Transport Group Holdings<br>Jetlink Ferries |

The Thomson Corporation

Thomson Regional
  Newspapers
*Scotsman*
*Western Mail*
*Belfast Telegraph*
(Total newspaper
circulation: 1.5 million)

Thomson Data
41 dailies (Canada)
121 dailies (USA)
Routledge

Thomson North Sea
Thomson Travel

Pearson (Cowdray)

Westminster Press Group
*Financial Times*
*The Economist*
*Northern Echo*
(Total circulation:
1.1 million)

Elsevier (France)
Penguin
Yorkshire TV
NAL (USA)
British Sky
  Broadcasting

Midhurst Corporation
  (USA)
Lazard Partners
Royal Doulton
Camco International (USA)

| | Main British press interests | Selected other media interests | Selected non-media interests |
|---|---|---|---|
| Lonrho (Rowland) | *Observer* George Outram and Co. Scottish and Universal Newspapers (Total circulation: 1.3 million) | Radio Clyde Border TV Radio Ltd (Zambia) Times Newspapers (Zambia) Melody Records (Zimbabwe) | Whyte and Mackay Firsteel Group Consolidated Holdings (Kenya) Constructions Associated (Zimbabwe) HCC Investments (South Africa) |
| Hollinger (Black) | *Daily Telegraph* *Sunday Telegraph* (Total newspaper circulation: 1.8 million) | Sterling Newspaper Group (Canada) TG & K Press Media (USA) Standard Broadcasting Corporation (Canada) | Hanna (USA) Ravelston Holdings (Canada) Argus (Canada) Norcen Energy Resources (Canada) |

*Sources: Who Owns Whom 1988:* Company Reports: Press Council Annual Report 1990.
*Notes:* [a]All circulation figures exclude freesheets and magazines and relate to the UK. [b]No dominant shareholder.

Press, 'Coverage of Thomson Organization activities in Thomson newspapers tends, certainly, to be drily factual.' It also resulted sometimes in newspapers' editorial columns being misused to promote the commercial interests of other companies in the same group. Thus, the *Observer* came under pressure from its parent company, Lonrho, to attack the Al Fayeds' dubious acquisition of the Fraser Stores Group. Lonrho had tried to purchase the company and wanted the Al Fayeds' take-over to be quashed by the government. This pressure took the form of requests that were difficult to refuse. 'In summary, Mr. Rowland [Lonrho's chief executive] would greatly appreciate any assistance', concluded one note, 'in persuading Mrs Thatcher to publish the report of the inspectors into the House of Fraser.' Between 1985 and 1989 the *Observer* printed a succession of critical articles about the Al Fayeds' take-over of the Fraser Group, culminating in the publication of a special, mid-week issue of the paper which revealed the details of the still-unpublished inspector's report which Rowland wanted to publicize. Journalists on the paper made a formal protest to their independent directors who concluded, after an investigation, that the *Observer*'s coverage of the Fraser Group take-over had 'tarnished' the paper's reputation.

This was not the only issue in which it was alleged that the *Observer*'s editorial policy was affected by its parent company's corporate interests. Lonrho had an indirect commercial interest in getting allegations published that its rival, British Aerospace, had bribed Saudi Arabian and Jordanian officials to secure the sale of Tornado aircraft. Lonrho executives planted the story at the *Observer*, and pressed for it to be given full play. Their requests were rewarded with prominent articles in the paper in March and April 1989. The head of the paper's investigative team, David Leigh, refused, however, to handle the story and subsequently resigned over the issue, declaring that the *Observer* 'had become a sick paper'. Still more damning, Anthony Howard, the *Observer*'s former deputy editor under the Lonrho regime, publicly attacked the editorial integrity of the paper. 'Without any overt pressure being applied', he wrote, 'there has developed a tendency to anticipate Mr Rowland's wishes and to cater for his interests.'

Editorial compromises at the *Observer* came under the public spotlight partly because its journalists made a fuss. Compromises sometimes occurred in other press groups without the same degree of internal opposition. When Murdoch newspapers gave disproportionate and largely uncritical coverage of the British launch of its sister company, Sky Television, in 1989, only journalists on one of his newspapers – *The Times* – made a formal protest. *The Times'* independent directors declined, much to their discredit, to investigate the protest beyond speaking to the editor.

But occasional abuses, arising from conflicts of interest, were less significant than the growing co-option of the press in support of the general interests and ideology of capital. The economic diversification of the press resulted in an intricate pattern of interlocking directorships in which senior newspaper executives came increasingly to work alongside other business leaders on the same boards. Other links also promoted the development of a shared outlook. Graham Murdock's pioneering research showed that in 1976–7 two-thirds of the chairmen and vice-chairmen of the ten largest press groups were educated at public school and/or Oxbridge, the recruiting grounds of much of Britain's industrial and financial élite.[5] Many top newspaper executives also belonged to exclusive London clubs (their favourites being White's and the Royal Yacht Club), frequented by élite members. All these affinities and points of contact – similar social origins, shared educational experiences, overlapping social networks, and close working relationships – fostered common ideological positions between controllers of the press and other groups within the capitalist class.

The economic absorption of the press subtly changed its relationship to the party system. The archetypal proprietors of the interwar period had been maverick politicians who viewed the world from the optic of Westminster and were heavily involved in party politics. In contrast, most of their successors after 1960 (with the notable exception of Cecil King and Lord Hartwell of the Telegraph Group, both throwbacks to an earlier period) were preoccupied with running large business conglomerates, and gave more intermittent attention to British politics.

Indeed for some post-war proprietors, newspaper ownership was little more than an investment in corporate public relations. It extended their range of business and political connections, increased their corporation's prestige, and, through judicious editorial appointments, contributed to the maintenance of public opinion favourable to private enterprise. As the Chairman of Atlantic Richfield (which spent $20 million subsidizing the *Observer*) explained to his shareholders in 1978:

Despite the social upheaval of the last few years, Atlantic Richfield's primary task remains what it has always been – to conduct its business within accepted rules to generate profits, thereby protecting and enhancing the investment of its owners. But . . . senior management recognise that the Company cannot expect to operate freely or advantageously without public approval.

The ownership of newspapers thus became one strategy by which large business organizations sought to influence the environment in which they operated. This strategy was pursued mainly on the basis of an arm's length relationship between newspapers and conglomerate newspaper companies during the 1960s. But in the more recent period, newspapers campaigned more actively for the general interests of big business, under closer proprietorial supervision. This development signified an important, long-term shift: commercial newspapers became increasingly the instruments of large business conglomerates with political interests rather than an extension of the party system.

Indeed a number of major press groups – Trafalgar House (which controlled for a time the Express Group), United Newspapers, and Pearson – gave in the 1970s and 1980s substantial donations to the Conservative Party. Owning (and in some cases subsidizing) newspapers was merely another way of sustaining the party which they believed best served their economic interests.

However, part of the lure of the national press for some proprietors was its social prestige. The ownership of national newspapers led to the bestowal of honorific titles on an almost automatic basis and provided access to an élite social world. It also offered a way of mainlining into the romance of Fleet Street which, as Leonard Woolf once observed, is 'a magnetic field of highly charged importance, influence . . . and vocational delusions'. These were clearly important attractions for Lord Thomson, who spent some £8 million subsidizing *The Times* (though part of this was tax deductible).

But what is clear is that the rewards of newspaper ownership were not defined solely in terms of profits. Indeed a growing number of national newspapers made substantial losses during the period between the ending of newsprint rationing in 1956 and the introduction of cost-cutting technology in the mid-1980s. Thus in 1966 five out of eight national newspapers made losses totalling £4.3 million. By 1975 four national dailies and six out of seven national Sunday papers made an even larger loss. In 1982 the national press was reported to have made a net loss of £29 million. Thus when conglomerates bought up the rotten boroughs of the national press, they were seeking more than just an immediate return on their investment.

## Compliance and resistance

The reassertion of proprietorial control did not go unchallenged. Strongest resistance occurred in the quality press largely because quality paper journalists had become accustomed to a greater degree of autonomy than their tabloid counterparts, and the new regimes represented a greater rupture with the past. Yet there was only one occasion when journalists actually succeeded in decisively defeating their proprietor, and that was when resistance was led by the editor supported by his staff.

When Tiny Rowland acquired the *Observer* in 1981, he clearly intended to introduce major changes. He told one group, for instance, that he wanted to improve the paper's coverage of southern Africa because its liberalism was abetting the advance of Communism. In traditional proprietorial style, he appointed a new roving Africa correspondent without consulting the editor.

However he was forced, like Murdoch, to accept new Articles of Association and independent directors at the *Observer*, designed to prevent him from interfering editorially. But whereas Murdoch moved with consummate skill at Times Newspapers, first encircling unwanted editors with people he could trust, Rowland blundered in with an ill-judged ultimatum that undermined his authority.

Donald Trelford, the *Observer*'s editor, wrote an article in April 1984 reporting that Zimbabwe's armed forces were torturing and killing their own citizens in the dissident Matabeleland province. This put Rowland in a difficult position since his corporation, Lonrho, derived £15 million of its profit from investments in Zimbabwe. Rowland also had an uneasy relationship with the Zimbabwe Prime Minister, Robert Mugabe, since he had backed his principal rival, Joshua Nkomo, in the recent elections there. Seemingly seeking to protect his commercial interests, Rowland instructed Trelford to withdraw his article.

Trelford refused and was backed in his stand by all his editorial staff and independent directors. In the highly publicized row that followed (in which Lonrho cancelled advertising in its own paper) Rowland had little real choice but to back off. Lonrho's corporate image, already tarnished by Edward Heath's celebrated attack on it as 'the unacceptable face of capitalism', would have been seriously damaged if Rowland had agreed to Trelford's offer of resignation. In the event, Trelford survived as editor. But his victory was only a limited one since he had subsequently to tread a difficult tightrope, balancing the demands of his proprietor with those of his suspicious and increasingly critical staff.

The partial success of journalists' resistance on the *Observer* was in marked contrast to what happened on the *Sunday Times*. This is worth reporting briefly because it underlines – what the academic literature on the media tends to ignore – the pressures and sanctions that managements can bring to bear on journalists. The *Sunday Times* evolved into a neo-Thatcherite paper in the early 1980s partly in response to the increasing influence of new right ideas in the early phase of the Thatcherite era. But the principal cause of change was a management-imposed shift of editorial direction. Murdoch's appointment of Andrew Neil as editor in 1983 was part of a general shake-up in the editorial hierarchy of the *Sunday Times* in which senior editors from the pre-Murdoch regime were gradually weeded out. This removed the buffer that had partly insulated reporters and feature writers from the full impact of the change in the paper's ownership. Neil's regime inaugurated, according to Claire Tomalin, the paper's former literary editor, 'a reign of terror'. 'I was extremely aware of a great deal of misery and bullying', she recalls. Her recollection of this period is echoed by other journalists we interviewed. For example, Peter Wilby, the paper's former education correspondent, recalls: 'There was a tone of fear . . . a horrible, "totalitarian" atmosphere.'[6]

Certain sorts of story – what Neil called 'wet' or 'lefty' stories – were discouraged or downplayed. Thus, Donald Macintyre, the paper's labour correspondent, had a running battle over his reporting of the miners' strike (1984–5) in which he was regularly pressed by the editor to adopt a less critical attitude towards the National Coal Board and the government. Sometimes Macintyre felt that the editor's criticism was justified; sometimes he argued back; but at other times, he admitted, he censored himself 'to some extent'. The trouble with arguing back, Macintyre explained, is that it 'starts to become counter-productive and you get to the point where you either had to leave or you just become a sort of joke'. Macintyre chose to leave voluntarily.

At times the pressure on journalists from the old regime was extremely abrasive. On one occasion, John Shirley, the paper's chief reporter (and right-wing Labour supporter) was denounced by Neil as a 'left-winger' and 'Trotskyist' in a voice so loud that the newsroom fell into a hushed silence. Shirley became so enraged by changes on the paper that he cancelled its delivery to his home. 'A lot of people were being bullied', according to the *Sunday Times*'s former features editor, Don Berry. 'Life was deliberately made unpleasant for them in the hope that they would go'. Thus Joan Smith, who had complained about the way in which her report of the Greenham Common anti-nuclear protest had been altered, was told by the news editor, Anthony Bambridge, on 25 January 1984: 'The editor feels you have got in a rut on nuclear matters. He would like to see you broaden your range. He would like to see you in the paper more often.' Smith asked how often and was told every week, ideally. She then pointed out that she had had 46 stories published in the past 44 weeks. Bambridge replied, 'You are to be congratulated. I am having a terrible time. You are not the only one who is thinking of leaving.' Two months later, Smith left the *Sunday Times*.

But the principal way in which the paper was propelled editorially to the right was through a cumulative process of attrition. This is graphically described by Isabel Hilton, the Latin American specialist at the *Sunday Times* until July 1986:

> What would happen is that you would write a story and it would disappear. The copy would vanish around the building and people would write little things into it and take out other things. It would eventually appear in a very truncated form with the emphases changed. It had all been done at stages along the way. To try and make a fuss about this on a Saturday when everything was very busy was very difficult.

The accumulation of pressures led some journalists to internalize controls. 'The sense of intimidation', according to Hilton, 'was so strong that people actually started censoring themselves because it is very unpleasant to get into this kind of argument all the time. It is not just a collection of incidents, it's a collection of incidents *and* the atmosphere, which in the end is so depressing. You stop functioning as a journalist. There are things you just don't bother to pursue because you know you just won't get them into the paper.'

Hilton eventually left. Her example was followed by many others, although not all went for the same reasons. In early 1981, there were some 170 journalists on the *Sunday Times*. At least a hundred journalists left the paper between February 1981 and

March 1986. This exodus included most of the best-known *Sunday Times* journalists from the pre-Murdoch era.

The changes in the *Sunday Times* during the period 1981–6 symbolized the shift towards a more hierarchical pattern of control in the national press. But the level of conflict at the *Sunday Times* and also *The Times* in the early 1980s was atypical. A number of factors generally minimized conflict. Proprietors usually had a free hand to choose the editors they wanted, and usually appointed them on the basis of short-term contracts only. Editors' freedom of action was generally curtailed by the house tradition of the paper, budgetary controls, management guidelines or an implicit framework of understanding about how the paper should develop. Increasingly editors in the changed managerial environment of the 1980s came to accept proprietorial intervention as legitimate. As Max Hastings, the current editor of the *Daily Telegraph* put it: 'I've never really believed in the notion of editorial independence as such. I would never imagine saying to Conrad [his proprietor], "You have no right to ask me to do this, I must observe my independence". '

A variety of influences also limited conflict in the newsroom. Journalists mostly internalized the norms and news values of their paper (though tensions sometimes increased if these were modified). Conforming to hierarchical requirements brought rewards in terms of good assignments, high exposure, promotion, and peer group esteem. Failure to conform invited escalating sanctions. As Anthony Bevins, a former political correspondent of the *Sun* and *Daily Mail* and now political editor of the *Independent*, puts it (with a measure of overstatement):

> It is daft to suggest that individuals can buck the system, ignore the pre-set 'taste' of their newspapers, use their own news-sense in reporting the truth of any event, and survive. Dissident reporters who do not deliver the goods suffer professional death. They are ridden by news desks and backbench executives, they have their stories spiked on a systematic basis, they face the worst form of newspaper punishment – by-line deprivation. . . . It is much easier to pander to what the editors want.

Accommodation was facilitated by other factors. Newsgathering continued to be based on routines organized around powerful groups and institutions adept at meeting the press's needs – most notably the various branches of the state. Prevailing news values accorded particular weight to these accredited sources, thereby

legitimizing heavy reliance on them. The structures of news-
gathering and professional norms thus tended to reinforce the
predominantly centre-right orientation of the national press.
National newspaper journalists also became increasingly well paid,
and relatively few of them had political convictions which were far
to the left. While there is no recent data about their political
attitudes, Tunstall's pioneering survey of specialist correspondents
in 1968 affords an indication of their outlook. He found that only 2
per cent of those working for right-wing Labour or centrist papers
said that they were 'well to the left' of their publications.

## Restoration of market controls

The market is viewed in many accounts of the post-war press as a
countervailing force taming and curtailing right-wing press owners.
This assessment ignores, as we have seen, the revival of proprietorial power in the 1970s and 1980s. It also misconceives the
way in which the market functioned. The market was not a
mechanism which impartially represented consumer demand, and
harmonized editorial and public opinion. On the contrary, it gave
added impetus to the right-wing drift of the post-war press in a
way that exceeded the rightward shift of public opinion because
the market mechanism was itself skewed to the right.

A key change in the functioning of the market occurred in the
late 1940s and early 1950s when newsprint rationing was greatly
reduced, finally culminating in its abolition in 1956. This had the
effect of restoring the national press's heavy dependence on
advertising. It also resulted in a net redistribution of advertising
away from the reformist press to its Conservative opponents. The
easing of the advertising space famine brought to an end the
artificial conditions in which left papers had been able to compete
on more equal terms with their rivals. Instead something approaching the pre-war pattern of advertising reallocation was re-
established in the 1950s. Most left papers attracted less advertising
per capita than their rivals because they were read, generally
speaking, by less affluent readers. The growth of working-class
affluence in the post-war period did not offset this because class
inequalities of income remained remarkably constant after 1945
until the 1980s when they slightly increased. Special factors also
led to a growing gap in support for down- and up-market publications in the 1960s and 1970s. The rapid growth of classified and

financial advertising particularly helped upscale papers, while downscale papers were more adversely affected by the rise of television as an advertising medium since their readers tended to be heavy viewers of commercial television.

Reformist newspapers reaching a mainly working-class readership thus suffered as a consequence of the removal of economic controls. Radical papers also encountered prejudice from some advertisers. A small number of advertising agencies admitted to the second Royal Commission on the Press (1962) that their clients sometimes vetoed left-wing publications. The ill-fated *Scottish Daily News*, founded as a radical co-operative in 1975, was told by an irate advertiser: 'I'm not going to keep a newspaper which, the first time I get a strike, will back the strikers.' A pre-launch feasibility study for the left-wing *News on Sunday* also indicated, on the basis of interviews with agency executives, that its politics would deter some advertisers.

But the evidence suggests nevertheless that political bias in advertising selection declined in post-war Britain. Advertising agencies came to rely even more on calculations of rival publications' cost effectiveness in terms of the readers that they delivered, based on increasingly detailed survey research into their characteristics and purchasing behaviour, and less on intuitive assessments of editorial influence coloured by subjective ideological judgements. This was reflected, for example, in the first two handbooks on advertising media planning published under the auspices of the Institute of Practitioners in Advertising. The first, issued in 1955, contained a whole chapter on the 'character and atmosphere' of advertising media, laden with speculative judgements about 'the intangible effects of accompanying editorial and advertising'. Its successor, published in 1971, was openly disparaging about this approach.[7]

## The death of radical papers

The impact of the relative redistribution of advertising away from down-market papers in the 1950s was exacerbated by a cumulative deterioration in the cost and revenue structure of the national press during the period 1957 to 1965. Increased competition led to rising levels of outlay. At the same time, circulations fell sharply because multiple household purchase of newspapers declined (mainly because papers were bigger and more expensive). As a consequence vulnerable papers became more at risk.

One of these, the *Daily Herald*, found it particularly difficult to attract advertising because its readership was overwhelmingly working class and disproportionately male and ageing. In 1945 its advertising revenue per copy sold (an index that takes account of differences in circulation) was more than that of either the *Daily Express* or *Daily Mail*. By 1964 it had dropped to less than half of either paper.

The *Daily Herald* also lost readers partly as a consequence of its continuing commitment to the Labour Party during the Conservative ascendancy of the 1950s. But its loss of advertising far exceeded its loss of sales, and was a more important cause of its downfall. In 1955 the *Daily Herald* had an 11 per cent share of both national daily circulation and advertising revenue. By 1964 its share of circulation had declined modestly to 8 per cent but its share of advertising had slumped to 3.5 per cent.

Indeed despite its loss of sales, the *Daily Herald* still retained a substantial following. It was not true, as Sir Dennis Hamilton suggested, that the *Daily Herald* 'was beset by the problem which has dogged nearly every newspaper vowed to a political idea: not enough people wanted to read it.' When it closed in 1964, it had a circulation of 1,265,000. This was more than five times the circulation of *The Times* of which Sir Dennis Hamilton was then editor-in-chief.

The *News Chronicle*, a long-established Liberal daily, succumbed in 1960 with a substantial circulation of 1,162,000. This was roughly on a par with the highly profitable *Daily Telegraph* buoyed up by up-market advertising. Similarly the *Sunday Citizen* (formerly *Reynolds News*) folded in 1967. It was a quality paper in terms of the relatively extensive coverage it gave to public affairs. But by 1965 it obtained per copy sold one-tenth of the advertising revenue of the *Sunday Times* because it did not appeal to an élite audience.

The closure of these three social democratic papers was part of an epidemic that also killed off the *Empire News*, *Sunday Dispatch*, *Sunday Graphic*, and *Daily Sketch* between 1960 and 1972. All these papers succumbed to similar pressures to those that decimated the centre-left press. They all had a predominantly working-class readership and, in terms of mass marketing, relatively 'small' circulations. They thus fell between two stools: they had neither the quantity nor the social 'quality' of readership needed to attract sufficient advertising for them to survive.

## Adjusting to the advertising system

One response of down-market papers to the economic realities of post-war publishing was to try to break out of their working-class ghetto. The editorial implications of this are graphically illustrated by the troubled post-war history of the *Daily Herald*.

The *Daily Herald*'s management responded initially to the paper's growing shortfall in advertising not by modifying its editorial policy but by seeking new and more imaginative ways of selling the paper to the advertising industry. In particular, it sought to combat the negative image of the paper's readers as poor by initiating research which showed that they were heavy spenders on certain products such as canned meat, desserts, cereals, and beer.

The diminishing success of this promotion encouraged the *Daily Herald*'s management to undertake in 1955 a fundamental review of the paper's editorial strategy and market position. Two clear options emerged from this review. One, partly inspired by market research into what people read in popular papers, was to devote less space to political and industrial coverage and more to human interest stories, photographs, and strip cartoons. This was identified as the most promising way to rebuild a mass circulation and, in particular, to 'bring in women – vital to the advertising department'.[8]

The second option, and the one that was eventually adopted, was to attract more advertising by seeking to upgrade the paper's readership. This strategy led to the appointment of John Beavan as editor in 1960 with the remit to lure former *News Chronicle* readers and, above all, to attract 'the intelligent grammar school boy'. The paper moved up-market, and included features about books, classical music, opera, and even ballet. It also loosened its ties with the Labour Party and the TUC, and moved politically to the right.

Yet despite these changes, the *Daily Herald*'s readership remained obstinately proletarian. Indeed even by 1963–4, only 13 per cent of its readers were middle class. Yet its owners were conscious that the traditional, loyalist union sub-culture from which the *Daily Herald* sprang was in decline. The paper's management, influenced by the Gaitskellite revisionism of the early 1960s, concluded that the cloth-cap, traditional Labour Party identity of the paper was putting off potential readers and that the only way to blast the paper successfully into the middle market was to relaunch it under a new name, the *Sun*. As a prelude to this, the TUC was persuaded to sell its share of the paper in 1964 to the International Publishing Corporation (IPC) which had acquired Odhams' shares in the paper three years earlier.

The intention behind the new launch was to construct a new coalition of readers composed of working-class, 'political radicals' (the old *Herald* readership) and young, upwardly mobile 'social radicals'. 'The new paper', according to an internal memorandum, 'is to have the more representative make-up essential to advertisers.'[9] But the difficulties inherent in this strategy were dauntingly revealed in pre-launch research which showed the enormous gulf that separated the two wings of the coalition.[10] 'Social radicals', defined largely in terms of their attitudes towards race, hanging, and issues like increasing access to (but not abolishing) public schools, turned out to be only marginally more inclined to vote Labour than Conservative or Liberal, and to be not greatly more likely to read the *Daily Herald* than the *Daily Telegraph*. Ranking high amongst the favourite reading of 'social radicals' were the society gossip columns of the *Daily Express* and *Daily Mail* expressing social values fundamentally at odds with the class-conscious, often resentful attitudes of many *Herald* readers recorded by Odhams' previous surveys.

These findings suggest that it would have been more sensible for the *Daily Herald* to have been relaunched as a more popular, working-class daily. But this strategy was rejected by IPC because it would have meant spending money attacking another paper in the same group, the *Daily Mirror*. Instead the launch proceeded along its preconceived lines, seemingly unaffected by the corporation's own research.

In the event, the editorial staff of the *Sun* never succeeded in finding an editorial formula which reconciled the two very dissimilar groups that they were seeking to attract. IPC's market research showed that the paper failed both to please old *Herald* readers and to attract young, affluent social radicals.[11] The paper struggled on as an underfinanced, deradicalized hybrid until it was sold at a low price to Murdoch in 1969.

The *Sun* was then reoriented towards a mass working-class market. The recasting was done with consummate skill, making the *Sun* Britain's best-selling daily. It greatly increased its entertainment coverage, in particular human interest reporting of show business and TV stars, developed a more explicit style of soft porn, and shrank its coverage of public affairs. It also evolved a complex editorial formula – mistakenly dismissed by some critics as simple-minded – which was both hedonistic and moralistic, iconoclastic and authoritarian, Conservative in its opinions and radical in its rhetoric. It also anticipated the Thatcherite era, articulating new right arguments even before Mrs Thatcher.

It was an ironic ending for a daily that had been the only consistent supporter of the Labour Party for over half a century. Revealed by market research to have had the most devoted readership of any popular daily as late as 1958,[12] it was first enfeebled and then converted into a paper which stood for everything which the old *Daily Herald* had opposed.

## Consensual pull of the mass market

Other reformist papers adjusted to post-war market conditions by muting their radical commitment in a bid to maximize sales. This pattern of accommodation is illustrated by the post-war history of the *Daily Mirror*. It emerged triumphant from the radical wartime and immediate post-war period to become in 1949 the top circulation daily paper. But the 1951 general election inaugurated a long period of Conservative ascendancy. Other indicators registered a change in the market environment. The *Daily Mirror*'s growth of circulation slowed down in the early 1950s, and began to fall after 1955. The paper also failed to maintain the substantial share of advertising it had won in the 1940s. Its management became increasingly aware that the tide of radicalism which had helped to sweep the paper to the top was receding, and began to worry about whether the paper was moving out of step with the times. It responded by steering the *Daily Mirror* more towards the centre of gravity in the mass market – the political centre. The class divisiveness of the paper's 'us and them' rhetoric of the 1940s softened in the 1950s and early 1960s into the more inclusive and acceptable rhetoric of 'the young at heart' against 'the old', the modern against the traditional, 'new ideas' instead of 'tired men'. The *Daily Mirror*'s commitment to the Labour Party remained but it changed in character. Increasingly it took the form of opposition to the Conservative Party rather than positive advocacy of a socialist alternative.

In the late 1950s, the paper also pursued, for a mixture of motives, young and upwardly mobile readers. They brought in additional advertising because they were particularly sought after by advertisers; they seemed to embody important, new social trends; and they were an accessible part of the market because their newspaper reading habits were relatively unfixed. The effect of this redirection was to make the paper's readership more socially and politically heterogeneous. By 1964 a third of the paper's readership opposed the Labour Party and its readership profile was considerably more up-market than it had been in the 1940s. This was perceived by the *Mirror*'s management to impose a limitation on the paper's radicalism. As Cecil King, then Chairman of the Mirror Group, explained in 1967,

> Today newspaper circulations are vast assemblies of people of all social classes and all varieties of political view. A controller who tried to campaign for causes profoundly distasteful, even to large minorities of his readers, would . . . put his business at risk.

However Cecil King's market fears, and those of his senior colleagues, perhaps rationalized their own personal inclinations. King's youthful radicalism had waned as he got older. Hugh Cudlipp, his close colleague and successor as chairman of the Mirror Group, subsequently left the Labour Party to join the SDP. Their centrism was reflected in the choice of political advisers to the Mirror Group in the 1950s and 1960s – Alfred Robens, George Brown, and Richard Marsh, all senior Labour politicians on the right of the party who defected to support the Alliance or the Conservative Party.

The *Daily Mirror* succeeded in recouping the circulation it had lost in the late 1950s until it was challenged by the renascent *Sun*. Between 1969 and 1985, its sales fell into almost continuous decline. The paper's successive managements responded defensively by cutting back on the *Daily Mirror*'s campaigning issue journalism. The paper also experimented with different populist registers in an attempt to find a new voice that would appeal to a younger readership. Both the *Daily Mirror*'s inner uncertainty and waning radical commitment were symbolized by its changes of masthead. Under the Maxwell regime, its old campaigning masthead slogan 'Forward with the People' was resuscitated in a consensual form as 'Forward with Britain'. This was replaced in turn with a slogan defining the paper's identity exclusively in market terms: 'Colour Newspaper of the Year'.

The deradicalization of the *Daily Mirror* was only one aspect of its post-war evolution. In some ways a more important feature of the paper's development was the declining attention it gave to public affairs, and the greatly increased proportion of space which it devoted to sport, pictures, and entertainment features. This shift was part of a more general transformation of the popular press.

## Depoliticization of the popular press

The commercial pressures reshaping the *Daily Herald* and the *Daily Mirror* affected more generally popular newspapers. They emerged from their cocooned existence in the 1940s, when newsprint rationing had curbed costs more than revenue and generated large profits, into a more competitive environment where the pursuit of readers became increasingly important. The scramble for circulation intensified when popular newspaper sales nose-dived during the 1950s and early 1960s, and the carcasses of dead titles littered the wayside to remind publishers of the consequences of failing to adjust to new market conditions. Thereafter, popular newspaper circulations continued a downward curve, though tabloid dailies registered a temporary recovery in the late 1970s and early 1980s. Contributing to this process were two trends: a slow decline in the proportion of adults reading national papers after 1967, and the modest growth of quality papers at the expense of the popular press. Popular newspaper publishers became conscious of swimming against the market tide.

Although advertising expenditure on the national press steadily increased, popular nationals' share of advertising declined gradually after 1953. More important, their advertising profit margins were seriously eroded during the 1960s and 1970s because most popular papers failed to increase their advertising rates in line with rising costs in an attempt to fend off competition from ITV. Popular newspapers responded to their mounting economic problems by doubling cover prices in real terms between 1962 and 1985. But this policy merely redoubled publishers' anxiety about losing readers.

However, the rise in costs was probably the principal driving force behind the pressure to maximize sales. National newspapers more than quadrupled their paging between 1945 and 1975. Their staffs also got bigger and were paid substantially more in real terms. Between 1946 and 1974, the annual costs of the average national and London daily increased fourteen-fold.[13] Expenditure was further inflated by the circulation war that began in 1981 and culminated in the award of top bingo prizes of £1 million in 1985. Soaring expenditure intensified the need to stay ahead in the circulation battle.

How this could be achieved was spelt out in extensive market research commissioned by increasingly anxious publishers. This revealed a remarkable constancy in what people read in national newspapers throughout the post-war period, notwithstanding the

Table 5 *The editorial contents of selected national daily and Sunday newspapers, 1936–76[a]*

| Percentage of editorial space | Daily Express | | | Daily Herald/ Sun | | | Daily Mail | | |
|---|---|---|---|---|---|---|---|---|---|
| | 1936 | 1946 | 1976 | 1936 | 1946 | 1976 | 1936 | 1946 | 1976 |
| Advertising (proportion of total space) | 43 | 18 | 44 | 42 | 17 | 40 | 46 | 18 | 36 |
| Editorial (proportion of total space) | 57 | 82 | 56 | 58 | 83 | 60 | 54 | 82 | 64 |
| Photographs[b] | 13 | 7 | 13 | 9 | 5 | 16 | 15 | 7 | 14 |
| Illustrations[b] | 4 | 4 | 5 | 2 | 4 | 6 | 5 | 4 | 5 |
| Public affairs news[c] | 14 | 29 | 12 | 23 | 34 | 8 | 15 | 27 | 12 |
| Public affairs features[c] | 4 | 10 | 6 | 10 | 11 | 6 | 4 | 12 | 8 |
| Finance | 10 | 4 | 7 | 6 | 1 | 1 | 9 | 3 | 10 |
| Sport | 22 | 18 | 27 | 19 | 20 | 30 | 20 | 19 | 23 |
| Human interest news | 20 | 20 | 16 | 14 | 14 | 14 | 14 | 19 | 17 |
| Human interest features | 10 | 6 | 12 | 8 | 4 | 20 | 15 | 3 | 10 |
| Consumer and women's features | 7 | 2 | 4 | 5 | 3 | 2 | 8 | 2 | 5 |
| Horoscopes, cartoon strips, quizzes, and competitions | 4 | 3 | 6 | 3 | 3 | 8 | 3 | 4 | 5 |
| Arts and entertainments | 6 | 4 | 7 | 6 | 4 | 7 | 5 | 5 | 9 |
| Other features | 5 | 5 | 4 | 6 | 4 | 7 | 7 | 6 | 3 |

| | Daily Mirror | | | Daily Telegraph | | | Sunday Express | | | People/ Sunday People | | | Sunday Pictorial/ Sunday Mirror | | | Observer | | |
|---|---|---|---|---|---|---|---|---|---|---|---|---|---|---|---|---|---|---|
| | 1936 | 1946 | 1976 | 1936 | 1946 | 1976 | 1936 | 1946 | 1976 | 1936 | 1946 | 1976 | 1936 | 1946 | 1976 | 1936 | 1946 | 1976 |
| | 29 | 16 | 42 | 47 | 35 | 48 | 51 | 16 | 56 | 38 | 22 | 44 | 24 | 25 | 46 | 46 | 36 | 49 |
| | 71 | 84 | 58 | 53 | 64 | 52 | 49 | 84 | 44 | 62 | 78 | 56 | 76 | 75 | 54 | 54 | 64 | 51 |
| | 21 | 8 | 18 | 8 | 2 | 9 | 14 | 4 | 13 | 11 | 4 | 21 | 26 | 25 | 20 | 3 | 3 | 12 |
| | 7 | 15 | 8 | 1 | 1 | 1 | 4 | 6 | 9 | 2 | 2 | 2 | 6 | 6 | 6 | 1 | – | 3 |
| | 10 | 18 | 9 | 19 | 40 | 26 | 8 | 20 | 5 | 10 | 15 | 2 | 7 | 10 | 5 | 20 | 28 | 16 |
| | 2 | 7 | 4 | 3 | 9 | 4 | 10 | 19 | 12 | 4 | 11 | 6 | 10 | 16 | 6 | 6 | 19 | 14 |
| | 4 | – | 1 | 20 | 8 | 20 | 5 | 2 | 2 | 1 | 1 | 1 | 2 | – | 2 | 7 | 2 | 10 |
| | 15 | 9 | 28 | 14 | 11 | 18 | 21 | 20 | 25 | 25 | 28 | 30 | 18 | 20 | 27 | 17 | 12 | 16 |
| | 21 | 29 | 17 | 14 | 12 | 13 | 15 | 11 | 12 | 18 | 15 | 13 | 11 | 14 | 13 | 7 | 5 | 5 |
| | 27 | 5 | 16 | 10 | 10 | 2 | 23 | 9 | 17 | 23 | 17 | 22 | 15 | 26 | 28 | 6 | 7 | 8 |
| | 6 | 4 | 2 | 3 | 1 | 5 | 4 | 2 | 10 | 3 | 3 | 5 | 8 | 5 | 5 | 4 | 2 | 11 |
| | 6 | 16 | 10 | 1 | 1 | 1 | 4 | 6 | 6 | 8 | 8 | 6 | 14 | 3 | 5 | 3 | 5 | 1 |
| | 4 | 1 | 8 | 6 | 3 | 10 | 3 | 4 | 6 | 3 | 2 | 6 | 7 | 3 | 6 | 25 | 20 | 15 |
| | 7 | 10 | 5 | 9 | 7 | 3 | 8 | 7 | 4 | 7 | 2 | 10 | 9 | 3 | 4 | 5 | 4 | 5 |

Notes: ªSample 252 issues. ᵇThese are also tabulated in terms of their content. ᶜDefined as political, social, economic, industrial, scientific, and medical affairs. All figures have been rounded off to the nearest whole number.

rise of television. The most-read items were found to be human interest stories and certain entertainment features. Public affairs coverage in newspapers obtained a smaller overall following, largely because it was of limited interest to women and young people. Within the broad category of politics, items about home politics and industrial news often had an above average readership among men. Even so, these more popular political stories were found to have less of a following among men than sport. Women's features, which brought in related advertising, were also shown to be heavily read by the majority of women.

The managements of popular newspapers responded by giving more space to content with a common denominator appeal. They expanded human interest content, entertainment features, sports, and women's articles (see Table 5).[14] This growth took place at the expense of public affairs coverage which declined, as a percentage of editorial space, by at least half in all our sample popular papers between 1946 and 1976. Indeed public affairs took up less space than sport in all these papers by 1976.

In effect the make-up of popular papers reverted back to its pre-war character in response to similar market pressures. However, the downgrading of political coverage was carried to even more extreme lengths in three sample papers – *The People/Sunday People*, the *Sunday Pictorial/Mirror*, and the *Daily Herald/Sun*. In the last case, public affairs as a proportion of editorial space was down by almost two-thirds in 1976 compared with thirty years earlier.[15] A supplementary content analysis also reveals that public affairs stories were less often chosen as lead, front-page articles in popular newspapers in 1976 compared with 1936.

The increasingly frenetic pursuit of readers also led to a general lowering of journalistic standards, as reporters came under mounting pressure to come up with good human interest stories. This led to a growing number of well-publicized excesses such as the invention of an overnight love tryst between Prince Charles and Lady Diana Spencer on a lonely railway siding in the royal train (*Sunday Mirror*), the fabrication of a fictitious interview with Mrs Marica McKay, the widow of the Falklands VC hero (*Sun*), the touching up of a photograph of 'Lady Di' to give a hint of nipples in a low-cut dress (*Sun*), the offering of 'blood money' to relatives and friends of the 'Yorkshire Ripper', Peter Sutcliffe (*Daily Mail*, *Daily Express*, *Daily Star*, and *News of the World*), and the pillorying of a child ('Worst Brat in Britain') without mentioning that he had a personality disorder due to contracting meningitis

(*Sun*). It also resulted in artificial flavouring and additive being injected into an increasing number of routine stories.

## Growing gap between quality and popular newspapers

In contrast to the popular press, quality papers continued to maintain their commitment to serious political coverage. The *Daily Telegraph* and the *Observer*, for example, actually increased their coverage of public affairs as a percentage of editorial space between 1936 and 1976, while reducing or merely continuing at the same level their human interest content (see Table 5).

But the increasing polarization between popular and quality papers was not due to a growing cultural gulf between élite and mass publics. On the contrary, studies commissioned by publishers regularly revealed that quality and popular paper readers were to some extent similar in their likes and dislikes. Thus to take but one example, the most read stories in Sunday quality papers during the period 1969–71 were human interest stories about ordinary people, followed by human interest stories about celebrities – precisely the most read stories in the *Sunday People* and *Sunday Mirror* during the same period.[16]

The growing divergence between quality and popular papers was a consequence of how they were financed. Quality newspapers were much more heavily dependent on advertising. They also differed from popular papers in that they did not obtain significantly more advertising if they sold more copies to a non-élite audience. There were thus strong economic disincentives against quality papers adopting editorial strategies with a wide public appeal (even if paradoxically more human interest stories would have appealed to many quality paper readers).

The bizarre dynamics of the newspaper market were highlighted by the alternating strategies pursued by *The Times* under a new owner, Lord Thomson. Between 1966 and 1969 *The Times* increased its circulation by 60 per cent through heavy promotion and a more popular editorial approach. However, a substantial number of its new readers were indigent students, lower middle and even working class. Advertisers objected to paying premium advertising rates to reach these new readers, many of whom could be reached more cheaply elsewhere, and they complained even more virulently about buying 'wasted' exposure to readers outside their target group. *The Times*'s advertising failed to keep pace with its growth of sales, causing it to incur a mounting loss. The paper then reverted to a more austere editorial policy, raised its price and changed its advertising campaign. It succeeded in jettisoning 96,000 in unwanted circulation between 1969 and 1971 as a deliberate act of policy.

This division of the press into élite and mass newspapers had important political consequences. The section of the press which provided the most detailed news reporting and analysis, and which most influenced broadcasters' and politicians' agendas, catered for a privileged audience and broadly reflected its class interests. However, market research repeatedly showed that there were also substantial minorities within the mass market who wanted to read public affairs news and analysis. But they were unable to sustain low circulation, serious newspapers, written from a different class perspective, because they lacked sufficient pulling power among advertisers. An élite press thus came to dominate by default the field of serious journalism, thereby reinforcing élite domination of political life.

This illustrates one way in which economic power and ideological power has been linked in Britain. What newspapers have been available for consumers to buy has been shaped through the medium of advertising by inequalities of income and wealth in society. This has resulted, in turn, in a press structure which has helped to sustain and legitimate these inequalities.

## Curtailment of choice

The escalating costs of publishing in the first four decades after the Second World War imposed a further limitation on the range of consumer choice. The rise in staffing, paging, and promotional expenditure in the national newspaper press barred market entry to all but major commercial interests by raising the level of investment needed to establish a new mainstream paper. This proved to be beyond the ready resources even of organized labour. During the 1970s and early 1980s the trade union movement discussed the possibility of starting a new national daily, and even commissioned through the TUC a detailed feasibility study. Reluctantly it concluded in 1984 that it lacked the funds to go ahead with the project despite the fact that its privately commissioned consumer research indicated that there was a substantial market demand for a new left daily.

The only new voices to be heard in Fleet Street merely amplified the existing chorus. In the half century before 1986, just four new national papers were established: the *Sun*, *Daily Star*, *Sunday Telegraph*, and *Mail on Sunday*. All these papers were or became Conservative, thus reinforcing the Conservative preponderance of the national press. They all originated from leading press groups, consolidating their oligopoly.

## The mythologizing of new technology

Between 1986 and 1989 a technical revolution took place in the national press. Computerized typesetting with direct input by journalists and advertising staff was introduced, and photo-composition fully replaced the manual casting of copy in hot metal type. Pages were designed and made up on computer terminals linked to plate making (an innovation that has yet to be adopted by all national papers) rather than being pasted-up on a board. Powerful, new web-offset machines, requiring fewer production staff, were installed by some publishers and some national papers also introduced colour printing. Facsimile transmission was adopted, which enabled the physical separation of editorial and production processes and the simultaneous printing of newspapers at different sites. This reduced distribution costs and facilitated the more intensive use of printing presses.

These technical innovations were accompanied by a revolution in the social organization of production. Thousands of printers were made redundant between 1986 and 1988, and the power of the print unions was broken. The old discontinuous process of production, in which shop floor control was effectively sub-contracted to craft unions, was streamlined into a low-cost, mass-production process controlled by management. In 1989–90, some publishers also made their journalists sign individual con-tracts, opening the way for the derecognition of the National Union of Journalists.

The introduction of new technology was funded principally in two ways. Reuters, jointly owned by leading press groups, was floated in 1984 and produced a windfall sale of shares. Most national publishers also sold their historic properties in the centre of London, and moved to cheaper sites. In 1989, the last national newspaper rolled off the last printing press in Fleet Street, marking the end of a historic tradition that goes back almost to the beginning of British journalism.

A skilled public relations campaign prepared the way for this transformation. Press managements argued that computerized technology would transform the national press by reducing costs. New papers would be easy to set up, and minority journalism would flourish with the aid of low-cost technology. These arguments were echoed by distinguished journalists and politicians on the centre-left as well as the right of the political spectrum in what proved to be a general mobilization of public opinion against Fleet Street's printers. 'Murdoch may have done more for the freedom of the press than a dozen Royal Commissions', enthused Bill Rodgers, Vice-President of the SDP, after the press tycoon shed his Fleet Street production workers. Only the intransigence of some in the print unions, argued Ian Aitken, political editor of the *Guardian*, prevented the emergence of 'entirely new newspapers representing all points of view'. His counterpart at the *Observer*, Robert Taylor, also wrote enthusiastically about how new technology would undermine 'the tyranny of the mass circulation press, with its mindless formula journalism appealing to the lowest common denominator'.

The man who initially embodied all these hopes for the future was Eddy Shah, a publisher of freesheets in the north-west and the victor of a famous confrontation with the National Graphical Association. He announced in 1985 to general acclaim that he was setting up a new national daily and Sunday paper in a green field site, miles from Fleet Street, using the latest in print technology. He was widely hailed as the harbinger of a new era.

But it was in fact Rupert Murdoch who made the first, decisive move by building a new printing plant in Wapping, East London. Although he told the print unions that he intended merely to print a new local daily there, he secretly established a large, new plant, costing over £66 million, capable of printing all his national newspapers. An alternative production workforce was recruited with the help of the maverick electricians' union and trained to operate the new technology. An alternative distribution system was also established through an Australian transport company, Thomas Nationwide Transport, to prevent effective sympathy action by organized labour. As a final precaution, Murdoch reconstituted his Wapping plant as a separate company so that picketing by his Fleet Street employees outside Wapping would be technically illegal.

Murdoch then issued an ultimatum to the print unions requiring them to accept a legally binding, no-strike agreement in which 'new technology may be adopted at any time with consequent reductions in manning levels' and in which anyone involved in industrial action during the term of the contract would be dismissed without appeal. The print unions, although agreeing belatedly to new technology and voluntary redundancy, refused to sign an agreement which they believed meant signing away their members' rights. A strike was called and Murdoch's Fleet Street production workers mounted a forlorn, nightly vigil outside the coils of razor wire surrounding the Wapping plant. Their frustration flared into occasional violence during ritualized mass pickets, which resulted in some print workers being jailed and their unions heavily fined. After more than a year, the strike was called off amid bitter recriminations. The whole episode had been an object lesson in tough multinational, business management in which Murdoch had used an Australian ally to help break a British strike in order to increase the cash flow for the expansion of his media interests in the USA.

His success was followed by a wave of redundancies in Fleet Street, as rival press groups introduced new technology. New papers were also launched in the period 1986–9, seemingly fulfilling optimistic predictions about the impact of new technology. But these predictions were based, as it turned out, on a myth: the widespread belief that overpaid print workers accounted for the major part of newspaper costs. In fact, production wages comprised only 21 per cent of Fleet Street costs before new technology was introduced.[17]

Shedding large numbers of print workers thus did not fundamentally change the economics of publishing. The launch and establishment of new national newspapers still required large resources. *Today* and *Sunday Today* were launched with an initial outlay of £22.5 million; the *Independent* with an establishment fund of £21 million; *News on Sunday* with around £6 million; the *Sunday Correspondent* with £18 million; and the *London Daily News* with an outlay of well over £30 million in its first year.

Outlays remained high partly because new technology was expensive but, more importantly, because it had only a limited impact in lowering operating costs. Consequently, newspapers still had to attain relatively high circulations in order to break even. This led to substantial losses during the period when new newspapers were building up readership in a market where the high proportion of repeat order sales delivered to the home made for consumer inertia.

Just how little things had changed was revealed by Shah's supposedly mould-breaking launch of *Today* and *Sunday Today*.

Shah's central problem – apart from his lack of editorial and managerial expertise – was, ironically, his lack of sufficient finance. A substantial part of his launch fund was swallowed up setting up a modern plant. This led him to economize on pre-launch preparations which contributed to the production problems and indifferent editorial quality of the early issues of his papers. He then ran out of money after only ten weeks and found it impossible to secure further credit, largely because the equity proportion of his capital amounted to only £8.5 million. As a consequence the first national newspapers to be launched by an outsider in half a century were taken over by a leading press conglomerate, Lonrho. Along with other subsidiary backers, Lonrho injected a further £24 million into the Today group, effectively doubling its establishment cost. *Sunday Today* was closed down and *Today* was acquired by the leading monopolist, Rupert Murdoch. Despite gaining a circulation of over half a million, *Today* was still trading at a loss in early 1990.

One problem Shah shared with other would-be proprietors was that he had to leap over the publishing equivalent of a high jump from a very short run-up. But the height of the high jump varied according to the depth of readers' pockets. At the bottom end of the market, a paper like the *News on Sunday*, using the latest technology, needed in 1987 a circulation of over 800,000 to break even. At the top end of the market, an upscale paper like the *Independent* required in 1988 around 400,000 sales to be profitable. This explains why most new papers were directed at an affluent readership that generated substantial advertising: they had to win fewer readers.

The net impact of new technology was modest because it did not change fundamentally the rules of publishing. Continuing high costs still restricted the ownership of newspapers to those with large resources: advertising still distorted the structure of the press. As a consequence, the technical transformation of the press did not produce an editorial transformation. The only new newspaper to extend the political range of the press – the radical *News on Sunday* – failed miserably because it was undercapitalized and editorially inadequate. Just two new popular national papers survived this expansionary period: the *Sunday Sport*, which pioneered soft porn in colour and almost parodied the excesses of tabloid journalism, and *Today*, which strengthened the press's in-bred oligopoly. The principal legacy of new technology was the emergence of three new quality newspapers – *Independent*,

*Independent on Sunday*, and *Sunday Correspondent* – the last of which survived for less than a year. These provided a refuge for journalists fleeing from Rupert Murdoch and Tiny Rowland, and raised the standards of quality paper journalism.

The indications now are that the expansionary period of the national newspaper press, brought about by new technology, is coming to an end. The opportunity for maverick outsiders to undercut print costs disappeared in 1986–8 when national papers rushed to adopt new technology. During this period, established papers pursued protectionist strategies that entrenched their position. They put on extra paging and, in some cases, whole new sections. (The prime example of this, the *Sunday Times*, caused between 15,000 and 20,000 trees to be felled with each issue in 1989.) They kept their cover prices low, and spent heavily on promotion when they were threatened by new launches. Thus, the national press spent a phenomenal £25.3 million on television advertising alone in January–March 1987. The effect of these anti-competition policies was to force up the run-in costs of new entrants. These had to start off with substantial paging in order not to appear too thin, charge a modest cover price to avoid looking too expensive, and spend heavily in order to be heard above the promotional din. The benefits of new technology in reducing costs and making it easier for new papers to be established were thus being eroded even during the period of its introduction.

In short, the technological revolution will be remembered as the revolution that never happened. It led to a cleaner, cheaper system of production and fatter newspapers. It gave a new impetus to an old tradition of centrist, bi-partisan journalism embodied by the *Independent* group. But what it did not do was significantly extend the political diversity of the press or enrich popular journalism through the proliferation of new papers aimed at minorities in the mass market.

## Retrospective

During the post-war period, the press became fully integrated into the core sectors of capital. Ownership ties between newspapers and business corporations were further cemented, at the top level, by institutional, social, and personal links, encouraging newspaper controllers and business leaders to adopt similar ideological positions.

The shift to a more delegated pattern of control in part of the national press during the 1960s was reversed during the 1970s

and 1980s. A new generation of predominantly right-wing proprietors emerged who adopted a more interventionist and personalized style of management. Yet, even in those papers where
proprietors were relatively inactive, control was still exercised
through the selection of senior management and mediated through
the structures of newsgathering and the influence of dominant
political values.

The impact of new, right-wing proprietors was reinforced by
the distorted operation of market forces. Rising costs and
advertising reallocations helped to decimate the social democratic
press, and contributed to the taming and depoliticization of the
radical papers that survived.

The rightward shift of the press was also a response to the
decline of the Labour Party. But the changing complexion of the
national press overstated the decline of the left and over-
emphasized the greater resilience of the right. This was reflected
in the yawning gap that developed between editorial and electoral
opinion, particularly from the 1970s onwards. By 1987, for
example, the Conservative Party had the support of 72 per cent of
national daily circulation but only 43 per cent of the vote.

Partly as a consequence of increasing concentration of ownership, the press failed also to reflect the growing diversity of
public opinion. Indeed the national press – although numbering
between 17 and 21 titles during the period 1969–87 – had
unanimous editorial opinions on a surprising number of issues.
For example every national daily and Sunday paper supported the
aborted union 'reforms' proposed by the government in 1969.
During the 1975 referendum every national newspaper supported
Britain's entry into the EEC. In 1980 every national paper opposed
the TUC's 'day of action'. In 1981 every national paper, which
expressed an editorial opinion, supported the more right-wing
candidate, Denis Healey, in the Labour Party's deputy leadership
contest. In 1985 all national papers applauded Neil Kinnock's
attack on the 'hard left' of his party.

The rightward drift of the press had significant political consequences. The closure of large circulation centre-left papers weakened an institutional prop that had helped to maintain a popular
radical culture in early post-war Britain. The *Daily Herald* had
provided reinforcement for a Labourist, trade union sub-culture;
*Reynolds News* had celebrated the collectivist self-help tradition
of the Co-operative movement; the *News Chronicle*, a paper
which had periodically upset its post-war owners by being too

radical, belonged to an older, ethical Liberal tradition. Together, these three papers reached, on their death-bed, an average issue readership of 9.3 million people.

The national press as a whole increasingly portrayed the unions in a way that weakened support for them. Its reporting of industrial relations tended to focus on strikes, which were regularly defined in terms of their harmful consequences rather than their causes. Thus Denis McQuail found that the three most frequently recurring themes in national daily reports of industrial disputes in 1975 were loss of output, loss of work by those not involved, and inconvenience or danger to the public. Implicitly, strikers were portrayed as being in conflict primarily with the public rather than with their employers. This selective definition was further sustained by under-reporting the role of management. Indeed, actions or statements by employers and their organizations accounted in 1975 for only 2 per cent of the main items of industrial relations reports in national dailies. McQuail found little difference in the pattern of reporting of industrial relations between right-wing Labour and Conservative papers.[18]

The press also mounted a sustained and effective attack on the Labour left. This culminated in the tabloid campaign against 'loony left' councils in 1976–7, the impact of which stemmed from a series of seemingly factual reports featuring left-wing councillors doing manifestly dotty things. Thus individual 'loony left' councils in London were alleged to have banned black bin liners as racist, proscribed the nursery rhyme 'Baa Baa Black Sheep', ordered its employees not to call each other 'sunshine', spent almost £0.5 million on '24 super-loos for gypsies', and insisted that gays should go to the top of the council house waiting list. Not one of these reports proved, on investigation, to be true.[19]

By contributing to the disorganization of oppositional forces in Britain, the press helped to stabilize the social order. Reaching a daily audience of two out of three adults even during the late 1980s, the national press generally endorsed the principal tenets of capitalism – private enterprise, profit, the 'free market', and the rights of property ownership. By regularly invoking the consensual framework of the 'national interest' and by projecting positive symbols of nationhood, in particular the Queen and sporting heroes, the press promoted national identification at the expense of class solidarity. The press also reinforced political and social norms by mobilizing public indignation against a succession of public enemies projected in stereotypical ways – youth gangs, squatters, student radicals, muggers, football hooligans, and union militants.

The press also built support for the social system in less direct and obvious ways. Its focus on political and state office as the seat of power tended to decentre capital and mask the central influence of industrial and financial élites. By regularly reporting political and economic news as disconnected events, it encouraged acceptance of the economic and social structure as natural – the way things are. Embedded in its entertainment features also were values and assumptions that were not as apolitical as they appeared to be at first sight. Its expanding consumer sections concerned with television, records, tapes, CDs, books, travel, motoring, fashion, health, homes, bingo, and personal finance tacitly promoted the seductive view that consumption is a way of expressing individuality and of participating in a 'real world' that transcends hierarchies of power. Its greatly enlarged human interest content tended to portray society as an aggregation of individuals, explain processes in terms of individual psychology rather than social structure, and offer moral rather than political solutions to problems. This conservative 'common sense' view of the world may well have contributed more than explicit political comment to sustaining the remarkably resilient social order of post-war Britain.[20]

## Notes

1. S. Koss, *The Rise and Fall of the Political Press in Britain*, vol. 2 (London, Hamish Hamilton, 1984).
2. The only partial exception to this was the *Daily Mail* which advocated a Conservative–Liberal coalition in the October 1974 general election.
3. MORI, June 1987. This excludes those who were undecided or intended to abstain.
4. The *Daily Worker/Morning Star* and *Newsline*, accounting for less than 0.1 per cent of national circulation in the early 1980s, have not been included as national papers since they did not have a proper nation-wide distribution. They have also been excluded in the assessment of national press content in the last part of this chapter.
5. G. Murdock, 'Class, power and the press: problems of conceptualisation and evidence' in H. Christian (ed.), *The Sociology of Journalism and the Press*, Sociological Review Monograph 29 (Keele, University of Keele, 1980).
6. My thanks to Brendan Wall for help in conducting interviews.
7. J. W. Hobson, *The Selection of Advertising Media* (London, Business Publications, 1955); J. R. Adams, *Media Planning* (London, Business

Books, 1971). There was, however, a reaction against overdependence on quantitative approaches in media planning during the late 1970s and 1980s.

8. '*Daily Herald* reader interest surveys recommendations', p. 8 (London, Odhams Ltd records, 1955).

9. 'Attitudes to newspapers and newspaper reading' (London, International Publishing Corporation (IPC) records, 1964), p. 3.

10. 'National newspaper readership studies: feature readership in national dailies' (London, IPC records, 1964).

11. 'Report of an investigation into the transition from the *Daily Herald* to the *Sun*' (London, IPC records, 1968).

12. 'Report of a survey to study attitudes to daily newspapers' (London, Odhams Ltd records, 1958).

13. Estimated from *Royal Commission on the Press 1947–9 Report* (London, HMSO, 1949), Table 4, p. 82, and *Royal Commission on the Press Interim Report* (London, HMSO, 1976), Table E5, p. 96.

14. A representative sample (twelve issues of dailies and six of Sundays per year) was selected in a way that gave appropriate weight to each quarter of the year, each week in the month, and each day in the week. A code-recode comparison of a representative sample of 1,491 items yielded 83 per cent agreement in their classification.

15. Our unsystematic impression is that the depoliticization of the popular press increased during the period 1976–85 but that this was followed by an increase in the proportion of space devoted to public affairs in some popular daily papers (most notably the *Daily Mirror* in 1990, under Roy Greenslade's editorship).

16. *Sunday Times*, Marketing Research Studies, 1969–71; Sunday Paper Readership Surveys, International Publishing Corporation Marketing and Research Department, 1969–71.

17. The latest available figure for the national newspaper press in the pre-new technology period, as reported in *Royal Commission on the Press Interim Report* (London, HMSO, 1976), Table E11, p. 101.

18. D. McQuail, *Analysis of Newspaper Content*, Royal Commission on the Press Research Series 4 (London, HMSO, 1977). The impact of this press coverage was reinforced by that of television. See Glasgow University Media Group, *Bad News* (London, Routledge & Kegan Paul, 1976) and *More Bad News* (London, Routledge & Kegan Paul, 1980).

19. Goldsmiths' Media Research Group, *Media Coverage of London Councils: Interim Report* (London, Goldsmiths' College, University of London, 1987).

20. For further discussion of this, see J. Curran, G. Whannel, and A. Douglas, 'The political economy of the human interest story' in A. Smith (ed.), *Newspapers and Democracy* (Cambridge, Mass., MIT Press, 1980).

# Part II

## *Broadcasting history*

# 8

# Reith and the denial of politics

There are two accounts of the origins of the BBC. The first is that the Corporation was the personal achievement of John Reith. The second is that its emergence was accidental. According to the first view the BBC's monopoly of broadcasting was an inevitable consequence of the Corporation's cultural mission, while for the second, as R. H. Coase has written, 'The problem, to which the monopoly was seen as a solution by the Post Office, was one of Civil Service administration. The view that a monopoly in broadcasting was better for the listener was only to come later.'

These theories appear to conflict. According to one view Reith made history fit his vision. According to the other, a great institution took a particular form because no one appreciated its future importance. Both, however, have a central flaw in common: they disregard political and social change in the world outside broadcasting.

### Discovering an audience, a director, and the money

Broadcasting – the transmitting of programmes to be heard simultaneously by an indefinitely large number of people – is a social invention, not a technical one. The capacity to broadcast existed long before it was recognized. 'Wireless telegraphy' was developed during the First World War for military purposes. It was used as a substitute for the telephone, but one with the disadvantage that it was impossible to specify the audience which heard the message. An American engineer, David Sarnoff, first saw the possibilities of radio in 1916. 'I have in mind a plan of development which would make radio a "household utility" like the piano or electricity,' he wrote. 'The idea is to bring music into the house by wireless.'

Yet for some time after popular broadcasting had started in the

1920s, wireless was regarded as little more than an experimental toy. It took Northcliffe, a pioneer in the commercialization of leisure, to demonstrate the potential audience for the new invention. He arranged a promotion stunt for the *Daily Mail*. Dame Nellie Melba was to be broadcast singing from Chelmsford. This event which began 'with a long silvery trill' and ended with *God Save the King* attracted a much larger audience than had been expected. It made the wireless manufacturers aware for the first time of a potentially huge market for them to supply.

In 1922 there were nearly a hundred applications to the Post Office from manufacturers who wanted to set up broadcasting stations. This demand created the need for control. As Peter Eckersley, one of the company's first employees, wrote later, 'The BBC was formed as an expedient solution to a technical problem. It owes its existence to the scarcity of air waves.' The Postmaster General solved the problems of radio interference by persuading rival manufacturers to invest jointly in one small and initially speculative broadcasting station: The British Broadcasting Company. John Reith was made its Managing Director.

How would the BBC have developed if its first director had been a career civil servant, a banker, or a Bloomsbury intellectual? Many of the features of broadcasting which are taken for granted today would certainly be absent. Reith's domination of the Corporation in its early days was massive, totalitarian, and idiosyncratic, and for many decades the traditions of the BBC seemed to flow directly from his personality. The British Broadcasting Company was set up as a business. Reith turned it into a crusade. 'Scotch engineer, Calvinist by upbringing, harsh and ruthless in character', as A. J. P. Taylor has described him, Reith used 'the brute force of monopoly to stamp Christian morality on the British people'. While waiting to find out whether his application for the directorship had been successful Reith wrote in his memoirs, 'I kept my faith alive night and morning and encouraged myself with the text "Commit thy way unto the Lord, trust also Him and He shall bring it to pass".' Later he was to exhort his staff to dedicate themselves to 'humility in the service of higher pursuits. The desire for notoriety and recognition', he warned, 'sterilizes the seeds from which greatness might spring.'

This ability to impose his will on staff was helped by his size. Churchill nicknamed him 'Wuthering Heights' and senior staff would stand on stairs to argue with him, 'so that I can see you eye to eye, Sir'. His administrative style, and indeed his private diary, were characterized by abuse. Memoranda sent to Reith would return peppered with 'rubbish', 'stupid', 'soft minded idiocy', 'he lies'. Frequently he saw his life in nautical terms: the Corporation was a ship and he was at the helm. He was pompous, humourless, arrogant, and, like most megalomaniacs, paranoid and self-pitying. Yet the near absurdity of his vision enabled him to foresee the power of the new service.

Broadcasting was to be financed partly by a tariff on wireless sets, and partly by a licence fee. These sources soon proved inadequate for the rapidly expanding station. Listeners evaded the tariff by building their own sets with cheap foreign components. They then evaded the full licence fee by applying for experimental licences. The BBC complained, and the manufacturers were angry that the monopoly of wireless production was not proving as profitable as they had hoped. Hence in 1923 the Sykes Committee was set up by the Post Office to inquire into the Company's finances. This rejected advertising as a source of revenue because 'The time devoted to it ... would be very small and therefore exceedingly valuable.' Radio advertising would interfere with market competition by favouring large firms. Instead the report recommended that a simple licence fee should be raised to finance the service.

The Crawford Committee, two and a half years later, unquestioningly accepted the necessity of a broadcasting monopoly, and recommended that the private company be replaced by a 'Public Commission operating in the National Interest'. The service was felt to have outgrown the petty limits of a business enterprise. 'Formed at a moment when broadcasting was still embryonic – regarded by many as a toy, a fantasy, even a joke,' the report argued, 'the company by strenuous application to its duties aided by the loyalty of its staff has raised the service to a degree which reflects high credit on British efficiency and enterprise.'

In 1926 the British Broadcasting Company closed, and the new British Broadcasting Corporation opened. Reith was delighted that the unique status of his organization was recognized. 'The Royal Academy and the Bank of England function under Royal Charter,' proclaimed the 1927 *Handbook*. 'So does the BBC. It is no Department of State.'

## The BBC as a public corporation

The BBC came to be seen, in the words of William Robson, as a 'sociological invention of immense significance', and a 'breathtaking administrative innovation'. Hilda Matheson, the first head of the Talks Department, wrote in 1933 that the Corporation was 'wholly in keeping with the British constitution, and it is more and more common to find it quoted as a possible model for the management of other national services for which private control and direct state management are equally unsuitable'. What, then, was the novelty of the BBC's organization and to what extent was Reith responsible for it?

Reith did not invent the notion of a public corporation. Neither did the Corporation simply emerge accidentally. Reith exploited a theory because it was convenient to do so. The Post Office, which played a critical role in the BBC's development, was itself an early example of a nationally run business. William Beveridge had commented in 1905 that the GPO was the 'one socialist experiment . . . that now works well'. Forestry, water, and electricity were all important public corporations set up in the years before the BBC was even thought of. Lincoln Gorden, the economist, wrote that by the 1920s, 'Public boards had become all the rage, politicians of every creed when confronted with an industry or a social service which was giving trouble or failing to operate efficiently – create a board.'

The First World War had been critical in establishing the conditions for the acceptance of a 'Public Service Utility'. Despite bitter opposition the centralized control of health, insurance, coal, and ultimately the rationing of food had been introduced. These were seen as exceptional wartime measures. By the 1920s, however, a generation of reformers who had been civil servants during the war were experienced in organizing the centralized distribution of resources. Indeed for a brief period after the war even the government accepted a more interventionist role. The BBC was formed in this period.

The development of the public corporation depended on the rejection of both market forces and politics in favour of efficiency and planned growth controlled by experts. Briggs has pointed out that the acceptance of the BBC and its monopoly was a consequence of the 'substantial and influential support' the Company received between 1924 and 1925. The monopoly remained in Reith's keeping because 'a large number of important people and

a large section of the interested public felt that it was right that
this should be so'. These influential people were those who were
personally impressed by Reith: the Post Office officials; the director
of the wireless manufacturers' association; even the Prime Minister,
Baldwin.

However, the idea of the BBC also had more general support.
There was a widespread dissatisfaction with the *ad hoc* nature of
industrial competition. Even in the 1920s, during the first post-
war slump, there was a sense that there must be alternative ways
to manage the distribution of resources. Men like Beveridge, who
had demonstrated the justice of centralized control in the arrangements for social security and in the rationing of food during the
First World War, were opposed to the social consequences of
industrial competition. In 1934 Beveridge was to argue:

> In a free market economy consumers can buy only that which is
> offered to them, and that which is offered is not necessarily that
> which is most advantageous. It is that which appears to give the
> best prospect of profit to the producer.

This kind of attitude, which Beveridge later developed and popularized in his broadcasts, was surprisingly widely held in the early
1920s. For example Sir Stephen Tallents, who was to play a
prominent role in the BBC as well as in the British documentary
movement, had worked on rationing with Beveridge, and held
very similar opinions. Reith's view that capitalist competition
was not wrong but could be inefficient was therefore hardly
original.

The BBC was to be used repeatedly as a prototype of the public
corporation, especially by Herbert Morrison. Perhaps the feature
which particularly attracted socialist writers was the BBC's distance
from the world of capitalist industry. The Corporation made no
profits. But in addition the goods it made, programmes, were in
theory accessible to an infinite number of consumers. It was also
a completely new enterprise with no capitalist inheritance to
weigh it down. As Robson wrote, 'The BBC is an engine of the
mind ... it represents socialized control not encumbered with
compensation.'

It was this aspect of broadcasting which Reith grasped. He
argued that it was in the very nature of the medium that it should
be available for all, for it 'ran as a reversal of the natural law that
the more one takes, the less there is left for others'. In
broadcasting, he wrote, 'There is no limit to the amount which

may be drawn off. It does not matter how many thousands there may be listening; there is always enough for others.'[1] In order to exploit broadcasting fully, Reith had argued, it must be governed by social and not financial priorities.

Thus considerations of profit would have restricted the service to the populous urban areas. Reith was determined that the BBC must serve the whole nation. However, Reith also saw that a national service was vital for the defence of the Corporation's monopoly. 'About a week ago', he wrote in 1923, 'we got wind of a projected attack.' This was to be 'based on the grounds that under the present system we had already reached the limits of our expansion. The deduction to be drawn was that the British people would never be supplied with adequate services unless the principle of competitive commercialism were admitted.' Reith rejected commerce because it would have diminished his empire and lowered its status. But he also believed it to be inefficient in the management of national resources. Many shared this view.

Even the government had come to see some kinds of goods as exceptional. In 1927 the film industry, suffering from foreign competition, was protected by import controls, because films were of 'outstanding national importance'. The BBC had been established because the government was anxious not to exercise unfair patronage by granting a monopoly to any one commercial company. But it had also been considerably affected by the report of a Post Office official, F. J. Brown, on a visit to the USA where 'an epidemic of broadcasting was raging'. Thousands of American companies had started broadcasting and President Hoover had demanded central control over the new technology, claiming that it was as if '10,000 telephone subscribers were crying through the air for their mates'. As a result of interference, Hoover declared, 'the ether will be filled with frantic chaos'.[2] The British government realized on the basis of the American experience that broadcasting was a new kind of resource whose management demanded a new form of administration.

The BBC was founded on a rejection of politics. From the start of broadcasting there had been anxieties that the service would become an agency of government propaganda. Sir Charles Trevelyan, a Labour representative on the Sykes Committee, asked the Company's lawyer whether 'for public reasons a government could intervene to prevent anything it regarded as undesirable being broadcast'. He was told that there might be control of the news, but that a government was unlikely to bother with concerts, lectures, speeches, or the weather.

While Reith believed that the BBC should be above politics, politicians at first believed the BBC to be beneath them. Direct public ownership was rejected because it was felt 'A Member might well shrink from the prospect of having to defend in Parliament the various items in a government concert.'

Reith despised politicians and disliked party politics. Although at various times he had political ambitions, he hated the 'toadying, the cringing pursuit of popularity' which he believed characterized politics. 'It is pathetic', he wrote, 'how apprehensive Labour leaders are of their followers and how little control they seem to have over them.' Reith often misjudged the significance of political events (he felt that the split and collapse of the Labour government in 1931 was unimportant, 'Silly, over money'). 'The whole horrid technique of politics should be abolished,' he wrote in his diary. 'Government of a country is a matter of proper administration, in other words efficiency. It need not be different in nature from the government of a business – only in degree' (29 November 1936). Perhaps the most significant feature of Reith's distaste was the sense that politics led to vacillation and compromise when firm government was needed. Reith was not alone in this view. Indeed an interest developed during the late 1920s and early 1930s, from the extreme right to the fellow travelling left – and including the Keynesian centre – in the benefit of planning.

'The Next Five Years Group' and Political and Economic Planning (known then as PEP!) were groups involving members with different political allegiances but who were agreed on the need for more social planning. 'It may be', wrote one reformer in *The New Outlook*, 'that the Party structures will act for some time as an obstacle in the way of new developments.' Macmillan summed up this position:

> Most of us recognize that the old system of free unplanned Capitalism has passed away. Most of us agree that a leap forward to complete state planning is politically impossible. But ... our search is for some practical scheme of social organization ... which is neither.[3]

On the left, the XYZ club and the New Fabian Research Bureau soon became the natural home for planners and economists.

It has been argued by Scannell and Cardiff that the BBC

legitimized its model of broadcasting, not by the huge audience the service soon attracted, but by reference to the élite of 'the great and the good who trooped into studios to educate and inform on every subject from unemployment to the Origin of the Species: Shaw, Wells, the Webbs, Beveridge, Keynes and Huxley – the roll call is endless'. Broadcasting, they argue, was dominated by a specific, reforming, fraction of the middle class. 'They saw themselves as superior to the aristocracy, for they were efficient and uncorrupt, and claiming to act for the general good, they presumed (naturally) to speak and act on behalf of the working classes.' Robert Skidelsky has argued that Keynes's economic theories provided the basis for a new liberal politics in the 1940s, which avoided class struggle and yet implied 'Keynes's most characteristic belief: that public affairs should and could be managed by an elite of clever and disinterested public servants' (*Encounter*, April 1979). The BBC provided a cultural institution which performed the same function. Indeed the economic and political structure of the BBC was also a product of the experience and beliefs of this reforming intelligentsia. Reith's view of what he intended the BBC to be, those pressures he perceived as threatening, and the alternatives he rejected, were typical of what has been seen as a 'middle opinion'. Indeed it might be claimed that the success of the BBC vindicated the view that a strong middle-class consensus lay beneath the dissent and turmoil of the 1930s.

However, this view should perhaps be modified. Marwick has admitted in an article called 'Middle opinion in the thirties' that 'They did not in their own day achieve much, these advocates of political agreement, the "soft centre" as they were not unjustly called.' Indeed, the 'great and the good' were, as Hugh Dalton wrote in 1936, 'more or less eminent persons who are disinclined to join any existing political party, but who are prepared to collaborate with others in writing joint letters to the Press, and in such organizations as the Next Five Years Group'. They were a band of leaders – but they had no followers. As Pimlott has argued in *Labour and the Left in the 1930s*, their policies might have developed 'into the basis of a powerful campaign for a British New Deal as a frontal assault on mass unemployment'.[4] But in fact the supporters of middle opinion were politically isolated. Keynes and Beveridge had to wait until the Second World War to see their ideas implemented. Yet the BBC was not merely a dream or a plan for reform. It was a rapidly growing institution. By the middle of the 1930s it had become an established and central component of British culture.

Perhaps pressures other than those of the liberal intelligentsia were at work in the making of the BBC? Certainly, unlike Beveridge's plans for insurance, the BBC cost the government no money. The personal connections of the BBC producers were with Bloomsbury literati rather than with liberal reformers. Reith was more an evangelist than a liberal. 'Anything in the nature of a dictatorship is the subject of much resentment these days,' he wrote in 1924. 'Well somebody has to give decisions.' While liberals planned, Reith bullied, wheedled, and built an empire. 'It is occasionally indicated to us that we are apparently setting out to give the public what we think they need and not what they want – but few know what they want, and very few what they need.'

Reith was authoritarian and successful. In the 1930s the new liberals were neither. Moreover, although they dominated broadcast talks, this category hardly dominated the BBC's output. Despite Reith's preoccupation with culture, contemporary critics most frequently accused the Corporation of philistinism. 'The company undoubtedly saw itself as a cultural force', wrote R. S. Lambert, 'by which it meant something constituted to avoid the postures of vulgarity.' Perhaps the BBC was less dominated by the concerns of the liberal intelligentsia and more successful in the 1930s because it was paternalist. Perhaps, also, it gave the public what it wanted rather more than Reith was prepared to admit. For, as the BBC *Handbook* shows, by 1934 the BBC was broadcasting more light music, comedy, and vaudeville than any other European station. It was hardly the stuff of social revolution.

## The BBC and political independence

How was the BBC's independence from partisan political pressure to be achieved? The directors of the private company were replaced by publicly appointed Governors in 1926. These were to be the trustees of the public interest. At first the Governors and Reith disagreed about how the responsibility should be divided between them.

Thus Philip Snowden's wife Ethel – described in Beatrice Webb's diaries as having 'caricatured social climbing' (19 March 1932) – arrived at the BBC expecting an office, a secretariat, and a full-time job. Appointed a Governor as a 'convenient

representative of both Labour and Women', she believed the
Director General should play an administrative role, and that the
Governors should make all policy decisions. Reith detested her,
and commented that she thought that 'there ought to be a board
meeting every day ... an abominable exhibition by her. A truly
terrible creature, ignorant, stupid and horrid.' He saw her as a
threat to his own position. Indeed he was quite correct to do so.
Hugh Dalton, the Labour politician, recorded in his diary (3
August 1930) that Ethel Snowden had asked G. D. H. Cole –
another Governor – to help her get rid of Reith. 'Who would she
suggest as his successor?' Cole had asked. 'I would gladly take it
on myself,' Ethel had replied.

Herbert Morrison wrote in his important work on nationalization,
*Socialization and Transport*, 'It is a matter of argument whether
the Director General of Broadcasting should, or should not, be a
strong personality.' Reith's views were quite straightforward: he
wanted to be in control, and he wanted the Governors to back up
his decisions.

The Corporation was supposed to be independent and non-
partisan: in practice it was not even indirectly accountable to
Parliament. In a Report on the Machinery of Government written
in 1918, the Webbs had opposed the increased use of public
corporations because

> when a board is set up without explicit status provided for
> ministerial responsibility to parliament – the situation is
> obviously unsatisfactory. Only ministerial responsibility pro-
> vides safeguard for the citizen ... and consumer.

However, these objections were not understood. The government
had felt in 1925 that 'The progress of science and the harmony of
art would be hampered by too rigid rules and too constant supervision by the state.' So, between Reith, anxious to avoid having
the content of broadcasting politically manipulated, and therefore
determined to evade political control, and the government, anxious
to avoid responsibility for trivia, the BBC was left with no
effective accountability. This omission came to be treated as
though it were a principle. Herbert Morrison later claimed to have
invented it. Robson wrote in 1935 that it was

> in strict conformity with the English tradition ... derived as a
> practical expedient to perform a particular function, without
> any concern for general principles – or indeed any awareness
> that questions of principle were involved.

It is perhaps better seen as the elevation of an uneasy compromise into an ideal type.

## The BBC and the General Strike

The BBC's practical interpretation of impartiality was soon tested during the General Strike in 1926. Reith knew that the survival of the Corporation (whose constitution had not yet been formally accepted) depended on its conduct during the crisis.

One effect of the strike was to create a national audience for broadcasting. At the end of 1926 Hilda Matheson was able to write, 'The public and wireless listeners are now nearly synonymous terms.' Beatrice Webb noted in her diary that 'The sensation of the General Strike centres around the headphones of the wireless set.' Although there were only 2 million licence holders these represented a far greater number of listeners, and 'communal listening' was a feature of the crisis as people gathered in halls and outside shops to hear the news.

The BBC seemed more important because of the absence of all other sources of information. An old age pensioner in the 1950s told Julian Symons that he still had 'the little homemade crystal set which worked lovely with the iron bedstead for an aerial . . . and which told me what was *really happening*'. Despite the inadequacy of its news the Corporation emerged from the strike with a national audience and increased authority.

Another effect of the General Strike was that the BBC invented modern propaganda in its British form. During the First World War persuasive techniques had been crude. All Germans were characterized as vicious beasts intent on murdering children and raping nuns. Anthony Smith has argued that a rejection of the

propagandists of the First World War, and the ensuing reaction against the black-out that they had perfected were among the profoundest influences on the men who came to lay the foundations of broadcasting in the early nineteen twenties.

The First World War view of propaganda was still accepted by many during the strike. Its main proponent was Churchill and its main instrument the *British Gazette*. This was a daily news-sheet that few took seriously, so evidently biased were its contents. Churchill wanted to commandeer the BBC, as the government had the right to do. Reith argued that if the BBC was taken over the strikers would merely close the service down. Apart from destroying 'the pioneer work of +3g years', by shattering public confidence in broadcasting, 'It was no time for dope, even if the people could have been doped.' He argued that to suppress information was likely to exacerbate the crisis. His most telling point was that by gaining the trust of both strikers and the government the BBC could positively facilitate a resolution of the crisis:

> In the end conciliations of some kind must supervene and . . . the BBC could act as a link to draw together the contending parties by creating an atmosphere of good will towards its service on both sides.

Reith argued that the trust gained by 'authentic impartial news' could then be used. It was not necessarily an end in itself.

He stated, however, that 'Since the BBC was a national institution and since the Government in this crisis was acting for the people . . . *the BBC was for the Government in the Crisis too.*'

Indeed it was Reith's own political judgement which controlled policy throughout the strike. Briggs has pointed out:

> He preferred mediation to showdown. If his views had coincided with those of the sponsors of the *British Gazette* he would have had fewer qualms about allowing the BBC to fall directly into the hands of the government. As it was, his personal conviction gave strength to his resistance on constitutional principles.

Reith, as another writer, Patrick Renshaw, has argued, 'would have supported the union against the owners. But he was certainly not prepared to support the TUC against the Government.' However, Reith's 'distinct' view seems very close to that of the most implacable opponent of the strike, Churchill. Martin Gilbert argues that Churchill was quite prepared to accept a conciliatory policy towards the resolution of the coal-miners' dispute with the owners; it was only the general and political strike he was opposed to.

Until 1926 the press had prohibited the BBC from collecting any news. The strike allowed the Company to develop a news service of its own. This reported statements by the strikers as well as the strike-breakers. One of the bulletins on 4 May started with the TUC statement, 'We have from Land's End to John O'Groats reports of support that have surpassed our expectations.'

During the strike no representative of organized labour was allowed to broadcast, and the Leader of the Opposition, Ramsay MacDonald, was also banned. These restrictions were imposed by the government. Reith thought them wrong, but said he could do nothing about them. Willie Graham, one of the strike leaders, wrote angrily to him:

> The Government emphatically deny that they interfere with the BBC in anyway. On the other hand the company states that it was not a free agent. I am sure that you will agree that it is impossible to make any sense of these two statements.

Called by some workers the 'British Falsehood Corporation', the BBC learnt how to censor itself during the strike in order to forestall government intervention. Nevertheless the General Strike marks the end of the propaganda based on lies and the start of a more subtle tradition of selection and presentation.

Throughout the strike the government had emphasized that the strikers were politically motivated and hence unconstitutional. The BBC emerged from the crisis with an ethic of political neutrality, which was expressed as much in the tone of its broadcasts as in any formal regulations. This was to have profound consequences for politics.

## Governments and the BBC in the 1930s

The General Strike initiated a pattern that was to recur throughout the 1930s: the BBC was forced to pass off government intervention as its own decision. In 1935 it was proposed to include talks by a communist and a fascist – Harry Pollitt and Sir Oswald Mosley, respectively – in a series on the British constitution. The Foreign Office protested, arguing that Pollitt could not be allowed to broadcast as he had recently made a speech supporting armed revolution. The BBC responded by referring the matter to the Governors, who declared that, 'More harm than good could be done if a policy were adopted of muzzling speeches.' A BBC official told the Foreign Office, 'We can't chuck Pollitt unless, under our charter, we are given instruction from government that he is not to broadcast.'

The Foreign Office remained adamant that Pollitt should not broadcast. They suggested, however, that the question could resolve itself into the undesirability of *Mosley* speaking.[5] The matter was finally brought to an end when the Postmaster General wrote to Reith pointing out that as the Corporation licence was due for renewal, it would be wiser to comply with government demands.

The BBC then asked for permission to say why the programmes had been banned.

The government reacted sharply. According to a Cabinet minute:

> It would be neither true nor desirable to state publicly that the talks would be an 'embarrassment to the Government' at the present time. But it would be true to say that 'they would not be in the national interest'.

Despite the feeling of Corporation officials like Tallents and Graves that the BBC's chances of survival were better if it were seen to be acting in strict accordance with the Charter, the series was dropped and no mention made of government pressure.

An even more remarkable example of the BBC's relationship with the government occurred in the period immediately before the outbreak of the Second World War. On 25 August 1939 the Labour leaders Hugh Dalton and Harold Laski, together with the General Secretary of the TUC, Walter Citrine, wanted to broadcast a direct personal message and warning to the German people. In an interview with them, the Director General of the BBC, Ogilvie (who had replaced Reith in 1938), refused to tell them whether their request would be granted. In the event, news that a 'statement' had been made was broadcast, but nothing whatsoever was mentioned about its contents.

Ogilvie, Dalton pointed out, clearly wanted to consult the Foreign Office but refused to admit this. The next day the Labour leaders complained to the Foreign Secretary, Halifax, of the way in which the BBC had treated them. By this time Ogilvie apparently claimed that he had told Dalton and Citrine that he was going to consult the Foreign Office.

Walter Citrine complained to Halifax that 'Our people are getting pretty fed up with being expected to shout with the government one day and being treated like a lot of children or nobodies the next.' He went on to say that Ogilvie (who had been a Conservative MP) 'might be good enough to help them [the Tories] collect material to rag Lloyd George with – but that doesn't satisfy me that he is fit to be Director General of the BBC'.[6] This incident demonstrates the continuous and insidious dependence of the Corporation on the government. It is not merely that the decision whether to broadcast the message was referred to the Foreign Office. In addition, Ogilvie was predicting Foreign Office policy, and indeed covering for it. Earlier, the BBC had been concerned to make government pressure on its decisions public. In 1939 it was protecting the Foreign Office, and passing off Foreign Office demands as its own policy.

Since 1927 the BBC had been strenuously courting government departments in an attempt to evade press restrictions on its reporting. 'We ought to be the arbiters of what Government news goes out,' wrote a Corporation official, 'not a commercial company like Reuters.'[7] A close relationship with civil servants grew up and government pressure was often exercised informally and personally. 'Vansittart would like the BBC to get pro-France in our news and stop using words like insurgent,' Reith wrote in his diary in 1937. The Corporation was most concerned that disputes with governments should not be resolved by the emergence of any official regulations.

This cautious self-protection was shrewd, and may have been the only strategy available. However, it made the BBC vulnerable to bullying. At various times it was implied that the licence fee might not be allowed to rise, or even that the Corporation's licence to broadcast might be terminated. As a result the most important constraint came to be the Corporation's anxiety to pre-empt the threats.

## The BBC, society, and programmes

During a decade of depression and industrial decline, the BBC grew, quadrupled its staff, raised salaries, and acquired vast buildings. One writer, D. G. Bridson, recalled his shock at being asked to work for the BBC. 'In 1935 I mentally bracketed it with Parliament, the Monarch, the Church and the Holy Ghost,' he wrote.

However, the Corporation also intended to become part of the Establishment. Its development into an authoritative institution was a complex process. This was expressed in the choice of outside broadcasters, and what they were allowed to say. It was also expressed in how the Corporation treated them, and its own staff. It was expressed in the distance between what it claimed to do and what it did.

In a decade of hunger marches and 'red united fighting fronts', the BBC regarded a succession of royal broadcasts as the triumph of outside broadcasting and actuality reporting. Broadcasting in the 1930s was dominated by state openings, royal anniversaries, visits, deaths and births, and by the Coronation. 'The floral decorations for His Majesty's broadcast', ran one press release, 'will be one bowl of hiskura (mauve) and a small vase of grape hyacinths.'

In 1923 Reith had exercised a servile cunning in his attempt to persuade the Dean of Westminster to allow the Duke of York's wedding to be broadcast. It would, he suggested, even have advantages 'from the devotional point of view'. Many who 'by sheer force of circumstance, or negligence had little to do with the Church' would hear the 'measured cadence of the sacred words'.[8] The experience, Reith implied, might change their hearts.

Reith's greatest coup was the annual Christmas message delivered by the Monarch. These events were usually preceded by an 'Empire programme', making contact with far-flung colonial stations. 'Goodbye Wilmington', ran one, 'and a Happy Christmas to you all . . . behind us the mountains which encircle Vancouver are still lost in darkness . . . though a faint radiance announces that dawn is on its way.'[9] George V's funeral resulted in an eighty-page BBC policy document, 'Procedures on the death of a sovereign'.

Reith and the Corporation did not merely present traditional pageantry to a wider audience. They established a new manner for royalty which was more appropriate to the twentieth century. Reith made suggestions for what royalty should say, and how they should say it. He recognized what kinds of occasion a royal presence would grace – and benefit from. One of the bitterest complaints of Reith's old age was his omission from royal Garden Party invitation lists. He felt he had 'done much to serve the House'. Indeed the BBC was responsible, at least in part, for moulding a new domestic and populist image for the Monarchy.

The BBC was a little less sensitive to the needs of trade unionists. One of the clearest aspects of what came to be known as the 'William Ferrie incident', was the incomprehension of the Corporation's bourgeois but liberal-minded staff, when confronted with a worker.[10] Ferrie, a communist trade unionist, was invited to reply to a talk given by Sir Herbert Austin, who had spoken on the immense improvement of working-class conditions during the twentieth century. This was in 1932. Ferrie committed the Corporation equivalent of original sin by departing from his written script when he reached the microphone. He began to tell the public how the BBC had censored him, and horrified Corporation officials rushed to fade out the programme. Ferrie later wrote:

I was particularly incensed at their demand that I should put across that the slogan 'Workers of the World Unite' is not a revolutionary slogan. I also refused to drop my h's and talk as they imagine a worker does.

His talk had quite clearly been altered to make it more politically acceptable. But the way in which it was done is even more revealing. The BBC censored him in ways that the officials would hardly have recognized as such. 'Your language', commented Mary Adams, 'was too literary and impersonal.' Ferrie, to her surprise, came 'in an agitated state', to see her at her Chelsea home. He arrived at the studio with three colleagues 'for support'. All of this seemed odd to middle-class BBC producers, even though Mary Adams was sympathetic to the union case. It seems in retrospect a perfectly regular way for a working-class trade unionist to deal with an institution that seemed bent on intimidating him.

The BBC was more intentionally autocratic in its treatment of its own staff. Reith would banish rebels from the centre of the empire to the periphery. 'You're a very dangerous man Harding,' Bridson recalls Reith telling one, 'I think you'd better go up North where you can't do so much damage.' Indeed by 1937 the only doubts about the Corporation's monopoly were centred on the rights of its staff. There were several symptomatic scandals during the 1930s. The first was the forced resignation of P. P. Eckersley, an engineer and programme innovator of enormous talent who had worked for the Corporation since 1926. Eckersley wrote his own epitaph, 'He had ideas: We stopped them.' He was obliged to resign because he was cited in a divorce case.

The second was over the pressure brought to bear on the editor of the *Listener*, R. S. Lambert, to discourage him from continuing with a libel action. Lambert was warned that he had no future career in the Corporation if he pursued the case. Later he argued that 'This opinion crystallized the dangerous doctrine that the individual owes more loyalty to his employer, than to his fellow employees.'

Reith's view was succinct. 'It's a mug's game', he wrote in a book called *Personality and Career*, 'to pull contrary to your boss.' In 1937 the Ullswater Report recommended, under pressure from Attlee, that a Staff Association should be set up, and for the first time the BBC's workers had organized representation.

The BBC saw itself as a humane and enlightened employer, which had always pursued strictly egalitarian and meritocratic appointment procedures. In 1934 an internal report commented complacently that there was 'a good proportion of women to men on the staff'. This was true, but most of the women were secretaries.

Hilda Matheson and Mary Somerville had set up the key Talks Department and the Education Service when the Company started. It was a woman's initiative which had started the Sound Archive. Women, however, were never announcers, rarely presenters, and the proportion of women in administrative and creative posts declined. Between 1926 and 1936 the Corporation's staff had increased fourfold yet, as the BBC's annual reports show, the number of women in creative jobs had risen by little more than one-third, and in senior administrative positions by barely one-quarter.

Nevertheless, the atmosphere in the BBC, a new exciting glamorous place where it was better, as Peter Eckersley remarked, 'to have discreet affairs than to remarry', is summed up by Maurice Gorham:

> The BBC secretaries were beginning to bloom though they reached full flower later. By that time many of them were pin money girls. It was a great sight to see them going out at lunch, high heeled, sheer stockinged, beautifully made up, talking disdainfully in high clear voices.

By the 1930s the BBC had become an august institution. It was not a crude agent of the status quo, rather it advocated acceptable change, in some areas, in certain circumstances, sometimes.

## The BBC and journalism

Indeed, by the end of the decade the sheer amount of news that broadcasting and the press were flooded with was so large that, had it wished to, a government could hardly have pre-censored it all. However, a new tradition in reporting imposed new criteria of selection on the news. Journalists stopped being passionate advocates, saw themselves rather as independent professionals, and their writing as a negotiated product of conflict between partisan views. This self-image and its practical consequences were most fully developed in the BBC. Reith was not opposed to conflict. On the contrary, he fought the press for the right to broadcast on contentious issues. But the BBC and the new 'professional journalist' retained a monopoly over deciding its limits.

## The BBC and appeasement

The BBC's brokerage was subject to pressure. In the eyes of the BBC's programme-makers, politics was an activity which only happened between major political parties. Two kinds of political dispute never reached the air waves: divisions within parties and the expressive politics of the streets. Winston Churchill, repeatedly excluded from broadcasting because his views were seen as eccentric, wrote to Reith saying he wished he could buy broadcasting time. He preferred the American commercial system 'to the present British method of debarring public men from access to a public who wish to hear'. In 1933 Churchill and Austen Chamberlain complained that the BBC 'had introduced an entirely new principle of discrimination into British public life, namely the elimination from broadcasting of any Members of Parliament who were not nominated by the Party leaders or the Party Whip'. Such a crucial innovation, they protested, should be decided by parliament, not arbitrarily imposed by the BBC.[11]

The most important dispute the BBC ignored, and one which cut across party loyalties, was that of the government's policy of appeasing German territorial ambitions. Churchill claimed that the BBC conspired with the press to exclude all opponents of this policy from any access to the public. Gilbert and Gott have suggested that appeasers were effective for so long mainly because of their success in keeping the opponents of German rearmament out of public office. However, the control of public knowledge and opinion was also crucial. An early reference to Polish rearmament lost a producer his job in 1932. Speakers were banned because of their hostility to the fascist states. Later, the BBC was to apologize for its attitude during the 1930s by explaining that, while mistaken, it was merely following the trend of opinion of the times. Yet the BBC's silence is extraordinary as it was itself making extensive plans for the Corporation's conduct and survival during a possible war.

Reith's diary first mentions preparations for war in 1933: plans for the physical protection of transmitters and broadcasting stations were in hand by 1935; Reith was involved in discussions over the organization of a Ministry of Information in the event of war by 1936; details of trains in which to send personnel from London were established by 1937. Thus the BBC was secretly preparing for a war which it did not officially expect, while the public were kept in ignorance of these cautious foresights.

## The BBC at the end of the decade

Reith resigned in 1937, restless and dissatisfied. The BBC no longer stretched him, and he hoped for something better which never came. Increasingly, as the prospect of high office receded, he regarded the Corporation which he had created with resentment. It had not, he came to feel, treated him well.

By the end of the 1930s the BBC seemed a natural and inevitable solution to the problem of administering a national broadcasting system. It had won the right to discuss controversial politics against the determined opposition of suspicious governments and a jealous press. But it developed unnecessary conventions, and had become too defensive. The real test of the Corporation's independence was to come during the Second World War.

## Notes

1. J. W. C. Reith, *Broadcast Over Britain* (London, Hodder & Stoughton, 1924), p. 52.
2. F. J. Brown, 'Broadcasting in Britain', *London Quarterly Review*, 145, 3 (January 1926).
3. H. Macmillan, 'Looking forward' in the Next Five Years Group, *The New Outlook*, 1 (8 May 1937).
4. See B. Pimlott, *Labour and the Left in the 1930s* (Cambridge, Cambridge University Press, 1977).
5. 'The citizen and his government' (1935–6), *BBC Written Archives*.
6. The unpublished diary of High Dalton (25–29 August 1939). For a further development of this affair, see J. Seaton and B. Pimlott, 'The struggle for balance: the BBC and the Labour Movement 1920–45' in J. Seaton and B. Pimlott (eds), *Politics and the Media in Britain* (Aldershot, Gower, 1987).
7. 'Relationship between the government and the BBC: the Foreign Office', *BBC Written Archives*.
8. Duke of York's wedding, *BBC Written Archives* (Royalty).
9. Christmas broadcasts, *BBC Written Archives* (Royalty).
10. The William Ferrie incident, *BBC Written Archives*.
11. The Churchill and Chamberlain complaint, *BBC Written Archives* (Churchill).

# *Broadcasting and the blitz*

The 'Dunkirk spirit' and the comradeship of the air-raid shelter during the blitz have long been part of our national self-image. How much was this myth and how much reality? Officials concerned with civilian morale in the Ministry of Information and the Home Office who had seen ordinary people as unintelligent and weak during the phoney war in 1939 came to see them as dependable, shrewd, and courageous by 1940. What was the cause of this change?

It is clear that the BBC, almost certainly the most important instrument of domestic propaganda during the war, conducted a campaign intended to convince the public of its own endurance and solidarity. The BBC emerged from the war as both a symbol and an agent of the victory. More than at any other time, the BBC was part of, and seen to be part of, the history of the nation.

## 'The people will break'

When war was declared in 1939 most people expected a cataclysm. Pre-war pessimism about popular morale had largely been forgotten, yet it had been common to many groups who were otherwise opposed to each other.

During the 1930s another war was felt to be imminent. The main aim of many politicians was to avert the repetition of a disaster like that of the First World War. Even pacifists organizing peace pledges came to feel, like Vera Brittain, that they were trying 'Canute-like to reverse the inexorable'. Indeed memories of the First World War dominated the British as they entered the Second.

The success of the fascist dictatorships had led to a growing distrust and fatalism about the political will of the 'masses'. J. A. Hobson argued in the left-wing *Political Quarterly*:

No one could have predicted the possibility of the collapse of all codes of decent conduct, all standards of justice, truth, and honour, not only in international affairs but in the revealed nationalism of the brutalitarian state, the facile acquiescence of whole peoples in the absolute domination of self-appointed masters, and the amazing credulity of the educated classes under the spells of the crudest propaganda. (January 1938)

Many on the left believed that the organization of the resistance to fascism would lead to totalitarianism at home. 'If you go to war to save democracy', Kingsley Martin wrote in the *New Statesman* (1 September 1939), 'you will give up democracy in doing so, and find that you are fighting for the overseas investment of your own capitalist classes.' Even after the outbreak of war Sir Charles Trevelyan, a former Labour Minister of Education, wrote privately, 'I have a deep-seated feeling that none of the people want to fight, and that the war will collapse.' It was thus felt by some on the left either that the workers would refuse to fight a war against fascism abroad, because it would only lead to fascism at home, or that they would not fight anyway, because of the iniquitous lack of justice in Britain.

The marches and demonstrations of the 1930s had led the right to believe that British workers were too anarchistic and socialist to be trusted to fight. Those in authority were also anxious about the effects of class division on morale. As early as 1926 a pioneering social scientist, Lasswell, had written, 'Governments of Western Europe can never be perfectly certain that a class-conscious proletariat will rally to the clarion of war.'

Indeed the whole concept of 'public morale', which so pre-occupied the government during the war, originated in the 1930s. It was a concept based on naïve psychological and sociological assumptions; in particular, that individuals' attitudes and behaviour were peculiarly susceptible to manipulation in the conditions of modern 'mass' society. 'Morale' was seen as single and malleable. The success of the fascist dictators had confirmed these views, and demonstrated that the urban masses acted in response to crowd psychology and not according to rational political calculation. One reason for this view of the masses, as Bruntz indicated, was the widespread belief that superior allied propaganda had helped to shorten the First World War. *The Times* in 1918 had argued that effective propaganda had hastened victory by a year, and consequently saved a million lives. Indeed, as

Shils pointed out, the Nazis may have overestimated the effect of propaganda because they concluded that 'If Germans failed to be tricked by propaganda this time, success was assured.' In addition, the decades between the two wars had seen the dramatic success of commercial propaganda in advertising. The people, then, were thought to be persuadable.

Parallel to this anxiety was the belief that the new technology of destruction, the bombing attack on cities, would lead to a collapse of civilian society. These fears were based on exaggerated projections of the number of deaths which could be expected for each ton of explosives dropped, and on the biased intuitions of military 'experts' about how civilian populations would respond to bombing. 'In simple terms', Titmuss wrote, 'the experts foretold a mass outbreak of hysterical neurosis among the civilian population.' Psychoanalysts argued that under the strain of bombing, people would 'regress', and behave like frightened and unsatisfied children. A group of eminent psychologists reported to the government that 'The utter helplessness of the urban civilian today when confronted with the simplest task outside his ordinary work is likely to be a potent factor . . . in the war effort.' Experts confidently predicted that for every survivor injured by bombs at least three others would be driven mad.

It was therefore widely believed that the British worker would be devastated by an attack from the air. Perhaps this fear explains the curious official ambivalence about the approaching war during the late 1930s. Detailed preparations were made for war, yet rearmers were still banned from the microphone. An atmosphere of dignity, gloom, and appeasement dominated broadcasting even after the declaration of war. Harmon Grisewood recalled that at the end of September 1939 the new Director General, Ogilvie, suggested that a lady cellist, playing a duet with a nightingale in a wood, should be broadcast to Germany. Ogilvie believed that the sound would induce peaceful and harmonious thoughts in the belligerent fascists.

## The first months of war

When the war started normal programmes were replaced by news bulletins interspersed with serious and appropriate music. 'Almost everything is obscured at present,' the *New Statesman* commented on 9 September. 'For the first days of the war the BBC monotonously repeated news which was in the morning

papers and which it had itself repeated an hour earlier. While each
edition of the papers repeated what had already been heard on the
wireless.' The news black-out was as complete as the black-out of
the streets. During the phoney war the BBC paid for nominal
independence by doing exactly what the government wanted. Jack
Payne noted that the music department was 'deep in memos', one
of which listed the eighty banned German and Italian composers,
including Monteverdi, who had died in 1643. Another BBC employee claimed that the only explanation for the failure of the
Germans to devastate Bush House was that 'no BBC administrator
had remembered to send Hitler the memo reminding him to have
it done'.[1]

When more varied programmes started from new provincial
centres in unlikely country houses, they were rather less well-
organized versions of what had gone on before. Basil Deane, who
ran the Entertainment National Service Association (ENSA), the
organization responsible for the entertainment of the troops, wrote,
'Public anxiety was not lessened by the forced gaiety of variety
artists whose personal jokes and excessive use of each other's
Christian names – syndicated familiarity – savoured of self-
advancement and was out of key with the national mood.' Many
early propaganda broadcasts had a peevish, hectoring tone. A
month after the outbreak of war a British Institute of Public
Opinion poll showed that 35 per cent of the public were dissatisfied
with the BBC and 10 per cent did not listen to it. In the winter of
1939 to 1940 Mass Observation reported that rumours were rife;
the people apparently did not believe the newspapers, the Ministry
of Information, or the BBC. They trusted only their friends.

The 'phoney war' forced the BBC to regionalize and extem-
porize. The most important change was the Corporation's dramatic
growth in size. In 1939 the BBC had 4,000 staff, by the beginning
of 1940 6,000, and by November of that year nearly 11,000. Roger
Eckersley, the staid brother of Peter Eckersley, wrote, 'I knew
directly or indirectly most of the senior staff up to the outbreak of
war. Now, I shared lifts with complete strangers.' It became
increasingly difficult to control the hordes of new staff and this in
itself led to a period of anarchy and change. The new employees
were quite different from the regular Corporation men. George
Orwell broadcast to the colonies and India, William Empson to
China, Herbert Read organized poetry readings, Edward Blunden
arranged talks, and Basil Wright and Humphrey Jennings made programmes on the principles of documentary. According to Orwell:

> The British Government started the present war with the more
> or less openly declared intention of keeping the literary intelli-
> gentsia out of it, yet after three years almost every writer,
> however undesirable his political history or opinions, had been
> sucked into the various ministries or the BBC. ... No one
> acquainted with Government pamphlets, the Army Bureau of
> Current Affairs lectures, documentary films and broadcasts to
> occupied countries ... can believe that our rulers would sponsor
> this kind of thing if they could help it.

The notion of a Corporation converted from philistine reaction to
progressive culture became part of the fable of the BBC at war. It
was a particularly public example of a common tension that
characterized much war work. Conservative administrative authorities were forced to work with creative intellectuals. Scientific
'boffins' invented curious bombs for the military; literary and
artistic 'boffins' did intelligence work. The Ministry of Information
was notorious for the strange collection of dilettantes, anthro-
pologists, and advertising copy writers which it employed. Duff
Cooper, who directed the ministry, wrote that a monster had been
created, 'so large, so voluminous, so amorphous, that no single
man could cope with it'.[2] 'Frustrated' was the word he came to
hate most: the plaintive cry of brilliant amateurs thwarted by
bureaucracy. Yet the intellectuals were more prepared to take
risks as they had no careers to jeopardize. The *Radio Times*
became filled with pictures of distinguished chemists putting
bicycle power to strange purposes, and professors of literature
'thinking' about future programmes; the image of 'boffin' at least
provided an accommodation and role for experts. For a brief
period it was respectable, and even useful, to be serious. Nevertheless the BBC, wrote Orwell, felt 'halfway between a girls'
school and a lunatic asylum'.

## Programme changes

The first radio personality of the war was not a patriotic politician
or a staunch common man, but Lord Haw Haw. By 1940 William
Joyce dominated German propaganda to England. His voice was
rich, apparently upper class, 'Cholmondely-Plantagenet out of
Christ Church',[3] and caused much speculation. It was difficult to
avoid Joyce's wavelength when tuning into British stations, as
Rebecca West recalled. 'There was an arresting quality about his
voice which made it a sacrifice not to go on listening.'

Everyone in Gosport knew that Haw Haw knew that their town hall clock was two minutes slow. In Oxford everyone knew when the Germans were going to bomb the Morris works; Lord Haw Haw had told them. The myth of the English aristocrat with inside knowledge of the German High Command – a kind of diabolical Peter Wimsey – was powerful. What Lord Haw Haw said was less important than what the British came to believe he had said.

It has been argued that Haw Haw was ineptly used by the Germans, who failed to keep him adequately informed about military developments. However, both the government and the BBC were seriously worried about the broadcasts. Robert Silvey of the Audience Research Department was commissioned to conduct a survey of Joyce listeners for the BBC. 'It produced highly reassuring results,' he wrote in the BBC *Handbook*. 'It showed that the British welcomed the new guest to the fireside as a diverting entertainment in the first bleak wartime winter.' But the survey included some less comfortable findings: by the end of 1939 over 30 per cent of the population was listening to Joyce regularly. The BBC's Home Broadcasting Board had sneered that only 'adolescents, and middle-aged women' listened to him. Silvey's work revealed that every kind of person heard the programmes. The reassuring feature of the audience, little understood at the time, was that Haw Haw's listeners were particularly discriminating ones. Most read one or more newspapers; 34 per cent of the listeners were *Times* readers. Those most exposed to enemy propaganda were those least likely to be taken in by it. Yet Joyce's ability to hold an audience demonstrated either that the BBC was failing to entertain or that its news was distrusted.

The fall of France in 1940 demonstrated the potential power of enemy propaganda. It was widely believed that German broadcasts were responsible for the failure of the French civilians to resist the German invasion, and for the strength of the French 'fifth column' of collaborators. British officials felt that radio was crucial, yet the BBC was too solemn, aloof, and boring. The problem was urgent.

### 1940 and cheerful patriotism

Dunkirk has been seen by most historians as a key turning point in the war. A massive defeat was turned into triumph, and the British, curiously relieved to be without allies, found a new determination to win the war. Calder sees Dunkirk as the point at which the 'old gang' of pre-war reactionaries was finally exposed. Found to be guilty they were thrown aside. After Dunkirk, he argues, people were concerned with winning the war, and ensuring a 'New Deal' for the peace. Mass Observation noted a steady growth of left-wing opinion from this period.

What is remarkable is the absence of any evidence of popular pressure for a negotiated peace. Rationally invasion seemed certain, and defeat, accompanied by appalling devastation, seemed likely. Yet where, during the 'phoney war' period, there had been a degree of indifference, now there was a closing of ranks. It was not that morale was high, nor that anybody believed Britain was likely to win the war: rather the war was accepted. The public decided to try and survive it as best it could.

Broadcasting contributed to this shift in mood. It ceased to be merely exhortative. It became more sensitive to popular feeling and, in consequence, more successful in moulding or at least channelling public opinion.

Dunkirk meant that the war changed from being an affair of soldiers abroad to one of civilians at home. It was quickly followed by the Battle of Britain and then the blitz. The kind of war that people had expected had arrived. Yet, though devastating, the catastrophic effects widely predicted in the 1930s did not occur. Survivors went on with what Churchill called 'their job of living through the blitz'. Even Mass Observation, which documented the panic and virtual disintegration of civilian life in the worst hit towns at some times during the winter, noted the remarkable capacity of the public to adapt to new conditions. In London, Tom Harrisson wrote, 'the unfailing regularity' of German attacks 'greatly raised the ability to adjust, and created the best organized centre in the country'.

The First World War was traumatic partly because the horror of a large-scale modern conflict had been far greater than anybody had ever imagined. The Second World War – especially on the civilian front – was bearable precisely because literature, memory, and rhetoric had led everybody to expect a repetition. Yet civilians in cities, like men in trenches, were prisoners. In the First World War the troops called trenches on the Western front by familiar names, Piccadilly, Liverpool Street, Elephant and Castle, Penny Lane. In 1940 it was the real places in Britain which suffered. They could not escape. There were civilian front and relief lines. In the First World War men would be regularly moved back from the front to security behind the lines. In the

Second World War (as Titmuss argued) the underprivileged survived the stress of attack partly because there was a variety of 'safety valves' they could use. The government never stopped the nightly 'trekking' out of the city centres, nor did it resist the takeover of tube stations as deep shelters. On any one night of the blitz seven out of ten Londoners slept in their beds. But in any single week during the blitz nearly everyone spent at least a night in the shelters or the equivalent. Civilians thus survived the stress partly because – like the soldiers in the First World War – they took some relief from the front.

The prevailing atmosphere in 1940 amongst the civilian ranks was, as in the 1914 army, one of 'us' against 'them'. The opposition was as much to the unbelievable bureaucracy of British administration, as to the Nazis themselves. Strachey expressed this mood when he wrote:

> There is no public record of the labour of the interdepartmental committee, of the co-ordinating committee, the Board of Enquiry, or of the Treasury minute, or indeed of the final Cabinet minute which settled upon the word 'incident' as the designation of what takes place when a bomb falls on a street.

One way of dealing with the Second World War was to refer firmly to the First. Like many of his listeners the broadcaster J. B. Priestley's own image of fighting was based on memories of 1914–18, and he particularly liked to draw parallels between trench life in the First World War and civilian mores in this one.

In his memoirs, Priestley referred to a folksong of the Great War:

> 'It's hanging on the old barbed wire
> I've seen 'em, I've seen 'em.'

... [E]ven the devilish enemy, that death-trap the wire, has somehow been accepted, recognized, acknowledged, almost with affection.

A similar point about public attitudes in the Second World War was made by John Strachey:

> No the people didn't call Germans Huns ... or dirty bastards. No one knows in what region of the unconscious the English people decided that their formidable enemy were best called Jerry. ... There is in it an acceptance of destiny; of a destiny to resist. There is a refusal to take the panoply of the German might at its own evaluation.

Both writers are pointing to an attitude of familiarity, though not of contempt, for the enemy. This had first developed amongst soldiers in the proximity of the trenches. In the First World War it had separated them both from those who lived in the security of high commands, and from everyone in the safety of home. In the Second, such irony was an appropriate attitude for civilians' nightly encounters with bombers.

To what extent did the BBC lead, follow, or play a part in the creation of a new rhetoric to handle the experience of being bombed nightly?

The war brought the blue joke and an anarchistic, almost surreal, assault on authority to the radio. Shows like ITMA (It's That Man Again) never challenged the basis of authority, rather they consolidated it by making a joke of its misuse. In the 1930s radio comics had been warned that there were to be 'no gags on Scotsmen, Welshmen, clergymen, drink or medical matters'. ITMA thrived on innuendo, and on a skilful nudging at the previously taboo.

The programme was based on a formula. It had a repertoire of characters with stock phrases. Funf, 'the enemy agent with the feet of sauerkraut', made a joke of the spy panic of 1940. 'This is Funf speaking,' he would intone muffled by a glass. 'After you Claude – No, after you Cyril,' RAF pilots would quip as they queued to begin the attack, using another ITMA catchphrase. Each programme had eighteen-and-a-half minutes of talk into which an attempt was made to pack 'at least one hundred laughs'.[4]

A great strength of the show was its topicality. The writers visited factories and army camps to pick up current slang. The programme would be rewritten up to the hour before it was broadcast in order to include jokes on the latest news. ITMA summed up public frustration and gave it vent. In an early show transmitted from Bush House, itself next door to the Ministry of Works, Tommy Handley issued a memo. 'To all concerned in the Office of Twerps. Take notice that from today, September the twenty-fourth, I the Minister of Aggravation, have power to confiscate, complicate and commandeer.' In 1940 there was a period of remorseless exhortation of the public by the government. Frank Owen noted in the literary magazine, *Horizon*, that he was obliged to pass thirty-seven government posters on the way from his house to the Post Office. The Ministry of Food was particularly active in impressing on the public the virtues of the carrot. An ITMA sketch took note:

*Door opens*. Voice: Do you know what you can do with a
carrot?
Tommy Handley: Yer.
*Door closes*.

Frank Worsley, the producer, thought that the humour of ITMA
was 'the closest radio had come to the everyday jokes that
ordinary people have always made. . . . The characters were not
trying to be funny in themselves, they were only funny in relation
to the situation.'

One of the show's most popular characters was 'Mrs Mopp, the
vamping vassal with the tousled tassel', a charlady who worked
for a pompous civic dignitary. 'Can I do you now sir?' she would
ask. Mrs Mopp was perhaps the most famous version of a familiar
figure of the period. She glares at German bombers during an
attack in an *Express* cartoon by Giles (20 November 1940).
'Never mind about it not being arf wot we're giving them – lets
git 'ome,' demands her husband. The same figure – phlegmatic
and grumpily imperturbable – was dug out of ruins. She was a
mythical figure, and real people were frequently credited with her
well-known characteristics. 'Mrs Wells is an obstinate woman,'
John Strachey wrote about one lady who survived an air raid.
'You may drop big bombs on her, you may kill her dearly loved
husband before her eyes, you may bury herself and her daughter
under her home: but you do not alter her.' People who signed
themselves 'Mrs Mopp' sent letters to the *Listener* and the *Radio
Times*; she was discussed in the *New Statesman* and she asked the
Brains Trust questions.

Mrs Mopp was an image of the working-class woman at war.
Her characteristics were an indefatigable appetite for work, and
stubbornness. She did not mean to be heroic, but simply to get on
with things. Titmuss saw her in 'a certain Mrs B., a beetroot-
seller by trade', who brings order and comfort to a shelter in
Islington but who returns daily to her stall.

When 'charladies' had first been mentioned in a broadcast in
1938 by John Hilton, the programme received hundreds of letters
correcting his language. He should have called them 'char-
women' for, wrote the aggrieved listeners, they were hardly
ladies.[5] By 1942 charladies were featuring regularly in BBC
programmes – recognition of a kind of the importance and power of
working-class women. 'Kitchen front' programmes were broadcast
'for the busy working woman – the charlady'. 'Mrs Mopp', said

Priestley on the radio, 'could easily believe there weren't any women in Germany . . . just tramping, bragging, swaggering males, silly little boys.' 'When I think of the country now,' said another speaker on the Home Service at the height of the blitz (*Listener*, 9 September 1941), 'I see representing the country an embattled Mrs Mopp shaking her fist at the sky. "I'll do yer," she says, "I'll do yer".'

The other woman the BBC gave the nation was 'the girl next door', Vera Lynn. She sang sweet but not sexy songs. The typical 'crooning' style implied an intimate relationship between the singer and her listener. The was hardly appropriate, and possibly embarrassing, to the communal listeners of the Forces Programme. Vera Lynn was the solution. A Vera Lynn song was a cross between a hymn and a pub song.

Yet nostalgia and sentiment were not thought by the BBC to be proper fare for fighting men. 'Why should we hear so much from Vera Lynn?' Deputy Director Graves wrote angrily. 'How can men fit themselves for battle with these debilitating tunes in their ears?' The BBC Board of Governors remarked testily, 'Sincerely Yours deplored – but popularity noted'.[6] Military authorities demanded something more martial, yet the show survived, simply because it had such a vast and enthusiastic audience. 'The girl next door' was loyal, sincere, faithful, ordinary, and unsophisticated. She was 'the mainstay of most war fiction', Tom Harrisson noted in a review of war literature written in *Horizon* (December 1941) and was the heroine of a number of films.

### 'The people are changing'

According to contemporary commentators, the war made the public more serious-minded. This view has been accepted by later historians. Perhaps it should be qualified. Robert Silvey certainly felt in 1946 that there was no evidence that public taste had 'deepened'. Val Gielgud, Director of Drama during the war, recalls that when a 1940 production of *Hamlet* was interrupted at the grave scene, the BBC was inundated with letters from people who wanted to know what happened next. Yet there was undoubtedly a shift in interest. The public appetite for news broadcasts became insatiable. Less predictably, the audiences for serious music increased sharply, and drama ratings doubled between 1939 and 1941. At the start of hostilities the BBC had assumed that the people would be 'too tired for much heavy stuff', and in too sombre a mood to appreciate variety. Both assumptions were revealing – and both proved wrong.

It was generally believed that the masses were becoming more informed, and the success of programmes like the Brains Trust was seen as evidence of this. 'One of the surprises of wartime radio', wrote Howard Thomas, the programme's producer, 'is that five men discussing philosophy, art and science, should have a regular audience of ten million listeners.' As many people listened to the Brains Trust as to the most popular variety shows. Such was the influence of current affairs and discussion broadcasting that the Brains Trust formula replaced orthodox debating in innumerable social clubs and societies. It was particularly popular with local Conservative Associations.

The Brains Trust panel consisted of three regular members and two visiting guests. The original trio were Julian Huxley, the scientist, the philosopher Joad, and Commander Campbell, a retired soldier. In retrospect Campbell seems like a character from Evelyn Waugh, or perhaps Captain W. E. Johns – an enjoyable overdrawn caricature with a background of exotic experience: he claimed to be able to sleep with his eyes open, to have solved the mystery of the *Marie Celeste*, to have seen and smelt sea serpents, and to have 'married' a South Sea Island girl by eating some fish with her.

Brains Trust questions were wide-ranging. 'Why should we learn algebra?' asked a class of Manchester schoolgirls. 'Why can you tickle other people but not yourself?' asked a bus conductor. 'What is hate?' enquired a schoolmistress. A group of RAF pilots who asked why flies could land on ceilings started a dispute which lasted months. To be mentioned on the Brains Trust was fame indeed. A week after *War and Peace* had been recommended by the panel it had gone out of print. This kind of impact was hard to ignore. In 1941 the Ministry of Food was exhorting women to make the new, economical, soya 'Joad in the Hole'.

The importance of the show was recognized by Whitehall in other ways. There was concern about the programme straying into delicate political areas, highlighted by the fact that Joad and Huxley were socialists. In 1942 questions on religion were banned because the churches complained that the programme had an agnostic bias. In 1943 the government banned the discussion of politics, and MPs were excluded from the panel. When Huxley attacked patent medicines and called for a National Health Service the Tories complained. After a period of increasing restriction the original panel were forbidden to appear together.

From 1943 each was allowed to broadcast only one programme in three.

The Brains Trust was somewhere between a culture and an institution. Like other programmes it provided a new currency of conversation. Women in shelters discussed Campbell's views on hypnosis. (He claimed it could be beneficial: 'I knew a man who put his wife to sleep with it at weekends.') In 1940 the *Listener* reported that Gilbert Murray's jokes were swapped in bus queues. 'Veni, Vidi, Vichy,' he had said. 'I came, I saw, I concurred.'

The success of the Brains Trust was the basis for many theories about public opinion during the war: left-wingers felt that a population interested in the panel's views on social justice would also be susceptible to socialism. Whether or not this was right, the programme presented to the listener an image of himself as engaged, participant, and capable of confounding experts. Perhaps the real significance of the Brains Trust was that it represented a shift not just in public attitudes, but in the Corporation's willingness to cater for them. Despite restrictions and political interference the Trust provided for and encouraged an immense public curiosity about the natural world, the world of affairs, and about questions of ethics, philosophy, and psychology, and in so doing it began to foster a less aloof and distant image of the Corporation.

Yet the most dramatic image of the radio at war is of families clustered around their sets listening with reverence to speeches by Churchill, the news, or J.B.Priestley's Sunday night talks. These commanded some of the largest audiences ever known. 'By 1941 over 50 per cent of the adult population listened to them,' reported Silvey. It is therefore worth considering them closely.

Before the war the BBC had rarely allowed Churchill to broadcast. The Corporation even censored him after the war had begun. He was considered too anti-German. Churchill had come to hate the BBC. Yet his speeches as Prime Minister, always delivered first to parliament, were perhaps the most dramatic events of wartime broadcasting. He claimed that he merely gave words to what people felt: 'The people's will was resolute and remorseless, I only expressed it, I had the luck to be called upon to give the roar.' Churchill believed that military success, rather than propaganda, was the only way to win a war. 'If words could kill,' he broadcast in 1939, 'we would all be dead already.' Despite his claim to the contrary, Churchill was of course an expert propagandist, and the government, whatever it said in public, remained desperately concerned with the public mood throughout the war.

If Churchill expressed confidence in the people, J. B. Priestley claimed to represent them. His first series of 'Postscripts' started after Dunkirk at the peak listening time after the Sunday evening news. The series turned him into a household name. 'I found myself', he wrote, 'tied like a man to a gigantic balloon – to one of those bogus reputations that only the media know how to inflate.'

Churchill combined an appreciation of practical problems with a deep, almost metaphysical romanticism, based on an appeal to honour, national pride, and a sense of history. Priestley was just as practical but looked to the future. He helped to give the war an aim beyond military victory by focusing attention on the world to be built in the aftermath. Priestley talked about a level of society with which Churchill had had little contact and of which he understood less. While Churchill talked of Henry V and quoted Macaulay, Priestley's examples were Falstaff and Sam Weller.

Priestley's success, however, had essentially the same foundation as that of Churchill. It was based on an appeal to traditional values; indeed, on an appeal to a traditional social order. Priestley's Postscripts make a virtue of getting on with the job in hand, even when there were no alternatives. Like Churchill, Priestley linked current events with the past. He reminded listeners after Dunkirk of Hardy's descriptions of the Napoleonic wars, and described it as another English epic. 'So typical of us, so absurd, yet so grand and gallant that you hardly know whether to laugh or cry.' Official propaganda, Priestley claimed, encouraged people to see the war as an interruption. It was, he said, rather 'a chapter in a tremendous history'.

Postscripts continually emphasized the rural nature of Britain. In the First World War officers read *The Field* and *Country Life* in the trenches, and war poets contrasted the seasons and images of nature with the war. Priestley, broadcasting to the most urbanized population in the world, referred in ten out of his seventeen talks to the country and nature. 'I don't think that there has ever been a lovelier English spring than this last one', he said at the start of the Battle of Britain, 'now melting into full summer.' Later, after the news that the British had been obliged to sink the French fleet, he started the broadcast by saying that he had seen two heartening things that week. 'The first was a duck and the second was a dig in the ribs.' The duck swimming with her ducklings, 'triumphant little parcels of light', was in a country pond; the dig in the ribs was given by Churchill to Bevin in parliament before the grim announcement. Priestley talked about factories and the blitz, British restaurants and London humour, but the village or the Welsh hills were more frequently the setting for his talks. Priestley provided his listeners with a way of handling their experiences. 'I don't like danger', he said in November 1940, when Londoners were facing their twenty-eighth consecutive night of bombing, 'but the fact that we are all at least within reach of danger seems to me a better, not a worse, feature of the war.' In the First World War men in the trenches, and the writers who recorded their lives, had survived its horrors by rejecting romantic heroism. In the Second, Priestley made the everyday and commonplace heroic.

Priestley demanded 'more flags and less red tape, hard work and high jinks'. He challenged the old order and called for more social justice. Like Ed Murrow later, he praised the courage of individuals and criticized their leaders for ineptitude. In his second series of Postscripts he proposed to talk about money, class, and equality. 'I received', he wrote, 'two letters.' One was from the Ministry of Information, telling him 'that the BBC was responsible for the decision to take me off the air'. The other was from the BBC saying 'that a directive had come from the Ministry of Information to end my broadcasting'. They were both anxious to make it clear that 'the order to shut me up had come from elsewhere'. The Minister of Information, Brendan Bracken, had seen Priestley earlier and warned him to say more about Dickens and less about the government. As with the Brains Trust there had been complaints in parliament about Priestley's socialism. Churchill felt it intolerable that the BBC should broadcast criticism of the government, and ordered Priestley to be gagged. Already, within the Corporation, the Controller of Talks had written to Ryan, the Controller of News:

> Priestley has definite social and political views which he puts over in his broadcasts. . . . The question which I want to raise is one of principle, whether any single person should be given the opportunity of acquiring such influence . . . merely on the grounds of his merits as a broadcaster, which are, of course, very great.[7]

Priestley's removal was widely greeted as a sign of government censorship. The *New Statesman* printed a selection of the letters of protest, 'representative of the many others we have received'. Even the *Radio Times* printed letters of complaint for several weeks.

The removal of Priestley showed how limited was the official concern for reform. Priestley's programmes proposed different priorities from the war aims laid down by Churchill. To talk of new orders and redistribution was, in the view of the government, merely to distract the public from the urgent business of winning the war. Yet it was at precisely this point in the war that even the officials in the Ministry of Information were beginning to urge the government to plan post-war reconstruction. The public, they argued, needed the prospect of a better future to enable them to cope with the rigorous present. Priestley had merely started the shift in propaganda a little early. Later it was to be taken up with growing enthusiasm by the government itself.

Harold Nicolson dismissed the talks as 'sentimental banalities'. Priestley himself was puzzled by their success. Subsequently they have been seen as a major contribution to a change in public mood. Yet the most notable feature of Priestley's talks was that a concern for ordinary people and their future emerged and was expressed by very traditional images of rural England, village communities, and nature. This was hardly the rhetoric of a revolutionary.

### The news

The most important wartime programme was the news. Information about the conduct of the war was the main determinant of morale on the Home Front. Indeed the BBC's claim to accuracy and objectivity was, in itself, a propaganda weapon – a demonstration of the superiority of democracy over totalitarianism. This was particularly true because the BBC – much more than the press – was the 'voice of Britain'. Unlike newspapers, its messages reached a wide foreign audience in neutral and occupied countries. Broadcast news also seemed to be an authoritative reflection of official policy and opinion. There were allegations on the left that the real facts of the situation were kept from the people; these were particularly relevant during the period of the 'phoney war' when many on the left expected imminent defeat. The Service Ministries, on the other hand, viewed radio news with suspicion for a different reason: they saw it as a threat to morale.

News, like everything else for the duration, was determined by the necessity of winning the war. The Corporation's sense of priorities was often very close to that of the government. There was narrow-minded and bigoted censorship. But some of the omissions which the BBC was later blamed for were more a result of the contemporary understanding of what could be done in the war, than of deliberate suppression. Thus, for example, the BBC did not so much fail to inform the public about the holocaust – indeed what it knew it told – rather this news was not given a prominent position, and there was little consideration of what might be done to save the remaining Jews. This was largely because the BBC accepted the government's views that the allied victory was the only 'realistic' condition for effective action.[8]

However, such was the demand for news that when little of the real thing was available because of military inactivity, the public created its own. Rumours acquired a special influence. The Ministry of Information waged a relentless and unsuccessful campaign against them. Mass Observation divided them into three categories:impressive, informative, and inhibited.[9] The first were a compensation for non-involvement in the war; the second were based on an attempt to improve the teller's prestige, and the third kind, the inquiry claimed, were based on fear. Mass Observation argued that rumours arose from a general distrust of published and broadcast sources, and so were a product of official censorship. But they may also have been a simple reflection of anxiety, a context in which to talk about the war. The BBC always argued that rumours could be stopped only by more comprehensive news.

Several departments contended for the right to control the BBC. Even more believed that they deserved it. The Ministry of Information was concerned to encourage morale at home; the Political Intelligence Department to scavenge information from abroad; the Foreign Office to maintain friendly relations with allies and neutral countries; while the Ministry of Economic Warfare was interested in the immediate effects on the enemy's industry and morale, even if this involved ignoring the interests of the neutrals.

At the start of the war an official wrote that the Ministry of Information 'recognized that for the purpose of war activities the BBC is to be regarded as a Government Department'. (He added: 'I wouldn't put it quite like this in any public statement.'[10]) This implies a rather different relationship between broadcasting and the government than that which the BBC claimed. Yet the control by the ministries was often irregular and contradictory. For a time even the BBC's Director Generalship was divided: one Director to say yes to the ministry (broadcasters joked) and the other to say no to the staff.[11]

The Ministry of Information, which had most direct control over broadcasts, had been the butt of much humour when it was formed: the inefficiency of its organization seemed to be surpassed only by the scale of its notional operation. It was believed to be staffed by brilliant but dotty amateurs. Nigel Riley (who resigned from the ministry) pointed out that in 1940 of 999 ministry employees only 47 were journalists. The ministry was supposed to build morale, yet until 1941 it based its judgements on little except hunches and intuition. Stories about the department's gentlemanly eccentricities were legion. One incident involved a ministry official dispatched to lecture in the provinces on the wickedness of gossip. Complaints came back that his speech had been almost entirely composed of long quotations in Latin. 'Oh', replied the department, 'Latin? It's usually Greek with him.'

Reith, who was appointed Minister of the Department in 1940, was deeply depressed by its pointlessness and disorganization. Nevertheless, before Churchill dismissed him later in the same year, he had begun to define the work of the ministry and to discipline its staff. Reith believed that it was essential to have news and propaganda controlled by the same authority. By the end of the war, Ian Maclaine has argued, the ministry was actively defending the press and broadcasting from the Service Ministries.

## Broadcasting and the press

Which did people believe more, the newspapers or broadcasting? Intellectuals certainly did not trust the Corporation. They recalled its role during the General Strike. 'What could possibly take the place of newspapers?' wrote the editor of the *Picture Post* (18 December 1940). 'There surely cannot be any sane man or woman who would argue that the Ministry of Information, or its near relation the BBC, have so far offered a serious alternative to the newspapers in conveying information?' Yet there were also grounds for distrusting the press. Newspapers had deceived the public in the interest of the Establishment over the abdication crisis.

The war heightened a long-standing rivalry between press and radio. The *Listener* was voicing a widely held BBC view in 1941 when it claimed that while radio was concerned to report events as they occurred, news in the press was regarded as entertainment. A Home Service talk in March 1941 maintained that newspaper stories might have come 'from a report from a Mexican correspondent of a Portuguese journal quoted in a Roman paper'. The public had little idea of the tricks employed by the press in presenting events.

Mass Observation reported that radio was the most important medium of information in 1941, and that by the end of the war it had replaced the newspapers for some kinds of news, particularly immediate accounts of battles.[12] When more systematic surveys asked people to rank the media on which they based their opinions, radio came far below personal experience and several points below newspapers. Yet between January 1940 and the end of the war in Europe the authority of the press fell steadily, from third to sixth place in people's ranking. In contrast the position of broadcasting remained constant throughout this period between fifth and sixth place.[13] By the end of the war people had come to trust broadcasting more – at least in comparison with other sources of information.

## Topicality and the BBC

The Second World War made topicality the dominant news value. German scoops had shocked the public and done much to discredit the Corporation at the start of the war. Topicality then became the key weapon in the BBC's defence against the expansionist censorship of the Service Ministries. The Ministry of Information recognized the importance of getting news on the air as quickly as possible. A memorandum ordered 'Action to strengthen confidence in BBC news. Confirmed items to be included in earliest available bulletins, even at the expense of friction with the Press.'[14]

From 1939 the BBC's news section grew rapidly, gathering material from an increasingly wide range of sources, including monitoring foreign broadcast sections. The BBC also developed the ultimately 'topical' news, the 'on the spot' or 'outside' broadcast. By late 1944 teams of broadcasters were regularly accompanying British units both in France and the Far East. Commentators developed a way of reporting conditions at the front which related the soldiers' experience more closely to their families at home. 'If you've got a brother or a husband or a sweetheart in Normandy today,' started one famous report from the war zone in 1944, 'there's a fair chance you might see your name riding along the dusty roads, your name on a truck, on a lorry, on a bulldozer, on a tank, somewhere in France.' The style of war reporting was also closely modelled on an earlier form of outside broadcasting:

sports programmes. A reporter describing a bombing raid on Hamburg was angrily compared by a *Radio Times* correspondent (30 September 1944) to 'someone at a Welsh Rugby International – not a person watching death and destruction'.

The war led to a victory for those who believed in the superiority of the scientific assessment of public opinion. At the start of the war the government believed that this could be tested by consulting pressure groups and opinion leaders. By the end of the war the public was being polled, probed, and tested by a multitude of official surveys. These new sources of information made it clear that in everyday matters of which the public had experience, it was essential that news should be given quickly and accurately. If people had been bombed out of their homes and their towns devastated, it was imperative that the BBC should be able to say so. Knowledge of the extent of destruction was an important factor in coming to terms with it. At the start of the blitz Maurice Gorham had written, 'The news sounded all the more alarming for being so vague.' But by November 1940, although scrupulously censored for information which might be useful to the Germans, it had become more precise. In Britain, at least, 'topicality' became the dominant news value as a consequence of the war.

### The 'manner' of the news

Before the war the BBC's announcers had been anonymous: this was felt to be more dignified. However, from the start of the war they were named, and this innovation excited considerable comment at the time. The change was introduced in order that, in the case of invasion, the public would not be taken in by orders issued by the enemy. After the war it was discovered that the Germans had carefully trained substitute announcers to sound like Alvar Lidell and Stuart Hibberd to be used during the proposed invasion of England. However, the BBC maintained some pre-war standards. The announcers, despite sleeping in a lavatory adjoining the studio, and living for days underground, continued to present the news in dress suits. When the BBC received a direct hit which made an audible thump in the middle of a bulletin, the announcer paused, a whispered 'Are you all right?' was heard, and then he continued, with Corporation-bred aplomb, to read the news without comment.

Before 1939 style had often seemed more important than comprehensibility in BBC news broadcasting; during the war ease of understanding became paramount. There was a new anxiety about syntax and vocabulary, and scripts were scrutinized for difficult words and constructions. The Corporation also became more sensitive about the voices of its news-readers. Clement Attlee, Deputy Prime Minister as well as leader of the Labour Party, complained that the monopoly of upper-class voices was likely to offend workers. Indeed this anxiety was shared, and a Home Morale Emergency Committee in the Ministry of Information suggested that 'something might be done to diminish the present predominance of the cultured voice upon the wireless. Every effort should be made to bring working-class people to the microphone.'

The Corporation responded by employing Wilfred Pickles, whose voice combined the properties of being both working-class and northern. Broadcasting had developed a unique pitch of speech in the 1930s and 1940s, a high and hard voice. One news-reader, Joseph Macleod, wrote that he had two voices. One was low, gruff, and Scottish. The other, which he always used when broadcasting, was 'young, suave, rather pedantic and intolerant, a voice in a higher register'. The war also made the tone of voice a more sensitive matter than before. Macleod lost his job, ostensibly because his style of announcing was too 'tendentious'. He was accused of putting too much emphasis on certain words, and apparently sneering at the government. He was dismissed, according to Harold Nicolson, soon after Bracken had 'spoken openly about the left-wing fanaticism of certain members of the BBC, especially in the news room'. Clearly the tone of an announcement could establish the public attitude towards the news. One news-reader wrote of the problems posed, for example, by announcing the suicide of the Commander of the *Graf Spee* after the ship had been lost. If the announcer sounded pleased the item 'would sound gloating. While if he sounded sympathetic it would sound fifth column.' The BBC's solution to this problem was that announcers should sound as 'official, neutral, and unaffected as possible'. The BBC announcer, it had been decided, should sound like a civil servant.

Another, more urgent, reason why announcers became so careful of their words and their timing was the problem of the sarcastic comments which German broadcasters had at first managed to slip in during pauses in bulletins. The only way to stop this was to read the news smoothly and unhesitatingly. By the last months of

1940 the only words a German commentator managed to intrude was an exasperated, 'Oh that's not fair!'

## The news, enemies, allies, and neutrals

Another, more romantic image of the Corporation at war was of the BBC as provocateur, spy, and supporter of resistance movements. The Corporation recruited many refugees to staff the foreign broadcasts, and these formed a new and exotic element within the Corporation's staid departments. 'The Hungarian Unit,' read a dry memo of the period, 'a duel averted by Duckworth.' A recurring tension in all of these sections was between the demands of the centrally controlled news service, and the interests of individual nations. The Danish section complained that they were not allowed to deal with events in Denmark itself in sufficient detail. According to Bennett, the correspondents who supplied the service with its information from neutral Sweden even organised a news strike in an attempt to change the BBC's policy.

Other countries complained that the broadcasts implicitly criticized the occupied countries. Listeners who took risks to hear the BBC felt that they should be complimented on their resilience, rather than condemned for their failure to do more. Indeed, like home broadcasting, the Foreign Service suffered from a tendency to exhort rather than inform or support in the first year of the war. Richard Crossman argued that too many of those employed in directing propaganda had come from the advertising world. 'Do you suffer from National Socialism?' was their line. 'Then buy British Democracy!'

Another tension was the extent to which the broadcasts should encourage (as one BBC administrator put it) 'listeners to *do* something rather than *feel* something'. It seemed presumptuous to instruct foreigners in sabotage when the British had little experience of it, and were themselves safe. More significantly, the dramatic success of the 'V' campaign, when in 1941 Dutch, French, Belgians, and Scandinavians in occupied Europe were asked to use the letter 'V' as a rallying sign, revealed the dangers of such a strategy. In one Vichy town, Moulins, graffiti Vs for 'Victoire' were so numerous that the Germans imposed fines and penalties on the whole town. In Prague 'multitudes of little Vs had appeared on all sides'. From Belgium it was reported that 'never had so much chalk been sold so quickly'. The campaign, initiated almost accidentally, was evidently a success. Its effects, however, were disastrous. It merely exposed those who were prepared to be active resisters to the Germans at a time when there was no possibility of any allied invasion. Men lost their lives in a campaign with no practical goal. In addition, the BBC was in effect making foreign policy. The campaign was stopped. Crossman later argued that it was a great mistake for those involved in psychological warfare to suggest that they have 'a mystical substitute for military action'. Broadcasting had to be as concerned with preventing resisters from acting unwisely as with prompting them to action when the right moment came.

It is not easy to assess the effect of the BBC's foreign broadcasts. Indeed it is difficult enough to decide what the overall impact of resistance was on the German war effort. Every clandestine listener, however, had already committed an act of resistance, and the BBC's service provided information – even if of a selective kind – to populations who were starved of news. The BBC's bulletins provided most of the material for the underground press in occupied Europe. M. R. D. Foot has concluded that the role of broadcasting was to 'keep the mechanism of the canal gates of freedom oiled and in decent order, till the water levels of fluctuating public opinion could move up and down again'.

This image of the heroic BBC was not, however, shared in the USA. 'To Americans, not very enthusiastic about British cooking, the warmed up remnants of the original meal were not very palatable. News bulletins – one half an hour long – often contained items from yesterday's American press,' wrote an academic, Emmanuel Katz, in 1944. The constant stress on the collapse of social barriers in Britain only emphasized how tenacious they had been, and to what extent they still survived. However, American public opinion was never wholly pro-British, and the attitudes towards broadcasting were part of a wider feeling about the war.

In matters concerning the allies the BBC's policy was dictated by government. When the Russians started to fight the Nazis, the cover of the *Listener* was devoted to a pageant in honour of Russia, while the *Radio Times* was packed with tributes to Russian workers. This was a period of extraordinary enthusiasm for Russia and all things Russian. As Elizabeth Bowen wrote of a character in her wartime novel, *The Heat of the Day*, 'The effect of her was, at first glance, that of a predominating number of London girls this summer when the idealization of Russia was at its height – that of a flying try at the Soviet comrade type.' However, the

BBC was told not to include the *Internationale* in the popular Sunday evening concert of allied national anthems. The Corporation abandoned the series rather than be embarrassed by the sound of the communist song.

## Conclusion: 'my country true or false?'

In 1939 the Home News Service editor had said that in the event of war the BBC would 'tell the truth and nothing but the truth, even if the news was horrid'. By the end of the war the Corporation was arguing that the pursuit of truth had been victorious. 'Today', the 1946 *Handbook* proclaimed, 'we can point to the history of broadcasting in Europe and say that certain good principles in broadcasting have defeated the worst possible principles.' During the war the BBC seldom lied if it could avoid doing so. Indeed as the war began with a series of devastating defeats for the allies it might have been difficult to disguise the situation. However, that the BBC could claim independence was at least partly because it suited the government that it should do so. For the government continually intervened in the conduct of the Corporation, and merely chose not to control it directly.

Veracity, however, was perhaps the only acceptable aim for a democratic news policy. More practically, telling the truth was probably the most effective propaganda with which to face a sustained war. 'You must hate propaganda to do it well,' Richard Crossman wrote, 'and we British did hate it and therefore took more trouble to conceal what we were doing.'

The contemporary judgement of the BBC's performance was enthusiastic. 'In a world of poison the BBC became the great antiseptic,' said Léon Blum, the French socialist leader. Recently the claims of broadcasters that they have independence have been challenged. 'Bias' and opinion are fundamental conditions of the production of news, not accidental pathologies. Hence the work of the BBC during the war has been viewed with greater scepticism. A belief in its independence is little more than a self-adulatory part of the British myth.

The BBC cannot simply be distinguished from its totalitarian opponents in terms of its intentions. In both Britain and Germany broadcasting was seen as a crucial instrument in the war effort. Indeed both countries even shared practical concerns: hopes should never be raised unless they could be met; controversy between enemy allies was, as Goebbels claimed, 'a small plant which thrives best when it is left to its natural growth'. He continued that 'News policy is a weapon of war. Its purpose is to wage war and not to give out information.' The BBC also viewed news as part of propaganda. However, the use of the 'news' weapon was determined by quite different constraints and pressures in a democratic society.

British home propaganda depended on an informed public. The BBC remained a civilian institution, whose employees saw themselves primarily as broadcasters. Once committed to a policy of informing the public, the war acted as an incentive within the Corporation for an improvement in the news services. Although the BBC broadcast optimistic official figures for enemy fighters shot down in the Battle of Britain, tended to treat raids on Germany as victories, cut, edited, and censored news, its main purpose remained that of telling people what was happening.

If the Service Ministries and the government were concerned to limit the amount and kind of information broadcast, the main pressure within the Corporation was to tell the people as much as possible. This did not mean telling them everything, but the heritage of obligations imposed by the Corporation's public service monopoly meant that the public knew more than might have been expected.

In Britain, Asa Briggs has observed, the mystique of radio meant little. In Germany, the new medium had been credited with almost magical powers of suggestion. These views affected the way in which broadcasting was used in both countries. The dominating image of the BBC during the war (indeed the dominating image of the war in Britain) was one of relentless domesticity. 'Every time I listen to these programmes I cry,' a factory worker told Mass Observation about a radio link-up between soldiers and their families. 'You hear the women giving the men their messages ... they can hardly get through sometimes.' Another describes her day. She gets back from work 'about nine o'clock, and they've got the wireless on. Dad's asleep in the chair – the kiddies are in bed.' Families were united around the radio; 52 per cent of respondents to one survey always listened to the news with their families, 76 per cent preferred to do so if possible. In Titmuss's classic account of the development of welfare policy during the war, he saw the security of the family as the crucial guarantor of good morale. By 1945 the radio had become an essential element of the image of the family in its home.

Before the war the BBC had regarded the regular expectation of particular kinds of programmes as 'lazy listening'. In contrast, during the war the BBC made considerable efforts to develop such habits. Regular programmes produced predictable audiences. The knowledge of these could be used in propaganda appeals and information campaigns. Indeed the predictability of the daily broadcasts was a kind of security in itself. 'At the moment, all similes for safety are slipping,' wrote C. A. Hodson in 1941. 'How can one say as safe as houses?' But the BBC at least seemed dependable. Modern programme planning, a matter of inducing habit, was at least in part a consequence of the war.

By 1945 the Corporation had apparently become less aloof. Programmes like ITMA, Hi Gang, and Worker's Playtime introduced a more vigorous tradition of speech and humour to broadcasting, one that was closer to the music hall tradition than the well-mannered 'variety' of pre-war programmes. They were part of a feeling that the British war, unlike that of the prudish Germans, was taken seriously, but never solemnly. Even government propaganda came to appreciate the 'common man's sense of humour':

> Those who have the will to win
> Eat potatoes in their skin,
> Knowing that the sight of peelings
> Deeply hurts Lord Woolton's feelings

exhorted the Ministry of Food. Humour was part of the protective self-image with which the British faced air attacks and the possibility of invasion. It was an image that the BBC helped to create, and was determined to encourage. Harold Nicolson even broadcast talks on the subtle superiority of British humour to that of the status-conscious Germans (*Listener*, December 1942).

There was, of course, another war which did not get much broadcasting time. This was one of apathy, and dingy making-do rather than cheerful resilience. Life in shelters was not always a protracted East End party; it was squalid, with inadequate sanitary arrangements, little food, and chaotic overcrowding. Novels of the period document the dreariness and austerity of life in Britain after several years of war, and newspapers campaigned against the petty-mindedness of official regulations and bureaucracy. The BBC did not campaign for the public on any of these issues.

However, the Corporation succeeded in producing a dignified but humorous image of what kind of people the British were. It was not that the BBC 'came closer to the people'. Rather it represented them as a liberal, compassionate, reforming administrator might have seen them. The BBC innovated within a repertoire of very traditional ideas. Subsequently it has been argued that there was a significant change in public mood during the war. The people became determined that there would be greater social justice after it. Certainly the war changed the BBC, and it changed public taste.

Yet the day after the war in Europe ended, the public changed again. The audience for the news dropped by half, and never returned to wartime levels.

## Notes

1. D. G. Bridson, *Prospero and Ariel: The Rise and Fall of Radio* (London, Gollancz, 1971), p. 269.
2. D. Cooper, *Old Men Forget* (London, Hart-Davis, 1953), p. 79.
3. Harold Hobson, *Daily Express* (14 January 1940).
4. T. Kavanagh, *Tommy Handley* (London, Hodder & Stoughton, 1949), p. 73.
5. *Listener* correspondence, *BBC Written Archives* (John Hilton).
6. Board of Governors' Minutes (5 July 1941), *BBC Written Archives*.
7. Maconachie to Ryan (6 September 1940), *BBC Written Archives*.
8. See for further development of this example, J. Seaton, 'The BBC and the Holocaust', *European Journal of Communication*, vol. 2, 1, 1987.
9. Mass Observation (October 1940), File 473, 'What the people are talking about today'.
10. A. P. Waterfield to W. Palmer, *Ministry of Information Files*, INF 1/238.
11. A. S. Hibberd, *This is London* (London, Macdonald & Evans, 1950), p. 307.
12. Mass Observation, *The Press and Its Readers* (London, Art & Technics, 1949), p. 41.
13. 'The British Institute of Public Opinion Survey, the attitudes towards the press and broadcasting and other sources of information (1940–5)' in H. Cantril (ed.), *Public Opinion 1935–46* (New Jersey, Princeton University Press, 1951).
14. *Ministry of Information*, INF 1/250, Home Morale Emergency Committee, Item 13 (22 May 1940).

# 10

# *Social revolution?*

It is a commonplace of twentieth-century social history that world war has been the agent, or at least the catalyst, of major change. What has been less noticed is the extent to which wartime forms of organization – born of the unusual conditions and needs of the moment – have created structural fossils in important areas of policy, surviving immutably in peacetime, but with no particular relevance to the post-war world.

Broadcasting and education provide interesting examples of this process. Both were drastically reorganized at the end of the Second World War. In each case the most striking feature of the reforms was the imposition of a 'tripartite' division, based on a supposed hierarchy of talent. The changes represented a sharp move away from a view of society as an aggregate of individuals towards an official concept of particular groups with separate needs.

## Broadcasting

Reith's programme policy depended on an assumption of cultural homogeneity: not that everybody was the same, but that culture was single and undifferentiated. He had been determined to avoid the mediocrity which he believed would accompany freedom of choice. 'It is occasionally indicated to us that we are apparently setting out to give the public what we think they need – not what they want,' he wrote in 1924. 'But few know whey they want and very few what they need.' Advisory panels of 'experts' were established to lay down canons of taste in music, and to adjudicate correct pronunciation. Their purpose was to give authority to cultural values, not to represent listeners' interests.

Reith believed that the function of broadcasting was primarily educative: its purpose was to train 'character'. According to this

view, your class of origin and what you learnt mattered less than
how you lived and how you learnt. This principle was the basis
for his programming policy. Men might be unequal, but they
could all try equally. Hence the Corporation defended a policy of
mixed programming, in which talks, light music, chamber music,
quizzes, vaudeville and plays succeeded each other. The service
was not planned to provide appropriate listening for different
interests, or to allow people to avoid what was serious in favour
of the trivial. Reith was determined that the audience should
encounter everything that broadcasting could offer.

Mixed programming determined many aspects of the Corporation's policy between the wars. In 1934 a BBC administrator wrote
that 'the most advantageous single extension or change in programme policy'[1] would be to stop broadcasting programmes at
regular times and so break the audience's conservative listening
habits. This was part of the Corporation's campaign against what
was contemptuously known as the 'tap' listener 'who wants to have
one or more very light programmes available at all hours between
breakfast and bedtime'.[2] 'The BBC', the 1932 *Yearbook* claimed,
'definitely aims at having an interval of four or five minutes
between programmes ... it is obviously irritating for a listener
who, switching on his set to hear, say, the news, finds himself
listening to the last minute of an opera or vaudeville turn.'
Listening was a serious business.

The BBC's belief in cultural homogeneity was a useful weapon
in the defence of its broadcasting monopoly, particularly against
the commercial wireless exchanges. These retransmitted a selection
of BBC and continental programmes to simple home 'speakers',
improving reception and making it cheaper. The number of such
stations had risen from 34 in 1929 to 343 by 1935. The BBC
argued, in the 1931 *Handbook*, that the relay system

> contains within it forces which uncontrolled might be disruptive
> of the spirit and intention of the BBC charter. The persons in
> charge of wireless exchanges have power, by replacing selected
> items of the Corporation's programmes with transmission from
> abroad, to alter entirely the general drift of the BBC's pro-
> gramme policy.

The BBC was defending its own position, and what it assumed
was a generally recognizable set of cultural values. Reith's objection
to audience research was also based on the principle of cultural
homogeneity. He did not want to know popular preference,

because of the danger that programme organizers would pander to it.

The BBC had a distinctive model of the listener. 'Broadcasting is not mass projection, though it seems to be so, it is an individual intimate business,' wrote Hilda Matheson, the first head of the Talks Department in the *Sociological Review* (no. 3, 1935). The personal relationship between listener and programme was elevated into a principle. The class and tastes of groups of listeners were irrelevant. Any variety in programmes was justified by the changing moods of the average listener and not by reference to the interests of different groups. In this way, 'entertainment' had its appropriate place: it was meant to provide periods of relaxation in the broadcasting diet of the Reithian 'average' listener.

The Reithian approach was paralleled during the 1920s and 1930s by similarly 'unitary' assumptions in state education. The content of state education between the wars was common to all schools: children merely received more or less of it. At the top of the ladder children had access to 'the whole world of learning', while at the bottom they had 'the hems of learning only'.[3] The curriculum was governed by notions of a 'general liberal education', a direct legacy of Matthew Arnold's philosophy of education.

Educational policy reflected the traditional psychology of the nineteenth century, argued the Spens Report on secondary education in 1938:

> with its emphasis on faculties and its belief in the doctrine of formal education and mental transfer which played an important part in perpetuating a curriculum common to all pupils.

It was assumed that most boys and girls were equipped with the same mental endowments, that most of them developed the same way, and at almost the same rate of progress. Although some scholarships were available to the academic secondary grammar schools, these were very scarce, and most pupils paid fees. University scholarships were even more rare. Yet all the children in grammar schools followed a pattern of education which was designed to secure university places which only 3 per cent of them actually attained. Even in non-academic secondary schools, the curriculum was merely a weaker version of the university-dominated teaching of the grammar schools.

State education, like state broadcasting, was (in theory) designed to enable the hard-working and able to develop those faculties which were regarded as common to all. In education there was also emphasis on the development of 'character', a nebulous and undefined moral concept, taken undiluted from the 'muscular Christian' ethos of leadership training which governed public schools. Until Cyril Burt's ideas on scientific intelligence testing were accepted during the 1940s and 1950s, the ideology of 'character' pervaded educational policy as well as broadcasting.

In many ways, of course, education and broadcasting are not comparable: for one thing, state education hardly grew at all during the 1930s while broadcasting developed very quickly. For another, broadcasting was centrally controlled with a national monopoly, while education was administered locally, and alongside (rather than in competition with) a prestigious private sector. Nevertheless, broadcasting and schooling as communicators of accepted values have enough in common for the similarity to be striking. The similarities in the organizational changes, which occurred as a result of the impulse for reform created by the Second World War, are more remarkable still.

## Reform, the war, and education

The needs of war radically altered education and broadcasting. The Education Act, 1944, which introduced compulsory secondary education for all, has been seen by many as the finest achievement of a great reforming minister, R. A. Butler, who based it on what he described to his biographer, Ralph Harris, as a 'sensationally ingenious report'. More recent assessments have been less enthusiastic. According to Brian Simon,

> Through the late 1940s and 1950s when so much might have been accomplished, the development of secondary education for all was restricted and distorted by the dead hand of a doctrine brought to a point during the depressed 1930s – the doctrine that in effect secondary education is not for all.

The Education Act recommended that schools be reorganized 'firstly to provide opportunities for a special cast of mind to manifest itself . . . indeed to develop specialized interests and aptitudes'.[4] The Act was not the result of radical political pressure, but of official initiatives within the Board of Education itself. In 1938 the Spens Report had suggested that 'It is becoming more and more evident that a simple liberal education for all is impractical.' It drew a distinction between those children 'who work with hands, work with tongue, or work with pen' and suggested that 'one child differs from another far more than is generally supposed'. The Norwood Report and the 1944 Act went further and argued that these differences were held in common by groups of children. They distinguished between three kinds, the child 'who is interested in learning for its own sake, who is interested in causes and who can grasp an argument. . . . [He] is sensitive . . . he is interested in the relatedness of related things . . . he will have some capacity to enjoy from an aesthetic point of view.' A child of this kind was to go to a grammar school, the distinct feature of which 'lies in the intellectual ideal which it upholds'. This category of school was to retain the values which had been intended for all schools before the war, and was to produce the new professional and managerial élite.

The second kind of child 'often has an uncanny insight into the intricacies of mechanisms, whereas the subtleties of language construction are too delicate for him. To justify itself to his mind, knowledge must be capable of immediate application.' These children would 'go into industry' and were to attend the new technical schools.

The third kind of child 'may have much ability but it will be in the realm of facts. He is interested in things as they are . . . he must have immediate return for his effort.' These residual children were to attend the new secondary modern schools. These schools were to be separate but equal and were, according to the report (incredibly) to have 'parity of prestige'. The purpose of the modern schools was distinct because these children would need education for their leisure: 'This homely aspect of education is often the basis of future happiness, and is as vitally necessary as it can be interesting.' It was implicit in the Norwood Report and the Act that there were children who could think, children who could do, and the rest.

This division of schools and children was not consciously based on any scientific evidence, but was justified on the grounds that 'these rough groupings have in fact established themselves in general educational experience'. Immediately the Act was published Cyril Burt attacked its underlying psychological assumptions. He argued that his own work had long since demolished the myth of separate 'mental types', and that the proposed reforms had overlooked the fundamental discovery of his work on intelligence: that anyone who was above average in any one aspect of intellectual performance was likely to be above average in all of them. 'It is difficult to see', he wrote, 'how even administrative necessity can lead us to discern the indistinguishable and to find three types of mind when they do not exist.' However, Burt's attitude was surprising, for the process of selection and division was to be carried out with his own 'scientific' intelligence testing. More strikingly, the proportions of children which it was projected would attend each kind of school closely approximated to Burt's 'normal curve' of the distribution of intelligence within the population. Indeed, in an article devoted to 'The psychology of listeners', Burt wrote: 'Politically no doubt all men are born equal. Mentally however, as the results of surveys incontestably show, the range of individual differences is far wider than had ever been suspected.'[5]

The classification of children proposed by the Act depended on the war experience of Burt's followers in training and assigning members of the armed services to appropriate jobs. Psychologists used increasingly detailed tests developed from Burt's work, not only to guarantee that the various services had equal shares of intelligent personnel, but also to distinguish between 'skill' and 'character', and to identify a whole range of special mechanical, logical, and clerical abilities. 'The value of vocational or educational classification', wrote Vernon and Barry about their work as psychologists during the war, 'lies not merely in the closer co-ordination of human capacity with job ... but also with their effects on morale.' Workers, they argued, were happier if they were not disturbed by association with those with abilities far beyond, or behind, their own. Thus during the war 'streaming' was developed and rationalized.

The effect of the war is also revealed in the provision of the new 'technical' schools. During the war there had been a shift in the subjects in which children were examined towards the sciences, in response to the increased need for technical skills. Lord Hankey wrote in 1941 that 'Technical colleges, although ill housed, ill equipped and understaffed had responded without hesitation to the needs of the services and industry and had magnificently reorganized themselves to train men and women for the war effort.' It was these experiences, a dramatic increase in the need for technical and scientific workers, and the reorganization of schools and training to produce them, which had led to the creation of the new 'technical schools' and the perception of the 'practically able' child.

In the Act it was expected that these new schools would take some of the children who would previously have gone to grammar schools, and direct them into more technical and industrial work. These schools simply failed to appear. This was partly because money was not available. Also during the war the government had been able to direct the allocation of the entire workforce; in a post-war world this was far more difficult. Moreover, hopes that private industry would seek technically educated school-leavers for training did not materialize; employers continued to prefer young people with a 'general' academic education where they could get them.

R. A. Butler had written in 1942 that

Education cannot by itself create the social structure of a country. I have to take the world as I find it and the world I find is one in which there is a very diversified range of types. Educational progress must be along the grain of human nature.[6]

Yet arguably the Act and its implementation was precisely an attempt at massive social engineering. It was not, as Simon has argued, merely a rationalization of the status quo, but marked a major change in the official perception of the child. It also represented a new recognition of class, and the fragmentation of culture. The old, liberal culture survived, but was confined to the curricula of the'professionals' in their grammar schools; while in modern schools children for whom exams were inappropriate were to be taught how to entertain themselves.

## Reform, the war, and the BBC

The war also revolutionized the BBC. During the war Reith's 'cultural unity' was abandoned. After a visit to the troops in France, Ogilvie, Reith's successor as Director General, had come back convinced that the morale of the forces would be improved by knowing that their families at home were listening to the same programmes with them, but also that the Corporation's whole programming would have to change. Ian Hay, a BBC comptroller, had written in 1939, 'We shall need a lot of entertainment before this business is over.' It was recognized that the new forces service would have to be quite different from a 'watered-down version of our peacetime programmes', for 'if we give them serious music, long plays, or peacetime programme talks they will not listen'.[7] The lure of the continental stations could not be ignored during the war and programme changes would inevitably have more long-term consequences. An official wrote ominously,

'We shall not be able to return to our Sunday policy when the war ends.'

More light music, comedy, crooning, and jazz were justified not only by the immediacy of wartime demands, but also, crucially, by a new model of the psychology of the listener. The first step argued that the service had to be changed because troops were listening to it communally in the mess or in camps. Then it was suggested that different programmes were appropriate to different occupations. Very quickly the audience research department was trying to establish which kinds of music had the best effect on factory production.

Modern wars change the status of entertainment: leisure is seen as an aspect of 'public morale'. This was particularly true in Britain after 1940. Nevertheless, the Corporation was anxious not to be accused of producing 'programmes fit for morons', and the *Listener* printed many letters on this subject. 'I think you will find this army more highbrow than you suppose,' wrote one officer (15 February 1941).

What had first been seen as a temporary expedient became a permanent feature when the General Forces Programme was changed to the Light Programme in 1946. Grace Wyndham Goldie commented on the consequences of this innovation for the internal structure of the Corporation: 'It is not only that this is lighter, more gay, fresher in its approach; but for good or evil it is more closely related to the box office than any broadcasting in England has ever been before' (*Listener*, 26 December 1940). Competition was introduced between various parts of the Corporation. It meant the recognition of distinct groups whose tastes the BBC was obliged to identify rather than to change. This internal reform was of more fundamental importance than that of the competition later offered by commercial television. An editorial in the *Listener* claimed that 'the position is that the Forces Programme is carefully planned and not a casual proliferation of high jinks for low brows' (13 March 1941). Yet providing the public with what it wanted had become central to the Corporation's plans.

The introduction of a 'Light' Programme inevitably had implications for the Home Service. As early as 1940 the Home Service Board had decided that the 'barometer of listeners' preferences' should be a regular item on its agenda. However, the Home Service also broadcast the main news bulletins, and came to be seen as the part of the BBC which was most concerned with 'citizenship, family and home'.

The final and most revealing innovation was the introduction of
the Third Programme. An internal memorandum in 1944 had
suggested that the BBC should provide three competing services.
Programme A 'should be of the highest possible cultural level,
devoted to artistic endeavour, serious documentary, educational
broadcasting, and the deeper investigation of the news, corresponding in outlook to a *Times* of the air'. Programme B, 'the real
home programme of the people of the United Kingdom', would
'give talks which would inform the whole democracy rather than
an already informed section, and be generally so designed that it
will steadily, but imperceptibly, raise the standard of taste, entertainment, outlook and citizenship'.[8] Programme C was to divert,
and needed little detailing.

The Third Programme was a survival of the Reithian ethic of
'mixed' programming. It emphasized that it should be judged by
the whole programming of the service rather than individual items.

> The daily broadcasting schedules rush by the listener like the
> scenery past the windows of an express train. ... The Third
> Programme from the beginning has arrived at a standard which
> has brought it into conflict with this ephemeral characteristic of
> broadcasting.[9]

Elsewhere, Harold Nicolson wrote, 'Every cultural pill is coated
with sugar; and an item which it is felt might be unpalatable is
tendered with a tone of apology, or with the horrid cheeriness of
the scoutmaster, the padre, or the matron.' The Third regarded
broadcasting as an art.

The 1950 White Paper on the future of broadcasting argued that
'listeners will now normally have a wider choice of contrasting
programmes', while Nicolson, who had been involved in the
creation of the Third, was at pains to point out that 'at no time, I
am glad to say, did we entertain the doctrine that the listening
public should be segregated between sheep or goats'. Sir William
Haley, the Director General who had originally thought of the
Third, put the classification clearly in a lecture given in 1948:

> Before the war the system was to confront [the listener] with
> pendulum-like leaps. The devotees of [Irving] Berlin were
> suddenly confronted with Bach. ... Since the war we have
> been feeling our way along a more indirect approach. It rests on
> the conception of the community as a broadly based cultural
> pyramid, slowly aspiring upwards.

This concept resembled the hierarchy of ability.

## Progress or rationalization?

By the end of the war British broadcasting and education had been radically reformed. Is it a coincidence that the two most important vehicles of national culture were reorganized almost simultaneously and in each case along very similar lines?

The reforms may have been made possible by the new weight given to public opinion by the war. However, in both areas of policy the form which the changes took depended on a new official way of looking at children on the one hand, and at listeners on the other. In this, distinctions were in effect being made between the tastes, abilities, and interests of different social groupings.

Listeners and children are not obviously analogous. Yet what is striking is the similarity in proportions of people assigned, quite independently, by education and broadcasting authorities to three categories. It is as though in the natural order of things there were three types of children and three types of listeners reflecting a three-way divide in society as a whole. It was expected that the population would divide as follows:[10]

| | |
|---|---|
| Grammar schools 5% | Third Programme 6% |
| Technical schools 15% | Home Service 20% |
| Modern schools 80% | Light Programme 74% |

In both cases the figures were based more on a hunch than statistics, and in both cases they proved wholly unrealistic. In education the technical schools barely got off the ground and completely failed to produce the technical administrators that had been expected; instead the grammar school section expanded. The estimate of the Third Programme audience of serious listeners was wildly optimistic; it never attracted more than 1–2 per cent of listeners. Neither projection was officially justified in terms of social class; yet in both cases what seems to have occurred is the imposition on social policy of official assumptions based on military and administrative experience.

There has been much discussion about the social effects of the war. Calder and Marwick have pointed to a major upheaval; Addison has suggested the culmination of a long, slow revolution in attitudes; Pelling argued that there was not much fundamental change at all. What is clear is that there was a dramatic and permanent increase in the power and scope of government. Whitehall's view of society and human nature, essentially meritocratic and hierarchical, pervaded policies which in normal times would have been fought out in the political arena. The reforms in both broadcasting and education reflected an approach to organization which had more to do with a civil service conception of the world as itself writ large, than with the reality of the world as it existed. Thus in Whitehall there were administrative, executive, and clerical grades (and in the services there were officers, NCOs, and privates). Officials found their own tripartite system natural and efficient. In creating new structures for the public they assumed a similar pattern of talent and need. In broadcasting, as in education, reforms contained a contradiction. On the one hand they were progressive in that they sought to cater for the whole society; but on the other they reinforced class divisions by giving new life to old hierarchical assumptions.

## Notes

1. Filson Young to Dawney, BBC Internal Memorandum, 'Programme policy', *BBC Written Archives* (3 March 1934).
2. 'Programme revision committee', *BBC Written Archives* (June 1934).
3. Board of Education, *Inspectors' Report* (1932), p. 12, para 7 [Cmd 4068].
4. *The Nation's Schools: Their Plans and Purposes*, Ministry of Education Pamphlet 1 (London, HMSO, 1945).
5. Sir Cyril Burt, 'The psychology of listeners', *BBC Quarterly*, IV, 1 (April 1949), p. 7.
6. Lord Butler, *The Education Act of 1944 and After*, The First Noel Buxton Lecture, University of Essex (Harlow, Longman, 1965), p. 21.
7. Ryan to Nicolson, BBC Internal Memorandum, *BBC Written Archives* (17 January 1940).
8. 'Programme development', BBC Internal Memorandum, *BBC Written Archives* (14 February 1944).
9. BBC, *The Third Programme: Plans for October–December 1944*.
10. Sources for education figures, Ministry of Education circular 731 (1944), quoted in P. H. J. H. Gosdon, *Education in the Second World War* (London, Methuen, 1976); and for broadcasting, *Listener* (February 1946), and BBC Internal Memorandum, 'Projection for the Third Programme', *BBC Written Archives* (14 May 1946).

# 11

# The fall of the BBC

In 1946, when television broadcasting was resumed, the BBC's popularity at home and prestige abroad were even greater than before, largely because of the wartime experience. Yet barely a decade later, the BBC's monopoly of the air waves was destroyed. Television and subsequently radio were placed on a new competitive footing. More than anything else, this has shaped the aims, structure, and output of all television programming over the last quarter of a century.

The change was not brought about by public pressure, but by a small group within the ruling Conservative Party. It was opposed by bishops, vice-chancellors, peers, trade unions, the Labour Party, and most national newspapers. Reith compared the introduction of commercial broadcasting into Britain with that of dog racing, smallpox, and bubonic plague.[1] The objections to commercial broadcasting were diverse, but most were anti-American, and opposed the encouragement of crude materialist desires. Criticisms of this kind were particularly vehement on the left. More recently, however, some socialist writers have taken a different view, arguing that commercial television was, in fact, a cultural liberator, taking the control of broadcasting out of the hands of a patronizing and paternalist establishment, and increasing the scope of genuinely popular influences.

### Austerity, monopoly, and the Beveridge Report

The BBC's prestige contributed to its undoing. The Corporation had assumed that it was invulnerable and so had the 1945 Labour government which consequently did not hurry to renew its licence. In 1947 Beveridge was asked to conduct an inquiry into the BBC's affairs. He might have been expected to sympathize with

Reith's legacy of benevolent, high-minded despotism at the BBC, for Beveridge had once claimed that his ideal society would be run by neither parliament nor dictators, but by professional administrators – 'social doctors' – who would organize society 'to adapt the social and economic relations of clients so as to produce the maximum economic health'.[2] However, as a liberal, Beveridge was highly critical of the Corporation.

He distrusted the tone and character of the BBC, which 'beginning with Londonization, going on to secretiveness and self-satisfaction, and ending up with a dangerous sense of mission became a sense of divine right'. He was constantly on the watch for 'the four scandals of monopoly: bureaucracy, complacency, favouritism and inefficiency'. Written in Beveridge's inimitable style, the report nevertheless finally recommended that the Corporation's licence be renewed, because the alternative, American-style commercial television, seemed far worse.

The recommendations of the Beveridge Report were ignored by the Conservatives after they beat the Labour Party in the 1951 general election. Instead, Selwyn Lloyd's dissenting minority report, which was in favour of commercial broadcasting, became the basis for the commercial lobby. Nevertheless, Beveridge's findings influenced the form of British commercial broadcasting. First, the report preferred spot adverts to sponsored programmes because they gave advertisers less control over programme content. 'A public broadcasting service', the report commented, 'might have its controlled and limited advertisement hour, as every newspaper had in its advertising columns, without sacrificing the independence of standards of broadcasting.' Second, the report advocated the regionalization of broadcasting and the decentralization of the BBC. These arguments affected the organization of the commercial system when it was introduced.

The commercial television lobby has been seen by some writers as a tiny group of back-bench MPs, 'who worked night and day on the project'. However, they were supported by the immense power of the great entertainment industries. Pye Radio, the largest West End theatre management, and J. Walter Thompson, the advertising agency, were all involved in the campaign. Although a member of the group declared in the House of Commons that 'Any suggestion that the Bill was fostered by commercial interests is a complete figment of the imagination of the Party opposite', the speaker at the time was a director of various electronics firms who expected to profit out of an increase in the market for televisions.[3] 'At what point', H. H. Wilson asked, 'were the members speaking as MPs representing their constituencies, and when were they speaking as directors, managers or employees of advertising agencies, market research organizations or radio and television manufacturers?'

However, the most important organizer of the lobby was a broadcaster, Norman Collins. He had been director of the Light Programme, and controller of BBC Television. When he was not appointed Chief Executive of Television, Collins resigned from the BBC. He told *The Times* that he had left

> because of a clash of principle . . . whether the new medium of TV shall be allowed to develop at this, the most crucial stage of its existence, along its own lines and by its own methods, or whether it shall be merged into the colossus of sound broadcasting.

The commercial lobby fought a hard and frequently unscrupulous battle. It was successful because important members of the government, including the Prime Minister, Churchill, were not prepared to defend the BBC. Significantly the campaign also had the active support of Lord Woolton. He had modernized the Conservative Party organization before the 1951 election and brought a new kind of candidate into parliament. This group represented industry and advertising rather than law or hereditary wealth.

Woolton wanted free enterprise to dominate the 'new age of post-war prosperity'. 'Our individual lives today', he complained in a broadcast, 'are hemmed in by no less than 25,000 controls.' He wanted to associate the party with the long-term material aspirations of the people, and believed that commercial television would help to do this.

The opposition to commercial television was organized by the National Television Council with Christopher Mayhew as its secretary. Support came from surprising quarters. 'The Establishment', wrote Henry Fairlie, 'came as near as it has ever done to organizing a conspiracy against the government of the day – a Conservative Government.'[4] This group objected to the cultural consequences of commercial television: it would 'vulgarize, bowdlerize, and coarsen', wrote one critic.

The argument became more fierce when it was learnt that in the USA the Coronation had been shown interspersed with NBC's television chimp, J. Fred Muggs, selling tea. A deodorant had been advertised just before the ritual anointment. Horrified MPs sug-

gested that if a commercial system were started here, royal tours
would be interrupted by commercial breaks extolling the makers
of the Queen's chairs and carpets.

Nevertheless the Act introducing commercial television was
passed in 1954 because most Tories believed that in some way it
would promote industry, commerce, and the free market. The new
service was named, by some genius of euphemism, 'Independent
Television'.

## Commercial television and the new world

'A whole new world has come,' proclaimed the first commercial
television *Yearbook* in 1955. 'We've won, and now we can really
get going,' said Norman Collins. 'The importance of the introduction of commercial TV goes far beyond any question of the
merits of commercial versus public service broadcasting,' wrote
Wilson, 'for it may also seem to symbolize a change within the
Conservative Party, and give expression to an accumulation of
influences which are securing the future of British society.' ITV
brought about a revolution, it has been claimed, because it
challenged the complacent pre-war conservatism of the BBC. The
Corporation was staffed by narrow-minded, middle-class professional bureaucrats who had little sympathy for working-class
interests. Norman Collins complained of the 'apathy, disinterest
and often open hostility towards the new medium' that existed
within the BBC. Lord Simon of Wythenshawe, chairman of the
BBC Governors, claimed that during the early 1950s only about
one-fifth of the business the Director General presented to the
board was concerned with television. Indeed in 1946 when Haley
was shown a television demonstration he had remarked that he
would not have one in his house.

The BBC, one producer wrote, regarded radio as 'the father
figure, established and responsible', while television was seen as a
'spendthrift tiresome adolescent'.[5] The BBC bureaucrats, secure in
the imperial comforts of Broadcasting House, deluged television
producers in the unheated wastes of north London with memos.
These detailed the proper procedures for the purchase of books and
why it was outrageous to suggest that book covers should be cut
up, even to be shown on the screen. The tensions were exacerbated
by the influx into television of cameramen, technicians, and directors who were used to the high living which characterized the
precarious film world. 'Disorder has been repeatedly reported from

the television studios ... new employees do not seem to have become one with the Corporation,' read one ominous memo of the period. 'Perhaps', another memo replied, 'a brief course on the history of the Corporation might be of assistance?'[6]

Indeed during the 1950s the Corporation appointments policy was apparently designed to keep the new service in order, rather than accelerate its development. Gerald Beadle was an amicable BBC administrator, quietly approaching retirement in the Western Region, when the call came. 'About 1953', he remarked, 'every BBC directorship in London was filled by younger men than me ... but then in 1956 something quite unexpected happened ... at the age of fifty-seven I was appointed Director of TV.' Beadle was to hold this post during the critical early years of commercial television.

Beadle was a typical example of the BBC administrator of this period. The Corporation man, as Burns has argued, did not work for the BBC, he worked *in* it – as a secular church of professional excellence. One writer noted that a Corporation producer 'breathes the BBC ritual welcome to eminent persons as they arrive' (to have their personalities 'brought out', rather than be put on the spot), 'How good of you to come!' (*Encounter*, October 1960). The Corporation saw itself as a particularly dedicated branch of the civil service, and this image affected its approach to television.

However, the BBC's performance during the 1950s needs scrutiny. Despite the overwhelming bureaucracy, a remarkable generation of television producers and directors started work during this period. They were to dominate the entire output of British television, on both channels, for the next twenty years. Even the Corporation's lack of interest in television had benefits. Because it was seen as relatively unimportant it was left alone. Goldie claims this allowed programme-makers far greater initiative.

The most serious charge against the BBC was that it starved the new service of funds. In 1950 the BBC's television budget was only one-half of that allocated to the Home Service. However, in the period of experimental broadcasts during the 1930s, television had been able to develop only because the BBC had been willing to subsidize it out of wireless revenues. (In the USA, where it depended on advertising funds, the service was forced to close because the pictures and reception were inadequate to attract a commercially useful audience.) The BBC also pursued a policy of national coverage and by 1956 98 per cent of the country was able to receive television. This was achieved only by a massive redistribution of resources away from the rich south-east, where there were many television owners, to the more remote regions. A national service was an investment which could not at first have been made by the commercial companies.

## Competition new and old

It has been argued that commercial competition changed the BBC. Competition forced the Corporation to consider public wants more seriously. 'The BBC will have to abandon the ivory towers for the beaches! People prefer fun,' wrote one critic (*Daily Mail*, 15 February 1957). Peter Black comments that a kind of myth developed, based on an image of 'the energetic thrusting showbiz visionaries elbowing aside the complacent bureaucrats of the BBC, by presenting a series of audacious novelties that blew the stale air of monopoly out of television and sent the invigorating breezes of free enterprise whistling through it'.[7] Others have argued that subsequently broadcasting has been dominated by the need to maximize the audience.

Yet competition came to the BBC long before Independent Television was thought of. The decisive break with Reithian paternalism occurred during the war, when the General Forces Network was established. Similarly the BBC had always been obliged to prove that the size of its audience legitimized its receipt of the licence fee. Indeed the BBC had been subject to competition from foreign commercial stations since the 1930s. It was the challenge of Luxembourg which had broken the dismal Reithian Sunday on the radio. However unctuously it was defended, the BBC had abandoned the concept of planned programming considerably before the introduction of Independent Television, while programme-makers have always been most sensitive to the competition offered by colleagues. Anthony Smith has argued in *British Broadcasting* that 'Producers within the BBC were more often conscious of an internal competition within the different sections of the BBC.' This, he claimed, led in the 1960s to 'an enormous flowering of talent and inventiveness'. Such internal pressure had the greatest effect on standards and innovation within both authorities.

In addition the threat posed by commercial competition was more limited than its advocates have suggested. At first the two authorities fought a bitter ratings war. They soon discovered that the public would watch anything in preference to a party political programme. (The parties reacted swiftly and ensured that these broadcasts were shown simultaneously on both channels.) When ITV offered the audience the Hallé Orchestra, the BBC's share of the audience rose. When the BBC offered the people *La Bohème*, the numbers watching fell to 2 per cent. However, both soon discovered the comforts of competition and the security provided by the dependability of the enemy's programming. It was found that documentaries and current events programmes achieved their maximum audience only if they were shown at the same time. As Burns commented, 'Competition now seems to be accepted as a fact of life for both the BBC and ITV, and is defended by both. There is one obvious reason for this; it makes life easier for them.' A rigidly conventional use of time and categories of programmes was reinforced by competition.

## Commerce and the audience

It is often assumed that ITV changed television because it won the battle for the audience. This is not the case. Indeed commercial television had little effect on the growth of the television audience, nor did it decimate the numbers watching BBC.

Between 1955 and 1956 the commercial companies struggled to acquire an audience. Howard Thomas wrote that by January 1956, 'The situation was very grim. The costs of running commercial television were enormous for the audience was simply not large enough to attract advertising revenue.'

However, the situation improved. In a well-publicized campaign in 1957 Sir Kenneth Clark was claiming a 79:21 preference for the commercial channel. In December of the same year, out of 539 programmes listed by TAM in the top ten ratings, 536 were from ITV and only 3 produced by the BBC. 'Once they had a choice', Black wrote, 'the working-class audience left the BBC at a pace that suggested ill will was more deeply entrenched than good.' The first *ATV Showbook* put the point more jubilantly: 'We've got the audience,' it proclaimed. Norman Collins said that the BBC would soon 'grind to a halt'.

Certainly the BBC panicked. *Ariel*, the staff magazine, became full of warlike metaphors about 'beating back the enemy' and getting into 'fighting formation'. As large numbers of staff left the Corporation for the higher salaries and more makeshift offices of the commercial companies, Sir Ian Jacob wrote, 'I doubt whether any organization in peacetime has been subject to comparable strain' (*Ariel*, 3, 1956).

Corporation officials became obsessed with maintaining a 30 per cent share of the audience. Television was typically being interpreted in terms of the audience distribution of radio. Furthermore its audience was being seen in terms of an obsolete distribution of the population between classes. According to this view, the commercial companies would concentrate on entertainment (like the Light Programme, which drew 68 per cent of the audience), leaving more serious programming to the BBC (like the combined Home and Third services which drew 32 per cent of the audience).

The apparent collapse of the audience posed a dilemma. The BBC might be destroyed because its share of the audience would no longer justify the collection of a licence fee from all viewers. Or the BBC might be destroyed because it would be forced to emulate the commercial programmes.

However, the argument about which service had won the largest audience was confused, in the first place because the two authorities counted their audience in different ways. 'For us,' wrote Robert Silvey, the head of the BBC's audience research, 'it meant people, and for ITV it meant TV sets. Our method was based on questioning samples of the population about their previous day's viewing; ITV's on metered records of when TV sets in a sample of homes had been switched on.' Although both methods showed trends in viewing behaviour, they could not be directly compared.

Indeed the commercial companies had not 'won' a 70 per cent share of the total viewing audience as Clark had implied. Rather this was the proportion of those viewers who had purchased a new television set which could receive both channels. At first this was a tiny fraction of the total audience. Even as late as 1960 the ITA estimated in its annual report that fewer than 60 per cent of licence holders had two channel sets. Given their considerable financial investment, it was hardly surprising that viewers with new sets at first preferred the novelty of commercial television. Nevertheless, throughout the period the BBC's total audience was over twice that of ITV.

Indeed the introduction of commercial television had no independent effect on the overall growth of the television audience.

As Table 6 shows this was fast but steady. The pattern of gradual growth was interrupted only once, when two years before the start of ITV the Coronation produced a dramatic rise in viewers. The BBC did not 'lose' an audience, nor did commercial choice increase the speed of audience growth.

Table 6   *Growth of television audience*

| Year | No. of new TV licence holders |
|------|------------------------------|
| 1946–7 | 14,560 |
| 1947–8 | 57,000 |
| 1948–9 | 112,000 |
| 1949–50 | 344,000 |
| 1950–1 | 420,000 |
| 1951–2 | 685,319 |
| 1952–3 | 693,192 |
| 1953–4 | 1,110,439 |
| 1954–5 | 1,254,879 |
| 1955–6 | 1,235,827 |
| 1956–7 | 1,226,663 |
| 1957–8 | 1,123,747 |
| 1958–9 | 1,165,419 |

*Source:* BBC Handbooks (1946–59)

## Public service: private enterprise

Commercial television in Britain was hardly revolutionary. Indeed it was carefully modelled on the BBC. The traditions of public service were inherited by the new authority.

The ITA was responsible for regulating the commercial stations and made no programmes. Like the BBC, ITV was licensed only for a limited period, a system which ensured that the whole of British broadcasting came under periodic review. Like the BBC it had a publicly appointed controlling board. 'The BBC triumphed', Peter Black wrote, 'because all of those chosen as members of the IBA might equally well have been BBC Governors.'

The new service was more limited than the BBC. It was banned from broadcasting its own opinions, and the injunction that it should observe 'impartiality in the treatment of all controversial issues' has been interpreted narrowly to imply a balance of views within each programme. As Smith points out, the prohibitions 'listed in the 1954 Act are broadly consistent with the general editorial policy of the BBC, but they have been used over the

years to oblige independent TV not to do certain types of programme'. Hence ITV has been given less political independence
than the BBC.

Thus Independent Television was made in the image of the
BBC. Introduced after a controversy which *The Economist* called
'a soufflé of high principles and politics' (15 June 1954), which
disguised a simple profit motive, commercial television was nevertheless formed as a public service.

## Commerce, finance, and television

Indeed television was so expensive it had always seemed likely
that it would have to be financed commercially. 'Had there been
no war in 1939', Briggs remarks, 'it is conceivable that commercial
TV would have come to Britain fifteen years before it did.' Even
in the limited experimental stage, television was an exorbitantly
expensive medium. In 1937 a BBC *Handbook* had estimated that
an hour of television cost twelve times as much to produce as the
most expensive programme on the radio. Even Reith, in his
evidence to the Selsdon Committee in 1934, claimed that he had
'no objection in principle to the sponsor system and we do in fact
do something which is near to that and might do it in the future'.
Sir William Haley wrote in 1945, 'Television will cost more than
the Corporation's usual sources of funds can easily provide.'
Beveridge had rejected sponsorship, but was not hostile in principle to some commercial involvement in television.

The BBC itself had been pressing for some kind of commercial
financing of television since the 1930s, partly because it was felt
that business interests could have little serious effect on what was
seen as a trivial means of entertainment. Within the BBC, television
was regarded as an extension of the Light Programme. As such it
might be expensive, but it could hardly be important. 'In terms of
the ethos which had been cultivated within the BBC during the
fifties', wrote Burns, 'Light Entertainment remained an unfortunate necessity, its marginal character inescapably perpetuated
in the adjective tagged to it.' Commerce, television, and programme policy had been closely linked since the 1930s.

## New programmes and the new style

Perhaps the most important innovation which ITV introduced was
the change of mood which it brought to broadcasting. The atmos-

phere of the new companies, owned and run by showmen like Val Parnell and the Grade brothers, was quite different from the stifling solemnity of the BBC bureaucracy. 'It was more like Klondyke than Maida Vale,' wrote Howard Thomas. When Thomas went to see Lew Grade at ATV about new programme ideas he would be met by a cloud of cigar smoke, and Grade would throw open a drawer bulging with receipts and bills. The haggling would then begin. Describing Parnell and Grade negotiating a new contract for ATV Thomas wrote, 'They sat like boxers pausing between the rounds of a heavyweight championship.'

Once ITV had begun broadcasting, it no longer had to fight the moral scruples of the establishment and its first priority was to capture an audience. 'Variety,' claimed the first *ATV Showbook*, 'although accumulating the largest number of viewers, has been taken to task by critics of commercial television who have asked for "more cultural programmes and less airy frolics".' The article continued, 'Many will agree with ATV chief executive Val Parnell when he says there is a lot of culture to be gained from watching a great clown performing.' However, it was not the big top or the *Commedia Dell'Arte* which drew the ATV audience, but rather the giveaway shows, Double your Money, Take your Pick, and Beat the Clock. The Labour MP, Tom Driberg, compared the audience's howl of laughter at one of these shows to that of the circus crowd in ancient Rome (*New Statesman*, 25 December 1959).

Independent Television did not, however, 'soundly beat the BBC at its own game', as a *Daily Mail* critic claimed in 1956. BBC drama, serials, and documentaries were consistently preferred to those of ITV. Consequently in 1956 news, documentaries, classical music, current events, and drama on ITV were cut by one-third. 'A craven definition of "serious"', Black claims, 'killed off promising programmes whose only offence was that though entertainment, they were a novelty.'

ITV's most important contribution to television was to develop a format for the news. The BBC bulletin had been read by an unseen newscaster accompanied by still photographs. Cardiff and Scannell argue that this failure

left a gaping hole in the very centre of television programme output. The function of a daily news service is not simply the continuous up to the minute monitoring, processing and defining of immediate national and international news events. It also serves to define the currency and topicality of events and issues for current affairs programmes.[8]

Independent Television News attracted an immense audience. It used journalists as news-readers, allowed them to write their own scripts, and showed them on the screen.

Robin Day, one of ITN's first newscasters, commented in his memoirs that 'The man on the screen had a further task, to win the professional confidence of his colleagues.' ITN developed television journalism in new directions, despite the limitations imposed upon it by the Television Act. The obligation to exercise balance proved particularly difficult. 'Any problems?' Day once asked the news director. 'Yes,' Cox replied bitterly, 'a call from a chap called Pontius Pilate who says his case has not been properly put.' The success of the ITN approach in turn provoked the BBC into improving its own news services.

However, ITV also inherited many traditions from the BBC. One disgruntled critic claimed, 'The BBC has precedents for everything, for handling a monarch's abdication, a State Opening of Parliament or a boy scouts' jamboree.'[9] The opening years of television seem little more than an extension of the wireless, where history was relentlessly marked by a succession of royal events (with outside coverage).

More significantly the BBC solved many of the political and social dilemmas that confronted television. The BBC showed the first televised election, and established the rules governing politicians' access to television, while the practical consequences of 'neutrality' and 'balance' in a visual medium were developed by a new generation of BBC producers and presenters. Goldie employed several young Labour ex-MPs defeated in the 1951 general election to make current events programmes. Later she claimed her choice was vindicated because Mayhew, Taverne, and Wyatt moved from the left to the middle and right of the political spectrum. These shifts in attitude might also demonstrate the power of the ethic of consensus which came to dominate television journalism. The commercial companies simply took over the conventions developed within the BBC. Both, wrote Stuart Hood, 'interpreted impartiality as the acceptance of that segment of opinion which constitutes parliamentary consensus. Opinion that falls outside that consensus has difficulty in finding expression.' Hood suggests that the median of acceptable opinion may shift, but the consensus, once arrived at, is always shared by both companies.

The BBC had also set precedents for the solution of technical dilemmas in television journalism before ITV started. New rhetorics of documentary and current affairs coverage were established. At first most cameramen had been trained in the cinema, and had little experience of journalism. 'In those early days', one producer wrote, 'I often discarded glamorous pictures of cherry orchards, or flocks of bleating lambs, or children dancing in playgrounds because, though improbably useful in a travelogue, they did nothing to a study of, say, the relationship of Yugoslavia to the USSR.'[10] She concluded that as pictures would always override words a style had to be found which ensured that they would reinforce rather than distract from the meaning of a piece. It was also recognized that the use of film raised problems of authenticity. Viewers could easily be led to believe that a film taken in the past actually portrayed events happening in the present. One solution was to use someone who had helped to make the film as the programme presenter. Reviewing the BBC magazine series Foreign Correspondent in the *Listener* (May 1959), Goldie had written that they

> were using film but we were not trying to make films. We wanted the programmes to be dominated by the personality of the commentator. . . . We were all feeling our way but when the series finished we felt that we had hit on a new form that had come to stay in television. The key to the new form is the use of film to illustrate a personal experience.

This form was quite opposed to the style of the British documentary movement, in which the film purported to represent an authoritative reality, rather than any personal view.

These innovations and cautious explorations of the specific properties and opportunities of televised politics and current affairs were made well before ITV started. They solved dilemmas that were common to any television service. ITV did not challenge or alter the rules established by the BBC; it merely helped to develop them further.

### End of a monopoly: vulgar new world

The introduction of Independent Television did not mark such a decisive break with the BBC. Rather the brash new companies owed more to the Corporation than has usually been recognized. The BBC had already begun to change in fundamental ways before ITV was started. The commercial station provided a stimulus for the maturing of a national television service. Sir Hugh Greene claimed that dramatic changes were to come later in the 1960s, and these were as much to do with a shift in the political climate as with any administrative innovations.

This is not to deny that the BBC had a radically different manner and organization from Independent Television. Like the British Raj, the BBC combined privilege and moral purpose. It was a world in which 'unsoundness' was a major crime. Independent Television provided an alternative source of employment for dissidents and had no deadweight of custom or dignity. Personnel moved continually and freely between the two authorities by the 1960s.

However, commercial television was also modelled on and limited by the BBC. Originally intended as a political counterweight to what was seen as the BBC's 'red' bias, ITV was as vulnerable to political pressure. The BBC depended on public support for the legitimacy of its licence fee, as ITV depended on it for advertising revenue.

It has often been claimed that ITV was a vulgar debaucher of cultural standards. In the pursuit of profit it merely pandered to the lowest common denominator of public taste. More recently a far more subtle case has been advanced which is not so crudely anti-commercial. This claims that ITV was rather an energizing, populist force which gave expression to working-class culture.

## Notes

1. J. C. W. Reith, *House of Lords* (22 May 1952), H. L.176: 1,293–451.
2. Quoted in J. Harris, *William Beveridge* (Oxford, Clarendon, 1977), p. 311.
3. Captain L. P. S. Orr MP, *House of Commons Debates* (22 June 1954), 529:327.
4. H. Fairlie, 'The BBC' in H. Swynnerton Thomas (ed.), *The Establishment: A Symposium* (London, New English Library, 1962).
5. G. Wyndham Goldie, *Facing the Nation: Television and Politics 1936–1976* (London, Bodley Head, 1977), p. 45.
6. 'Television staff policy', *BBC Written Archives* (1955).
7. P. Black, *The Mirror in the Corner* (London, Hutchinson, 1972), p. 115.
8. P. Scannell, 'The social eye of television', *Media, Culture and Society*, 1, 1 (1979).
9. H. Fairlie, 'TV: idiot box', *Encounter* (August 1959).
10. G. Wyndham Goldie, 'TV report', *Listener* (23 October 1968).

# 12

# Class, taste, and profit

Post-war affluence was measured in consumer durables. Cars, refrigerators, and washing machines made it easier to do what had always been done. Television changed people's social life and habits. Commercial television was believed to alter their aspirations and values as well.

In the late 1950s and early 1960s television was central to a debate about supposed changes in the British class structure. The growth of a mass television audience and the setting-up of a commercial service were seen as agents of a revolution that was eroding class distinction and increasing social mobility. Television has more often been seen as a destructive than as a creative force. In the 1950s many regarded it as a threat to traditional ways of life, and hence to the basis of traditional political loyalties.

In 1962 the Pilkington Report summed up this debate. The Director General, Sir Hugh Greene, later called the report 'the most important piece of work on the purposes of broadcasting which has appeared in this or any other country'.[1] Pilkington attempted to establish the criteria for producing – and judging – good broadcasting. In fact the report was very much a product of its time, and was constrained by current sociological fashions.

## The myth of the disappearing working class

During the 1950s it was argued that affluence was destroying the working class. The general elections of 1955 and 1959 seemed to support the view that there were no longer two nations: fewer and fewer people were prepared even to support the Labour Party. Two complementary explanations were put forward. According to the first, as the working class had become richer it was actually disappearing through assimilation into the middle class.

According to the second, a working class had continued to exist but prosperity had undermined an awareness of its own interests: capitalism was successfully eradicating the consciousness (though not the reality) of class.

The first view was particularly popular among right-wing Labour politicians (who used it to justify an attempt to remove socialism from the party's constitution). 'The steady upgrading of the working class,' wrote Anthony Crosland in his book *The Future of Socialism*, 'both occupationally and still more in terms of political and social aspirations, renders Labour's one-class image increasingly inappropriate.' It was also widely held by social scientists who invented the inelegant term 'embourgeoisement' to describe the alleged process. As Butler and Rose wrote after the 1959 general election, 'It is more than ever possible to speak of the Conservatives as the country's usual majority party ... the Labour Party has to face the fact that its support is being eroded by the impact of age and social change.'

Between 1951 and 1958 real wages rose by 20 per cent. The proportion of manual workers who owned their own homes rose from 32 per cent to 39 per cent in the four years before 1962.[2] Between 1951 and 1964 the number of television sets rose from 1 million to 13 million. Indeed as televisions were clearly not useful, the widespread ownership of sets merely appeared to confirm what Crosland called the 'pubs, pools and prostitutes' view of the working class which was seen to 'waste all its higher income on alcohol, tobacco, gambling and fun ... if not actually women'.[3]

During the same period working-class habits also changed. People went on more holidays, went to the cinema less frequently, began drinking more at home and less at pubs. As these goods and habits had previously been the prerogative of higher social classes, it was assumed that their use also entailed middle- and upper-class views and beliefs.

The second explanation of the decay of the working class depended on the centrality of culture. The rituals which were a source of strength to working-class life were disappearing, partly (so it was argued) because of the homogenizing influence of television. Paradoxically working-class culture was celebrated just as it seemed to be about to vanish. Indeed its condition was detailed by a generation of academics whose origins were working class, but all of whom had been upwardly mobile.

'To live in the working class', wrote Richard Hoggart, 'is to belong to an all-pervading culture, one in some ways as formalized and stylized as any that is attributed to the upper classes.'[4] Jackson and Marsden in their book on working-class life argued that two and a half centuries of urban life 'have established distinct working-class styles of living with very real values of their own. Values which are perhaps essential to society and which do not flourish that strongly in other reaches of society.'[5] In a chapter headed 'An acceptance of the working-class life', they remarked that obliterating these values and way of life, 'can be so quick in a technological society ... the mass media, the central planning office, the bulldozers are all characteristic instruments of change'. In a related series of studies Wilmott and Young compared the warm closeness of a Bethnal Green working-class community with the more isolated life of a new suburb. In the East End the emphasis was on the informal collective life and the extended family, the pubs and the open air market. 'There is a sort of bantering warmth in public,' they claimed, which in the new suburb, Woodford, was reserved for the family home. There seemed to be more uniformity in gardens, attitudes, and behaviour in Woodford than in the East End. 'Maybe uniformity is one of the prices we have to pay for sociability in a more mobile society,' they concluded.[6]

Television was important because it was seen as replacing old communal forms of leisure with isolated and standardized entertainment. 'In many parts of life', Hoggart argued, 'mass production has brought good: culturally the mass produced makes it harder for the good to be recognized.' Indeed for writers like Hoggart culture was the most important aspect of a society's achievement.

Hoggart applied F. R. Leavis's concern with the moral quality of élite literary culture to a broader problem of working-class life. For Leavis, Annan wrote, 'The analysis of the text is only important in so far as it reveals the profundity or morality of the writer's moral consciousness.'[7] Leavis was concerned to evaluate the purpose of literature. 'Where there is not in the literary critical sense a significant contemporary culture', he wrote, '*the mind* is not fully alive.'[8] Hoggart was concerned to judge modern working-class culture. He concluded that 'Most mass entertainments are in the end what D. H. Lawrence described as "anti-life". They are full of corrupt brightness and improper appeals and moral evasions.' Progress had been reduced to material improvement: 'It only offered an infinite perspective of increasingly good times. Technicolour TV, all smelling, all touching, all tasting TV.'

Thus the Pilkington Report was the product of two contemporary concerns: that the working class was being absorbed into the middle class, and that working-class culture was decaying because of the industrialization of leisure. Raymond Williams wrote that 'From 1956 to 1962 there was an intense development of ideas in the field of culture and communication, and by the time of the Pilkington Report this had reached the level of open and conventional politics.'[9] The committee had been asked to review the development of television. In fact they did much more, producing a report which judged the nation's culture. Television, the report argued, was 'one of the major long-term factors that would shape the moral and mental attitudes, and the values of our society'.

Yet the working class did not disappear, and neither did working-class culture. There is little evidence that people lose a sense of their social identity simply because they become comparatively better off. Indeed the really remarkable feature of the period was not affluence – the rise in living standards looks far less impressive when it is compared with the growth in other European countries – but full employment. For the first time there was work for everyone, and it gave working-class culture, taste, and life a confidence which it had rarely had before.

The Pilkington Report depended on a sentimentalization of an earlier 'golden age', just as Hoggart and Wilmott and Young had before it. Indeed it demonstrates a puritanical distaste for the effects of improved material conditions. Although its concern with the influence of television on social and cultural behaviour is important, the standards by which it judged the mass media were based on false premises about the nature of working-class life.

## The power of the media

The Pilkington Report also depended on a crude view of the power of the media to influence individual behaviour. Advertising, and in particular its newest and most dramatic form, the television commercial, was regarded as immensely persuasive. The effect of advertising was dramatized by the contrast with the war, when advertising had not only been limited, but also pursued rather novel goals. A cartoon by Fougasse in 1942 wryly made the point: it compared the huge pre-war billboard extolling the public to 'Eat more and more Meatio' with the tiny wartime poster which read, 'Save Meatio, don't use more than you need!'[10] In this context the post-austerity explosion of advertising amazed the public, and academics and politicians became very sensitive to its effects.

Television advertising in particular was regarded as sinister. It was often equated with 'brain-washing' techniques which had been exposed during the Korean war. 'It may well be', wrote Daniel Bell in the *Listener* (December 1956), 'that our fears are excessive, that the pliability of the consumer, like that of the "indoctrinated" communist youth, is an exaggerated fact.' The fashion for 'motivation research' seemed to suggest that advertisements relied on an appeal to people's irrational and subconscious feelings in order to sell goods. The model of the consumer as a rational hedonist was replaced by another in which many goods were purchased not for their intrinsic worth or usefulness, but in an attempt to assuage anxieties. Marketing, dependent on the 'eight hidden needs' (most of which could be reduced to one – sex), was claimed to have dramatic effects. 'The ability of advertisers to contact millions of us simultaneously through television has given them the power to do good or evil on a scale never before possible,' one persuader put it.[11] Leavis wrote that 'a new brand of applied psychology . . . and a highly specialized profession' had been developed. 'Years of carefully recorded and tabulated experiment [led advertisers] to develop their appeal in the confidence that the average member of the public will respond like an automaton.'[12] Television advertising, which reached people in the defenceless privacy of their own homes, seemed to assume that consumers were unable to introspect sufficiently to understand their own motives.

The working class were felt to be the group most vulnerable to the ambitions of advertisers. 'There is one kind of person who seems particularly responsive to advertising: the man or woman who is moving up from one class to another,' Mark Abrams argued in a broadcast in 1956. 'These people – and there are an incredible number in Britain – have to shed their old buying habits and acquire new ones. The class-destroying function of modern advertising is cumulative,' he suggested:

> The initial effect is to encourage people to want to buy consumer goods formerly enjoyed by their social betters. As they achieve this and become more socially mobile, advertising and television provide them with knowledge that enables them to fill their new role.[13]

Indeed the first television commercials seemed to confirm this view of the direct impact of the media on behaviour. Shops almost immediately sold out of the advertised goods, and jubilant market researchers discovered that the public recalled the commercials long after they had first been shown. But this was only a temporary effect.

Indeed later research has shown how complex the relationship between media message and audience behaviour is. The public is not a passive empty box merely waiting to be filled with the injunctions of advertisers. How people react to what they see is determined by their class, age, and the beliefs they already hold. Nor is the public subconscious so easily manipulated as many assumed. As one contemporary market researcher pointed out, surveys which concluded that housewives did not like macaroni which cooked to a wet sticky mass because wet sticky masses aroused sexual guilt in them were not treated with the scepticism they deserved.[14] Some critics reacted cautiously to the power of advertisements: 'I cannot think so poorly of British Fathers', wrote Tom Driberg in the *New Statesman* (20 December 1958), 'as to accept the diagnosis proclaimed by one ITV advertiser last week, "Every daddy *deserves* a Brylcreem home dispenser for Christmas".' However, most critics believed it to be overwhelming. Advertising executives were credited with a power they would have been delighted to exercise, but which was far in excess of their rather unpredictable performance.

This overestimation of the manipulative power of the media influenced the Pilkington Report. It led to a crude view of the public – particularly the working-class audience – as passive, gullible, and misled.

### Real and false wants

The Pilkington Report dismissed expressed public preferences as unreal and the product of commercial manipulation. A Labour Party report on advertising written in 1962 developed some of these arguments. Advertising, it claimed, could not be defended by the assertion that it merely reflected the times. For, in order to make advertisements, individuals were obliged to make decisions. In so far as advertisers determined what was shown they were responsible for their choices. Some people, the report argued, had claimed that advertising 'reinforces attitudes of materialism, only too prevalent in society'. In the committee's opinion,

This charge is probably the opposite of the truth: for it seems more likely that what advertising does is to interfere with the appreciation of material goods to the extent that it substitutes for a genuine assessment or perception of their qualities, vague sentiments and fantasies.

The choices that were expressed under these conditions were consequently not 'real'.

The Pilkington Report's assessment of commercial television depended on a similar view of the exploitation of working-class false consciousness for profit. The argument was based on two premises. First, that the public's expressed choice was not a real one because it had not been offered the entire range of possible options from which to choose. It made its choice of television programmes from a culture already limited by the imperatives of profit. Second, the public was in itself limited: the choices it made were deformed by the inadequacies of its education, wealth, and leisure. The working class has, of course, been particularly damaged in these ways.

The report's attitude towards cultural choice was particularly clear in its discussion of entertainment. ITV defended itself by arguing that its programmes were popular. Pilkington replied that

to give the public what it wants is a misleading phrase ... it has the appearance of an appeal to democratic principle, but the appearance is deceptive. It is in fact patronizing and arrogant, in that it claims to know what the public is but defines it as no more than the mass audience, and it claims to know what it wants, but limits its choice to the average of experience.

The commercial companies suggested that there was no need to consider entertainment as it was so unimportant. However, for Pilkington, the individual programme was analogous to the text for the literary critic. As such it was as essential to judge 'trivial entertainment' as more serious programmes. Pilkington found most entertainment programmes unsatisfactory.

However, as Crosland pointed out, it was patronizing and perhaps unwise to dismiss expressed public wants as irrelevant. He argued that the range of newspapers and television programmes was 'still considerable, certainly wide enough to offer genuine comparison'. Indeed most people, for most of the time, chose the escapist, the diverting, or the trivial. Policy should not ignore these needs, but should also seek to encourage minority interests.

The Pilkington Committee's fears that the public was passive led it to consider audience preferences as little more than the expression of commercial manipulation. Consequently the report became insensitive to public taste. Indeed it endorsed the BBC's popular music policy when this was clearly out of touch with what people wanted to hear, as the success of the pirate stations soon demonstrated.

### Entertainment, politics, and advertising

The Pilkington Committee was romantically committed to a concept of folk culture. Its emphasis on the importance of the 'authenticity' of cultural products meant that many other considerations were ignored. For instance television entertainment programmes often implicitly supported particular political values. Yet the report's emphasis on the cultural purposes of programmes has meant that long-term political consequences have rarely been discussed. In addition the report depended on a series of misleading images about the nature of working-class life and culture which affected its tone and distorted its recommendations. Often Pilkington seemed perilously close to despising what was popular and entertaining, and approving only that which was rigorous and demanding.

This was unfortunate, because the report's identification of programmes as the central focus for any assessment of broadcasting is crucial. Moreover, its recognition of the structural effects of advertising on the quality of programmes is original and shrewd, and still pertinent a generation later. In addition, attempts by Pilkington to mitigate the impact of advertising by giving the third channel to the BBC, and by strengthening the power of the ITA over the companies were important factors in improving the commercial service. In particular, the report, which had been wonderfully orchestrated by Sir Hugh Greene, also gave the BBC the *élan* and confidence which were the basis for its most exciting expansion in the 1960s.[15] For the first time, the Corporation attempted to make broadcasting something like a quality popular newspaper. This is perhaps the most challenging model for a national broadcasting service.

# Notes

1. Sir Hugh Greene, 'The future of broadcasting in Britain', Granada Guildhall Lecture (1972), p. 24.
2. M. Pinto Duschinsky, 'Bread and circuses: the Conservatives in office 1951–64' in V. Bogdanor and R. Skidelsky (eds), *The Age of Affluence* (Harmondsworth, Penguin, 1970), p. 55.
3. C. A. R. Crosland, 'The mass media', *Encounter* (November 1962).
4. R. Hoggart, *The Uses of Literacy* (London, Chatto & Windus, 1957), p. 16.
5. B. Jackson and D. Marsden, *Education and the Working Class* (London, Routledge & Kegan Paul, 1962), p. 223.
6. P. Wilmott and M. D. Young, *Family and Class in a London Suburb* (London, Routledge & Kegan Paul, 1960), p. 129.
7. N. Annan, 'Love among the moralists', *Encounter* (February 1960), p. 37.
8. F. R. Leavis, *The Common Pursuit* (London, Chatto & Windus, 1952), p. 192.
9. R. Williams, *Communications*, revised edn (London, Chatto & Windus, 1966), p. 10.
10. Fougasse (pseud. C. K. Bird), *The Changing Face of Britain* (London, Methuen, 1950), p. 15.
11. V. Packard, *The Hidden Persuaders* (Harlow, Longman, 1957), p. 259.
12. F. R. Leavis and D. Thompson, *Culture and Environment* (London, Chatto & Windus, 1953), p. 48.
13. M. Abrams, 'Advertising', *Listener* (15 December 1956), p. 1,089.
14. M. Abrams, 'Motivation research', *Advertising Quarterly* (November 1959), p. 311.
15. See M. Tracey, *A Variety of Lives: The Biography of Sir Hugh Greene* (London, Bodley Head, 1983).

# How the audience is made

Commercial television produces audiences not programmes. Advertisers, in purchasing a few seconds of television time, are actually buying viewers by the thousand. The price they pay is determined by the number of people who can be expected to be watching when their advert is shown. Hence advertisers regard programmes merely as the means by which audiences are delivered to them. The sequence of programmes in any evening, week, or season reflects the quest of commercial customers to get the largest or most appropriate public they can. 'The spot is the packaging,' wrote a market researcher in *Advertising Quarterly*, 'the product inside the package is an audience.' These are the realities which help to determine what kinds of programmes are made, when they are shown, and who sees them.

Commercial television was introduced in the 1950s because it was claimed that it would bring competition into broadcasting, and make the service more responsive to popular demands. The Independent Television channel was supposed to break the narrow élitism of the BBC's cultural policy. Indeed once it had been given a regional structure, it was also supposed to promote provincial culture and oppose the BBC's metropolitan bias. Finally, commercial television, its advocates claimed, would be less vulnerable to political pressure. Unlike the BBC, its finances would be independent of official control.

Few of these hopes were fully realized. The allocation of the franchise areas in which commercial companies were given the right to broadcast was designed to produce a system in which four (later five) of the largest and wealthiest regions made most of the programmes for the national network. The smaller companies made most of their programmes for local consumption; only a few of their products were to be shown nationally.

The first commitment of the commercial companies was to make a profit. Hence they were concerned to minimize the financial risks involved in making programmes. The smaller regions, whose audiences were not so attractive to advertisers, could not afford to invest in expensive programmes unless they were guaranteed a national showing. Similarly the large networking companies needed to be able to show their programmes in every region in order to cover their costs. Consequently decisions about which programmes were to be networked became centralized.

This centralization was formally established when the Independent Television Companies Association (ITCA) was set up in 1971. This decided which programmes were to be shown on the national network, and how much the smaller companies had to pay towards the costs of the major programme producers. The smaller companies, however, complained that the ITCA was dominated by the five major programme networking companies.

## The Independent Broadcasting Authority

Yet British 'commercial' television was not merely a product of market forces. If financial pressures were the only influence, the programme-makers' aim would always be simply to reach the largest possible audience for the smallest amount of money.

In practice this would have meant a diet of American soap opera, variety shows, filmed series, quizzes, and chat shows, based on proven formulae, endlessly repeated. 'Minority' programming would cater only for groups defined primarily in terms of their consumption patterns. Current affairs would have been confined to news bulletins, and advertising spots would have been longer, more frequent, and more intrusive. In addition, even more programmes would have been bought from abroad – particularly the USA – and fewer programmes made in Britain or directed at a British audience. Commercial broadcasting did not develop all of these features in Britain, because of the framework of public regulations within which it was obliged to operate. Nevertheless, these pressures remain the dominant features of a commercial service.

The Independent Broadcasting Authority (IBA) exerted a major influence on commercial television. The powers of the authority were widened following the report of the Pilkington Committee (1962), but the most public job of the IBA was to license television franchises, and to reallocate these periodically. The authority was also required to ensure 'balanced programming', 'due impartiality' in the treatment of controversial issues, and a high quality in programme production as a whole. To enforce its recommendations the IBA could determine the broadcasting schedule, prohibit the transmission of particular programmes, or even revoke the franchises of offending companies. In addition, the IBA monitored and controlled the amount, timing, quality, and content of advertisements shown on commercial television.

When commercial television started in Britain in 1956, there was little idea of what form it would take. 'All we had in the beginning', recalled Sir Robert Fraser, the first Director General of the ITA, 'was an Act of Parliament, an untested authority, a little prefab in a mews by Marble Arch, and a bit of money we had to pay back.'[1] Nevertheless, the new controlling authority quickly developed a commitment to public service. Thus in the first months of broadcasting, as Sir Kenneth Clark recalled, the IBA threatened to make current affairs programmes itself to counter a proposal to abandon such programmes by the commercial companies. The determination of the authority to maintain minority programming in peak viewing time was similarly demonstrated when it came to reallocate franchises. In 1967 some of the original commercial franchises were not renewed. As a result, programme scheduling on ITV had an important though secondary goal, that of securing the reallocation of franchises. 'Advertisers understand that current affairs and news programming is a condition of the survival of the commercial television companies,' wrote one advertising executive recently. 'It is no good complaining about them.'[2]

The IBA also intervened in the construction of the programme schedules, requiring that one-third of all material broadcast by commercial TV companies should be 'serious non-fiction, sensibly distributed over the week as a whole in appropriate times'.[3] Without this intervention, a service which many people relied on as their primary source of news might have carried very little current affairs coverage.

The IBA's intervention also helped to maintain a wider range of cultural output than would otherwise have been the case. In 1956 'serious programming' accounted for 19 per cent of the companies' schedules. This rose to 26 per cent in 1959, and 36 per cent in 1965, a proportion which was maintained. However, official figures were inflated by the growing number of programmes which were classed as serious documentaries, but which were on entertainment topics (such as Alan Whicker's series). In addition, there were an increasing number of consumer-oriented programmes (on cars, holidays, and gardening, for example), some of which scarcely qualified for their official classification as 'serious and informative'. Nevertheless, programming on commercial television undoubtedly included more serious material because of the IBA's influence, and many of these programmes gained large audiences. The most striking example was ITN's News at Ten, which was enormously innovative in its presentation of news and which regularly featured in the IBA's yearly 'Top Twenty' popularity ratings.

The Authority was also important in maintaining the standards of entertainment on commercial television. It limited the number of cheap American imports and the frequency with which programmes were repeated. The IBA also assisted the smaller regional companies by charging the more profitable regions a higher rent for the use of the television transmitter which it owned, and thus made them subsidize the rental of the poorer companies. In addition, through its position on the committee which decided which programmes were shown on the central network, it ensured that some of the regional programmes were shown nationally.

## Regions and audiences

The Television Act, 1954, had not specified how commercial television was to be organized. It had laid down no principles to guide the allocation of contracts. When commercial companies began to submit proposals to the ITA they suggested many different ways of dividing commercial broadcasting between competitors. Thus some contractors offered to provide particular kinds of programmes, all the light entertainment, or all the music; others proposed to make the programmes for particular times of day, 6–9 pm or 3–7 pm. However, Sir Robert Fraser decided that the system should be based on regional companies. In this way, he intended to prohibit the growth of a centralized monopoly based on London, and to 'give real creative power to the regions'.

Yet the principle of the federal structure seemed threatened from the very start. During the first two years commercial television was so expensive to run, reached such a small audience, and was so unprofitable that there was little interest in the smaller regions. It was during this disastrous period that Roy Thomson acquired

Scottish Television at a very low cost. It was only when this company overcame its initial difficulties that the other regional services began to develop. Thomson, famous for having said that owning a commercial station was like having a licence to print money, soon made Scottish Television profitable. 'I like monopolies', he said, 'when I operate them.'[4]

Regional commercial broadcasting has survived, but in a form that makes sense in economic rather than cultural terms. Thus Tyneside and Teesside have little in common apart from geographical proximity. Yet they were given a combined television station because only the joint purchasing power of their audience was sufficient to make up a marketing unit. A more serious case was that of Harlech Television, supposedly a Welsh station, but actually required, for commercial reasons, to cater for a large English audience as well. It has been argued that some regional television stations, for example Border Television, may have strengthened, or even created, a sense of local identity. However, most of the regions have no real justification except in marketing terms. Apart from London, television regions have not even approximately coincided with local authority areas. This has at least inhibited the discussions of local political issues.

The regionalism of commercial television appears less firmly rooted in popular needs than in the convenience of the market.

Indeed the most important response by the commercial companies to regional differences within Britain was to identify and sell distinctive characteristics in marketing terms. 'Granada has the skilled workers: surveys prove it!' read an advertisement in a 1959 trade magazine. 'Westward where women cook,' read another in *Campaign* in 1962. In 1979 Southern Television was pointing out that its A, B, and C1 housewives cook, and have time to be *femmes fatales* afterwards (*Campaign*, 5 July 1979). The differences between the habits and tastes of the various regional audiences became an essential feature of sales campaigns. In 1962 one writer claimed that 'The television regions made scientific selling more possible than ever before.'[5] New products could be launched in regions where they were most likely to be successful, and advertising campaigns could be tested by pilot surveys in a particular region. In the same way regional television meant that additional advertising pressure could be applied in any area where sales were slumping. The most important effect of the regional structure of commercial television was to change the marketing map of Britain.

## Franchises and owners

The cost of developing commercial television was at first so great that franchises had to be given to syndicates which had the resources to undertake the necessary capital investment. This brought an important change in the kind of people who controlled broadcasting. Hitherto in the BBC responsibility had been vested in professional administrators whose social origins, training, and attitudes reflected the 'public service' philosophy of the Corporation. Independent television introduced a new type of executive, business-oriented and entrepreneurial, geared to the commercial criteria of the sponsors. Thus while the BBC was directed by Sir William Haley, who had started his career as a journalist on the *Manchester Guardian*, and who became editor of *The Times*, Associated Television's first director was Lew Grade, a show business and theatre impresario.

By the time that the franchises were reallocated in 1967, commercial television had become highly profitable, and consequently the justification for allowing it to be controlled by speculative capital no longer held good. Indeed such vast profits had been made from a publicly owned asset, the air waves, that the prospect of their reallocation created a flood of applications. There was an atmosphere reminiscent of Klondyke gold fever. Many of Britain's major corporations financed 'prospecting' companies composed of theatre managers and entertainment moguls spiced with a few peers or eminent members of the BBC. Although changes were made in the new franchises, instead of widening control, the redistribution, in practice, merely consolidated the power of the great media empires.

This pattern continued until the 1980s, the government encouraged the oligopolistic tendencies of the broadcasting industry itself – in the name, of course, of freedom. If one contradiction of this period was that free market rhetoric was accompanied by interventionist practice, another was that talk about a media market-place was accompanied by its virtual eradication. Technological change, with its requirement of long-term investment and large-scale capitalization, produced a bureaucratic jungle of profit-taking conglomerates which now own huge shares in all the media which the public consumes.

By 1990 the small number of corporate owners were not competitive in a sense that could be conceivably expected to produce an improved product: but their financial rivalry undoubtedly imposed pressure to produce a cheaper one. That meant an almost inevitable lowering of standards: it is cheaper to buy in agency news than to send a reporter to the scene, it is cheaper to buy in internationalized soap opera than to make your own drama, and so on.

The victims of media concentration are variety, creativity, and quality: while the future proliferation of broadcasting channels in the hands of a shrinking band of operators is certain to make matters worse.

## Ownership and control of television

However, the control of commercial television companies could not simply be equated with ownership. Those who actually produced commercial television programmes enjoyed a significant degree of autonomy. But, most important of all, the pressure of market forces imposed powerful constraints on what could and could not be broadcast. These operated irrespective of the formal ownership of commercial television. In a study of the way in which programming is determined in the USA, Wolf argued that ownership does not explain the differences in programming between stations. 'It may be', he suggested,

> that those who saw such influences labored under a false analogy between the small town newspaper editor who may have shaped every word in his paper, and the television corporate executive, who according to the analogy controlled what was shown on the air.[6]

Indeed he concluded that in the USA the more diversely owned companies were less likely to take the networked programmes, particularly the news, current affairs, and documentaries, and more likely to replace them with old movies, old quiz shows, or old operas. They did this simply because of the pressure to attract the largest possible audience.

The economic and social organization of broadcasting is very different in Britain from that which Wolf describes in the USA. There, the more diversely owned companies were the smaller and less successful ones, which were more vulnerable to market pressures. Nevertheless, the inevitable pursuit of profit within a commercial system must have some similar consequences for the programming decisions which can be made in any country. Market forces operate as a continual limiting pressure on any commercial broadcasting system. Yet it is also clear that more socially diverse patterns of ownership could be an important factor in creating the conditions for more adventurous and varied programming.

## The audience that advertisers want

The most important pressure on television scheduling and programme-making is that of advertising expenditure. If television companies sell audiences, what kinds of audiences do advertisers want, and how are they packaged to attract sales? Indeed how does the real purpose of producing audiences for advertisers affect the apparent purpose of producing programmes for audience consumption?

The American system of programme sponsorship, in which advertisers pay for individual programmes, was rejected when commercial television started in Britain on the grounds that it gave advertisers direct power over programme content. Instead only 'spot advertising' was permitted. Advertisers could buy time slots only between or within programmes. At first, advertisements were limited to an average of six minutes per hour. Later, when it was seen that this led to an accumulation of advertisements in peak viewing times, which had above average amounts of advertising, it was decided to limit advertisements to no more than seven minutes in any one hour.

The decision to adopt restricted spot advertising had been hailed as a victory for public service broadcasting. 'The prohibition of sponsorship was an inspiration of the Television Act', declared Fraser, 'since it established the supremacy of the editorial principle.'[7] Spot advertisements were compared with newspaper advertising. They were seen as guaranteeing the independence of programme-making from the influence of advertisers: no rational person, it was argued, supposes that what newspapers publish in their editorial columns is determined by advertisers. Spot advertising would protect the editorial integrity of commercial television. 'Advertising will be an asset worn as a bright feather in the cap of free TV,' Sir Robert Fraser wrote, 'not as a soiled choker around the throat.'

Sponsorship of all programmes except news and current events was finally permitted in 1988. However, on the ITV channels there continued to be a fierce battle about who could sponsor what – and considerable anxiety about potential commercial abuses of the authority of some programmes. Such niceties, of course, were not part of the satellite broadcasting regime. Here there were few restrictions on sponsorship and far more advertising was allowed. Indeed, one of the oddities of the intense political campaigns of the period was the BBC's failure to point out, in its own defence, that while the British public enjoys some adverts, repeated research has shown how irritating they find too many. Historically, the British public has enjoyed and endured less advertising per hour of viewing than any American or European viewer. They may be appalled when the full commercial diet of adverts reaches them in the mid-1990s.

However, during the 1980s, powerful interests complained to a sympathetic government that the ITV companies and the IBA were using their monopoly too effectively. Between 1981 and 1989, the advertising revenue of commercial television doubled in real terms, fierce competition for air time raised the price of advertising, and increased the discretionary power of companies. Thus there was great commercial pressure to create alternative sources of air time: cable, satellite, and a competing commercial terrestrial Channel 5 were proposed, in order to bring down advertising costs. Advertisers believed they had a strong interest in breaking the economic basis of the existing ITV companies' cultural power.

Hostile critics argued that the IBA had become too closely identified with the ITV companies. A new body, the Independent Television Commission, was set up to preside over the 'deregulated' commercial system, but with far more limited powers than its predecessor. Thus franchises for ITV (which after 1993 will be known as Channel 3) were to be auctioned. Auction winners will then hold franchises for ten years. The ITC will have little authority to demand changes in programme performance. Thus while the Commission is obliged to ensure that public sensibilities about images of sex or violence are not offended, it has limited authority with which to perform the more critical task of ensuring that good programmes continue to be made and shown by companies desperately trying to recoup the huge capital expense of their franchise bid.

The IBA's powers, however imperfectly exercised, stemmed from its economic sanctions within the ITV system. Since its inception, the ITC has developed imperialist ambitions. Clearly it would like to use its controls to bring traditional public service criteria to bear on the enlarged commercial sector. Indeed, the

ITC is probably responsible for a profound metaphorical change in ministers' language. In 1986 guarantees of programme quality were to be a 'factor' in allowing applicants to enter the auction for Channel 3 franchises; by 1987 they were being discussed as a 'hurdle'; they rose during 1988 to a 'fence'; and by 1990 they were confidently described as 'a barrier to the inferior'. But metaphors alone will not control commercial pressures to maximize profits, and it remains to be seen how far the ITC can realize its ambitions.

Yet many of the pressures exercised by advertisers on the content of programmes have remained remarkably consistent since the start of commercial broadcasting. The extent to which they affect programmes and schedules depends on the ways in which they are balanced and regulated.

Thus it is clear that even spot advertising does not preclude advertisers from calculating how the editorial content of programmes affects the impact of their advertising message. 'After all', as an advertiser wrote as early as the 1950s, 'an advert is seen as part of a programme' (*Campaign*, 14 March 1956). Advertisers have prior knowledge of programme schedules which are published each quarter in advance of their transmission. They thus know the general character, if not the precise content, of the programmes with which their advertisements will be shown. There have been cases in which advertisers have avoided certain programmes on the grounds that their content is unlikely to dispose viewers to respond favourably to their advertisements. This is most common when the content of the programme clashes directly with the appeal of the advertisement (for example airlines have withdrawn advertisements from appearing in documentaries about air disasters). However, it has also occurred when a programme is thought to have associations that detract from the broad image of the product.

In contrast, some programmes may be preferred because they provide an editorial environment conducive to a favourable response to particular advertisements, or because their prestige is thought likely to enhance that of the product or service advertised within them. Thus advertisements for newspapers appear near the news, and those for beer are often placed close to programmes on sport. The very fact that such intuitive judgements associated with programme content can influence how advertising time is bought must affect the decisions made by the companies about scheduling.

This pressure is, however, marginal. The main consideration of advertisers is not the programme environment of their advertisements, but the size and composition of the audience that the programmes will attract. Advertisers buy television time in two ways. Sometimes they buy a 'guaranteed audience', that is a fixed number of viewers. This may be made up of many small sections of the audience and spread over a whole range of programmes with low ratings. Alternatively it may be composed of a few large audiences during peak viewing times. In either case, what is bought is viewers. However, advertisers may also purchase particular advertising slots. The television companies may oblige advertisers to buy a 'package' of slots, composed of some of the peak viewing times the advertisers want, but combining other less attractive slots. Nevertheless, advertisers are more in control of the kinds of audiences their campaign will reach if they buy specific slots.

Commercial television rapidly became the leading advertising medium for mass consumer products and so was under pressure to put on programmes with an appeal to a mass audience. However, many patrons of commercial television have sought to reach particular constituents within the mass market, in particular women (who are the key decision-makers in many consumer purchases) and young people. Since commercial television derives its revenue from advertisers and not from viewers, the commercial system is thus led towards catering for these groups. Thus the success of commercial breakfast time television depends almost entirely on its capacity to attract an audience rich in consuming housewives.

Market research can provide a detailed breakdown of the audience profile for particular programmes. A massive investment is made in monitoring how many and what categories of people watch each programme. This research assists the television companies to produce programmes that will deliver the required audiences, and to provide them with an accurate measurement of the audiences which they have sold.

Research also helps advertisers predict from advance programme schedules what audiences they can expect to buy. This research takes the form of continuous monitoring of a representative sample of viewers, providing detailed figures for programme viewing analysed in terms of the size and class of audience. It is supplemented by additional surveys that analyse other more specialized characteristics of viewers. This research has established that certain types of programmes – soap operas, situation comedies, the main news bulletin, and variety programmes – have a generalized appeal that transcends differences in social class, age, and sex. It also reveals that other types of programmes – most notably political documentary programmes and serious drama – are not watched as much by women and young people. The results have shown a remarkable stability of viewing preferences since the introduction of commercial television. There has been little change in the pattern of mass viewing, apart from a small shift away from variety and sport.

The way in which commercial television time is sold generates pressure for quantity of audience, rather than quality of audience appreciation. It has even been suggested that some advertisers prefer television programmes not to be too involving, for fear of detracting from the impact of their advertisements. This has been called the 'Let's-give-the-public-the-shows-they-*least*-like-so-they'll-watch-the-ads' theory.[8] The widespread use of video-recording machines has made research into the effects of advertising even more complex. Little is yet known about the extent to which the public uses this technology to avoid adverts. But it is assumed that 'spooling on' is a common habit.

The IBA attempted to offset the pressure for quantity of audience by circulating the companies with a weekly Audience Appreciation Index, which monitors the quality of audience response to individual programmes. This index has consistently shown that information programmes are more highly appreciated than those concerned with entertainment. There seems to be an inverse relationship between audience size and audience enjoyment.

However, it is doubtful whether this intervention had much influence on the time-buying decisions of advertisers, as no connection has yet been established between the audience's enjoyment or involvement in programmes, and their responsiveness to advertisements shown at the same time. The implications of audience appreciation research have only lately begun to be developed. It has been argued that within the two categories of information and entertainment programmes, those with large audiences tend to have higher appreciation scores than those with small audiences. Indeed some market researchers have come up with the less than remarkable finding that the more demanding a programme is, the better it has to be before people will watch it.[9]

The pressure on commercial television to maximize audiences naturally leads to a preference for 'entertainment' as opposed to 'serious' programmes. Within the broad category of entertainment there is a preference for programmes which have previously demonstrated their appeal to women and young people. Hence there is a bias against showing sport at some times of the day, as it mainly appeals to men. Commercial pressures have also led programme-makers to emphasize the personal and human interest aspects of documentary stories. Thus structural social problems are treated in the form of individual case studies. This kind of programme reaches a wider audience, particularly amongst women, than other documentary styles. The prominence given to certain types of programmes on commercial television is a direct consequence of the pressures generated by advertising for the production of certain types of audiences.

Advertising also generates a strong pressure for the television companies to produce predictable and regular audiences, as well as to maximize them. While the ratings for any particular programme may be hard to predict, because they depend so much on factors outside the control of any commercial company (in particular what the BBC is showing), viewing patterns over a year, as well as the categories and sequences of programmes, have been easy to predict.

Advertisers rely on programme schedules to produce the audiences which they pay for. This has encouraged attempts to use the sequence of programmes in order to manipulate the size of an audience over an evening. Consequently programmes with a broad audience appeal are shown early in the evening, in an attempt to capture viewing families for a particular channel for the rest of the night's programmes. Scheduling attempts to expand and consolidate the mass audience throughout the evening. It is this pressure which leads to the screening of 'minority' information programmes outside peak viewing times, and to the 'twinning' of BBC and ITV schedules for current affairs programmes. By doing this the companies may minimize choice, but they also minimize the loss of audience from programmes that get low ratings. In addition, current events programmes are thus seen by a far larger general audience than would otherwise be the case.

The proliferation of broadcasting channels which was so enthusiastically advocated by advertisers will, however, make many of these calculations increasingly insecure. Already the use of videos makes the assessment of impact of adverts more difficult. Accelerating fragmentation of the great national audiences previously enjoyed by the duopoly may provide, as some have argued, many new specialized concentrations of consumers, or it may provide nothing more than smaller, more unpredictable audiences. Indeed, the most enthusiastic advocates of 'deregulation', the advertisers, have begun to be anxious about the future effectiveness of advertising on TV at all.

Whatever happens, there is evidence that these commercial attempts to manipulate the audience are only partly successful. Goodhardt has argued that most families watch television sporadically. The 'inheritance factor' (or the likelihood of watching the programme that comes next) seems effective for only one programme, not the whole evening's viewing. Nor would it seem that people become loyal to a channel because they are addicts of particular series. Out of forty serials screened in the spring of one year only 54 per cent of people who saw one episode of any serial also saw the next. Most of the people watching the second half of the story were different from those who had seen its beginning.[10]

Nevertheless, the commercial companies necessarily continue to try and maximize their audiences. The pursuit of the largest possible audience is not in itself harmful. But if it is narrowly interpreted, it may lead to schedules that are cautious, conservative, and very rarely break established patterns.

The needs of all advertisers using commercial television are not the same. Some have sought more specialized groups within the mass audience, and the financial significance of this kind of advertising is growing. This is indicated by the growth of corporate advertising, in which giant companies are merely concerned to project an image of their activities rather than any specific product. In addition, there has been an increase in consumer durables and motor advertising. These categories have risen as a proportion of total television advertising expenditure from 7 per cent in 1968 to 30 per cent in 1988.[11] This has been accompanied by a fall in food, drink, and household advertising directed at the mass market. Furthermore, there has been a growing tendency even amongst mass-market-oriented advertisers towards directing their campaigns at particular segments of the market.

The impact of this shift, however, has been muted by the difficulties involved in translating the aims of marketing strategies into buying television time. There have been fashions in market research which determine how the audience is offered to the advertiser. In the 1950s and 1960s motivational research was dominant. 'Beecham's buyers are a little more likely to strive, and are a little more neurotic,' stressed an Associated Rediffusion survey in 1962. 'Compared, that is with Aspro, Anadin and

Disprin buyers, however, they are noticeably more extrovert.'
Increasingly, though, there was a trend towards pilot studies of
particular products and towards attempts to segment target
markets with a fine precision.

However, despite attempts (by Leo Burnett and the British
Bureau of Market Research in particular) to develop 'psycho-
graphic' profiles of television viewers, such methods remain impres-
sionistic. No satisfactory method has been developed that enables
advertising men to select time slots in a way that allows them to
reach the types of personalities believed to be particularly susceptible to their advertising campaigns. Consequently commercial
television companies have not been obliged to cater for particular
groups (at least those defined by psychological categories) to any
great extent.

Advertisers have been most interested in reaching 'light viewers',
who are like the 'floating' voters in election studies. The success
of a campaign may depend on the proportion of light viewers,
who might not otherwise know about the product, that it can
reach. For a time, light viewers were regarded as being particularly selective in their television watching habits. This was
partly because a large proportion of light viewers were middle
class, and were believed to be discriminating.

However, this view has now been challenged. Goodhardt has
suggested that light viewers do not tend to watch particular types
of programmes, nor do they prefer low-rating minority programmes. They tend to be as unselective as heavy viewers, but
merely watch less television. Hence support of minority programmes does not seem to be a means of reaching the light
viewer. On the contrary, it appears that advertising on high-rating
programmes represents the most efficient way of reaching light
viewers. Another study suggests, furthermore, that the pursuit of
light viewers is in itself misguided. What matters is not how
many advertisements of a particular product are seen, but how
many in relation to the number of advertisements of a competing
product.[12] The light viewer sees less than the heavy viewer of *all*
the competing products on television. It may, therefore, be better
to reach him or her through other advertising media.

A further problem for the advertiser is that neither minority
programmes nor particular *genres* of programmes can be relied on
to deliver specialized audiences. Goodhardt's analysis of the house-
wife audience for twenty different categories of programme showed
that only Westerns are positively sought out by any viewers.

Westerns were the only kind of programme with a slightly higher
level of 'duplication viewing' – that is the likelihood of a viewer
seeing more than one programme within this category – than could
be explained by channel loyalty or overall rating figures. Most
people, Goodhardt's work suggests, see further programmes of any
particular *genre* only because they prefer one channel, or because
the programme has a high rating, not because they are specifically
interested in its content. 'People who watched one arts programme', according to Goodhardt, 'had no more tendency to see
another arts programme than to see, say, a Western or a religious
programme, or a sports programme with a comparable weighting.'

This characterization of television audiences as indiscriminate
and promiscuous in their viewing habits has been challenged. Sue
Stoessel argued that the results of Goodhardt's research were
misleading because they aggregated behaviour over several weeks.
This obscured major changes in viewing behaviour from week to
week. It is only by examining these detailed changes in viewing
behaviour, she suggested, that preferences for individual programmes could be revealed. An analysis of changes in viewing
figures over successive weeks reveals the effects of positive
choice and preference, as does an analysis that distinguishes
between audience behaviour in the different regions. In London,
she argued, light viewers are more heavily concentrated amongst
the audiences of some specific programme types. There are
significant groups of viewers, at least in the London area, who do
choose to watch programmes because of their content.[13]

This debate is likely to continue. The apparent failure of different categories of programmes to divide audiences into conveniently
specialized groups has important implications. It may reduce the
potential for commercial television to create new patterns of
programmes. A low-rating current affairs programme has little to
offer advertisers if it delivers, not a discriminating élite (like a
'quality' national newspaper), but large numbers of heavy viewers
so hypnotized that they cannot even summon the energy to switch
off the ballet or Third World poverty programme offered at the
margins of peak viewing times.

Indeed the audiences for specialized programmes do not necessarily share other characteristics which would make them marketable packages for sale to advertisers. A shared interest in Westerns
does not imply, for instance, a propensity to trade in a new car
each year or a tendency to be a young couple setting up home for
the first time. On the other hand, if Stoessel is correct, there is a

market for élite and quality advertising in television, but it may not be most efficiently reached through this medium.

Indeed in so far as advertising has promoted minority programming hitherto, it has tended to be in a form that produces groups of viewers which are marketable. Travel programmes, and those about cars and cooking, have all developed partly because they cater for audiences with a shared interest in buying certain sorts of products. The advertising for cable and satellite television depend on the development of this commodity-based 'narrowcasting'. The greater choice of channels will, it is suggested, offer advertisers more refined groups of audience interest. However, those with less material interests in common have been, and will continue to be, less favoured.[14]

## Public regulation and the public interest

In the past the IBA played an important role in mitigating the adverse effects of advertising on broadcasting. Nevertheless, at times the Authority was passive. For example it was reluctant to ensure that companies adhered to the programme policies on which they won franchises. It was difficult for the Authority to be more active in its surveillance, partly because its statutory obligations were imprecise in many areas. However, political realities limited its power more fundamentally. The commercial television lobby is highly organized and politically effective. It employs public relations officers and cultivates an able group of MPs. In addition, many newspapers are sympathetic to the commercial television lobby. Its interests are also protected by an extensive network of contacts based on the interlocking directorships linking commercial television companies to other banking and industrial organizations. In contrast, the IBA was less effectively organized as a political lobby, and its powers of supervision – which were inevitably the product of political negotiation – were consequently constrained. Finally, the IBA would be 'punished' for its interventions into schedules or programme decisions. Thus, having been required to present more balanced programming over Christmas, the companies could retaliate by showing programmes which got only very low ratings.

However, the aims of the IBA were furthered by the presence of the BBC as a 'public service' institution, committed to broad social and political objectives rather than to the maximization of profit. There was in Britain a great convergence between public and commercial broadcasting in which the two systems influenced each other.

In addition, for much of its history commercial television was in a strong bargaining position in relation to advertisers. ITV was able in the past to resist some advertising pressure precisely because it was in a seller's market. Companies sold advertising time in ways which reduced the pressures to maximize audiences. The high profits and monopolistic position of commercial television created an environment in which the IBA could be more effective.

## Swinging sixties and sober seventies

In the 1960s and 1970s television came of age. Since 1970 there has been a remarkable revolution not in the technology but in the content of broadcasting. In this period, television rapidly developed its own forms – in the treatment of politics, interviews, documentaries, and plays – which were quite different from the earlier styles of radio or film. During the 1960s television humour began to take the form of satirizing itself – an indication of how widely the conventions of the new medium had been publicly absorbed.

This was partly a product of a more generally liberal mood, which made a wider range of possibilities available for broadcasters. After Pilkington, the BBC became a more adventurous organization. At the same time, the independent television companies became more secure, because more profitable. By the 1960s, moreover, television had taken over from the cinema a mass working-class audience.

In many ways the vast size of the television audience has posed problems for the medium. There is a continual pressure to screen programmes that will attract the highest audiences and cause offence to the fewest numbers of viewers. Yet the attempt to reach a big audience while meeting 'public service' criteria has been a creative tension.

Some commentators, like Stuart Hood, Michael Tracey, Anthony Smith, and even Sir Hugh Greene, have seen the period since the early 1970s as one of increasing caution in television. Not only has the reporting of the troubles in Northern Ireland provided many problems for the broadcasting institutions, but also the BBC and ITV have become more vulnerable to government threats over a broad range of issues.

## Channel 4, minorities, and money

Yet it was a reinterpretation of the public service principle which produced Channel 4. The ideas behind the creation of this new channel were a product of the tensions identified during television's most creative and expansionist years. But it was also influenced by the political problems of the period. However, by the time the station opened there had been a change not only in the general economic climate but also more damagingly, in the conditions of competition for television audiences.

Channel 4 'publishes' programmes made by independent production companies. It does not make any programmes of its own, although it does commission them. Originally it was financed by the existing commercial companies who supplied much of its material. As it did not sell its own advertising time it was somewhat removed from the direct pressures experienced by the rest of the commercial sector. The 1990 Broadcasting Act changed this: the channel is now to be made more vulnerable to advertisers' interests. However, it is still obliged to screen programmes for the various 'minority' interests that are not well served elsewhere in the television system.

The minority-based rationale of Channel 4 had a number of origins. Perhaps the most important was the experience of even the most distinguished and 'marketable' producers and directors that it was impossible to work, in Britain, outside the BBC or ITV companies.[15] Those who wanted to make programmes that did not conveniently fit into the patterns of viewing developed by the duopoly, or those who simply wanted a greater control over their own material, found it difficult to raise the necessary finance or find buyers for what they made. It was argued that there evidently were audiences within the mass of viewers with more distinctive tastes and needs, but the existing channels allowed these consumers little opportunity to demonstrate their preferences. A new pattern of differently organized production companies, liberated from the limitations of the ITV or BBC systems, would be able to find and develop these more specialized audiences. Therefore any innovation in the television service ought to make it possible for 'independent' producers to explore the interests of these minorities.

It was also strongly argued that television had failed to reflect Britain's contemporary cultural diversity. Reformers emphasized the needs of the various Black and Asian communities, as well as those of minorities like the young and the old, for programmes which dealt with their concerns and ways of life. Any new service, it was suggested, should produce material for these social and ethnic minorities.

Finally, some market researchers believed that the blunt instrument of television advertising could, by the 1980s, be refined. A new channel could offer programme incentives that attracted discriminating 'minorities' of selective television viewers and could sell them the things they had particular interests in. For the first time television would be able to deliver higher concentrations of the more affluent consumers that advertisers wanted.

The logic of Channel 4 looked appealingly neat. It would offer greater freedom of choice, and serve minorities neglected elsewhere. Unfortunately the minorities that producers, social reformers, and advertisers were interested in were somewhat different.

Channel 4 represents an important (and perhaps the last) reinterpretation of the public service role of broadcasting. In this version, the freedom of creative individuals to risk making the programmes they want to make is seen as the guarantor of public good. It was a Labour government which decided to back the new channel (although a Conservative one presided over its birth). Labour support was based on a feeling that the political consensus developed by the existing broadcasting services was too restrictive. Consequently the channel was given the opportunity to create new conventions for dealing with controversial and political issues. It is not obliged to balance views within a programme, but only over the whole schedule and over time. It can, therefore, broadcast more clearly partisan material.

However, the channel's capacity to innovate depends on the politics of money. The only ultimate defence Channel 4 has for its new style and new programmes is their ability to attract advertising revenue. By the 1980s the Conservative government was using the success of Channel 4 to attack public service broadcasting, by demanding that greater numbers of programmes should be produced by 'independent' companies. Yet Channel 4's innovations had been completely dependent on the development of public service ideals.

In the late 1980s both the BBC and ITV companies were obliged to take an increasing proportion of their programmes from the 'independent' sector; by 1993 this is expected to account for 25 per cent of their output. This has led to the emergence of some culturally important and commercially successful companies – and of innovative programmes. 'The Media Show', the astutely topical series on Stalin, and many others were made by production companies outside the duopoly. However, whether such companies are actually independent, except in the formal sense, is dubious. A recent survey by the London Business School showed that they were all financially precarious with low profit margins.[16] People set up independent television companies because they want to make programmes – not because they want to make money. The study also showed how completely dependent these companies were on the patronage of the established channels. The new satellite companies were, as yet, hardly interested in their quality products.

The limitations of commercial broadcasting are largely the result of the economic pressures to which it is exposed. That British commercial television has been in some ways superior to others is due to the public service traditions and institutions that have so far determined its development. Nevertheless, the implications of a comment by Sidney Bernstein, the television industrialist, should always be borne in mind. 'Commercial television is a very unusual business,' he said, '. . . you don't necessarily make more money if you provide a better product.'

Yet the market and the audience for television programmes is altering dramatically under the impact of a whole series of technological changes. Whether the advantage of increased variety will be enough to offset the dilution of resources remains to be seen. Indeed this period may yet be regarded, in television terms, as a lost golden age.

## Notes

1. Sir Robert Fraser, *ITA Notes* (October 1970).
2. P. Todd, 'Scarcity of TV time!', *Campaign* (26 January 1979).
3. *IBA Annual Report* (1978).
4. R. Thomson, *Contrast: Television Quarterly* (winter 1961), p. 107.
5. Associated Rediffusion, 'Cold and flu remedies', *Market Profiles*, 6 (1962).
6. F. Wolf, *Television Programming for News and Current Affairs* (New York, Praeger, 1972).
7. Sir Robert Fraser, *ITA Notes* (January 1970).
8. C.E. Setlow, 'TV Rating, there just might be a better way', *New York Times* (31 December 1978).
9. T. P. Barwise, A. S. C. Ehrenberg, and G. J. Goodhardt, 'Audience appreciation and audience size', *Journal of the Market Research Society*, 21, 4 (October 1979), p. 269.

10. G. J. Goodhardt, A. S. C. Ehrenberg, and M. A. Collins, *The Television Audience: Patterns of Viewing* (Farnborough, Saxon House, 1975).

11. Tables of advertising expenditure in *Admap*, No. 2, 1988.

12. A. Roberts and S. Prentice, 'Reaching light TV viewers', *Admap* (March 1979).

13. S. Stoessel, reply to Roberts and Price, 'The real weight of light viewers', *Admap* (June 1979), p. 277.

14. M. Johnson, 'Narrow-casting – problems and opportunities', *Admap* (June 1983).

15. See S. Lambert, *Channel 4* (London, British Film Institute, 1982).

16. *Independent Television Production: Finance and Dependency*, London Business School Report (Dec. 1989).

# *The information society: video, cable, and satellite*

Video, cable, and satellite technologies, and their attendant communication novelties – ways of transmitting entertainment, words, pictures, data, voices, and other services in huge variety, over vast distances, at ferocious speeds – have been discussed in such extravagant terms, and introduced with such little debate, that their wider social and economic implications have been ignored. We are in danger of seeing emerging patterns as necessary, or even more dangerously as technologically determined, and accepting the consequences fatalistically.

Sixty-year-old audience habits are changing. But the impact will go far beyond what people do with their leisure. The information revolution affects what goods the nation produces, and Britain's survival as an industrial nation. It will affect how the national image is developed and our political priorities both at home and abroad. Many believe that current developments will accelerate the emergence of global cultures and economies, at the inevitable expense of national identities. The various new broadcasting (and 'narrowcasting') technologies are closely related to problems of opportunities produced by the increased capacity of modern communications to monitor, collect, store, and sell information about all the processes in society, but in particular to record the actions and preferences of every individual citizen.

There is also the likelihood of direct impact on political behaviour and institutions. Every previous innovation in communications, from the emergence of the mass circulation press through the development of radio and television, has profoundly altered not only how politics is understood in societies, but the nature of political negotiation itself. Such an immense set of changes as are now occurring will inevitably revolutionize political expectations, behaviour, and institutions. We, as yet, can only speculate about the likely effects: but they will clearly influence the future of democracy.

Experts have been divided between the neophiliacs and the cultural pessimists. Neophiliacs write of the disappearance of class (by which they mean that traditional types of work will be replaced), the disappearance of workplaces (as the work-bench is supplanted by the home computer terminal), and the eventual relocation of the production process to the developing world as the management of information (about production and consumption) becomes the key commodity in the technologically advanced economies.

Such predictions seem premature. Neophiliac arguments bring to mind an earlier debate about the arrival of the 'post-industrial' society. Comments by Anthony Smith and John Howkins belong to the same tradition as Daniel Bell and Alain Touraine,[1] who argued that the expansion of the service sector, increasing expenditure on the production of knowledge, and ever larger investment in research, together with changes in the technologies of production and leisure, were creating a new social order. *Plus ça change:* as Krishan Kumar has argued, similar developments become apparent early in the history of industrialization, and do not represent any qualitative change.[2] Many of the neophiliac predictions of future patterns are based on naive extrapolation from current trends, and ignore the idiosyncrasies of historical development.

The pessimists, on the other hand, see changes in mass commercial culture as a subversion of 'standards'. In the discussion of broadcasting technologies, the new 'cultural' pessimists, such as Nick Garnham and Richard Collins, join hands with the 'industrial' pessimists like Henry Braverman,[3] who share concern over the impact of computer and information technology on employment. Thus broadcasting becomes the fulcrum of a wider social and economic upheaval. The pessimists see little evidence for the emergence of new cultural patterns and much evidence for the irreparable damage to old ones.

In practice this 'revolution' represents the continued industrialization of the service sector. New technology performs old tasks more efficiently: in particular the sorting, correlating, and ordering of information in bureaucracies. Many of the current problems in broadcasting policy concern the next stage: the domestication of the computer.

Indeed from both sides of the British political spectrum great, and perhaps unrealistic, hopes of industrial revival have been pinned on the exploitation of new communications technologies, particularly of cabling. On the one hand those on the left have argued that the provision of a national cable network is similar to the laying down of the other great service infrastructures of industrial society: water, rail, and road. It has been persuasively suggested that markets for goods and products increasingly exist not in physical space, but between those who are in contact via the networks of cable communication. Goods and services can be produced anywhere and to any specification with the complex exchange of data provided by cable facilities. It has thus been argued that the state should invest in a massive programme of cable provision in order to provoke a dramatic new regional and national economic revival. Advocates of this strategy point to the success of recent French governments' attempts to modernize communications. Using the notion of 'informatics', the French have argued that access to, and understanding of, the most modern means of communication is part of being a contemporary citizen. Consequently, French policy makers have suggested that the state must educate the people and provide the means for the fullest possible public participation in this technology. The French government has also based its policy on the belief that the industrial possibilities of cable systems can only be developed if the technology is in the widest possible use. Thus in France there has been a typically 'dirigiste' development of cable and telephone services by the state, according to a clearly laid-down plan, with little room for liberal 'free market' principles.

However, those on the right have also been concerned to develop cable and computer services. Indeed, much recent broadcasting policy, as we shall see, has been directed at encouraging private, individual investment in cable and when this failed, it hoped to substitute satellite service. There has been no commitment in Britain during the 1980s to an extension of citizenship rights or knowledge. Indeed, the direction of broadcasting policy which it might be argued should always be considered along with education, has been to exaggerate the divisions between groups of people. British broadcasting policy was previously based on the concept that it had to make the same rights available to all audiences, citizens, voters. This is no longer the case. Increasingly policy is based on one right only: the 'right' to pay for extra services. Thus Conservative policy makers, while also emphasizing the importance of cable communication, have been prepared to reduce the access to information and services of most citizens in the belief that development could most efficiently be led by those who can pay for it.

There is also a key economic problem (a reflection of distinct patterns within the British economy) which influences policy decision within this area. The Conservative government during the 1980s, although it wished to encourage the private acquisition of cable television (so that the public would at least become a potential market for the other goods and services cable might offer), was also concerned, rather belatedly, with the provision of advanced communications to the financial and banking sector. So dominating now is this interest in the British economy, that fulfilling its urgent needs for greatly expanded new information services became an overriding but unstated priority within government policy. Many of the decisions in this area were thus, covertly, determined by the perceived interests – or by the pressure exerted – by this sector of the economy.

The effects of the development of increasingly interdependent technologies of telephone, data, and broadcasting services have all, in England, been used to diminish the democratic access to these services. Thus, traditionally, heavy (business) telephone users subsidized lighter (domestic) subscribers' long-distance calls, which tended to be shorter and less frequent. As the costs of communication became an ever-more important item in commercial budgets, the pressure to reduce costs and to influence policy increased. Domestic subscribers now subsidize businesses. Broadcasting policy too, has been determined more by concerns to protect, for instance, the domestic electronics industry, than by an interest in the political and cultural obligations of broadcasting.

The problems posed by this kind of development are common to all countries. Few countries, however, have such strong broadcasting traditions as Britain, or such determined neophiliacs at the helm. When the Conservative government came to power in 1979 an official ideology of non-interference in the market was buttressed by a vigorously neophiliac view of information technology. A key Cabinet Information Technology Advisory Panel (ITAP), including experts in electronics and industrialists but nobody with any broadcasting experience, concluded that industrial revival was to be stimulated by 'cabling up' the nation. The necessary conditions for this economic miracle (a large proportion of homes linked to high-quality cable networks), it was argued, would best be created by providing an alluring range of television channels for the eager public. That these would inevitably offer a consistent diet of old films, sport, American soap opera, and light entertainment was regarded as incidental.

In 1982 the committee urged the adoption, not of North American models, but of the most sophisticated cabling system that would permit households to receive and use several hundred different channels. Thus the nation would be lured into the new infrastructure by stealth: having paid for cabling in order to receive more entertainment, television users would find themselves linked conveniently to a variety of multipurpose networks with opportunities for computerized shopping, working, and learning. 'It is as if', one commentator has suggested, 'the Roman Senate had sanctioned, without debate, the proposition that improvements to the supply system of the Roman legions should first be introduced by speeding up the chariots in the hippodrome.'[4]

So solid was the expectation of a virtually insatiable appetite for television, that official calculations have been based on the assumption that the technological leap forward could be accomplished without support from public funds. Britain is the only country in Europe which expects the entire capital cost of laying a cable system to be paid for by the sellers and consumers of the recycled programmes and films. In West Germany, France, and Japan, state investment in a comprehensive cable system has become a major, and expanding, element in the annual budgets.

Apart from the problem of initial finance, there are other grounds for wondering whether neophiliac hopes are not premature. Thus in the USA – where the success of cable had been seen as providing a model for Britain – the cable revolution seems to be failing, or at least stabilizing. In the last half of the 1980s more cable stations closed in the USA than opened.

Indeed 'popular' programmes aimed at mass audiences, supposedly the basis of cable expansion, have failed to find adequate markets. Where cable has succeeded commercially there has been a price. In 1989 the most profitable American cable network offered its viewers an unremitting 'choice' of five movies repeated 179 times – all within the space of six months.[5] The pressure of real or supposed mass taste has been inexorable: even in Manhattan, with its sophisticated viewers, CBS was forced to end the brief experiment of providing one quality station.

Indeed, in Britain there is an additional factor, more powerful than in the USA: video. The proportion of video-owning homes is already twice as great in Britain as in the USA and, despite the recession, video ownership continues to grow faster in Britain than in any other European country. By 1990 approximately one family in three possessed a video: a development not taken into account by official calculations at the beginning of the decade. Satellite television services, launched with immense publicity, have so far done little but lose their backers money. Unconstrained by the public service obligations, the first, Sky Television, owned by Rupert Murdoch, provided four channels pitched relentlessly at the supposedly popular tabloid market: a children's channel which offered nothing but cartoons, a film channel (for which, in addition to a dish, you have to buy a decoder), and two other channels showing replicas of exhausted formula programmes, mostly presented by familiar formula faces. This service so far has hardly added to the 'choice' the sovereign consumer could indulge in. In 1990 a competing, allegedly 'quality' service, British Satellite Broadcasting, began to operate, but soon merged with Sky. So far, cable and satellite services have been unsuccessful here. In addition to these satellite services there are plans to launch a new commercially financed Channel 5 later in the 1990s, while it is also proposed to auction Channel 3 (Independent Television) companies to the highest bidders. These changes mean that the behaviour of the television audience as well as television production values and finance are bound to alter. Nevertheless, there is evidence that in the battle for public viewing hours, these new 'viewing' opportunities face a more formidable task than had been expected. Certainly in Britain there had been no cable 'revolution' by the start of the 1990s,[6] nor was a post-industrial society much in evidence.

## The end of public service broadcasting?

One reason for believing that cable and satellite – with or without government intervention – will not reveal an as yet untapped demand for a wider range of television programmes is that since 1979, and following an American trend, the number of 'live' television viewing hours per British inhabitant has actually declined. Between 1980 and 1989, there was a decline of nearly two and three-quarter hours, with particularly large reductions during bank holidays when ratings are normally highest. Christmas 1982 saw a staggering 22 per cent average drop since the previous December, with barely any recovery a year later. During the

1980s Christmas viewing figures never recovered their previous levels.

As we have seen, part of the reason is the parallel growth of video: time previously spent on current programmes is now devoted to video cassettes. (Significantly, 75 per cent of video usage is for BBC and ITV programmes at non-networked times, a statistic that throws doubt on the thesis that there exists a pent-up demand for material not presently available on existing channels.) Since, however, the downward trend preceded the take-off of video, other factors – boredom with the medium for example – were presumably also involved. If so, pressure on the networks may not cease when video ownership reaches saturation point.

Certainly satellite, cable, and video in combination will accelerate the decline in audiences for existing networks: more viewing opportunities will mean fewer viewing hours. One change is a move away from 'family viewing'. Early evidence from satellite television showed that rather than arguing about what to watch together, family members were separating to watch different programmes. Thus apparently while fathers watch sport (in the sitting room), mothers are now relegated to viewing soap operas in the kitchen, while teenagers consume pop video channels in their bedrooms.[7] The take-up of satellite and video demonstrates that the public is willing to spend a higher proportion of its disposable income on entertainment, but this fragmentation of the audience has barely been explored by advertisers and its wider social implications have, as yet, hardly been considered. As ratings fall, something will have to be sacrificed in the bitter struggle for survival. An early victim is almost bound to be public service broadcasting, not of course just the BBC, but the whole range of quality programmes and perhaps even the possibility of innovative broadcasting. The public service ideal depends for its realization on funding. In the new hyper-competitive climate, funds will be in short supply. Indeed, by the beginning of 1990, even advertisers, who had been so clamorous in their demands for more advertising time, were becoming anxious about the likely *over-supply* of time in the 1990s. As the White Paper on the Development of Cable Systems and Services pointed out, one hour of home-grown documentary could cost £20,000. By contrast, an hour of American soap opera could be bought for as little as £2,000. We may expect, therefore, a trend similar to that in the cinema of the 1940s and 1950s: fewer programmes made in Britain, and an ever-expanding proportion of imports.

Here Thatcherite market liberalism will have particularly disastrous effects. With the abolition of quotas for foreign programmes, there will be little to restrain cable and satellite stations from importing much and commissioning little. With no rules to enforce a balanced diet of programming, the new stations will naturally turn, like their American counterparts, to the lowest common denominator of pop, chat, soap, and sport. Perhaps the wider range of viewing which satellite, cable, and video will provide will lead to an imaginative exercise by viewers of 'freedom of choice'. Existing evidence, however, suggests the opposite: audiences will not have the freedom to consume anything other than an even greater concentration of pop, chat, soap, and sport than now.

If this analysis is correct, a shift of power within the networks is likely to follow. Where broadcasting is protected through subsidy, monopoly, or legislative requirements, producers can be given their head; where commercial pressures necessitate a heavy reliance on imported package deals and low-budget formula programming, producers will be reduced, in effect, to corporation men: executives carrying out company policy. With less money available, making fewer 'original' programmes, initiative will be at a low premium. In particular, there will be little incentive to make programmes about British subjects, political, social, or cultural, purely for domestic consumption. Indeed it is ironic that much of the privately commissioned research for the satellite stations has shown just how wise the consumer is, and how badly served by neo-liberal belief in market forces. The public has found the existing satellite services repetitive, limited, and based on all too familiar styles and formats. They also recognize that the BBC, ITV, and Channel 4 offer a greater variety of programmes, and of course they still continue to watch far more of these than the satellite stations, albeit increasingly to their own schedules on video.

Some people do, of course, have specialist interests which satellite channels may serve. Nevertheless, so far the public remains more discriminating as a body of viewers than as newspaper readers. Yet, it seems oblivious to the likely disappearance of the services it values most. Under the current regime, market forces, not consumer interests, will come to determine programme making.

There is a further danger or at least an area of uncertainty. Until recently the economics of television was determined by an invariable: people bought television sets to watch programmes put out by the networks. The relationship between programme-maker and viewer, through the medium of a single-purpose instrument, and the role of public policy in regulating programme content, were based on this simple truth. The old relationship is rapidly weakening and soon will hold no more. Watching 'live' programmes ('live' in the sense of received from the ether) is already only one of the purposes of a television set. When it becomes increasingly common to use television not only for video, but also to make hotel reservations, monitor electricity consumption, and place bets, 'live' viewing may become a comparatively minor factor in the calculations of those who buy, sell, and produce television sets, with inevitable consequences for those who make programmes as well. At the same time, the obligations of public policy become more difficult to define when the 'content' of television is no longer so evidently a single 'cultural' product.

## Politics and new technology

There will also be consequences for politicians and political parties. Broadcasting, and especially television, has been a vehicle of political integration, establishing what Denis McQuail has called the 'common coin of values, ideas, information and cultural expression'. Arguably television has set the political agenda: ordering public priorities and arousing public concern for good or ill.

Key to this process has been the national audience. The power of television has been based to a considerable degree on lack of choice: almost any nationally networked programme is certain to count its viewers in millions. Cable, video, and satellite have increased the range of 'choice' without necessarily increasing variety or quality of subject matter (perhaps, as has been argued, reducing it). A larger number of highly competitive commercial stations will fragment: the national audience will vanish. Here we should avoid premature judgement. Such a change might have beneficial results or bad ones. Given the centrality of broadcasting to modern politics, however, it is virtually certain to alter the nature of the political game. Already some effects of increased 'choice' on political culture can be seen. The recent proliferation of quality newspapers (although it has so far improved the standard of them all), has nevertheless lessened the impact of each. In the long run, this diminished authority will undoubtedly influence both the role and the standard of these newspapers. A similar process is taking place with television: the fragmentation of the national audience means that the significance of any one programme or channel may be greatly reduced in the future. It is important not to be confused here. It is not being suggested that the media will have less effect: just that their effects will be different.

These effects, however, remain speculative. Will national coverage be reduced in importance relative to local issues? Such a development might be positive. It might provide citizens with greater awareness of what affects them directly, and give more scope to local campaigns and pressure groups. On the other hand, the example of the existing local press gives little ground for optimism. Lack of initiative, cost, and the fear of writs have discouraged the vast majority of newspapers, including the big-circulation regional dailies, from acting as anything more than publishing houses for politicians' handouts.

If, therefore, a diversity of local television stations produces an increase in local political reporting, the benefits remain uncertain. What does seem likely is that the present 'privileged' status of news and documentary, which has been a prominent feature of public service television, will be eroded. Political coverage at least held its own as inter-channel competition increased: between 1956 and 1976 the time devoted to politics quadrupled on average. Channel 4 increased the variety and range of political programmes. But this trend began to be reversed in the late 1980s. During the 1987 general election, campaign coverage on the two major channels (BBC1 and ITV) was restricted to little more than a series of interviews with leading personalities: examination of campaign issues was relegated to BBC2 and Channel 4. Cable stations with small budgets and instant commercial targets are scarcely likely to widen the range or deepen the level of discussion. Indeed for all its failings, television coverage of politics in Britain has been serious and sustained. As Scannell has argued, broadcast politics has widened access to political processes. Indeed it may be argued that political programmes with the depth of reporting of the quality press (though with its definition of the limits of political discussion) are served out, for largely historical reasons to do with the public service origins of the BBC, to a Sun-and-Star-buying public. It seems likely that the commercial pressures of cable and video may ensure that, instead of deriving political information from television, large numbers of people will, in effect, be deprived of any reliable political information at all.

Even if there is no reduction in the time allotted to current
affairs and documentary programmes, cuts in budgeting are bound
to have a deleterious effect on quality and, in particular, originality.
National and international reporting all too easily becomes a
collaborative exposure of the viewpoint of the spokesman for a
particular interest, provided that the interest in question has Establishment approval. The reason is cost as much as bias: investigative
journalism, digging beneath the surface and asking uncomfortable
questions, involves more time, resources, and financial risk. Here
competitive pressures are likely to be the enemy of imagination,
professionalism, and above all, that which is controversial and
radical.

## Censorship

Some political effects of the new technology are speculative.
Others are already frighteningly apparent. One development in
the second category is the closing of doors which many had
regarded as permanently unlocked: the reimposition of censorship
in a new form, made the more dangerous because it is occurring
in response to a public mood that owes much to fear of the new
technology itself.

While dismantling 'public service' standards in broadcasting,
and claiming to liberalize and free the system, the Thatcher
government in fact presided over the introduction of an accumulation of supervisory quangos to control videos, satellite, cable, and
terrestrial broadcasting. All are concerned primarily with the
exclusion of 'offensive' imagery. The movement started with the
video recording bill. This introduced a system of bureaucratic
pre-censorship of a kind unprecedented since Oliver Cromwell's
'licences of the press'. Ostensibly it was concerned with pornographic and violent home videos dubbed by the press as 'video
nasties'. In practice the implications have been wider. The legislation set aside the earlier 'interpretative' view of screen images,
held by the British Board of Film Censors (BBFC). This view was
concerned with evaluating the meaning and intention of scenes,
and emphasized that it was in context that any given act had to be
judged. This view was replaced, in effect, with an index of
prohibited acts. All videos have to be submitted to the board, and
may be liable for censorship if they contain any material which
deals with 'human sexual activity', 'images of human sexual
organs' (potentially even if the films are made as part of training

programmes for medical staff), or 'mutilation, torture, or other acts of gross violence' (like scenes of war and sporting events). Defence on the grounds of artistic or literary merit has been increasingly set aside.

Film censorship has a long and in some respects a hilarious history. The BBFC, however, had come to see its role as one of 'leading public taste as much as curbing it'. More recently, its board of nominees, for the first time directly appointed by the Home Office, have tended to apply specific standards of permissible and non-permissible sexual or violent acts. This style of regulation has come increasingly to determine considerations in all the other regulatory bodies. Thus there has been a decisive shift in public policy towards the media: away from the encouragement of the good towards the deletion of what government-appointed committees regard with distaste.[8]

Perhaps the availability of unpleasant material to the public, especially young people, will be reduced by all these supervisory bodies. However, the history of censorship in general reveals little evidence of a beneficial effect on public morality or mental health. But whatever the possible benefits, the dangers of illiberalism are manifest: thus, for example, coverage of wars, deliberately and rightly intended to shock, may well be restricted.

## Conclusion

Should we, therefore, side firmly with the cultural pessimists against the neophiliacs? The answer is that much depends on the behaviour of broadcasters and programme-makers and, more particularly, governments, in the face of technological advance. Both neophiliacs and cultural pessimists emphasize the *power* of new technologies. Machines and inventions are not inherently powerful, nor is the use to which they are put inevitable. While the new technology brings with it many dangers, as well as many opportunities, its impact will depend crucially on how it is managed. We should be able to make the choice, but in order for the choice to be a real one there will have to be changes in policy – and soon.

## Notes

1. See, for example, A. Smith 'The fading of an industrial age', in J. Curran, H. Smith, and P. Wingate (eds) *Impacts and Influences*, (London, Routledge, 1987).

2. K. Kumar, *Prophecy and Progress* (Harmondsworth, Penguin, 1978).

3. See, for example, R. Collins, N. Garnham and G. Locksley, *The Economics of Television* (London, Croom Helm, 1987).

4. *Parliamentary Information Review*, No. 2, Cable and Services (June 1988).

5. S. Hearst, 'The development of cable systems and services', *Political Quarterly* (Autumn 1983) p. 388.

6. In societies where the state was prepared to take a more 'dirigiste' role, like France and West Germany, the revolution was more advanced. See, for instance, G. Nowell Smith, *The European Experience* (London, British Film Institute, 1989); or Nick Costello, 'Telecommunication and cable in France, America and the UK', *European Commission Special Paper*, No. 3 (Jan. 1990).

7. MORI/NOP survey, *Satellite Television and Family Viewing* (Jan. 1990).

8. For an expansion of this see J. Seaton, 'Down with Aunt Tabitha: a modest media proposal', in B. Pimlott, A. Wright and T. Flower (eds), *The Alternative: Politics for a Change* (London, W. H. Allen, 1990).

# Part III

## *Theories of the media*

# 15

## The sociology of the mass media

Do newspapers, broadcasting, and mass entertainment matter? Do they change society or merely reflect the changes created by others? This chapter will argue that the media do have an independent influence, but not in the sense that has often been assumed. The power of the press and broadcasting is not necessarily greatest when the political involvement in the media is most apparent.

One (determinist) tradition has stressed the relationship of the media with the governing class. It has argued that the media play an important part in modern society. Another (empirical or pluralist) school has looked at the response of audiences to the media, and has concluded that other social pressures overrule any independent effect. These two approaches have been regarded as opposed to one another. In fact, as we will show, they are not incompatible.

### The Frankfurt School and the power of the press and broadcasting

'Propaganda, propaganda, propaganda,' Hitler said after the unsuccessful Munich *putsch* in 1923. 'All that matters is propaganda.' Although the Nazis emphasized the importance of oratory and public meetings, they were also fascinated by the emergence of the new technologies of mass communication in the USA and Britain. In particular they saw radio and film as a means of extending the influence of demagogy.

When Hitler came to power in 1933, a group of German intellectuals opposed to the new regime – and seeking to explain the fascist success – turned their attention to the role of the media. The so-called 'Frankfurt School' of writers argued that the roots of the fascist or 'authoritarian' personality were to be found in the nature of the family. However, in explaining what made a population potentially fascist, or why there was no revolt before the Nazi regime began to use widespread force, they also saw the press, radio, films, and even comics and popular music as reinforcing these early influences. The new mass media strengthened the habits and attitudes which made people susceptible to fascist arguments.

## The USA, mass culture, and Europeans

Many members of the Frankfurt School became refugees and settled in the USA, for which they developed a profound distaste. Disorientated and homesick they reacted against every aspect of the American way of life. They concluded that American mass culture was an irreversible force which was destroying superior European cultural traditions. What was worse, mass culture produced precisely the kinds of personality traits that made the population vulnerable to fascist domination. The Frankfurt writers believed, incorrectly, that the USA was also about to become fascist, as Germany had done before.

However, their reaction to mass culture is better understood as part of a more general European response to the USA. The Frankfurt analysis of the role of the press, films, and later television is very similar to that of the literary critic F. R. Leavis. Broadcasting, Leavis argued in 1932, was 'little more than a means of passive diversion but one that made active recreation, especially active use of the mind, more difficult'. And, in an essay called 'Mass civilization and minority culture', he concluded that 'The prospects of culture, then, are very dark. There is less room for hope, in that a standardized civilization is rapidly enveloping the world.' Many of Leavis's views on the USA during this period had been formed by reading a book by Robert and Helen Lynd called *Middletown*. This described the increasing isolation of individuals, social fragmentation, and the pervasiveness of the profit motive in a typical American town.

Thus the Frankfurt School writers shared with many other European social and literary critics a revulsion against American culture. Much of the work of writers like Marcuse and Adorno on the media was based on a rejection of that which was modern, mass, and American.

### Liberalism and the individual and the emergence of fascism

The Frankfurt critics, both in Germany and later in the USA, were concerned to explain the failure of liberalism, and of the liberal emphasis on freedom of speech, expression, and creativity. Writers like Adorno, Marcuse, and Arendt (although she can only loosely be described as a member of this group) pointed to what they saw as the weakness of these concepts in practice. These ideals, the Frankfurt writers believed, had degenerated into a corrupt and selfish individualism. The mass media had played a major part in this process: manipulating society by vulgarizing its culture. In an essay called 'The end of Utopia', Marcuse wrote, 'Today we have the capacity to turn the world into hell and we are well on the way to doing so.'

According to the Frankfurt School the unique individual personality was being destroyed by society. Adorno wrote in *Prisms* of the illusory importance and autonomy of private life which conceals the fact that it 'drags on only as an appendage of the social process'. The celebration of the home, family, and the individual which characterized liberal thought and bourgeois life in the nineteenth and twentieth centuries was already decayed. 'Nothing proved easier to destroy than the privacy and private morality of people who thought of nothing but safeguarding their private lives,' argued Arendt.[1] Totalitarianism was seen as both a cause of this process, and an effect of it.

The Frankfurt School saw the loss of individuality as the cause of dependence on great mass organizations. This analysis implied that society had returned to a more primitive form of association. The interdependence of highly specialized individuals, or what Durkheim called 'organic solidarity', had been succeeded by a new and barbarous homogeneity. Only a 'mechanical' cohesion was possible, dependent on similarity and standardization. Horkheimer argued that, paradoxically, individuality was impaired by the decline in the impulse for collective action. 'As the ordinary man withdraws from participating in political affairs, society tends to revert to the law of the jungle, which crushes all vestiges of individuality,' he wrote.[2] In this analysis the Frankfurt theorists were claiming that totalitarianism emerged as a result of corrupt social institutions and the decline of liberal principles.

There was also another explanation of the success of fascism, which might be characterized as a paranoid theory of change. In this a stealthy process of substitution occurs. This constitutes a

Gresham's law of culture and personality, in which bad inexorably drives out good.

The mass media are the key agents of this process. They replace real cultural values with their 'look alikes'. This view that the media provide an ersatz inferior culture is an important element in the Frankfurt explanation of totalitarianism, which assumed that many of the changes brought about through the media would be fought if they were recognized. Horkheimer wrote in *The Eclipse of Reason* that

> Just as the slogans of rugged individualism are politically useful to large trusts in society seeking exemption from social control, so in mass culture the rhetoric of individuality, by imposing patterns for collective imitation, subverts the very principle to which it gives lip service.

Adorno, in a book called *The Jargon of Authenticity*, explains how the 'mass media can create an aura which makes the spectator seem to experience a non-existent actuality'. This subversion of values is a process which Hayek (a writer who came to rather different conclusions) also observed. 'To make a totalitarian system function effectively,' he wrote, 'it is not enough that everybody should be forced to work for the same ends. It is essential that people should come to regard them as their own ends.' The easiest way to do this, he argued, was to substitute new meanings for familiar and respected values, like liberty and freedom.

There is a third explanation of the success of totalitarianism in the work of the Frankfurt writers. In this totalitarianism emerges as the inevitable product of capitalism: the final subjugation of every aspect of life to commercial values. 'The individual now reproduces on the deepest level, in his instinctual structure, the values and behaviour patterns that serve to maintain domination,' wrote Marcuse.

Thus the School suggests three competing explanations of the emergence of fascism. The first sees totalitarian success as a consequence of the attrition of institutions. As Lasswell wrote, 'The Nazis came to power because of weak democracy.'[3] The second suggests that formerly vital values were hollowed out, and replaced with deluding substitutes. The third that fascism did not emerge by default but by evolution.[4] But whatever the explanation, the Frankfurt writers were agreed on one point: the new mass media were not merely a tool of totalitarianism, they were a major reason for its existence.

## Entertainment

Above all else (according to the Frankfurt School) radio, film, popular music, and television share an overriding concern to entertain. This was the ultimate form of corruption. Indeed for these writers, 'entertainment' occupies much the same kind of role as self-abuse in pre-Freudian medical literature.

Entertainment promised relief and relaxation but, Rosenberg argued, 'Far from dispelling unrest, all the evidence on hand now suggests that mass culture exacerbates it.' Indeed the atomized individuals of mass society lose their souls to the phantom delights of the film, the soap opera, and the variety show. They fall into a stupor. This apathetic hypnosis Lazarsfeld was to call the 'narcotyzing dysfunction' of exposure to the mass media.

Entertainment thus led to blindness and lunacy. 'It is becoming increasingly plain', wrote Adorno in *The Authoritarian Personality*, 'that people do not behave in such a way as to further their interests, even when it is clear to them what these interests are.' People, it was argued, became insensitive to their own needs.

'The unreal delights and the frenzied fascination' of the mass media prevented them from acting collectively. They became the irrational victims of false wants. Marcuse argued that addiction to the media resulted in an absolute docility: the public had 'been enchanted and transformed into a clientèle by the suppliers of popular culture.' Reisman developed the analogy in *The Lonely Crowd*: 'Glamour in politics, the packaging of the leader, the treatment of the events by the mass media, substitutes for the self-interest of the inner directed man the abandonment to society of the outer directed man.'

## Industrialization and leisure

The Frankfurt School argued that leisure – empty time filled with entertainment – had been industrialized. The production of culture had become standardized and dominated by the profit motive as in other industries. In a mass society leisure was constantly used to induce the appropriate values and motives in the public. The modern media trained the young for consumption. '"The sphere of pleasure" has itself become a sphere of cares,' Reisman argued. Leisure had ceased to be the opposite of work, and had become a preparation for it.

The repetition of the forms of the mass media resembled the

monotony of the assembly line: what Adorno called 'The ever-changing production of what is always the same'. In this process, it was argued, culture is consumed by the process of industrialization. Marcuse pointed at the practice of listening to serious music while doing other things (the phenomenon of 'Bach in the kitchen'). Music presented as 'classic', he suggested, 'comes to life as other than itself'. The fact that modern methods of reproduction have increased the quantity of music, art, and literature available to the public does not mean that culture spreads to the masses; rather that culture is destroyed in order to make entertainment.

'At its worst mass culture threatens not merely to cretinize our taste', argues Rosenberg, 'but to brutalize our senses while paving the way to totalitarianism.' Lazarsfeld and Merton put the case succinctly: 'Economic power seems to have reduced direct exploitation and to have turned to a subtler type of psychological exploitation,' they wrote of the USA in the 1950s. Overt totalitarian force was increasingly obsolescent. Radio, film, and television seemed even more effective than terror in producing compliance.

## Complexity and mass culture

The Frankfurt School argued that although the messages of the media might be simple, explaining them was not. The overt content of any programme, film, or newspaper was merely the basis for interpretation. The mass media appeared to confirm the traditional values of British puritanical middle-class society. The real message they communicated, however, was one of 'adjustment and unreflecting obedience'. It was necessary to analyse not only the content, but also the form of the media and the way in which they were used. 'The trouble with the educated philistine', wrote Arendt, 'was not that he read the classics, but that he did so prompted by the ulterior motive of self-perfection.' Nothing, for the Frankfurt School, was what it seemed. It was always worse.

Their view of the illusion of apparent social relations was part of a developing analysis during the 1940s. Lasswell's *Psychopathology and Politics* had claimed 'that the significance of political opinions is not to be grasped apart from the private motives which they symbolized'. Political motives 'derive their vitality from the displacement of private effects upon public objects'. Later, in a bleak article written in 1941 on 'The garrison state', Lasswell also suggested that although 'instrumental democracy may be in abeyance the media will doubtless continue to purvey the symbols of mystic democracy'.

Indeed capitalist culture was so powerful that it could even use opposition to further its own interests. As Benjamin wrote in *Illuminations*,

> We are confronted with the fact . . . that the bourgeois apparatus of production and publication is capable of assimilating, indeed of propagating an astonishing amount of revolutionary themes without ever seriously putting into question its own continued existence – or that of the class which owns it.

It follows from this that only that culture which was not assimilable and difficult to understand could be the source of genuine opposition.

### Mass society theorists and the power of the media

The concern of Adorno, Arendt, and their colleagues with the direct psychological impact of the new media was in part a product of their experience in Germany. The rise of Hitler encouraged the Frankfurt School to view all mass audiences with suspicion, as though they were indistinguishable in behaviour and malleability from the crowds at a Nazi rally.

These writers also, however, developed another more long-term concept of the power of the media. Marcuse commented in *One Dimensional Man*:

> Objections are made that we greatly overrate the indoctrinating power of the media and that by themselves people would feel and satisfy the needs that are now superimposed upon them. This objection misses the point. The preconditioning does not start with the mass production of radio or TV. The people enter this stage as preconditioned receptacles of long standing. In this more complex view the public do not abdicate rational consideration of their interest blindly. More subtly, the whole basis of rational calculation is undermined.

Nevertheless, even this more complex explanation has a simple goal. 'Ideology for the Frankfurt School works one way,' Swingewood has commented, 'that is from above, seeping into working-class consciousness as an alien and conservative force.' Even leisure had been reduced to an adjunct of capitalism, its sole purpose 'the restoration of the human labour force for labour',[5] while all

human needs had been redirected into 'consumption' – the destructive exhaustion of resources rather than their creative use. As
a consequence the Frankfurt School saw the function of the
media, whether in the long run or more directly, as controlling the
public in the interests of capital.

It is here that the Frankfurt analysis is most vulnerable. What
appears to be a particular account of the media is actually a view
of capitalist institutions in general. Indeed the very strength of the
Frankfurt analysis is dissipated in its generality.

## Pluralism: the role of personal influence on the reaction of the audience to the media

The power of the media, and the pessimistic Frankfurt model of
industrial society, were tested, challenged, and apparently refuted
by American empirical researchers. A series of major surveys
seemed to show that the media had very little influence on popular
opinion.

In an odd way, the small town American gossip came to the
rescue of democracy. Survey findings seemed to prove that people
were not the isolated atomized automatons suggested by mass
society theory. Thus the inhabitants of places which sounded like
the locations for John Ford movies – Eerie County, Decatur,
Elmira, and Rovere – appeared oblivious to, rather than hypnotized
by, the blandishments of media propaganda. Far more important
influences were provided by friends, neighbours, and drinking
companions – whether people were deciding which presidential
candidate to vote for or what brand of cornflakes to have for
breakfast. It was personal contact, not media persuasiveness, that
counted.

Market research methods were used to investigate whether the
press and broadcasting had an effect on public attitudes. However,
the concept of an 'effect' which was used in this research was
very limited. Media messages were compared to 'bullets' and the
only effects evaluated were immediate changes in audience attitudes.

### *Conceptualizing the power of the media*

Nevertheless, empirical research as a whole has at least begun to
question the way in which we understand the effects of the media.
Thus writers on the press and broadcasting have credited the

media with the power to 'influence' or 'persuade' their audience, to 'change attitudes', or even to 'affect behaviour'.

Yet these terms are imprecise and obscure. What is it to persuade or influence? All of the terms which are used to describe what the media do have a behaviourist basis, in which a single and external force – the media – has an impact on a single subject – the person. The empirical studies, in a very limited way, have re-examined these concepts. In a narrow attempt to measure effects they have at least dislodged terms which otherwise have been unquestioned.

The empirical work is inadequate. The theories which underlie our understanding of the media might be revealed more usefully than in an attempt to measure problematic phenomena. Indeed the early survey tradition of the 1940s and 1950s eventually abandoned interest in the media. However, it is possible to discuss the problem of how the power of the media might be conceptualized in examining the empirical work. For, as yet, there is no adequate vocabulary to describe the relationships between the media, individuals, and society.

## Reinforcement

Early surveys seemed to show that the media did not change people's minds. 'Paradoxically campaign propaganda exerted one major effect – by producing no overt effect on voting behaviour at all – if by the latter "effect" we naïvely mean a change in vote,' wrote Lazarsfeld in 1944. In fact the media confirmed people in the opinions which they already held. Propaganda marshalled the faithful. It did not 'win over' the wavering or the opposed.

As election campaigns progressed, however, people became more interested in politics, but only because more of them had made up their minds. 'Thus they became both more likely to pay attention', wrote Schramm, 'and less likely to be converted as the campaign goes on.' Previously it had been assumed that 'floating' voters, in their attempt to arrive at a rational decision, would be the most avid consumers of information. But, because they were undecided, they appeared to be uninterested. 'As a group', wrote Trenaman and McQuail later in 1961, 'the "don't knows" were less well informed than consistent voters by as much as 25 per cent . . . showing a general lack of information, and not just an ignorance of particular policies or the policies of one particular

party.' However, even 'reinforcement' was insufficient on its
own.

## Personal influence

The research showed that the audience was not homogeneous, and
society was not a simple, centrally controlled hierarchy. There
were strong defences against people being persuaded in spite of
themselves. Further, some members of the audience had a role in
the persuasion of others. Ideas, it was argued, 'flow from radio
and print *to* the opinion leaders, and *from* them to the less active
sections of the population'.[6]

The power which personal contact exercised over people's
views was examined by Katz and Lazarsfeld in a study of women
'opinion leaders'. The study, done in the late 1940s, seemed to
show that some individuals of high social status had little effect
on other people's views, while some of low status were important
opinion leaders. Personal influence 'intervened' between the
message of the media and its reception by the public. Consequently
it impeded any attempt at mass indoctrination by the media. What
could be more satisfactory than to find that in a democracy wealth
and power do not buy opinion?

It was also argued that opinion leaders were not a narrow élite.
The same study showed that a high proportion of women were
exercising influence over others in matters of marketing, fashion,
movies, and politics. Moreover, the diffusion patterns of influence
and the characteristics of opinion leadership were different for
each area.

Thus it was concluded that the media had little or no independent
effect on public opinion. Indeed rather than changing attitudes,
behaviour, or the world it seemed that they merely confirmed the
status quo.

## Findings the researchers ignored

In fact it is possible to look at the findings of these surveys in
another way and draw quite different conclusions. What appears
insignificant when buried in a range of figures dealing with
breakfast cereals and film stars becomes more interesting if taken
on its own. Status and opinion leadership, for example, were not
correlated in most areas, except public affairs. Here high-status
women appeared to exercise considerably more influence than

low-status women. The assumption that consumer behaviour and political behaviour obey the same rules is not supported in these findings. Hence it would be dangerous to take for granted that the media – as opposed to opinion leaders – shape opinions about consuming and opinions about voting in identical ways.

Election surveys of the 1940s and early 1950s are also open to reinterpretation. 'Not every public opinion change involved a personal contact,' Lazarsfeld, Berelson, and Gaudet admit in their study *The People's Choice*. 'Fifty-eight per cent [of the changes not the changers] were made without any remembered personal contact and were very often dependent upon the mass media' (these changes were widely distributed amongst those who changed their views at all). This effect was ignored.[7] It was concluded that the media had little influence. Becker and McCombs have also shown other contradictions in these studies. In the Eerie County survey a high proportion of electors who intended to vote Republican at the start of the campaign but who were exposed to Democrat propaganda switched to Democrat by polling day. Yet this finding was also ignored.

These studies did not show that the media had no effect, although this is what was concluded from them. They showed only that people did not necessarily change their minds because of direct media exposure. The media – as the studies empirically confirmed – raised interest, fixed opinions, and, crucially, informed the electorate. Most of what people knew about campaigns they had learnt from the media.

## Understanding and information

Indeed during this same period, another approach to studying the effect of the media, that of experimental psychology, began to develop a rather different model of media influence from that of the surveys. 'The power of the media to persuade, at least where there is a democratic controversy,' wrote Poole, 'is very much less than is usually assessed, but their power to inform is enormous.' A series of psychological experiments carried out by Hovland during the 1940s examined the effects of films designed to inform American soldiers about the war in Europe. The films had little effect on 'morale' or 'motivation to serve'. Yet after they had seen the films the men talked significantly more about what was happening in Europe, and this knowledge persisted for weeks. 'The hammerlike blows of frenzied oratory', Hovland concluded, 'may produce acquiescence and later recrimination: autonomous decisions made under the cumulative pressure of facts do not exact this price.' The theory which lay behind this 'propaganda of facts', he points out, 'is not far removed from the logic of progressive education'.

These experiments also showed that people were particularly vulnerable to persuasion about subjects of which they had no direct experience. Moreover, the willingness of the public to believe what it is told is precisely related to the degree of trust it has in the source of the message. Since few people have first-hand experience of politics, and broadcasting is regarded as an especially authoritative source, these findings would suggest that the effects of the media on political opinion may be particularly strong.

Hovland later argued that the distinction drawn between his experimental results and those of survey research was misleading. His work showed that between one-third and one-half of the people he tested 'actually changed their views'. Yet the surveys had concluded that communications had little effect on attitudes. Hovland argued that some of these differences could be explained because laboratory studies examined immediate responses to media messages, while the surveys were typically conducted long after exposure. But also, he argued, the laboratory studies 'deliberately try to find some types of issue susceptive to change', while surveys attempted to assess the impact of the media on 'socially significant attitudes which are deeply rooted in prior experience and involving much personal commitment'.[8] That is to say, the surveys had investigated those attitudes least likely to be altered in the short term.

## The active audience

Studies of the purposes for which members of the audience use the media, and the gratification they get from this use, have also emphasized that public response is varied and not homogeneous. Thus McQuail *et al.* have argued that people use the media for diversion (including escape from routine and unpleasant problems); for developing personal relationships (including substitute companionship); for confirming their personal identity; and for keeping themselves informed. It is implied that if people use the media to satisfy different needs they will also interpret and use the same media message in many different ways. Nevertheless, in the case of political communications, the most frequently expressed use of the media is that of surveillance, or using the media to acquire information.

Indeed the findings of the 'uses and gratifications' research are not incompatible with a stronger interpretation of the role of the media. Given the differences in education, work, and leisure opportunities it would be surprising if the audience response to the media was unitary. The problem is rather to integrate evidence about the differences in the quantity of people's media exposure; about variations in popular interpretations of the media; and about differences in the extent of recall, with other evidence about social divisions. Thus Katz asks, 'What needs, if any, are created by routine work on an assembly line and which forms of exposure will satisfy them?' It is also possible to ask whether the use of the media reinforces or ameliorates social differences. In either case, an explanation of variety in media use is an important part of any more adequate explanation of the power of broadcasting and the press.

## Pluralism: the effects of what the audience knows

More recently attempts have been made to understand the effects of the media on knowledge as well as on opinion. Survey research had apparently shown that the media had little effect on attitudes; new evidence seems to show, by contrast, a dramatic impact on the range and depth of perceptions.

### Changes in politics

Underlying these new approaches – and perhaps not unrelated to them – were changes in political behaviour. 'Party allegiance', wrote Blumler, 'which was once the rock of Gibraltar of the reinforcement doctrine of political communications effects has increasingly become its shifting sands.' The class basis of party support was apparently eroding in all the western democracies.

Consequently as the consistent voter became more rare, the nature of the 'floating' volatile voter changed. Previous research had shown floating voters to be an ignorant and apathetic section of the electorate. Recent research provides a different profile: undecided voters are seen, typically, as increasingly likely to be better informed than the majority.

Indeed if class continues to become a less accurate predictor of voting decisions, the media will play a more important role in political choice. By the 1980s television had become the dominating source of election information for nearly all voters. Yet this is the medium which might be expected to have the greatest effect on long-term political allegiances. For as class and social networks become less important as the determining source of political reinforcement, it has been suggested that voters will rely more heavily on information to make up their minds.

Views may become more strongly held because they are reinforced by the media. However views may also wither and die because they receive no public reinforcement. Martin Harrop argues that this negative power of the media – selectively to neglect some ideas – is a critical, and little recognized media effect.[9]

Thus the media have an authoritative relationship with their audience. This is one of dependence and trust and it provides the media with a potentially independent power base in society and one that may have become more powerful recently.

## *Agenda setting*

In addition attempts have been made to discover the effect of the media in determining priorities: how far press, radio, and television coverage could change a sense of which events were more important. On the basis of a study of the emergence of issues during an American presidential campaign, Becker and McCombs argued that such an influence was major, but gradual. There was a distinction, however, between the effects of the press and television. With newspaper influence there was a delayed reaction. 'The newspaper agenda of political issues in June is a predictor of voters' agendas in October,' they claimed. With television the impact was last minute, but immediate. By the end of the campaign, television had become the most important determinant of voters' ideas.

The media's ordering of priorities particularly influenced voters without strong views. Yet television's coverage of politics has now penetrated sections of the electorate who previously were little affected by political communication because they were uninterested. Consequently the agenda setting by the media seems to be becoming more significant to a larger proportion of the electorate.

The media's agenda of issues may be quite different from that of the political parties. As Seymour-Ure has shown, media coverage made a speech on immigration delivered by Enoch Powell to a small audience in a church hall familiar to 86 per cent of the population two days later. Before the speech only 6 per cent of a Gallup Poll sample thought immigration an issue of national importance; afterwards 27 per cent thought it was important, and nearly 70 per cent of the public believed that the government would have to take 'a harder line'. In effect, Seymour-Ure writes, Powell had 'won himself a national constituency, a platform in the media from which to state his views on most subjects with the certainty of having an audience'.

Neither Powell, nor the media, created the race issue in Britain. Nevertheless, argues Seymour-Ure, the publicity surrounding his speech at a crucial moment (during the debate on the controversial Race Relations Bill) pushed immigration to the front of the political stage, a position it has kept ever since.

The political effects of the media on public opinion are complex, and need to be examined in their historical context. The media may exert great influence over one group, but have little impact on the other members of a society. Thus in many recent revolutions, the press and writing – despite close censorship – has been crucial in establishing cultures of opposition to authoritarian regimes amongst the educated classes. This was an essential condition of the success of the liberal revolution in Portugal in 1974. Yet, there, after the revolution, a dramatic change in the political direction of the media (from right to left), between the first and second democratic elections, had no effect on voting behaviour at all.[10] Similar patterns seem to be developing after the Eastern European revolutions of the late 1980s.

The first studies of the effects of the press and broadcasting had undermined earlier assumptions about the power of the media, suggesting that audiences were, after all, free. Anybody, it seemed, could make almost anything out of any message. Yet a re-examination of the evidence has thrown doubts on this view. It has been suggested that the media may not persuade the public directly; nevertheless they affect what people know, and what they think is important.

## Media organizations

Of course, research into public responses to news and information is not the only way of considering the political role of the mass media. Another approach is to look at how news is produced: the

processes of news-gathering, sifting, and editing, and the administration of news and entertainment organizations. The virtue of this
method is that it helps us to understand what pressures shape the
commodity presented to the public. Its limitation is that in considering how rival interests balance one another, there has been a
tendency to ignore the broader problem of those important but
powerless interests which have no influence at all.

## *Making news*

News rooms are always under pressure: the unexpected is always
about to happen, the scoop is only a telephone call away. This is
the professional self-image. However, for journalists (as for
politicians, doctors, and firemen) crises that are frequent enough
develop a pattern: the unexpected becomes the predictable.

Journalists solve these pressures by developing a set of rules.
Tuchman argues that 'the routinely non-routine is constituted in
practical tasks: in work'. Tuchman, however, also suggests that
objectivity is little more than a protective 'strategic ritual', a set
of conventions about the origins and presentation of facts that
allows journalists to defend their selection of newsworthy events
and interpretations. In an extreme form, Tuchman's definition of
news precludes any distinction between relatively good or bad
journalistic practices. Nevertheless, this interpretation highlights
the way in which accuracy is by no means the same thing as
objectivity.

The events that are honoured by being made news are those
that are easy to obtain. They are by no means necessarily the most
significant events which have occurred. In order to get made into
news, events have to happen in places convenient for the news-
gathering agencies, to be of a recognized and acceptable kind,
come from a reliable and predictable source, and fit into journalists'
framework of news values. These rules and habits have become
worldwide and, as Golding and Elliot argue, 'News changes very
little when the individuals that produce it are changed.' Even the
international flow of news is determined not by the importance of
events but by the organization of the news-processing industries.

The popular image of journalists (elaborated in many movies)
as intrepid hunters after hidden truths is hardly realistic. Specialist
reporters in particular are closely involved with, and indeed
dependent upon, their sources. Thus crime reporters identify with
the police, defence correspondents with the services, and

industrial relations experts with the trade unions.[11] But, in addition, journalists, who are better seen as bureaucrats than as buccaneers, begin their work from a stock of plausible, well-defined, and largely unconscious assumptions. Part of their job is to translate untidy reality into neat stories with beginnings, middles, and denouements.

The values which inform the selection of news items usually serve to reinforce conventional opinions and established authority. At the same time, a process of simplification filters out the disturbing or the unexpected. The need of the media to secure instant attention creates a strong prejudice in favour of familiar stories and themes, and a slowness of response when reality breaks the conventions.

## Pseudo-events

Many items of news are not 'events' at all, that is in the sense of occurrences in the real world which take place independently of the media. An important development alongside the mass media has been the growth of organizations, professions, and skills aimed at manipulating the media.

In a pioneering study (*Public Relations and American Democracy,* 1951) J. A. R. Pimlott reviewed attempts to control news and public opinion in the USA. Prompted by his own experience as a civil servant closely involved with the implementation of Labour's post-war programme in Britain, he was concerned with the use of public relations to win support for central planning and social reform – in particular the New Deal. He also considered the dangers which public relations presented. The book takes issue with the '*laissez-faire* school' argument that free competition ensures a fair hearing for both sides of every major issue. In many cases, the author pointed out, it is 'nobody's business to put the other side'. In the early 1930s American unions had complained that because of inadequate resources, they were unable to compete with the publicity of employers. Pimlott felt that there was some justice in the trade union case during the Depression, that 'more than ever before strikes are being won or lost in the newspapers'. His conclusions were pessimistic. It was impossible to control the growth of public relations by government intervention. Nevertheless, newspapers could help 'by transferring some of the energy which they devote to attacks upon government propaganda to attacking the misuse of public relations by private industry'.

Indeed the notion that 'events' compete for attention in the press and broadcasting is misleading. Often the media are desperately anxious to secure enough content (of the kind they want) to fill their space or time.

In this way, much of what is perceived as 'news' is little more than free advertising. 'Not for nothing does the trainee journalist have to sit as part of his qualifying exams a test in how to write a press handout,' writes McBarnett. The local press is particularly vulnerable to pre-digested news. Much of what appears as 'political news' is in fact written by councillors, candidates, and MPs. The same process also determines much of what appears nationally, leading to what Boorstin has called 'pseudo-events' – activities whose only real purpose is to secure and control media coverage.

## Entertainment

What is entertainment? All media industries compete to create it. Even with news and documentaries, the pressure to be 'entertaining' – to hold audiences by being immediately accessible and stimulating – overrides other considerations. A high proportion of media content has no other aim but to amuse, flatter, excite, mystify, or titillate the public and so keep its attention.

Thus Michael Tracey has argued that the most prominent anxiety of producers of political television was not the sensitivity of their relationships with the political élite, but rather the development of an entertainment formula. Discussion programmes were composed as much for dramatic excitement as for political balance. 'Did you see her on women's lib?' he quotes a producer enquiring. 'Marvellous woman. Never stops talking. Liable to throw something.'

Yet just as little 'serious' material is presented without a sugar coating, so too there is nothing – or almost nothing –that can be deemed 'pure' entertainment. Soap opera, comedy, variety, and pop may not be intended to have any effect on the views of their audiences. But, it can be argued, there is scarcely a joke or a lyric that does not reflect a social attitude, and one with political consequences.

Some writers have suggested that entertainment encourages political passivity. Giltin has argued that it often 'provides a legitimation of depoliticized forms of deviance, usually ethnic or sexual, and a delegitimation of the dangerous, the out of bounds, the violent'.[12] The resolution of social problems typically presented in fictional programmes may influence how they come to be seen in the real world.

It is not only the content of the media which may have implications for attitudes but also the form of programmes. Dyer has argued, in his discussion of light entertainment, that the way in which stars are presented, pictures shot, and the studio audience used, may all affect the meaning communicated by programmes. In so far as 'leisure' is seen by programme-makers as being opposed to work, then entertainment 'has to do something about the reality of work, it has to have an attitude towards it'.

## Audiences

It is often argued that the mass media 'reflect' society because they are obliged to please their audiences. Yet many researchers have commented on the apparent remoteness of producers from their potential viewers. 'It is not so much that people don't know what the audience wants,' Alvarado and Buscombe write, 'as that in the actual process of production people were working more to please themselves.'

However, while writers on political broadcasting have seen this ignorance of the audience as a problem – 'the vital missing link', as Tracey calls it – writers on creative and fictional broadcasting have seen it as a safeguard. 'A model of popular television', write Alvarado and Buscombe, 'which sees it either as a cynical manipulation, or a straightforward identity of tastes between producers and audience, would be an over-simplification.'

The demands of the audience do not, then, exert any direct pressure on producers. Producers have only a vague image of those who watch their programmes. Yet they have a clear, if unconscious, notion of who they are actually addressing: well-informed, critical, professional people like themselves.

## Institutional pluralists

One argument has been that television in particular is not so much a player in the political game as the referee: setting the rules and arbitrating between contending forces.

This view of the political role of the media has been expressed most clearly by Anthony Smith. 'Television', he argues, has become the Theatre of Politics in both senses of the term. Like the theatre of classical times its structures combine into a memory system. Its disciplines incorporate the moral norms of politics as these apply at a given moment of history.

Thus the nature of the rules and their application reflect the politics of the time. The decision about whether to interview a terrorist on television, or the choice of 'controversial' topics for discussion, precisely indicates the political mood as it is perceived by producers and editors. Changes in the relationship between 'current affairs', 'comment', and 'news', or what is seen as 'hard fact' determine the manner in which information is presented to the public. In this way the limits of the permissible, the acceptable, and the appropriate constitute a series of snapshots of prevailing attitudes.

These pressures, however, are always seen by these writers as emerging from a free market of influence. Reviewing research into media organization, Blumler has argued that 'Researchers may be near the heart of competition through communication that is waged in a democratic pluralist society.' Burns has suggested that the politics of broadcasting are the politics of accommodation, while Smith, in his book *The Shadow in the Cave*, argued that 'If broadcasting is to be used as a tool for the intelligent exchange of cultural products, political information and controversial disquisition, it needs to be left flexible and left alone.'

Yet 'negotiation' and 'amplification' are inadequate metaphors for a process in which so much power has come to be invested in the message carrier itself. Hirsch and Gordon have argued that commercial pressure has limited the range of opinion expressed in the quality press. 'The picture we suggest of the quality press is a band of opinion occupying the broad centre of British politics from about half way into the moderate left through to the edges of the extreme right.' But broadcasting has usurped the role of the popular press as a supplier of political information to the mass audience, while preserving the same 'consensus band' of opinion as the quality newspapers. Thus the audience of BBC or ITV news includes most readers of the *Mirror* and the *People*: but these programmes' political values (not just their concern with information) are closer to those of *The Times* and the *Observer*.

That the media order events, and discriminate between them, is not in itself evidence of their systematic effect on public understanding. But while some groups can bring powerful pressures to bear on the work that the media do, others can bring none. The market for information is no more free than any other.

## The new determinists: class and market

Another view of the press and broadcasting is that they reinforce and legitimize the present structure. The media, it is argued, distract public attention from real problems by manufacturing events and inflating trivial issues. However, the press and broadcasting, the new British cultural critics have suggested, do not merely express the interests of the dominant class. This is not only because this class does not always have one simple unitary interest, but also because the media at times reflect other interpretations of society.

However, it should be noted that these writers – many of whom have been associated with the Centre for Contemporary Cultural Studies at Birmingham – rarely question the concepts of 'lived experience', culture, struggle, resistance, or social control in their work. These ideas are accepted as self-evident and unproblematic, and used as the basis for explaining other phenomena. This inadequacy limits the work of these writers.[13]

### Ideology

Ideology, writes Stuart Hall, 'entails the proposition that ideas are not self-sufficient, that their roots lie elsewhere'. Indeed while the audience for the media contains most members of society, only a few groups have any control over what the media produce. Hall concludes that they 'reproduce the definition of the powerful, without being in a simple sense in their pay'.

Hall argues that the media do not simply trick their audience: to some extent they must meet its needs. The independence of the media is at times quite genuine. For instance Hall suggests that broadcasting organizations have 'a wide measure of autonomy in their programming'.[14] However, this independence, though not a device, is actually serving a highly sophisticated function within a complex system. Precisely because the media produce material which is good, impartial, and serious, they are accorded a high degree of respect and authority. Since, in practice, the ethic of the press and television is closely associated with a homogeneous establishment this provides a vital support for the existing order. In this way, the apparent autonomy of organizations like the BBC 'veils and mystifies the structure of constraints'. Independence, Hall argues, is not 'a mere cover, it is central to the way power and ideology are mediated in societies like ours'. Thus we seem to have a more sophisticated instance of 'false consciousness'. The public are bribed with good radio, television, and newspapers into an acceptance of the biased, the misleading, and the status quo.

Hall emphasizes that the media change the world. They do not passively reflect class interests that have already been well developed. The media often articulate interests not previously expressed. That they do so is not because of the intentions of those who produce them. Rather it is a consequence of the situation and function of the press and broadcasting. The media, Hall suggests in a 1977 essay, help us 'not simply to *know more* about "the world", but to make sense of it'.

The mass media are not, according to this approach, crude agents of propaganda. They organize public understanding. However, the overall interpretations they provide in the long run are those which are most preferred by, and least challenging to, those with economic power.

### Class, culture, and experience

Part of this approach to the power of the media has been a concern with the way in which different classes experience their position. The work of E. P. Thompson and that of Raymond Williams has been an important influence here. Both of these writers have been concerned with the nineteenth-century reaction to industrialization (although this has often been mistaken for a reaction to capitalism). Thus Thompson has written about working-class movements which opposed industrial developments, and Williams has examined the social criticism implied in the aesthetic reaction to industrialization of the Romantic movement. Barnett has argued that Williams puts too much faith in the political force of cultural opposition. 'Where economistic strategies rely upon the spontaneous momentum of industrial struggles to accomplish the overthrow of capitalism,' he suggests, 'Williams's book contains a cultural argument that is logically similar.'[15] In this way the independence of working-class culture has come to be seen not only as a source of opposition to capitalism, but also as leading to a socialist rejection of it.

This tradition has led the cultural critics to focus on working-class response to, and use of, the media. Thus Finn and Grant argue that people are 'not merely on "the receiving end" of their objective class position'. Classes take over, interpret, and use ideologies which are presented to them: they make them their own. This is particularly true of the ideas transmitted by the media.

According to this view, the working class is imprisoned by an ideology it often rejects. Many workers are not taken in by the view of society handed down to them. This can be seen from 'oppositional' behaviour which is generally not overtly political. Thus Willis has considered the division in a boys' comprehensive between those who are subservient to the imposed system and take exams, and those who regard the examination system as a confidence trick that will not help them. Willis argues that the second group of disrespectful layabouts actually have a better understanding of the world and their place in it. He suggests that 'Oppressed, subordinate and minority groups can have a hand in constructing their own vibrant cultures and are not merely dupes.'

Yet the relationship between working-class culture and political action is hardly inevitable. The relationship between lifestyle and class is also more difficult to explain than these writers have implied. In addition, those who have written about the sociology of art, literature, or film have found no simple correlation between the social origins of artists, writers, and film-makers and the political implications of their work. Indeed, as Garnham has pointed out, just because cultural goods are made within the capitalist system it 'does not follow that these commodities will necessarily support the dominant ideology'. This is not to argue that there is no relationship between class, cultural products, and experience; only that a direct relationship cannot be taken for granted. At the same time, even if it is true that experience of the media has become an intrinsic part of working-class culture, it cannot therefore be automatically assumed to be good.

## The market

The pluralists largely ignore market pressures. The new determinist writers, in contrast, give them a crucial role. However, the determinist analysis of working-class culture leads to a contradiction. Goods – including the products of the media industries – are produced, it is argued, not to meet needs but to earn profits. Hence the goods are often worthless or inappropriate in themselves. However, workers are not necessarily enslaved by the distortions of the market. By appropriating what the system throws up, the working class preserves its cultural autonomy. Thus claims Willis, 'from the rubbish available within a pre-constituted market', working-class groups 'generate viable cultures, and through their work on received commodities actually formulate a living and lived out concretized critique'.

The work of Willis, Hebdige, and others provides an analysis of particular groups within the working class. Yet on the one hand, any attempt to generalize these conclusions to 'working-class culture' has to be treated with caution because of the narrow base of the research; on the other, the new critics seem to want to have their cake and eat it. Is television a subtle form of exploitation, the more sinister for being good? Is it 'rubbish available within a pre-constituted market', to use Willis's phrase for consumer goods in general? If the former, then it is hard to see how – or why – the working class should adopt oppositional 'concretized critiques' of it in their lifestyles. If the latter, and working-class culture manages to incorporate or appropriate the media product and remain 'viable' and 'lived out', then how thorough is the exploitation?

Pop music produces an interesting example. Is rock 'n' roll an expression of youth culture? Or is it a prime instance of capital discovering a new market and exploiting it? Few people would want to say that rock is intrinsically bad, or that it is not an important element in working-class life. No industry is more brazenly oriented towards quick, easy profits; in few are market pressures more immediate. Yet it is hard to sustain the argument that rock is handed down 'rubbish'.

Pop or rock fans are hardly an oppositional body taken *en masse*. As Frith points out, they are well aware that the product they buy is made and sold primarily to make profits. The reality is that rock is not simply a market-oriented concoction of the recording studios of Decca or EMI. Nor is it authentic folk music living an independent life in the community. Nor, for that matter, is it a distortion of a musical tradition plucked out of its native environment. Rather it is the product of a complex set of relationships in which music, fans, the media, profit takers, and distribution systems all play a part.

### News values and power

The new cultural critics are most interesting when they deal with the content of the media and its relationships to power. *Policing the Crisis: Mugging, the State, and Law and Order* by Hall *et al.*, for example, both describes the career of a category of news story, cases of 'mugging', and also analyses its influence on the judiciary, the police, and the public.

The authors show how the media created anxiety by giving a new name to an old offence. This in turn precipitated an aggressive sentencing policy which was seen as a necessary response to an earlier mistakenly 'soft' attitude towards offenders. Yet as Hall and others show, not only had the rate of increase in crimes of violence actually declined in the period before the emergence of the mugging story, but also far from becoming more lenient, sentences had steadily become longer. The curious inversion of facts, the authors argue, can be explained only in terms of the media's most general function of reworking ideology and maintaining the status quo.

The new cultural critics emphasize that their explanation of this process does not imply any deliberate conspiracy. 'Within its limits', Hall has written, broadcasting, for example, 'shows little evidence of intentional bias, but the trouble is the matter of unwitting bias'. Rather the coincidence of interests between the media and those with economic power is secured by professional and organizational values, and a shared perspective of the way in which society is organized. Thus Murdoch, writing about the reporting of an anti-Vietnam rally in 1968, argued that 'despite this element of autonomy, the basic definition of the situation which underlies the news reporting of political events very largely coincides with the definitions provided by the legitimate power holders'.

## Social control

Thus the media are seen by the determinists as one powerful agency of social control – as a means of inhibiting opposition to the social order. In a similar argument, Bourdieu has described the function of the education system, which he sees as justifying the established order, by

> using the overt connection between qualifications and jobs as a smokescreen for the connection – which it records surreptitiously under the cover of a formal equality – between the qualifications people obtain and the cultural capital they have inherited – in other words through the legitimation it confers on the framework of this form of heritage.

Differences in the use of the media, the distribution of tastes and preferences, are thus more than a mere expression of class. They are a vital means of making people accept different class opportunities, and those interpretations of events which are the least challenging to existing social arrangements.

Indeed in the analysis of the cultural critics, the media perform a special role in addition: they maintain and repair consensus as the nature of the status quo changes. Thus the crime of 'mugging', launched and amplified by the press, did not emerge accidentally. Rather it arose 'in the middle of a general moral panic about the rising rate of crime. Far from triggering into existence what did not previously exist, it clearly focuses what is widespread and free floating.'

The concept of social control seems to imply an imminent crisis, one that will eventually erupt but which is at present controlled. The emergence of the 'mugging' story is therefore interpreted merely as a symptom of a more fundamental crisis, one in which there has been a collapse in the willingness of the public to accept the authority of the state. The individual discrete 'moral panics' of the 1960s are seen as having been superseded by a more general breakdown. The only rationale, it is argued, for

> entrusting the management of the corporate capitalist state to a social democracy is either (1) that in a tight squeeze it can better win the collaboration of the working-class organization for the state, or (2) that if there is going to be a crisis Labour might as well have it!

In this way there is a danger that social structure is anthropomorphized: it becomes an active agent in pursuit of its own persistence.

However, despite the limitations of the concepts of social control, the determinist explanation of the role of the media is revealing. The media do not merely express the interests of the ruling class, rather they have an independent function in ordering the world. The media do not merely 'reflect' social reality: they increasingly help to make it.

## Conclusion

As we have seen, the pluralist analysis of the effects of the media contains as apparent contradiction. On the one hand, it seems to show that the media do have an influence, both on what people know and on the political system. On the other hand it seems to suggest that, so far from having an independent power, the media merely reflect the balance of forces within society. Thus the pluralists are left saying that the press and broadcasting function as an ideological market-place, a focus for competing pressures without an impact of their own. At the same time in taking a favourable view of 'pluralist' balance, this position tends to ignore the extent to which the weaker and unorganized groups are excluded from the process altogether.

Is the determinist approach any better? The cultural critics share the pluralists' view that the media have a key political role, stressing the way in which press and broadcasting shape public understanding. They differ from the pluralists in their preoccupation with the real or supposed role of the media as an instrument of class domination.

Thus the determinists have pointed to a major weakness in the pluralist case: the model of a freely competitive market-place of ideas breaks down because some groups are unable to compete. At the same time the empirical evidence of the pluralists gives powerful backing to the determinists' conviction that the media exert an important and uncontrolled influence. Yet the determinist explanation in terms of class manipulation and exploitation is too mechanistic, obscuring a series of complex relationships which have yet to be explained.

## Notes

1. H. Arendt, *The Burden of Our Time* (London, Secker & Warburg, 1950), p. 331.
2. M. Horkheimer, *The Eclipse of Reason* (London, Oxford University Press, 1947), p. 135.
3. H. D. Lasswell, 'The garrison state', *American Journal of Sociology*, 46 (1941), p. 462.
4. This 'strong' interpretation they share with F. Hayek, *The Road to Serfdom* (London, Routledge & Kegan Paul, 1944). He indicts socialism, they blame fascism.
5. H. Arendt, *The Life of the Mind,* vol. 2, *Thinking* (London, Secker & Warburg, 1978), p. 93.
6. E. Katz and P. Lazarsfeld, *Personal Influence: The Part Played by People in the Flow of Mass Communication* (New York, Free Press, 1955).
7. P. Becker and M. McCombs point this out in 'The development of political cognition' in S. H. Chaffee (ed.), *Political Communication:*

*Issues and Strategies* (Beverly Hills, Calif., Sage, 1975).

8. C. I. Hovland, 'Reconciling conflicting results derived from experimental and survey studies of attitude change', *American Psychologist*, 14 (1959), p. 11.

9. M. Harrop and A. Sharp, *Can Labour Win?* (Harlow, Fabian Research Bureau/Longman, 1989).

10. For a further development of this case, and a consideration of its more general implications, see J. Seaton and B. Pimlott, 'The role of the media in the Portuguese revolution' in A. Smith (ed.), *Newspapers and Democracy: International Essays in a Changing Medium* (Cambridge, Mass., MIT Press, 1980); J. Seaton and B. Pimlott, 'Political power and the Portuguese media' in L. Graham and D. Wheeler (eds), *In Search of Modern Portugal: The Revolution and its Consequences* (Wisconsin, University of Wisconsin Press, 1983); B. Pimlott and J. Seaton, 'The Portuguese media in transition' in K. Maxwell (ed.), *The Press and the Rebirth of Iberian Democracy* (Westwood, Conn., Greenwood, 1983).

11. See J. Seaton, 'Trade unions and the media' in B. Pimlott and C. Cook (eds), *Trade Unions in British Politics* (Harlow, Longman, 1983).

12. T. Gitlin, 'Prime time ideology: the hegemonic process in television entertainment', *Social Problems*, 26, 3 (1979), p. 111.

13. James Curran does not share many of Jean Seaton's reservations about the writers discussed in this part of the chapter.

14. S. Hall, 'The external/internal dialectic on broadcasting', *4th Symposium on British Broadcasting Policy* (February 1972).

15. A. Barnett in R. Williams (ed.), *Politics and Letters: Interviews with the New Left Review* (London, New Left Books, 1979), p. 98.

# 16

# *The liberal theory of press freedom*

According to classical liberal theory, the freedom of the press is rooted in the freedom to publish without being subject to pre-publication censorship by the state. This ensures that the press reflects a wide range of opinions and interests in society. If a viewpoint is not expressed in the press, this is only because it lacks a sufficient following to sustain it in the market-place. As the heroine puts it in Tom Stoppard's play, *Night and Day*, 'The *Flat Earth News* is free to sell a million copies. What it lacks is the ability to find a million people with four pence and a conviction that the earth is flat. Freedom is neutral.'

This neutrality of the market makes the press a representative voice of the people. 'The broad shape and nature of the press', argues John Whale for instance, 'is ultimately determined by no one but its readers.' This is because newspapers and magazines must respond to their readers if they are to stay in business in a competitive market.

Some liberal theorists compare the operation of the market to the processes of political representation. Newspapers, they contend, must submit to the equivalent of an election every time they go on sale whereas politicians seek election only at infrequent intervals. The press should thus be seen, according to this argument, as the fourth estate of the realm – an institution that represents the public and is uniquely accountable to it.

Three political 'functions' of the press are usually stressed in liberal theory. The press provides a forum of public debate about the issues of the day; it articulates public opinion arising from this debate; and it forces governments to take account of what people think. The press is thus the agency through which private citizens are reconstituted as a public body exercising informal supervision of the state. In addition, liberal theory posits other political roles for the press. It educates citizens, enabling them to make informed judgements at election time. It provides an independent channel of political communication between different groups in society. And the press also champions the individual against the abuse of executive power and the misdeeds of the powerful.

Embedded at the heart of liberal theory – although often obscured by layers of well-rehearsed argument – is the assumption that press freedom is a property right. It is generally assumed that proprietors have a legitimate right to manage directly their publications, or to delegate authority to others, as they see fit. However, the hidden hand of the free market ensures that proprietors' pursuit of their private interests corresponds to the public good. For, as we have seen, liberal theorists argue that the freedom to publish and compete in an unrestricted market produces a press which is diverse, accountable, and representative.

This theory of press freedom has been attacked by radical critics on the grounds that it masks the way in which capital is privileged in the seemingly open contest of the free market, and obscures the fact that the press tends to report and interpret the world in ways which are consonant with the interests of dominant groups.[1]

But perhaps more significantly, some liberal commentators have also criticized the traditional theory of press freedom. One line of attack has been to challenge the legitimacy of proprietorial control on the grounds that the creation of vast press empires has led to the concentration of too much power in a few hands. Editors, according to this argument, should determine what is published without interference from proprietors. Others have mounted a more far-reaching assault on classical theory, arguing that it is now out of date and no longer fits the facts of an industrialized, monopolistic press. In some versions this comes close to – indeed merges with – radical critiques of liberal theory.

The nature of these criticisms and misgivings will be illustrated by comparing the reports of three successive Royal Commissions on the Press, published in 1949, 1962, and 1977. The last two reports represent, as we shall see, staging posts in a progressive process of disenchantment with conventional views of the free market that underpin the liberal theory of press freedom.

## Freedom to publish

'Free enterprise', declared the first Royal Commission on the Press, 'is a prerequisite of a free press.' Underlying this belief was a relatively untroubled conviction that the unrestricted freedom to publish produces a diverse and representative press. The Commission expected to find that 'the press as a whole gives an opportunity for all important points of view to be effectively presented in terms of the varying standards of taste, political opinion, and education among the principal groups of the population'. Wartime economic controls were blamed for preventing new publications from springing up to meet changes in public demand. Anticipating the time when these controls would be removed, the Commission rejected dividend control because it might inhibit the creativity of the market. It also dismissed proposals for assisting the launch of new papers on the grounds that they were unnecessary.

The 1977 Commission was forced to make a different assessment of the market. As the Commission put it bluntly, 'Anyone is free to start a daily national newspaper, but few can afford even to contemplate the prospect.' It also noted that the national press was overwhelmingly right wing and manifestly unrepresentative. Indeed 'in February 1974 ... the share of newspaper (national daily) circulation held by papers supporting the Conservative Party was 71% greater than Conservative votes as a percentage of the votes cast.'

High entry costs were found to curtail the freedom to publish in other sectors of the press. Even establishing a new local evening paper in a town with no direct competition would cost in 1977, according to the Commission, between £2 million and £3 million. The cost of launching a new magazine in the main consumer sectors was also found to be high. As for new paid-for weeklies, there are 'not many places left with the right conditions to provide a permanent market'.

The assumption that 'anyone' is free to start a new paper has been an illusion ever since the industrialization of the press. That it is an illusion was exposed in unsparing detail by the last Commission. This part of its report thus dislodged a key foundation stone sustaining the traditional theory of press freedom.

## Proprietors and chain ownership

The 1949 Commission argued that proprietors should be free to conduct their publications as they wished. This was justified principally on the grounds that proprietors had the right to safeguard their financial investments in a high-risk industry. It was also assumed that their freedom underpinned the wider freedom of the press as a whole.

Underlying the Commission's approach was the assumption that chain ownership would not develop into a major problem. 'There is no reason to expect', declared the Commission,

> that the aggressive expansion of chain undertakings [in the daily and Sunday press] which characterised the early period will be resumed. Neither in the local nor in the periodical press nor in the news agencies do we expect a significant trend towards further concentration of ownership.

The 1962 Commission was obliged to revise this assessment. It found that the share of circulation controlled by the major chains had 'substantially increased' in all parts of the press. The leading three proprietors' share of the national daily press had soared to 89 per cent. There were, it added, 'spectacular movements towards concentration of ownership' in the periodical press. Only amongst local weeklies was concentration 'negligible'.

In 1977 the third Commission was forced to revise even this conclusion. The greatest acceleration of chain ownership had occurred, it reported unhappily, in the local weekly press. Furthermore, new acquisitions had resulted in the same three proprietors dominating both the national daily and Sunday markets unlike before.[2] The Commission also highlighted a phenomenon which had previously received little attention – the emergence of sub-regional monopolies in which all 'competing' local morning, evening, and weekly papers were owned by the same group.

These changes in the press prompted a reassessment. Whereas the first two Commissions had taken for granted the right of proprietors to determine editorial policy, the third Commission talked of the need to 'protect editors and journalists from owners'. The exercise of proprietorial power no longer appeared legitimate on the grounds accepted by its predecessors – that of guaranteeing the diversity of the press. Indeed at a time when just three men controlled over half of total daily and Sunday newspaper sales in Britain, proprietorial authority was tacitly recognized to threaten editorial diversity.

## Proprietorship of the fourth estate

This shift of attitude towards proprietorial authority was also influenced by changes in the character of press ownership. The first

Commission had advanced as a subsidiary justification for proprietors the argument that they safeguarded the autonomy of the press. 'It is undoubtedly a great merit of the British press', declared the Commission, 'that it is completely independent of outside financial interests and that its policy is the policy of those who own and control it.' The Commission thus invoked the classical liberal view of the press as an independent fourth estate, uncompromised by vested interests.

But during the take-over boom of the late 1960s and 1970s most of the British press was bought up by or diversified into interests outside publishing. All but one of the leading publishing groups in both Fleet Street and the regional press became part of larger conglomerates with holdings in fields as diverse as North Sea oil, transport, mining, construction, engineering, finance, and the leisure industries. 'Rather than saying that the press has other business interests,' the last Commission concluded unhappily, 'it would be truer to argue that the press has become a subsidiary of other industries.'

This clearly undermined the case for proprietorial control as a guarantee of the press's autonomy to which the 1949 Commission had paid such a fulsome and, in retrospect, embarrassing tribute. It also cast in a new light the 1949 Commission's contention that proprietors had the right to safeguard their financial interests, whatever the circumstances. If a newspaper's investigative journalism jeopardizes its parent conglomerate's interests, should the controller of that conglomerate have the right to suppress it? Should the freedom of the press be located in the property power of large business organizations whose activities should be subjected, according to liberal theory, to fearless press scrutiny?[3] These were questions which clearly troubled the 1977 Commission, and partly explains why it was much less enthusiastic about 'the rights' of proprietors than its predecessors.

### Competition, consumer choice, and new technology

The first Commission attached great importance to the role of competition in making the press accountable. Due to competitive pressures, argued the Commission, 'whatever a paper's purpose and however it is owned, it cannot escape the necessity of offering the public what some at least of the public will buy'.

Although the Commission was troubled by the large number of newspaper closures during the inter-war period, it took comfort in the belief tha  u  s had been only a temporary phenomenon caused mainly by extravagance and lack of adaptability. 'In the provincial press as a whole,' it concluded, 'there is nothing approaching monopoly and we can see no strong tendency towards monopoly.'

The Commission's optimism was confounded by events. The total number of newspaper titles continued to decline (see Table 7). The cities in the UK with a choice of directly competing local morning or evening papers was reduced by 1974 to only London, Edinburgh, and Belfast (see Table 8). In 1975 only 18 per cent of towns with a local paper had a choice of weeklies under separate ownership, a proportion that was little over half of what it had been in 1961. In short, competition – the *deus ex machina* of liberal theory which makes the consumer 'sovereign' and proprietors accountable – had been seriously eroded in much of the regional press.

The last Commission found some solace in the emergence of freesheets, a development which has become even more pronounced

Table 7   *The number of newspaper titles, 1921–88*

|  | 1921 | 1937 | 1948 | 1961 | 1976 | 1988 | Percentage reduction 1921–88 |
|---|---|---|---|---|---|---|---|
|  |  |  |  |  |  |  | % |
| *National press* |  |  |  |  |  |  |  |
| National daily | 14 | 11 | 11 | 10 | 9 | 12 | 14 |
| National Sunday | 14 | 10 | 10 | 8 | 7 | 9 | 36 |
| *Regional/local press* |  |  |  |  |  |  |  |
| Morning | 41 | 27 | 27 | 22 | 20 | 18 | 66 |
| Evening | 93 | 83 | 80 | 77 | 79 | 74 | 20 |
| Sunday | 7 | 7 | 6 | 5 | 6 | 8 | (14) |
| Weekly and bi-weekly | 1,485 | 1,303 | 1,307 | 1,219 | 1,072 | 801 | 66 |
| Freesheets | – | – | – | – | 185[a] | 896[b] | – |
| Total[c] | 1,654 | 1,441 | 1,441 | 1,341 | 1,193 | 922 | 44 |

*Sources: Royal Commission on the Press 1947–9 Report*, Appendix 2, Tables 2–3; *Royal Commission on the Press 1961–2 Report*, Appendix 3, Tables 3 and 5; *Royal Commission on the Press 1974–7 Final Report*, Annex 3, Table 4; *Press Council Annual Report 1988*, Table 1 and Table A.

*Notes:* a. This relates to 1975. b. In addition there was one local daily and one Sunday freesheet. c. Excluding freesheets.

since it reported. However, the rise of freesheets has caused a further reduction in the number of paid-for weeklies (see Table 7). Due to their dependent relationship to advertisers, freesheets do not constitute an important independent voice. Ironically many of them are now also published by the major chains. In 1988 the five largest publishers of freesheets were responsible between them for 338 free newspapers: the same publishers also controlled a further 243 paid-for papers.

The contraction of the press troubled both the 1962 and 1977 Commissions. But what disturbed them even more was evidence that there was a built-in impetus towards market distortion. 'The natural tendency', concluded the 1962 Commission, 'of the economic factors affecting [newspaper] production and sale is to diminish the number of papers where competition is close.' This pessimistic conclusion was based on its analysis of the unequal competitive relationship that often developed between strong and weak papers. Successful papers, the Commission found, enjoyed a double advantage over weaker competitors: they had generally lower unit costs due to economies of scale, and more revenue. This enabled them to outspend their rivals; win more circulation through higher spending; and drive their weaker rivals into debt by making them incur additional expenditure in an attempt to stay competitive. The 1977 Commission broadly endorsed this view, although it drew attention to 'countervailing forces' offsetting

Table 8   *The number of urban centres with competing local dailies,1921–88*

|  | Urban centres with a choice of: | |
|---|---|---|
|  | Local morning paper[a] | Local evening paper |
| 1921[b] | 15 | 27 |
| 1937[b] | 6 | 10 |
| 1948 | 4 | 11 |
| 1961 | 2 | 9 |
| 1974 | 2 | 1 |
| 1988 | 2 | — |

*Sources: Royal Commission on the Press 1947–9 Report,* Appendix 2, Table 1; *Royal Commission on the Press 1961–2 Report,* Appendix 3, Table 4; N. Hartley, P. Gudgeon, and R. Crafts, *Concentration of Ownership in the Provincial Press,* Royal Commission on the Press 1974–7, Research Series 5 (London HMSO, 1977), Table 6.1; *Press Council Annual Report 1988,* Table 1.
*Notes:* a. Excluding London. b. Excluding Ulster.

scale economies. The Commission also pointed to further ways in which powerful press groups had increased their domination of the market. Economies of consolidation had enabled them to buy out rivals at above the market rate. Their large financial resources and accumulated expertise had also equipped them to be successful innovators. The 1977 Commission found that only two out of a sample of twenty-four local weeklies launched between 1961 and 1976 had originated from independent publishers. It also discovered that over half the consumer magazines with a circulation of over 30,000 started between 1966 and 1974 had come from just four publishing groups. 'The larger companies', the Commission's research team concluded soberly, 'are better placed to incur the considerable costs that are required to enter some markets.'[4]

The last two Commissions came, in effect, to the uncomfortable conclusion that there was no free market solution to the central problem they had diagnosed: namely that the processes of competition reduced competition. The 1962 Commission reluctantly concluded that increased efficiency in the press – although desirable in itself – offered no panacea. Cost saving, it argued, might offer a weak publication temporary respite, 'but the important point', it stressed, 'is that reduction in costs, however desirable in itself, will not, if equally applied to all newspapers, improve the relative position of the weaker publication'. Similarly the 1977 Commission emphasized that potential savings could be achieved through the introduction of new technology. But it too concluded that this would not neutralize the dynamic inequalities inherent in competition between weak and strong papers. 'Even if all newspapers accomplish the change [in technology]', concluded the Commission, 'competition may still result in some papers closing since the new technology does little to alter the relative position of competing titles.'

Subsequent developments since its 1977 report do not justify overturning this verdict. Nor do they vindicate the Panglossian hopes that accompanied the introduction of technology, at least as far as the newspaper press is concerned.[5] Contrary to what was widely predicted, computerized technology has not significantly reduced the market share of the three leading publishers; it has not extended the ideological range of the newspaper press; it has not reinvigorated popular publishing through the proliferation of new, minority papers: and, while it refuelled competition in some press sectors, by making it cheaper to start papers, even this gain is being eroded. Rising levels of expenditure in the press industry are now increasing the total investment needed to establish new papers as going concerns.

## Reform or reinterpretation

The last two Commissions' reports reveal the gradual weakening of beliefs that have legitimized the press for over a century. The incorporation of the press by big business and the growth of chain ownership has cast doubt on the legitimacy of proprietorial control by undermining the traditional arguments advanced to justify it. Market distortions have also undermined the processes which are said in liberal theory to produce a press that is politically diverse, representative, and accountable.

In these circumstances the last two Commissions had perhaps two available options, given their liberal-conservative make-up. They could endorse the status quo and seek to legitimize it by updating traditional liberal theory. This would have meant following the pattern of the USA where liberal theory has been skilfully reworked in a way that takes account of the monopolistic structure of the American press.

Alternatively they could propose a major programme of reform which would make liberal representations of press freedom correspond more closely to reality. This is the strategy which has been adopted in most European countries where a variety of schemes have been introduced in an attempt to 'repair' the free market. These have ranged from subsidies to assist the launch of new publications to grants and tax concessions designed to prevent newspapers from closing.[6]

## The Commissions' programme of reform

Perhaps the closest the Press Commissions came to adopting an interventionist strategy was to advocate an anti-monopoly policy. This was tentatively initiated by the 1949 Commission which proposed that the Monopolies Commission should monitor changes in press ownership with increased vigilance. This had no discernible effect.

Its successor recommended in 1961 the setting up of a Press Amalgamations Court. A variant of this proposal became law in 1965. It required all large press groups to obtain the permission of the Secretary of State before they were allowed to purchase any newspaper. The effectiveness of this legislation may be gauged by the fact that not one of the fifty acquisitions of newspaper companies by major press groups during the period 1965–77 was disallowed.

The 1977 Commission argued that press anti-monopoly legislation should be greatly strengthened. Its advice was ignored by both Labour and Conservative governments. Consequently anti-monopoly law again proved to be ineffectual when it was put crucially to the test in 1981. Permission was given to Rupert Murdoch to buy *The Times* and *Sunday Times*, thereby giving him control of 30 per cent of national daily circulation and 31 per cent of national Sunday circulation, without the take-overs even being referred to the Monopolies Commission.[7]

The impact of successive Press Commissions in this area has thus been limited. They have manifestly failed to restrain the rapid growth of press concentration that has taken place. Yet, while promoting ineffectual mergers legislation, the last two Commissions opposed proposals for divesting the major press groups – originating from the centre as well as from the left of British politics.[8]

### Restriction on joint media ownership

The first Press Commission urged that the ownership of the press and broadcasting should be kept separate. No attention was paid to its views when commercial television was introduced in 1954. The second Press Commission criticized the press's heavy involvement in commercial television but was prevented from making any explicit recommendation by its terms of reference. Contrary to the spirit of its report, press groups continued to retain large shareholdings in commercial television. Indeed they were even given a prescriptive right to participate in setting up local commercial radio stations in their circulation areas when independent radio was introduced in 1972.

This prescriptive right was ended by the Broadcasting Act, 1981, at the recommendation of the 1977 Press Commission. The IBA also adopted a policy of reducing press interests in broadcasting (although these are still very extensive) in response to the urging of both the 1977 Press Commission and the Annan Committee on Broadcasting. But the Press Commission's main recommendations in this area have been ignored. Press groups have not been debarred from having interests in local radio stations in their main areas of circulation and they have not been excluded from ITV franchises in those areas where they are dominant.

## Press Council

The Press Council was perhaps the most concrete reform to come out of the Press Commissions. However, it bore little relationship to what was originally advocated. The initial blueprint, proposed by the 1949 Commission, was for a powerful 'General Council of the Press', which was to be a well-funded and widely respected public body concerned not only with investigating complaints but also with such matters as the recruitment and education of journalists and the promotion of substantial research into the press.

The Press Council was finally set up in 1953, in an enfeebled form. Its shortcomings were roundly criticized by the 1962 Commission which urged government legislation if the Press Council failed to reform itself. This produced some improvements – notably, the appointment of an independent chairman and the annual recording of basic press statistics. However, the 1977 Commission was sharply critical of its performance, and attacked both the quality of its adjudications and their lack of impact. 'We hope', concluded the Commission, 'that in the future the Press Council will be more vigilant in demonstrating the independence and impartiality to which it lays claim.'

The 1977 Commission made twelve recommendations for a complete shake-up of the Press Council's organization and procedures. Nine of these – including most of the important ones – were rejected. The Press Council continued much as before.[9] Its central weakness remained unchanged: it was a toothless watchdog which was not taken seriously by the papers which it most often criticized. In 1981 the National Union of Journalists, which had been pressing for reform of the Council, withdrew from it as a mark of the union's lack of confidence in the Council's proceedings.

Only the threat of press legislation generated a fresh impetus for reconstructing the Press Council. In 1989 the government set up the Calcutt Committee to investigate whether a privacy law should be introduced. This triggered a new bout of reforming zeal on the part of the Press Council, which announced in 1989 a major overhaul of its proceedings including ironically the adoption of some of the recommendations of the 1977 Commission. However, the Calcutt Committee was so unimpressed by the performance of the Press Council that it recommended its disbandment in favour of a new body, the Press Complaints Commission. While it is too early to form a judgement about this new agency, established in 1991, it is clear that the Press Council failed to fulfil the purpose for which it was founded: the effective promotion of 'a sense of public responsibility and public service' in the press. After 37 years, the crowning achievement of the Press Commissions' reformism died unmourned.

## Miscellany

The 1949 Commission advocated that broadly based educational courses for journalists should be started, which would promote higher standards of professionalism. What emerged were courses that were narrowly vocational and encouraged uncritical acceptance of traditional values in the industry. The last Commission advocated a widening of journalism education to little effect. Most of its detailed proposals were ignored; its chosen instrument of change, the Printing and Publishing Industry Training Board, was later abolished by the Thatcher government.

Press Commissions have also advocated other reforms – that newspapers should prominently display the name of their owner, that they should declare an interest when reporting on economic activities in which their parent or associated companies are financially involved, that Fleet Street papers should receive cheap loans to assist the introduction of new technology, and that the press should abide by a Charter of good practice drawn up by the last Commission, which would be policed by a reformed Press Council on a voluntary basis for a trial period. No attention has been paid to any of these proposals.

In short, successive Royal Commissions have had very little influence on the press. Most of their proposals have been ignored. The few reforms that have been introduced have proved relatively ineffectual. In so far as the Commissions have exerted any real influence, it has been largely negative in discouraging the adoption of any of the reformist measures implemented elsewhere in Europe.[10] They have thus contributed little towards relieving the problems identified in their reports through a programme of reform.

## Reworking liberal theory

However, the significance of Royal Commissions on the Press was not confined solely to their influence on public policy. They also drew together different sources of evidence and different views in new processes of synthesis. They had therefore unique opportunities for modifying and updating theoretical justifications of the press in a form that took account of changes in its structure and ownership.

There is one passage in the last Commission's report which is of particular interest in this context, since it seems to indicate a new approach:

> We define the freedom of the press as that freedom from restraint which is essential to enable proprietors, editors and journalists to advance the public interest by publishing the facts and opinions without which a democratic electorate cannot make responsible judgements.

By defining press freedom in these collective terms, the Commission appeared to be modifying the traditional concept of press freedom as the property right of proprietors. The novelty of this approach was seemingly confirmed by the clauses in the Commission's proposed Charter which upheld the freedom of conscience of individual journalists and the right of editors to accept any contribution 'notwithstanding the views of his proprietor'.

But this new approach was not sustained. The overriding concern of the Charter, reflected in numerous, detailed prohibitions, was to protect proprietors and their editors from journalists and their principal collective organization, the National Union of Journalists. The traditionalism that really informed the Commission's attitude towards the press was further revealed by its discussion of how proprietors might be prevented from abusing their power. It accepted the Newspaper Publishers Association's argument that 'in reality editorial and managerial decisions were inseparable' and that writing certain freedoms into editors' contracts – such as the right to criticize the activities of other parts of the organization to which their papers belonged – was 'too constricting'. On the wider issue of internal democracy, urged by some as an essential safeguard against the abuse of proprietorial power, the Commission made the extraordinary admission that it had 'not examined the issues raised in such a way as to enable us to express a view on this complex and disputed subject'.

The Commission's reworking of liberal theory was inconsistent as well as faltering. For instance it portrayed the issue of the union closed shop in the press as a simple conflict between 'two valid but competing demands': on the one hand, the desire of employees to improve their earnings and conditions of work and,

for those on the other side, what matters most is the freedom of the press because they cannot 'conceive a civilized society that does not regard as its first priority the right of a man to express what he believes in whatever form he thinks appropriate, subject to the control of the law'.

In accepting this simplistic representation advanced by the Newspaper Publishers' Association, the Commission was falling back on the classical liberal premise that the unrestricted freedom to publish guarantees 'the right of a man to express what he believes'. It was thus endorsing a view which it had previously contested.

The Commission failed to construct a new set of persuasive arguments which would replace traditional liberal apologetics. But its euphemistic re-presentation of the concept of press freedom as a collective freedom from restraint, and its tentative acknowledgement of the need to curtail proprietors, was nevertheless significant. It reflected the last Commission's uneasy awareness that the rhetoric of liberal press theory no longer corresponded to the reality of the contemporary press.

The same uneasiness is reflected in the Commission's tentative espousal of a philosophy of public service. Newspapers, the Commission argued, should behave 'with proper restraint'; the press should be like broadcasting and recruit more graduates; young journalists should go on improving courses and 'learn about society'.

Indeed the Commission seemed intent, at times, on transplanting the public service rationale of broadcasting to the press. But its moves in this direction were inconsistent and contradictory. It wanted a public service orientation but was opposed to the framework of public regulation that underpins it. It favoured a more balanced, responsible approach to journalism but was also committed to the tradition of partisanship and outspoken comment upheld by the free market tradition of the press. Unable to define precisely what it meant by professionalism, the Commission was not very successful at promoting it. But its flirtation with the idea of public service was nevertheless revealing: it was an attempt to co-opt a different theoretical tradition in a bid to bolster the increasingly threadbare classical theory of press freedom.

## Commissions' escapism

Unable either to rationalize away or to reform the problems they identified, the Press Commissions took comfort in the belief that the importance of the press has been greatly exaggerated. This argument was explicitly stated by the first two Commissions, and implicitly stated by the last one when it stressed the growing importance of the broadcasting media. By implication, the failure either to prescribe practical remedies or to declare the patient fit did not greatly matter.

Admittedly critics of the press have sometimes overstated its influence. But the Commissions' downgrading of press influence runs counter to the new consensus of informed opinion. The minimal effects model of the press is rooted in American research conducted in the 1940s and 1950s and is now rejected by most contemporary researchers into the press.[11]

All three Commissions also sought to diminish the problems they encountered by adopting a narrow, functionalist perspective. They discussed the role of the press exclusively in terms of its contribution to society as a whole: newspapers were portrayed in unproblematic terms as informing, educating, entertaining, and representing the public. They thus took refuge in nineteenth-century liberal conceptions of the press, and its near blood relation, the functionalist sociology of the immediate post-war period. In this way, they avoided asking awkward questions about the relationship of the press to power groups in society which might have propelled them towards a different analysis.

The ways in which the Press Commissions reconciled themselves to failure – both at a practical level and in terms of reinterpretation – have a curiously old-fashioned look about them. They are rooted in the discredited, intellectual fashions of yesteryear, scarcely a firm foundation for continued evasion in the future.

## Weak opposition

The lack of a coherent and convincing set of ideas legitimizing the present pattern of press ownership leaves proprietors potentially vulnerable to attack. However, they have not been exposed in the post-war period to a sustained political attack of the sort mounted with considerable effect by Stanley Baldwin and the Conservative establishment in the early 1930s.

The most probable source of such a campaign is the labour movement. Its attitude towards the press changed when it ceased to own part of it, following the closure of its mass circulation papers in the 1960s. Alienation turned into growing hostility when the national press supported a series of aggressive campaigns against the trade unions from the mid-1960s onwards. The first sign of a political shift occurred in 1974, with the publication of a Labour Party Study Group report, *People and the Media,* most of whose proposals became official policy in the 1970s. But it was not until 1983 that the Labour Party first included a programme for reforming the press in a general election manifesto. Its more right-wing 1987 manifesto also contained proposals for press reform, including a commitment to limit press monopolies and assist with public money the launch of new publications.

But Labour leaders refrained from launching a sustained attack on press monopolists, partly for fear of the political damage that an antagonized press could inflict. They have not even sought to publicize the party's manifesto commitments on the press (even though the most radical of these originates from Kinnock himself).[12] In reality, the only section of the labour movement actively to seek public support for press reform were the press unions, and they were not very successful, partly because they were themselves widely regarded as an illegitimate vested interest. Their most effective action was to help set up in 1979 the Campaign for Press and Broadcasting Freedom. But while this pressure group had some measure of success, it never succeeded in generating a public debate about press freedom and the role of proprietors as its union sponsors had originally hoped.

Disquiet about recent changes in the press was one of the factors that led to the launch in 1989 of *British Journalism Review,* backed by a large number of distinguished journalists. But although this worthwhile journal has initiated a valuable discussion about what is good and bad about contemporary journalism, it has given relatively little attention to institutional reform. Its response has been cast in 'professional' rather than 'political' terms, thus underlining the reluctance of journalists to become involved in any campaign to change the structures of the press.

Public criticism of the press also increased. In 1975 (according to MORI), more than half the adult population of Britain claimed to believe what they read in the papers: in 1989 fewer than two-fifths did so. When asked to differentiate between sectors of the press, people were even more critical. Gallup found in 1989 that only 12 per cent thought that tabloids like the *Sun* were truthful, and only 25 per cent said the same of the middle-market papers like the *Daily Mail.* But the growing volume of public criticism has given rise to demands to curb rather than to reorganize the press.

In the absence of a popular campaign from the left, press freedom will continue to be equated with the property rights of proprietors, perhaps more from the force of habitual assumption than considered conviction. Indeed, the widespread belief that new technology is revitalizing competition has probably strengthened their position. There are also indications that publishers are becoming concerned about growing public criticism. In late 1989 the Press Council called on them to take sanctions against employees who are the subject of Council censure. Proprietors may yet win new acclaim – ironically as champions defending the public from the papers they own.

## Notes

1. This is the underlying theme of part I of this book.
2. The Commission was less troubled than it might have been partly because its analysis of the evidence concealed the full extent of the trend towards concentration of ownership. Its main report did not examine chain ownership in terms of total daily and Sunday circulation as its predecessors had done, and did not take properly into account the long-term development of press concentration in the period before 1961.
3. In this context it is worth noting Colin Seymour-Ure's argument that the transfer of control of the press from political parties to unaccountable capitalist conglomerates with an interest in the outcome of government policy has undermined the legitimacy of the press. (See his 'National daily papers and the party system' in *Studies on the Press,* Royal Commission on the Press Working Paper 3, London, HMSO, 1977).
4. N. Hartley, P. Gudgeon, and R. Crafts, *Concentration of Ownership in the Provincial Press,* Royal Commission on the Press 1974–7, Research Series 5 (London, HMSO, 1977); *Periodicals and the Alternative Press,* Royal Commission on the Press, Research Series 6 (London, HMSO, 1977).
5. See chapter 7, pp. 119–23.
6. Still the best available general survey of alternative European press subsidy schemes is A. Smith, 'State intervention and the management of the press' in J. Curran (ed.), *The British Press: A Manifesto* (London, Macmillan, 1978). For a more recent account of the most developed and successful social democratic policy on the press, see Olof Hulten, *Mass Media and State Support in Sweden* (Stockholm, Swedish Institute, 1984).
7. The government's failure to refer News International's acquisition of Times Newspapers to the Monopolies Commission was nonetheless probably a breach of the law, even in its unreformed state. See H.

Evans, *Good Times, Bad Times* (London, Weidenfeld & Nicolson, 1983).

8. Proposals for divestiture came from, among others, Sir Geoffrey Crowther (Royal Commission on the Press, Oral Evidence, vol. 1, p. 5, London, HMSO, 1962), and Professor Jeremy Tunstall (Royal Commission on the Press 1974–7, unpublished evidence), both from the broad centre of the political spectrum.

9. Arguably, the public was better off with the Press Council than without it. However, the case against the Council is well put in G. Robertson, *People Against the Press: An Enquiry into the Press Council* (London, Quartet, 1983).

10. However, the 1977 Commission contained a minority report, signed by two members, proposing a National Printing Corporation and a Launch Fund to assist the establishment of new publications. These recommendations were ignored.

11. P. Dunleavy and C. Husbands, *British Democracy at the Crossroads* (London, Allen & Unwin, 1984) and J. P. Robinson and M. R. Levy, *The Main Source* (Beverly Hills, Calif., Sage, 1986) are examples of recent assessments of press influence. This said, a number of factors do significantly limit the impact of the press. For a more cautious assessment, see J. Curran, 'The boomerang effect: the press and the battle for London, 1981–6' in J. Curran, A. Smith, and P. Wingate (eds), *Impacts and Influences* (London, Methuen, 1987).

12. See chapter 19, pp. 354.

# 17

# Broadcasting and the theory of public service

British broadcasting was started as a public service, and this proved as creative commercially as it was innovative culturally. Indeed, every stage of its development, from the emergence of the BBC, through the introduction of commercial television, to the founding of Channel 4, depended on a set of linked and radical expansions. First, at each stage a novel source of finance was discovered. In turn the growth of broadcasting was financed by the licence fee, advertising revenue, and then a tax on the profits of the commercial companies (but one devoted to making programmes). These sources of finance did not compete with each other, and were key to the possibility of political independence. Each stage produced new audiences for broadcasting – the BBC creating an image of its audience as 'participants' in the great affairs of the nation, commercial television popularizing the medium, and Channel 4 decisively registering and enhancing the interests of minority audiences. Finally of course, at each stage new kinds of programmes and styles of addressing audiences were evolving. Until the the 1980s, broadcasting in Britain was not fettered but liberated for cultural and political expansion by the requirements of public service.

The principle of public service – which has always been fought over and continually reinterpreted – was not the paternalistic and abstract rule which critics have suggested. Nor has it been damaging to entrepreneurial initiative. Indeed, public service regulation has secured the survival of a successful broadcasting industry, one which has become more significant economically and which has become an important exporter of programmes while continuing to discuss and mould national issues. It has of course also never been perfect. Broadcasters have often failed to perceive the public interest and, even more frequently, have been too acquiescent to political pressure. Broadcasting has often been used by dominant political actors. Nevertheless, it has provided a flexible means of managing and developing an important utility which has been both commercially successful and served the public.

In the 1980s 'public service' became unfashionable. Yet those who derided it often had a financial interest in weakening it, or, alternatively, disliked the political autonomy of broadcasting. However, public service is not a static or dated ideal, it is one we need to redefine and develop. What were the origins of the principle and how did it come to be undermined?

Broadcasting in Britain – monopoly or duopoly – always depended on an assumption of commitment to an undivided public good. This lay beneath all official thinking on radio and television until the 1970s. In 1977 the Annan Report abandoned this assumption, and replaced it with a new principle of liberal pluralism. The ideal ceased to be the broad consensus – the middle ground upon which all men of good sense could agree. Rather it became, for Annan and those who supported and inspired him, a free marketplace in which balance could be achieved through the competition of multiplicity of independent voices. The result has been confusion and crisis, from which no new received doctrine has yet emerged.

So, by 1982, the Hunt Report on the introduction of cable television could begin to modify the principles of balance and quality even further. These were relegated to a part of the national service in the BBC and ITV. Although both the Hunt Report and the subsequent White Paper advocated some safeguards to protect the British system from the damaging effects of foreign satellite transmissions, and to guarantee the rights of the networks to televise events of national interest, the basis of public service broadcasting was abandoned. Thus cable television, free from constraining ideals, was left to produce programmes that 'were sufficiently attractive for the public to buy'.[1] The 1990 Broadcasting Act suggested that contenders for broadcasting franchises should produce 'sufficient amounts of quality programmes', but not only was this undefined, it only occupied two paragraphs in the Act. By contrast, conditions governing the financial arrangements for the auction of franchises took up fifteen pages.

However, the most obvious long-term symptom of the change in the status of the concept has been a shift in terminology. The concept of public service is elaborated in all broadcasting reports before that of the Annan Committee. As early as 1923 the Sykes Report argued that broadcasting was 'of great national importance as a medium for the performance of a valuable public service'.[2] The next report – that of the Crawford Committee in 1926 – suggested that in view of the scale, significance, and potentialities of broadcasting, the duties and status of the Corporation which it had just created 'should correspond with those of a public service, and the directorate should be appointed with the sole object of promoting the utmost utility and development of the enterprise'.[3]

Later reports developed the consequences of this view. 'The influence of broadcasting upon the mind and speech of the nation', commented the Ullswater Report, made it an 'urgent necessity in the national interest that the broadcasting service should at all times be conducted in the best possible manner and to the best possible advantage of the people'.[4] In 1950 the Beveridge Report on broadcasting characterized the ideal of public service more actively. 'Like the work of the universities,' Beveridge suggested, 'the work of broadcasting should be regarded as a public service for a social purpose.'[5] The Pilkington Report, which considered both the BBC and the commercial service in 1962, added to this definition: 'The concept of broadcasting has always been of a service, comprehensive in character, with the duty of a public corporation of bringing to public awareness the whole range of ... activity and expression developed in society.'[6] Indeed the organization of commercial television was as much a product of the ideal of public service broadcasting as the BBC's had been originally. Thus successive reports developed the idea of broadcasting as a public service – catering for all sections of the community, reaching all parts of the country regardless of cost, seeking to educate, inform, and improve, and prepared to lead public opinion rather than follow it.

The Annan Report, however, broke with this tradition for the first time. This change was noticeable, both in the evidence which was presented to the committee, as well as in the conclusion of the report. Even the reformers, whether of the left or right, disregarded the public service principle entirely. The BBC referred to it in only the most apologetic tone. The Annan Committee itself took a pluralist view: broadcasting should cater for the full range of groups and interests in society, rather than seek to offer moral leadership. 'For the individual life is a gamble, he is entitled to stake everything, if he desires, on one interpretation of life,' it argued. 'But broadcasting organizations have to back the field, and put their money on all the leading horses which line up at the starting gate.'[7] In one elegant metaphor, the whole basis of public service broadcasting had been dismissed.

Indeed the Annan Report's reinterpretation of public service unintentionally left British broadcasters defenceless against the threats posed by recent technological developments. By so transforming public service it left no grounds on which to manage or control the impact of the inevitable introduction of cable, video, or satellite broadcasting. Since 1977, reports and White Papers on the future of these very technologies have not even attempted to assess the impact of unregulated competition for audiences, revenues, and programmes on the television system as a whole. Thus it was possible for the Hunt Report to suggest that viewers' willingness to pay for cable television simply constituted a new source of revenue. It was claimed that this would not divert resources from existing channels. (However, it was not apparently thought necessary to support this assertion by either evidence or argument.)

By contrast there was a radical development in the 1986 Peacock Report, which reinterpreted the role of the market in broadcasting.[8] While advocating what Samual Brittan, a leading monetarist journalist and theorist and member of the Peacock Committee, called 'the goal that British Broadcasting should move towards a sophisticated market system based on consumer sovereignty', the report perceived public service commitments as actually protecting consumer sovereignty. Brittan commented that 'The existence of a tax-financed BBC and the IBA regulation of commercial television were justified by Peacock as a second best, but very successful, attempt to replicate artificially the programme structure of a true broadcasting market.' More than that, the committee took up the elaboration of the public service ideal developed in Channel 4 provision, and suggested that a mature broadcasting service would operate like the publishing industry. 'Prepublication censorship, whether of printed material, plays, films, broadcasting or other creative activities or expressions of opinion, has no place in a free society', the report argued, and recommended that the government 'embark forthwith on a phased programme for ending it'. Brittan went on to point out not only that the report widened the scope of its enquiries far beyond its original brief of considering the introduction of advertising on to the BBC (which it rejected), by assessing the future of broadcasting and how that could be best managed in the context of technological developments, but also that the report demonstrated the fundamental social significance of broadcasting. As Brittan commented

Peacock exposed many of the contradictions in the Thatcherite espousal of market forces. In principle, Mrs Thatcher and her supporters are in favour of de-regulation, competition, and choice. But they are distrustful . . . of plans to allow people to listen to and watch what they like, subject only to the law of the land. They espouse the market system but dislike the libertarian value judgements involved in its operation: value judgements which underlie the Peacock Report.[9]

The Peacock Report put public service back on the agenda at just the point when the broadcasting organizations seemed to have abandoned it.

Indeed this abandonment by the broadcasting organizations is a problem, for the authority of British broadcasting has always depended on the pursuit of public service. Indeed by relinquishing any claim to this, the broadcasting institutions have put into jeopardy a whole set of complex relationships between themselves, the state, their audiences, and their programme policy. What caused this crisis? What are its consequences?

## The state and broadcasting

One cause of the collapse of the principle of public service broadcasting has been the deterioration in the relationship between the state and broadcasting institutions. In the Sykes Report, Charles Trevelyan argued that 'We consider such a potential power over public opinion and the life of the nation ought to remain with the state.' Because broadcasting was so important it was seen as 'essential that permission to transmit, and the matter to be transmitted should be subject to public authority'.

Air waves were a scarce resource which did not obey national boundaries. Consequently the state was obliged to control the right to broadcast in all societies. In the early British broadcasting reports, however, there is a consensus that state regulation is the best guarantee of broadcasting independence and accountability. As the Crawford Report put it, only the state could license the BBC to be 'a public corporation acting as trustee for the national interest'.

In the 1920s the problem of the relationship of government with broadcasting was dealt with by making new rules and creating new machinery. It was taken for granted that the control over the administration of an organization could be kept quite

separate from whatever the organization did. Hence it was possible for broadcasting to be politically accountable, and yet
remain independent of any political influence. The Sykes Report
noted that any detailed control of the work of the Corporation
would make a government 'constantly open to suspicion that it
was using an opportunity to its own advantage'. It was therefore
decided that the minister responsible for the service would be able
to answer questions in the House on matters of principle and
finance, but he should not be held responsible for the programmes
themselves. Later the problem seemed to disappear. Complaints
about government intervention were rare, and the issue of excessive
interference no longer seemed to exist.

In 1936 the Ullswater Report commented, 'We have no reason
to suppose that, in practice, divergent views of public interest
have been held by the Corporation and government departments.'
Pilkington argued in 1962 that 'The practical resolution of the
problem was made easier because the first priority of the department concerned with exercising the government's responsibility
(the GPO) is with technical matters.' No conflict had arisen
between broadcasters and governments over the definition of
public interest.

However, by the 1970s this pragmatic argument was felt to be
inadequate. Imperceptibly the problem had become one of defending broadcasters against the state. The relationship was increasingly
characterized as one of vigilant and stealthy hostility. A cold war
had been declared between them.

This was partly a consequence of the changing nature of politics
in Britain. In a world of increasingly sophisticated news reporting
this posed problems for both the BBC and the IBA. 'Politics' and
political balance could be treated simply in two- or three-party
terms in the 1950s. By the 1970s this was no longer the case. The
emergence of centre parties made the work of 'striking a balance'
far more difficult for broadcasters. In addition many fields which
had previously been regarded as non-controversial and administrative had moved into the political arena. But also because of a
proliferation of parties, interests, and pressure groups, because of
a widening gap between the major parties and, most of all,
because of the rise of issues – of which Northern Ireland was the
most critical – for which the gentlemanly and constitutionalist
assumptions of the early rule-makers could not cater. The
problem of providing 'balance' in dealing with treasonable activities in Ulster – when, whether, and under what conditions to

interview terrorists or members of illegal organizations, how to discuss the issue at all – forced the broadcasting directorates to make new rules and, in effect, to add to the corpus of Britain's unwritten constitution.

The questions which the public asked about broadcasting, the Annan Report claimed, were becoming 'more critical, more hostile and more political'. At the same time, there was a new public mood, 'at once inflationary in the expectation of what political power could achieve, and deflationary towards those in power who failed to give effect to these expectations'.

The interests of governments had come, by the late 1970s, to be seen as inimical to those of broadcasting. The distinction between the broadcasting bureaucracies and what they produced had been challenged. Previously the quality and balance of a company's programmes were believed to be guaranteed by the good order of the administration. This view was now replaced by one of increasingly detailed suspicion. More than that, broadcasters' institutionalized caution about the power of governments had developed into a rejection of all kinds of intervention by the state.

This has had profound consequences for the legitimacy of the public service broadcasting organizations. The Annan Report argued that the authorities have a dual role: on the one hand they exist to ensure that broadcasters operate in the public interest and are responsive to public opinion, particularly as expressed in parliament. On the other hand, they exist 'also to defend broadcasters from undue pressure from whatever quarter'. But these are not complementary obligations; rather they are contradictory. The authorities are supposed both to reflect political pressure and to resist it. It used to be possible for the authorities to perform these two functions when the interests of the state and the broadcasting organization were seen as similar, if not identical. However, once their interests are opposed, the two aspects of the authorities' role are increasingly difficult to reconcile.

## Accountability and broadcasting

This situation would matter less if other mechanisms designed to relate broadcasting institutions to society seemed less perfunctory. Since 1926 they have all suffered from attrition.

Reith rapidly turned the Governors, supposedly 'the trustees of the national interest', into creatures of the Director General. In both commercial television and the BBC, the Boards of Governors depend for their information upon the organizations they were designed to supervise, and they have no independent secretariat or research function. The Governors have remained relatively power-less, and do not see their job as one of representing external interests or views. Similarly the role of the advisory committees was ingeniously reinterpreted. Reith ensured that these acted as specialists (whether in music, speech, or religion) who merely offered their advice over particular policy issues to the Corporation, rather than experts in broadcasting as such.

Indeed the only independent source of power left within these supposedly governing bodies is that of the Chairman of the Board. This power derives from the Chairman's close personal association with the Director General – or the administrative head of the independent service. Yet this intimacy leads to what Heller has called 'the tendency of broadcasting authorities to identify their interests, and by implication the national interest very closely with the survival of the organization they supervise'.[10]

However, in the 1980s a series of political crises in which the role of broadcasting was crucial – the Falklands War, continuing trouble in Ireland, disputes about the interpretation of foreign events, and profound disagreements about the management of the economy – all exposed the potential vulnerability of the governing body and the Chairman to political influence. Indeed, the Con-servative government sought to dominate the governors more directly than any previous administration, by swamping the board with its own supporters. In the 1980s, the problem was not so much the identification of the Chairman with the institution, but rather the identification of the Chairman with the government in power.

Yet the broadcasting organizations had given up so much of the ground themselves. By the 1980s the IBA was to claim that accountability was only a minority interest. The Annan Report had endorsed a system which was little more than a pious rhetoric. 'On balance', the report concluded '. . . while some improvements could be made, the relations between government and parliament and the broadcasting authorities do not require much adjustment: the chain of accountability is adequate.' Annan apparently believed that accountability was a purely abstract idea – one which includes no reference to the public. But the paragraph nevertheless ends, 'We do not consider, however, that the relations between the broadcasters and the public are satisfactory.' If, as Annan suggested, broadcasting is to abandon the independence of public service, and be based, rather, on a principle of representative pluralism, then the inadequacy of the Governors, and advisory committees, becomes even more serious.

## Independent professionals or men with an interest?

The independence of broadcasting from the state has recently been seen as the most important condition of the service's accountability. This independence has in turn been reduced to the freedom of programme-makers. Yet as Beveridge once commented, 'To whom is a broadcaster responsible? If it is only to his own conscience the decision might better be described as irresponsible.'

This emphasis on broadcasters' rights is a consequence of focusing the assessment of broadcasting on individual programmes. Pilkington was the last report to elaborate the tradition of public service, and it also argued that 'A service of broadcasting should be judged, not by the stated aims of the broadcasters, but by its achievements.' The Annan Report endorsed this approach.

Nevertheless, broadcasting and broadcasting institutions cannot be understood merely as a collection of separate programme 'texts'. As an ACCT Report commented, judging broadcasting organizations by their product 'was like being asked to evaluate the Milk Marketing Board by drinking milk – relevant, but not adequate'.[11]

Broadcasting is a process which cannot be entirely understood from its products. Few would claim that the whole nature of the capitalist enterprise can be understood from the shop floor of one factory. Neither can all the pressures which condition broadcasting institutions be revealed by an examination of what Tracey has called 'the world of determination of a television programme'[12] – however important that study might be. The emphasis on programmes as the most important criterion for judging broadcasting reinforces the arbitrary role of professionals at the expense of more general considerations of public service.

The Annan Report claimed that 'Good broadcasting would reflect the competing demands of a society which was increasingly multi-racial and pluralist.' In turn, this variety could be secured only by giving the 'talented broadcasters' greater freedom of expression.

However, broadcasters are not necessarily influenced by a wide variety of interests. Much recent research has shown how little producers and directors consider their audience. The only information about viewers which seriously affects producers is knowledge of the size of the audience. This is not because audience research is incapable of providing more complex detail, but because to know more would put producers under even greater stress. 'For a sociologist', comments Burns, 'it was rather like watching the whole practice of medicine being reduced to the use of a thermometer.'[13] Producers value the opinion of their colleagues most, but they see very little even of them.

The public interest cannot simply rely on the quality of broadcasters, because to do so is to ignore the pressures which determine broadcasting choices. 'When one stresses the role of individuals manning the system,' Garnham argues, 'one is tempted to await a Messiah who will come over – and help transform the system.'[14]

However, the relationship of broadcasters to their organization has also altered. Burns argued that there had been a considerable change in attitude since the 1960s. Then staff expressed a devotion to public service 'and a belief in the BBC's normative role in the cultural, moral and political life of the country'. By the 1970s this had been replaced by a commitment to professional values. Indeed as Kumar points out, the emergence of professionalism as the dominating ideology is the product of a particular moment in the evolution of broadcasting organizations. Even the notion of 'lively broadcasting' which determines the professionals' judgements 'expresses a particular stance towards the audience, a judgement of what the audience can and cannot take, which reflects a particular conception of the purposes of broadcasting'.[15]

Indeed the new 'scientific management' of broadcasting organizations has greater power than earlier administrations, whose main concern had been to protect and assist programme-makers who had far higher status within the organization. 'Because of the need to allocate time and resources economically,' Burns argues, 'working relations became impersonally functional.' The steady march of rational managerialism had led to a withering of institutional ardour.

Indeed, professionalism is now being superseded in many broadcasting organizations by crude financial managerialism. The pursuit of profit rather than excellence is more likely to dominate decisions in the next decade. Government reforms, culminating in the 1989 Broadcasting Bill,[16] and the proposal to auction Channels 3 and 5 to the 'highest bidders' (who in order to bid may have to pass a programme quality 'threshold', but who will be awarded franchises solely on their ability to raise the largest amounts of capital)[17] will inevitably reduce the power of pro-gramme-makers. These pressures are already evident: in the past broadcasting administrators had often been programme-makers first; in a 1989 survey of new appointments to top posts in television the majority of posts were given to 'accountants, bankers, and financial managers'.[18] Consequently not only were the talented programme-makers upon whom Annan, for instance, rested the future of broadcasting less committed to public service than before, but also they had become less important within broadcasting organizations. Indeed, current proposals for the re-structuring of broadcasting in the 1990s can only diminish their power even further.

## Independence and the theory of broadcasting

The significance of broadcasting independence is also disputed. One side suggests that the independence is functional and must be extended to guarantee accountable broadcasting. The other argues that this same independence poses a serious threat to political institutions, whose control over broadcasting should be strength-ened. Working from the same assumptions about the role of the media, Anthony Smith and Colin Seymour-Ure have arrived at diametrically opposed diagnoses and solutions.

According to classic liberal theory the independence of a journalist depended on his ability to follow the uninhibited dictates of his conscience. According to Smith, this is an illusory ideal. In discussing the 1968 crisis in French broadcasting he argues that, 'The ORTF strikers had stumbled across the central dilemmas of broadcasting and were demanding in the name of freedom . . . a right which no broadcaster has ever really achieved – the right to be an individual member of a Fourth Estate.' In its place Smith puts forward a far more sophisticated and powerful version of the theory, in which the independence of broadcasters is not an individual right – but rather a functional necessity.

Broadcasters are not free, but are 'brokers and megaphones, impresarios and mediators', he suggests. The 'independence' of broadcasting institutions from political control was one solution to a dilemma all broadcasting systems had to solve: namely the necessity not only of regulating the right to broadcast but also of ensuring that broadcasting served the interests of all sections of society. For, Smith suggests, 'The institutions of broadcasting inaugurated a special problem of unlegitimized and unselective

power.' Broadcasters are obliged to negotiate political conflict –
and not take sides in it – precisely because of the immense and
dangerous nature of their power. In stable systems countervailing
interests would always be able to enforce damaging sanctions if
broadcasters became partisan.

This model implies that all political interests in society can, in
practice, be reconciled. It is a logical extension of broadcasting
institutions' own view of their role as arbiters that they come to
see conflict and opposition as the products of failures in communication. Nevertheless, if there are real differences in interest,
incompatible policies, and irreconcilable principles, then the role
of the broker becomes untenable.

However, the functional independence of broadcasting institutions has many of the same policy consequences as the older liberal
individualism. For, Smith argues, the way to meet recent criticisms
is to give broadcasters more independence. The more perfectly
broadcasters can do anything they want, the more adequate the
service will be. As he is reported as commenting to the Annan
Committee:

> If I am free to say anything I want to say except the one thing I
> want to say then I am not free. . . . In broadcasting . . . a single
> prohibition imposed on a national broadcasting authority or
> within it tends to corrode the whole output.

Colin Seymour-Ure views the 'independence' of broadcasters
rather differently. The independence of the press – no longer the
client of political parties – and 'now part of vast corporations who
may have very direct interests in the outcomes of policy decisions'
is vulnerable because it is compromised by ownership. Broadcasters, moreover, having abandoned the protection of 'public
service' ideology are also susceptible to accusations of bias.
Seymour-Ure argues that:

> Some Labour politicians used to take comfort in the fact that
> although the press might be disproportionately conservative, at
> least broadcasting was balanced. This is no longer true. No
> doubt broadcasters are not wilfully biased. But the simple fact
> of deciding their own programme content may in the extreme
> case lead to a projection of party politicians and leaders that
> might run entirely counter to the parties' own views.

He suggests that the current interpretation of broadcasting independence has seriously damaged the political system.

The ideal of broadcasting independence – unlimited by any obligation to public service – has become increasingly inadequate. It has contributed to a growing anti-government ethos. It is hostile to many forms of political partisanship. It may inhibit political change and development. It may be that, as Seymour-Ure comments, the period of mass-based party organization is ending, for one effect of television in many countries seems to be 'the erosion of intervening structures between representatives and electors'. Nevertheless, any increase in the autonomy of broadcasting institutions may have more serious political consequences than had been expected. Rather it is the democratic processes which need support: not because broadcasters are malign but because of the inexorable pressure of broadcasting independence on the handling of politics.

## Choice versus public service?

Double think, according to George Orwell, is the 'power of holding two contradictory beliefs in one's mind simultaneously and accepting both of them'. Through successive regimes, *double think* has nevertheless precisely defined the attitude of politicians towards broadcasting. On the one hand there are people (government ministers, for instance) who tend to believe that the worse excesses of broadcasting, as of the trade unions, should be curbed. There are others (shadow ministers, for instance) who look to broadcasting as a means to correct political bias.

Never, however, have the contradictions been so glaring as in the past decade. The politics of the 1980s have been orchestrated in a language of freedom, choice, non-intervention, withdrawal of the state: yet the 1980s were deformed with successive governmental limitations on the public right to be informed. Where individuals have sought to challenge state manipulation of the news the government showed neither mercy nor moderation in making an example of offenders. Indeed, the effective range of discussion and investigation is probably narrower here than in most modern democracies – including France, Sweden, West Germany, and possibly even the USA. It may not be long before the former Eastern bloc leaves us behind in the matter of broadcasting freedom. Who can imagine the Home Office giving a foreign camera crew *carte blanche* to film what they liked in the Maze Prison – in the way that the Soviet authorities recently provided open access to a Western team in one of the USSR's remaining political gaols?

In addition to this, during the 1980s the Conservative government blatantly used television for government propaganda – with a massive increase in public sector advertising. Between 1980 and 1989, commercial television revenues doubled in real terms, and the proportion of advertising revenue generated by the public sector over that period quadrupled, indeed by 1989 it had become the largest single buyer of television advertising.[19] If the ostensible purpose of the advertising was the sale of shares in the shortly to be privatized public sector industries, it also furthered the ideology of privatization.

Throughout the period, public service broadcasting was compared unfavourably with 'the real choice offered to consumers by a more effective market'.[20] Successive reports, government green papers, and bills proposed to 'set free broadcasters from the narrow constraints of control' and it was repeatedly argued that satellite, cable, and a deregulated broadcasting system would offer the public a greater choice of programmes more sensitively tailored to their wants by the competitive pressures of the market. In part, of course, government policy was attempting to adapt to a new situation in which cable and satellite would deliver such a multitude of channels and services that the previous regime of regulation would become practically impossible. But more than this, policy was driven by a profound hostility to the principles of public service broadcasting.

Yet the ideology of 'choice' was absurd. Commercial broadcasting is based, not on the sale of programmes to audiences, but on the sale of audiences to advertisers. Thus the introduction of more competitors will reduce advertising revenues both by spreading them between a greater number of channels and by splitting potential audiences into even smaller groups. As the main incentive will remain the attraction of the largest possible audience, the competing channels, less constrained by regulation to produce a variety of programmes, will tend to show more of the same or similar programmes.

Indeed, if one contradiction of Thatcherism was that free market rhetoric was accompanied by interventionist practice, another was that talk of the market-place was accompanied by its virtual eradication. Technological change – with its requirement for long-term investment and large-scale capitalization – has produced a bureaucratic jungle of profit-taking conglomerates, which own shares in all the media which the public consumes. The small number of corporate owners are not competitive in a sense that could conceivably be expected to produce an improved product; but their financial rivalry will undoubtedly impose pressure to produce a cheaper one. That means an almost inevitable lowering of standards, since it is cheaper to buy in internationalized soap opera than to make your own drama, and so on. The result is likely to be a lesser variety of the kind of programmes that many of us watch some of the time, and some of us watch most of the time, but which do not attract top audience ratings. We are all, on occasions, members of minorities. Thus the victims of media concentration are variety, creativity, and quality, while the pro-liferation of broadcasting channels in the hands of a small band of operators, 'liberated' by government policy from the obligations of public service variety, is likely to make matters worse. 'Choice', without positive direction, is a myth, for all too often the market will deliver more – but only more of the same.

## Conclusion

Broadcasters have come to see the state as their enemy. Yet broadcasting institutions ultimately depend on the state for their legitimation. This authority cannot be replaced by a pluralist ideal of reflecting social and cultural variety. Indeed the adoption of this principle has left broadcasters peculiarly vulnerable to the more general attack on public service broadcasting.

Moreover, arguments with quite different aims from those of the broadcasters, but apparently related, are being used to under-mine broadcasting responsibility and independence. Thus neither the emphasis on the authority of the viewers' right to choose from a greater variety of programmes, nor the elaboration of some aspects of the local and regional role of the media, let alone the distinction between a 'service' the public will pay for and a public service, are intended to strengthen the creative autonomy of broadcasters. On the contrary, they are arguments which enhance the power of commercial interests in determining the patterns of broadcasting provision.

Thus without a commitment to public service, broadcasters are increasingly vulnerable to detailed political interference in the content of programmes. Broadcasting in Britain has in the past had a considerable degree of autonomy from other institutions: it has not in any simple sense been biased. This autonomy is now threatened, partly because the consensus about what constitutes the 'middle ground' of agreed opinion has broken down, partly because the reliance on the skill of professional broadcasters which has replaced it is unjustified, and partly because of the erosion of public service broadcasting. Broadcasting needs to find a new relationship to the state – and a new form of commitment to public service, and indeed a new definition of public service that will work in the conditions of increased competition.

## Notes

1. *Report of the Enquiry into Cable Expansion and Broadcasting Policy* (Hunt Report, 1982) [Cmnd 8697].
2. *Broadcasting Committee: Report* (Sykes Report, 1923) [Cmnd 1951], X, 13, para. 21.
3. *Report of the Broadcasting Committee* (Crawford Report, 1926) [Cmnd 2599], VIII, 327, para. 49.
4. *Report of the Broadcasting Committee* (Ullswater Report, 1936) [Cmnd 5091], VII, 617, para. 7.
5. *Report of the Broadcasting Committee* (Beveridge Report, 1951) [Cmnd 8116], IX, 1, para. 217.
6. *Report of the Committee on Broadcasting* (Pilkington Report, 1960) [Cmnd 1755], IV, 259, para. 23.
7. *Report of the Committee on the Future of Broadcasting* (Annan Report, 1977) [Cmnd 6753], XVI, para. 311.
8. *Report of the Committee on Financing the BBC* (Peacock Report, 1986) [Cmnd 9824], II, para. 636.
9. S. Brittan, 'The fight for freedom in broadcasting', *Political Quarterly*, 58, 1 (March 1987).
10. C. Heller, *Broadcasters and Accountability*, BFI Television Monograph 3 (London, British Film Institute, 1978), p. 39.
11. ACCT report, quoted in C. Heller, *Broadcasters and Accountability*, BFI Television Monograph 3 (London, British Film Institute, 1978), p. 50.
12. M. Tracey, *The Production of Political Television* (London, Routledge & Kegan Paul, 1978), p. 13.
13. T. Burns, *The BBC: Public Institution and Private World* (London, Macmillan, 1977), p. 137.
14. N. Garnham, *Structures of Television*, BFI Television Monograph 1 (London, British Film Institute, 1973), p.21.
15. K. Kumar, 'Holding the middle ground: The BBC, the public and the professional broadcaster' in J. Curran, M. Gurevitch, and J. Woollacott (eds), *Mass Communication and Society* (London, Edward Arnold/ Open University, 1977), p. 232.
16. Broadcasting Bill, Bill No. 9, December 1989 (London, HMSO, 300906).

17. See Martin Cave, 'The conduct of auctions for broadcasting franchises', *Fiscal Studies* 10, 1 (Feb. 1989), pp. 17–31.
18. 'New managers, new talents', *Vision* (Dec. 1989), pp. 15–31.
19. 'Television advertising by sector', *Campaign* (July 1989).
20. S. Velachesky, 'Broadcasting choice', *Hobbart Papers on Liberal Economics* (June 1989), p. 7.

# Part IV

## *Politics of the media*

# *Contradictions in public policy*

## Introduction

To inform, to discuss, to mirror, to bind, to campaign, to challenge, to entertain, and to judge – these are the important functions of the media in any free country. The purpose of public policy should be to enable the media to perform them more effectively. Yet historically, very different traditions of promoting these ideals or indeed pursuing no ideals at all have developed in public policy towards the press and broadcasting. Newspapers have been seen as part of the market, while broadcasting has been regulated in order to achieve at least some of these goals. Recently, however, there has apparently been a revolution in official thinking about the media. It has been argued that broadcasting ought also to be managed by market rather than official forces. The state is now seen by some as having a dead hand, and regulation as an impediment to innovation.

Nevertheless, however loudly the discussions of the 1980s were carried on in terms of 'liberating' or removing official constraints, one basic point was clear. You cannot reform by doing nothing. A government policy which sought to make changes was interventionist even when it claimed not to be. Policy towards the media has been just as authoritarian recently as in the past.

The 1980s were the 'me' decade. Political, economic, and social revival were supposed to be led by the individual's pursuit of self-interest. Nowhere was this new principle in public life more dominant than in thinking about the media. The 'individuals' whose self-interest was particularly valued were those of the existing media barons. In the new age, entrepreneurs, seeking to maximize their own profit were more likely, it was claimed, to produce a broadcasting service genuinely sensitive to what audiences – customers – wanted. A decade of reform was intended to make broadcasting just like the newspapers.

Thus the reorganization of broadcasting services proposed by the 1990 Broadcasting Act and the management of the introduction of new media services were all based on the rhetoric of dismantling regulation. The contradictions between public thinking about the press and broadcasting were to be finally resolved: the market was to reign.

However, as Samuel Brittan has pointed out, the 'radical' reformers of the 1980s were less bold in their actions than their words. They were too timid to let the public express its taste: in case it liked what they thought was bad for it. In practice, although financial restraints to produce good national broadcasting were discarded, they were replaced by a bevy of regulatory quangos, censoring material for respectability. Even more ironically the decade ended with a belated, ineffective, series of initiatives, some from the newspapers proposing a self-policing code of ethics, others like the recommendations of the Calcutt Committee designed to curb the worst irresponsibilities of the 'free' press from outside. Even the press barons apparently recognized that their newspapers' exploitation of individual tragedy, extravagant lies, and persecution of scapegoats, had come to outrage the public (the sovereign 'consumer') so much that they had to be at least seen to regulate the worst of these excesses.

Indeed, by the beginning of the 1990s not only was the need to control the press seen to be more desirable and possible, but it was also clear that beneath a veneer of market reforms, there remained a resilient consensus that public policy had to ensure that broadcasters produced a better, wider range of programmes than the market alone would permit. Many of the proposals for broadcasting reform, were, in effect, modified by a commitment to traditional requirements that broadcasters be impartial, informative, and representative. Perhaps the time for a unified policy for the media is ripe – but not a policy of spurious freedom, rather one of regulated responsibility? For the first time it is possible to ask that the media be not merely slicker or richer, but better.

However, it is also important to identify the contradictions in existing public policy, the extent to which thinking about the press and broadcasting is different, or more remarkably similar.

## Efficiency

Some official attitudes towards the media have changed remarkably little over the last sixty years. One recurrent theme has been the emphasis on greater efficiency. Thus in 1949 the Gater Report on the British Film Industry called for more effective financial planning, while the second (1962) Press Commission urged that better machinery for negotiation should be established, a point also stressed by the Prices and Incomes Board report on the press in 1967. In the same way the Annan Report (1977) concluded that 'clear lines of decision making, fewer chieftains, better communications' were the most important remedies and the Peacock Report on the BBC (1986) argued that 'the assessment of efficiency is one of our Committee's chief aims'. Such comments, few of which have ever had any significant effect, have become part of the ritual of investigation.

Most government reports have also taken an optimistic view of the independence of journalists and programme-makers, and their capacity for autonomous reform. Thus two Royal Commissions have stressed in identical words that 'on the quality of the individual journalist depends not only the status of the whole profession of journalism but the possibility of bridging the gap between what society needs from the press and what the press is at present giving it'. Similarly the Annan Report argued that 'The strength of British Broadcasting lies in the creativity of people who make programmes.'

Hence successive reports have suggested better recruitment policies, improved training and education, and greater integrity and responsibility amongst communicators as the best ways to improve the media. Annan proposed an Open Broadcasting Authority which would show programmes made by 'small independent production groups', a term which is reminiscent of the 'small independent producer' which film policy has been unsuccessfully trying to help since the Moyne Report in 1936. In the same way, three Royal Commissions have attempted to secure a more varied press by encouraging individual entrepreneurs. Even the Calcutt Report (1990) on privacy suggested that newspaper ethics depended 'on the calibre of the individual conscience'. A somewhat narrow view of the causes of tabloid exploitation.

This emphasis on individuals – as opposed to structures – has led to a neglect of the role of financial limitations. Thus for many years public money was used in an attempt to finance independent

film producers. Yet, because there was no reform of the organization of film distribution and exhibition, this money merely increased
the profits of the large production companies. Public finance
reinforced those monopolistic tendencies within the film industry
which it had been intended to mitigate. Similarly the Annan
Committee proposed an Open Broadcasting Authority to introduce
more adventurous minority programmes, yet failed to suggest
how the finance of the new authority could be arranged to protect
it from the economic pressures which inhibited experimental
programming on the other channels. Channel 4 has produced a
multitude of small, innovative production companies, but all
dependent on the patronage of a few commissioning editors.
Indeed the Peacock Committee, appointed by a government hostile
to the BBC, nevertheless made an important contribution to the
survival of public service broadcasting precisely because for the
first time its main object was to consider the financial structures
that underlay the cultural considerations.

Thus, Channel 4's early success in assisting the renaissance in
the British film industry was more a result of regularizing the
product than of providing the finances. By giving individual, one-
off, British art movies a secure, predictable audience on television, systematizing their careers through the art movie theatres,
and making it possible to present each film as part of a successful
series, the channel facilitated the independent producers' capacity
to raise film finance. Channel 4 helped to raise the hopes of a
network of able, creative, and important film-makers. However, it
failed to solve the financial crisis. In other European countries
with successful film industries state finance has been easily
available – a critical factor in artistic and commercial success.

Therefore, government reports retained a number of basic
assumptions over the years, glossing over or ignoring problems
which their recommendations failed to solve. Yet the essential
conservatism of official policy was less important than its contradictions. Good policy is not necessarily consistent policy, but one of
the most curious features of government relations with the media
has been the way in which reports on the press, broadcasting, and
film industries have often conflicted sharply with one another.

## The state as a threat

A common feature of much official thinking about the working of
the media has been a liberal suspicion of the state and a determina-

tion to reject state intervention. In the last decade this has grown
in Britain to a crude abhorrence of all regulation. Of course, in
practice, many of the most economically successful societies,
Japan and Sweden among them, modify market forces both in
industry and in the media for political, social, and economic ends.
The French have revolutionized their press and broadcasting in
the last ten years – by state fiat. The 'neo-liberal' suspicion of the
state, coupled with some anxiety about the effects of the market,
has been repeatedly expressed in official reports on the press. In
Britain the last Royal Commission on the press argued:

> We are strongly against any scheme which would make the
> press, or any section of it, dependent on government through
> reliance on continuing subsidies from public funds. We are also
> opposed absolutely to the establishment of any body which
> could, or might have to, discriminate among publications in
> such a way as to amount to censorship in the sense of preferring
> to support some publications and not others.

The MacGregor Commission, like its predecessors, rejected any
form of public support that was either selective or which led to
economic dependence on the state. These principles were invoked
in opposition to proposals for financial reform of the press. In
addition, it was believed that they would forestall any further
discussion of economic intervention. 'Suggestions [for financial
reform of the press] were put to the two previous Royal Commissions', stated the report, 'and, although rejected, have continued
to be advocated. We hope, perhaps optimistically, that ... we
may have finally laid them to rest.'

The two principles have been expressed in technical arguments.
On the one hand most schemes for subsidizing newspapers involved
providing aid for small or insecure publications; since this meant
a 'selective' award, they have always been rejected. On the other
hand, schemes that did not discriminate in favour of the weaker
publications have been rejected because they were ineffective. As
the second Press Commission put it, 'If the subsidy were available
to all newspapers, it would leave their respective competitive
positions unchanged. If it were discriminatory it would involve in
an obvious way the dangers of government interference in the
press.'

Practical proposals for press reform have therefore been seen as
politically unacceptable, while politically acceptable ones have
turned out to be impractical. Consequently any interventions in

the economic conditions of the press have been dismissed.

Yet the principle of selectivity, which the Royal Commission found so dangerous, has been central to much public policy on communications. 'No public body', argued the third Press Commission, 'should ever be put in a position of discriminating like a censor between one applicant and another.' However, this was exactly what the Independent Broadcasting Authority did when awarding radio and television franchises. The new franchise-awarding body for television has also devoted much energy to modifying the lottery of the auctions, precisely to allow it to discriminate between plausible and exploitative contenders for the right to a Channel 3 contract. The same has been true of the National Film Finance Corporation when granting loans to production companies, and of the Arts Council when making grants (including some to small press publications). Channel 4 has 'commissioning editors' who discriminate between projects and companies sometimes on political grounds. Indeed the Economic and Social Research and Science Research Councils have also always discriminated among research projects, including politically sensitive ones, in awarding grants. It may be that the discrimination exercised by these bodies has been politically acceptable because they have not been concerned with news. However, there have been a number of scandals about the political motivation of decisions affecting information collection. Indeed, it is increasingly difficult to separate 'news' from information, research, and opinion – the production of which several of these organizations are involved in.

Moreover, previous examples of economic intervention by the state in the press have not been examined by the Royal Commissions. Yet there is little evidence that economic regulation of the British press during the Second World War, or press subsidies in other democratic countries, have led to covert political censorship. At the same time the state continues to intervene in the market for newspapers. Newspapers receive a considerable government subsidy in the form of zero-rating for VAT, which makes a number of marginal publications dependent on government for their continued existence. Also, a number of local government authorities provide funds for small community newspapers. This is a form of selective aid that contravened the Commission's principles. Indeed it might well be argued that selective aid given directly by any level of government to its potential critics, unmediated by any independent agency, is liable to abuse. There is much hypocrisy in this area, and official thinking needs re-examination.

The negative view of the state held by successive Royal Commissions on the press contrasts with their positive view of the market. Having rejected selective public subsidies because they might be open to political manipulation, the Commissions did not apply the same criteria to advertising. Thus advertising subsidies are discretionary, keep alive some publications, and favour right-wing newspapers. Similarly the political consequences of the exorbitant expense of launching a newspaper were not recognized. These have, of course, been reduced by new technology. However, the market tended to be seen as natural, inevitable, and politically neutral: public intervention on the other hand was always seen as politically biased.

## The benign state

In contrast to Royal Commissions public reports on broadcasting continue to invoke a more positive state. Conservative paternalism and an Arnoldian concern with moral and cultural values originally contributed to this view. A corporatist tradition also played a part, equating central planning with the rational and scientific use of resources, and so did a radical belief in the redistribution of power and wealth through state intervention. Certainly broadcasting has been seen as so powerful a political instrument that the state has been unwilling to abandon its close relationship with it. Even radical Thatcherite hostility to existing broadcasting organizations failed to undermine the practical necessity of involvement by the state in broadcasting affairs. Despite the liberal rhetoric, government policy has been more cautious than many critics feared.

All of the nine major reports on British broadcasting argued that a publicly appointed agency could act in the public interest, because it could be independent of all sectional interests, including that of the government. As the Crawford Committee (1926) put it, 'The actual commission should be persons of judgement and independence, free of commitments, and ... they will inspire confidence by having no other interests to promote than those of public service.'

Broadcasting has been repeatedly presented in reports as serving the public interest by being subject to regulations framed for the public good and controlled by people committed to the best interests of the entire community. The BBC at least was to be financed from licence revenue and was therefore, in the words of the Pilkington Report (1960), under 'no obligation, express or implied, to pursue any other objective other than that of public service'. Public regulation was seen as both necessary and desirable even after the introduction of commercial television.

This conception of public service has depended on a number of principles. First, that broadcasting services should be made available to everyone in the UK, and not merely developed in areas where it was easy or cheap to do so, or restricted to those who could pay for them. However, this principle has now been breached, and it is likely that access to broadcasting will increasingly depend on the ability to pay. Nevertheless, the full impact of these changes is not yet clear. Second, public service broadcasting should produce a wide variety of high-quality programmes because it would not be so subject to the pressures that make for low standards and uniformity. Lastly, that public regulation should ensure broadcasters' accountability through the relationship of the authority with parliament.

Reports on broadcasting have also been hostile to the effects of the market. The Crawford Committee (1926) argued that 'No company or body constituted on trade lines for profit . . . can be regarded as adequate . . . in view of the broader considerations which now begin to emerge.' The Ullswater Committee (1936) regarded commercial advertising as incompatible with 'the intellectual and ethical integrity which the broadcasting system in this country has attained'. Much of this opposition has been based on the belief that what the Beveridge Committee (1951) called 'competition for numbers' results in standardized programming. This view has been justified by references to the deplorable condition of commercial broadcasting in the USA. 'Experience in other countries', concluded the Pilkington Report in 1960, 'is that this kind of competition, so far from promoting the purposes of broadcasting, or extending the range of programmes, or helping to realize the potential of the medium, serves rather to restrict them.'

Despite increasing anxiety about the nature of the relationship between the government (and party politicians in general) and broadcasters, the necessity of state regulation was never questioned in public reports on television or radio until 1986. State control was portrayed as the best way of guaranteeing that broadcasting did not become an instrument of narrow sectional interests.

The notion of a 'public good' implies a commonly accepted consensus of opinion within society. Thus the Annan Report introduced a variety of reforms with the intention of encouraging a more sensitive balance. Annan remained committed to the notions of 'common interest', 'impartiality', and 'balance' on which public service broadcasting is based.

However, the belief that publicly regulated broadcasting could 'maintain cultural standards' arose in a period when values were more secure than they are now. As the Annan Report commented, 'The ideals of middle-class culture, so felicitously expressed by Matthew Arnold a century ago . . . found it ever more difficult to accommodate . . . the variety of expression of what is good.' The Annan Committee found it harder to define what 'good' broadcasting was than did Pilkington. Nevertheless, Annan did make qualitative judgements, finding the BBC's output, on balance, superior to that of ITV. Annan was opposed to the unrestricted commercial control of broadcasting, and saw the fact that ITV made 'some programmes which both stimulate and entertain, and are not concocted in order to drug their audience into an uncritical stupor' as a product of public regulation. Even the Peacock Report turned out to be a surprisingly staunch supporter of public service ideals. Regulated broadcasting, it argued, had led to a 'mixed diet' of programmes at 'a low cost', and it was particularly concerned to protect 'the interweaving of information, education and entertainment that has broadened the horizon of a great number of viewers'. The reform of broadcasting services proposed for the 1990s still requires the national networks and franchises to produce 'sufficient quantities of quality broadcasting'. Indeed, there is some evidence that redefinition of 'public service' is occurring, particularly for instance in the reorganization and reinvestment in news services within the BBC. These have consciously become more serious and better researched in an attempt to capture a different audience – and to distinguish the service from commercial competition.

Thus there has been an unresolved contradiction between the approaches adopted in the press and broadcasting reports. The idea that government should give money to a publishing corporation, even one with a publicly appointed managing authority, would have been opposed by all the Royal Commissions on the press. Yet this is precisely what the Annan Committee proposed when it suggested that a government grant could be given to start an Open Broadcasting Authority. Moreover, this is precisely what the Conservative government did when Channel 4 was launched.

The Conservative administration of the 1980s intended to resolve this contradiction permanently by making broadcasting subject to market forces – just like the press. Incidentally it also no doubt sought through financial reorganization to rid itself of what it perceived as a political irritant in the BBC. The Peacock Committee was established to consider substituting advertising revenue for the BBC's licence fee, and to look into the further 'deregulation' of broadcasting. With considerable ingenuity, the report in fact produced a defence of 'public service broadcasting' on the impeccable grounds that it had most perfectly promoted the aims of a neo-liberal policy. 'Public service institutions', the report commented,

> have been necessary to provide the viewer and listener with what he or she wants as a consumer. The BBC and the regulated ITV system had done far better in mimicking the effects of a true consumer market than any purely *laissez-faire* system financed by advertising could have done.

Peacock argued that there was an important category of programme, not merely of minority interest, and not restricted to narrow political and cultural ghettos in content, that consumers as voters and citizens had a significant interest in seeing preserved. These programmes, however, would be destroyed by exposure to market forces. 'More than that', the report went on to argue, 'we are clear that the component in consumer welfare which represents exposure to programmes which expand their range of tastes and preferences is of major importance.' Public service broadcasting for the Peacock Committee, in a classic definition entirely consistent with the traditional British view of the role of broadcasting, is about 'knowledge, culture, criticism, and experiment'.

In the past the attitude of broadcasting reports to pay-TV revealed a fundamental hostility to market pressures. By linking a cable television service to a pay-as-you-watch scheme, it is possible to establish a market-based system of broadcasting use which would be comparable to the press and film industries. Such a system has already been introduced in the USA and Canada. Its advocates argue its merits in much the same terms as the advocates of the capitalist press. Cable-based pay-TV, they argue, guarantees independence from state control and offers a wide choice of programmes. Thus they suggest that it forces programme-makers to respond to the interests and needs of consumers who pay only for what they want to see.

Previous Committees of Inquiry into broadcasting rejected these arguments. They pointed out that pay-TV would increase the cost of broadcasting to the consumer. It would discriminate against those who could not afford it and for whom it would not be profitable for pay-TV operators to cater. Above all, it would impoverish public service broadcasting. Not only would it divert revenue from existing services and increase their costs, but also it would result in a reduction in programme choice, for pay-TV operators would merely compete to attract the largest number of subscribers. They would have no obligation to consider programme standards. The whole basis of balanced programming and public service broadcasting would be undermined.

The Peacock Report, while suggesting that some more direct form of finance will be necessary to protect public service broadcasting by the end of the century, also rejected 'pay-TV' in its crude form. Rather, it argued, people should subscribe to a 'channel' of programmes, buying not individual programmes but rather a mixed diet of programmes for a fixed period. Most consumers, it suggested, would find this more convenient. But crucially this form of protection would support the continuing opportunity for broadcasters to provide the audience with programmes which would not otherwise survive the pressure of market forces.

Recent government policy has sought to increase the influence of market pressures on broadcasting by the way in which it has advocated the introduction of satellite television. Nevertheless, policy has been influenced by a continuing commitment to protect broadcasting from the full effects of unregulated market competition. Thus cable services are largely paid for by subscription, not on a programme-by-programme basis. In their present form they have been unsuccessful in attracting audiences. In addition, unlike the American system, the cable stations have been obliged to relay BBC and ITV programmes; and have been prohibited from interfering with the networks' schedules. Finally, the cable stations have to maintain standards of 'taste' and 'decency', and to follow the regulations governing advertising content laid down by the BBC and ITV.

Satellite stations have also had some of these restrictions imposed on them. Perhaps the most serious development to date is the permission they have been given to buy up exclusive rights to public events. Nevertheless, in seeking to control some of the effects of pay-TV and to consider the economic conditions for the production of public service broadcasting, public reports have continued to reject in part the market-based rationale for information that has determined policy towards the press, and have argued instead that public service regulation at the moment makes the market in broadcasting more 'perfect': regulation increases choice.

## The government and lame ducks

Finally, government intervention has often been justified as an exceptional measure that will make subsequent interference unnecessary and restore a stable and competitive market. Thus in 1927 a Board of Trade inquiry into the film industry had advocated special measures to deal with 'unfair, devious and improper trading' by American competitors. This report resulted in the Cinematograph Act, 1927, which banned block booking (when good films were sold only in a 'package' with a number of less desirable Hollywood products) and obliged the distributors and exhibitors to purchase and show quotas of British films. But the ban was intended to be only a short-term measure, to promote 'free and equitable trade'. In 1948 the National Film Finance Corporation was set up to provide loans for film production. It was seen as a response to a temporary inability of British film producers to obtain private investment capital. The Eady Levy, introduced during the same period, was also designed to promote national film production through a tax on box office takings which was supposed to fall most heavily on successful foreign imports. In the same way the last Royal Commission on the press recommended that newspapers should be offered cheap loans in order to pay for the introduction of new printing technology during a period of financial crisis.

This tradition was carried on by the Conservative administration during the 1980s. Even this adamantly 'free market' government launched, in 1990, a 'salvage package' for the British Film Industry. This was too little, too late, and too short term. With the emergence of a European market for films many continental film producers wanted to make joint films with British companies in order to break into the lucrative American market. However, the paucity of film finance in Britain made these deals very difficult to organize. The government, having ignored the developing crisis in the British industry, despite a commercial and creative explosion in the early 1980s, suddenly performed a U-turn and proposed a short-term finance scheme. Thus the government is again spending public money on films – but not according to any systematic plan that is likely to secure the industry's future. The money may be spent (probably ineffectively), but only for a single 'rescue' operation.

Yet schemes initially proposed as short-term expediencies have tended to become permanent. The 'temporary' measures to control the import of films introduced in 1927 were strengthened in 1938, further added to during the 1940s, and abandoned only in 1983. Similarly the National Film Finance Corporation was forced to write off many loans and so become a continuing source of state finance for the film industry. The Eady Levy survived until 1984, even though it reinforced American domination of the British film industry by subsidizing American-backed films which were only nominally British. The rationale for the levy changed, and it came to be seen as a way of maintaining employment in the British film industry. All these one-off interventions have led to a more permanent government involvement in the industries than had been originally intended. They might all have been more successful if they had been designed to meet long-term problems rather than short-term crises.

## The variety in policy goals

British communications policy has traditionally pursued contradictory goals. Thus the IBA Act of 1973 required that 'a proper proportion' of the programmes shown should be made in Britain, which led to a rule that no more than 14 per cent of commercial broadcasts should be foreign (excluding Commonwealth countries). 'Foreign' was subsequently redefined to apply to countries outside the EEC in the 1981 Broadcasting Act. The BBC in turn voluntarily adopted this quota. In addition the IBA prevented foreign, and in particular American, investment from controlling too large a share of British commercial television. The Annan Committee supported this protectionist policy, and added that 'foreign holdings in television companies should be severely limited.' Indeed the Committee criticized the IBA for its permissive attitude towards Commonwealth investment in local radio. Even the 1990 Broadcasting Act expresses residual 'concern' about the possibility of a completely foreign-owned broadcasting system, though it proposes few measures to prevent it occurring.

Conversely, unregulated foreign investment in the newspaper industry has been accepted by successive Royal Commissions (admittedly because of the unwillingness of others to invest in such a marginally profitable area). Public reports on the press, however, have expressed little concern for the potential political implications of this development. Furthermore, foreign investment, particularly by Americans, has been encouraged in the British film industry. As the 1968 review of film legislation suggested, the National Film Finance Corporation should be maintained, 'as it constitutes a real attraction for foreign investment'.

Many regulations continue to exist to maintain standards in broadcasting. The IBA attempted to mitigate the effects of 'competing for numbers'. Backed with the sanction of withholding licences, the IBA ensured that some of the advertising revenue generated by programmes reaching large audiences was invested in programmes for smaller audiences. However, the same principle did not apply in the allocation of film funds through the Eady Levy. This tax on cinema takings was paid to production companies in proportion to the box office revenue for their films. It constituted a bounty distributed according to market demand, rather than quality. 'The levy', concluded the 1968 Board of Trade review, 'should not be used to breed indifference to economic reality.' This seems to imply that the consideration of cultural or qualitative standards would be economically harmful. Although during the 1980s it was argued for a time that any consideration of 'cultural standards' was merely paternalistic caution, and as damaging culturally as it was inhibiting commercially, by the beginning of the 1990s the terms of discussion had changed again. There was a fierce and unresolved debate about the quality of broadcasting in the new conditions of greatly increased numbers of service providers. Quality, control, and regulation were clearly back on the broadcasting agenda.

Many public reports have argued that the media are not like other industries, and should be treated as special cases. As the Palache Committee (1944) put it, 'A cinematograph film represents something more than a mere commodity to be bartered.' Nevertheless, there is little discussion about how the traditional economic goal of maintaining full employment should be balanced against the wider objectives raised by the media's special role. In the case of film policy, priority has been given to the support of employment in the industry. In the case of the press, however, the main concern of Royal Commissions has been to maintain its diversity. In the case of broadcasting, there may even be belated recognition that the industrial success of an increasingly important industry has actually depended on some form of regulation.

## The politics of information and the politics of entertainment

Policy reports have also differed in the way in which they have approached the media. Royal Commissions on the press have been almost exclusively concerned with the current affairs content of newspapers, and policy proposals have dealt largely with the political function of the press. They have paid scant attention to the economic precondition for healthy political dispute, and virtually none to less august matters such as advertising, women's pages, and human interest stories. In contrast, broadcasting committees have considered the whole range of broadcasting. They have discussed the role of television and radio in wider social and cultural terms, and their recommendations have been intended to improve the general quality of programmes. The Peacock Committee was clearly part of this tradition.

This difference of approach may have arisen when current affairs reporting in broadcasting was severely limited. Until the Second World War the press, anxious about competition from the BBC, attempted to restrict the range of news that could be broadcast. In addition the Corporation, wishing to avoid charges of political bias, was also very cautious about political comment or opinion. Thus broadcasting came to be seen as a medium of entertainment for which 'cultural' and not 'political' standards were appropriate.

However, this has led to confusion in public policy. On the one hand, it is felt to be important that politicians' control over information and news is very restricted, not only because politicians might use any such power to further their own ends, but also because the news media may help to control politicians. On the other hand, there has been little concern about political control over entertainment, leisure, and culture. Public policy towards these areas has largely been concerned to secure a variety of cultural expression reflecting national life. Yet the distinction between the media of 'information' and those of 'entertainment' has now almost completely broken down. Hence the different political approaches which have developed to deal with broadcasting and the press are no longer adequate.

Recently there has been a reduction in the amount of current affairs and political news carried by the press. Moreover, the proportion of broadcasting time devoted to news and information has increased. BBC radio and television now carry more current affairs content, as a proportion of total output, than does the popular press. Of course, broadcasting has usurped the press in many aspects of reporting.

In many ways, however, the 'cultural' focus in reports on broadcasting has allowed them to consider the wider social and political consequences of the media. Thus in 1960 the Pilkington Committee recommended a ban on television advertisements 'appealing to human weakness'. Yet two years later the Royal Commission on the press did not even consider the content of newspaper and magazine advertising, let alone recommend its reform. Similarly the Annan Committee recommended that the joint ownership of commercial broadcasting companies and record or music publishing companies be banned, on the grounds that there was bound to be a conflict of interest between them. The third Royal Commission on the press, also reporting in 1977, made no such recommendation in relation to the musical press and record production.

## Pressure groups and policy

Public inquiries have also been exposed to different pressure groups and economic interests in each of the media. In the absence of an integrated approach to communications policy (or even comparable terms of reference for media inquiries), this has inevitably resulted in contradictory recommendations. The last two Press Commissions, for example, influenced by a powerful press lobby, supported the principle that one company could own several media industries, and subsidize the more vulnerable enterprise from the profits of the other. Thus the Press Commissions' approval of limited press holdings in profitable television and radio franchises. Similarly the Prime Minister's Working Party on the Film Industry (1977), closely influenced by the views of the industry, also proposed that television should finance film-making. On the other hand, the Annan Committee was exposed to a broadcasting lobby which was hostile to the idea that broadcasting should subsidize less profitable media industries. The Annan Report consequently opposed the view that 'like an aged parent, the film industry has a right to look to television to support it in its old age.' It therefore rejected the proposal (which had already been accepted by the Working Party on the Film Industry) for an allowance for film investment to be made out of the television levy. In addition reports on the press have often ignored the cultural consequences of financial structures.

The uncoordinated way in which policy for the media is formulated has meant that reforms have been proposed and implemented for one industry, which have then had unforeseen effects on the other media. For example, the decision to introduce commercial television had important repercussions for the press, many of which are still being worked out. Many of the major advertising agencies informed the 1962 Press Commission that commercial television had diverted advertising funds away from the press (and, in particular, from the general magazine press). It is difficult to assess the precise impact of commercial television on the advertising revenue of the press, as some losses may have been offset by the influence which television may have had in raising the total amount that was spent on advertising. On the other hand, the increase in advertising expenditure may have been caused not by television but by the ending of newsprint rationing and the general economic growth which characterized the period. However, it is clear that the amount of television advertising has grown much faster than display advertising in the press. Moreover, the competition from commercial television caused newspaper managements, for a long time, to keep the increase in advertising rates below the rise in costs. Newspaper profits from advertising were thus steadily eroded.

Despite this experience, the Annan Committee proposed to start a second television channel dependent on advertising revenues, without considering its consequences for newspapers. It seems to have been assumed that the new channel would compete mainly with quality newspapers and specialist magazines for advertising revenues. In turn the Peacock Report considered the extension of advertising to the BBC. Yet the implications of such a proposal for the press were hardly considered by the reports.

This confusion has a long history. In 1977, for instance, while the third Press Commission was considering how to help unprofitable quality papers, the Annan Committee was simultaneously proposing to make them even more vulnerable. The Hunt Committee took the process even further, for its recommendations about the finance of cable television posed a serious threat to the local press. Yet again, many of the proposals embodied in the Broadcasting Act were prompted by interests of the advertisers who wanted more advertising time to bring down advertising costs. Indeed, a major reorganization of broadcasting was proposed, based on the propaganda of this lobby, rather than on any evidence about the distribution of advertising revenue, or the impact not just on broadcasters, or the public, but on the advertisers themselves, of such a huge expansion of advertising opportunities. While the proposals were advocated during a period of economic expansion, they seem likely to be implemented during a period of economic recession: had the proposals been based on facts rather than interests, they might have been more cautious.

## The need for an integrated approach

Of course, a degree of variation in approach to the different media could reasonably be justified in terms of the contrasting characteristics of the media themselves. However, in practice, the conflicts and contradictions which have been described are a product, not of rational differentiation, but of the piecemeal way in which communications policy has emerged.

Some thirty public bodies are involved in formulating and carrying out British media policy. In practice this proliferation of responsibility has led, at times, to its unacknowledged concentration – in the hands of the Prime Minister. This has not resulted in any greater co-ordination, but rather in the erratic pursuit of narrowly defined political objectives with little reference to their overall effect on the media.

Since the late 1970s media policy, and particularly that governing the introduction of new technologies, has been determined by narrow and unthought-out commercial considerations. The view of broadcasting as providing a national service for the nation's good has been abandoned. The justification for this destruction has been commercial expediency. Yet there are few signs of the new, British industrial revolution that, for example, cable and satellite were supposed to introduce.

The need for a coherent news, information, and communications policy is now critical, for many of the principles on which media policy has traditionally been based are being undermined by new technological developments.

Thus British broadcasting has been obliged to maintain cultural standards, properly balanced programming, and equality of access. Yet there is no way of controlling video-recording according to these principles.

Similarly, the development of teletext (the transmission of

printed material of a great variety on to television screens) has intensified the competition for classified advertising, while proposals for a regional structure for Channel 5 might well have dramatic effects on the advertising revenues of local newspapers and specialist magazines which, until now, have largely been insulated from the effects of television. In turn, the way in which teletext is developed will have important implications for the future of broadcasting, and change the nature of postal and telephone communications services. This blurring of traditional demarcations between the media provides new opportunities. But it also poses problems for communications policy, which seems hardly to have been considered.

Indeed the development of schemes which link computers to satellites and which are capable of transmitting unprecedented amounts of commercial, political, and industrial information internationally, makes any kind of national regulation increasingly difficult. Such schemes are being developed by multinational corporations like IBM, which are concerned with information as a commodity, not with its political implications. Just as 'freedom of speech' was invoked in the 1950s by American film exporters during their expansion into a world market, so 'freedom of information' is now being used to facilitate American domination of the market for facts. The only way in which these developments can be properly monitored, let alone regulated, is through the development of a comprehensive policy for communications. Indeed a national communications policy, sensitive to the commercial and political implications of information, is a prerequisite for the development of any international policy. It is also needed to ensure that British media industries take proper advantage of their commercial opportunities.

## A unified policy for communications

A single Ministry of Arts, Communications, and Entertainments (ACE) needs to be created. This would be responsible not only for the mass media, but also for the post, telephone, and information technologies. It would thus be able to oversee and control the entire commercial development of these critical industries. The ministry would also deal with the interrelated areas of the arts, public libraries, publishing, sports, and recreations. This reorganization would entail the merging of responsibilities currently dispersed between the Cabinet Office, the Home Office, and the

Department of Trade and Industry, as well as the Department of Education and Science.

This rationalization would facilitate the development of an integrated policy, committed to more clearly defined goals, that could properly consider the political and economic implications of developments (including the increased concentration of economic power across all the media by a few large companies) in the information industries. The creation of the proposed ministry would also be a recognition of the role which the media, information, arts, and sport have in contemporary society. It is a role which is likely to have increasing importance in the future. A coherent, ambitious, and visionary policy for the communication industry – one tolerant of political difference and genuinely concerned with the whole variety of new commercial and cultural possibilities – is now more vital than ever before.

# 19

# *Alternative approaches to media reform*

When the first edition of this book appeared in 1981, relatively little had been published on media reform apart from government-sponsored reports. This has changed. The media have become politicized as an issue, and the emergence of satellite TV has prompted a debate about the future of broadcasting. There is now an intimidating plethora of articles, pamphlets, policy papers, reports, speeches, and books about media policy. This chapter is intended to provide a convenient summary of this literature. It tries also to chart different points of entry into the debate about media policy by mapping the main strategies for reform and describing the thinking that underlies them.

At one level, policy discussion about the media is dominated by the debate between two opposing camps: disciples of the free market versus supporters of the public service approach. But within each of these two camps there are divergent tendencies. In the public service corner there is a split between traditionalists, who want to preserve the broadcasting system more or less as it was in the late 1980s, and radicals, who argue that public service broadcasting needs to be redefined and find expression in new institutional forms. Within the free market camp, there is also a broad split between those who oppose media regulation beyond the 'normal law of the land' and social market liberals who favour limited public intervention to secure specific public goals. These differences are presented in an ideal-typical form in Table 9.

However, the debate about the media is also polarized between paternalists and libertarians. This creates a second axis that cuts across the divide between advocates of the free market and public service. The result is a complex configuration of policy positions, which can be viewed at a glance in the simplified diagram on page 368. But for the sake of expository clarity, we will outline

Table 9  *Public service vs. free market approaches to media reform*

| | Public service | Radical public service | Social market | Free market |
|---|---|---|---|---|
| *Media role* | Cultural leadership/ channel of political information/social responsibility | Public sphere/ political negotiation/ cultural diversity | Consumer enrichment/ political representation | Consumer gratification |
| *General approach* | Public corporation/ public agency regulation | 'Popular' control | Market intervention where necessary | *Laissez-faire* |
| *Terrestrial broadcasting* | BBC/regulate franchised broadcasters | End government patronage/new structures and guidelines | Independent production quotas/Public Service Broadcasting Council/monopoly control | Deregulate |
| *New TV* | Stress on programme regulation | — | Stress on economic regulation | Develop with minimal bureaucracy |
| *Press* | Regulate franchised newspapers | Lease publicly owned print facilities monopoly controls | Launch fund/ selective grants/ | Voluntary self-regulation |

first the debate between free market and public service supporters, and then consider separately the arguments advanced by paternalists and libertarians. Only then will we try to piece the two together.

## Free market approach

The starting point of the free market approach is that consumers are the best judges of what is in their interests. Media policy should be geared therefore to creating the conditions of greatest possible competition in which consumers can exercise sovereign control. This produces a media system which gives people what they want: a diverse output to choose from; a 'discovery mechanism' by which consumers can extend their tastes and interests by shopping around; and, above all, media which are independent of government. Indeed there is no fundamental conflict, according to some neo-liberals, between the ideals of public service and the free market. 'All provision for the consumer on a competitive basis in a non-distorted market', writes the *Financial Times* journalist, Samuel Brittan, 'is a *public service*' (emphasis supplied).

Since the press is organized on free market lines, most neo-liberals see no need for reform. When confronted with evidence of press concentration and market distortion, they usually argue that new technology and the ending of restrictive trade union practices are in the process of reinvigorating competition. In any case, the threat to press freedom posed by state intervention is, according to many neo-liberals, more dangerous than the shortcoming that it is intended to remedy.

Although neo-liberals are generally conservative in relation to the press, they are radical when it comes to broadcasting. The three main defects of public service television, they maintain, are that it is unresponsive to popular demand because it is dominated by a small élite; it is vulnerable to government pressure because it relies on state-sponsored privileges; and it costs too much because public service monopolies are a natural victim of trade union exploitation. Some also argue that public service broadcasting provides a protected haven for radicals. This is in marked contrast to the competitive environment of the press where the consumer is sovereign and where, consequently, unpopular radical views get short shrift.

Most neo-liberals argue, therefore, that broadcasting should be 'deregulated' and reconstituted along the free market lines of the press. Publicly owned broadcasting should be privatized. Regulation of commercial broadcasting should be abolished. Broadcasters should be subject, like publishers, only to the law of the land.

Neo-liberals support this argument by pointing out that the traditional technical justification for public service broadcasting, based on the need to allocate and regulate scarce airwave frequencies, has been overtaken by events. The emergence of multichannel cable and satellite television has resulted in there being now more television channels than national papers to choose from in some areas. Some commentators also pursue the press analogy by arguing that the technology exists for encrypting channels and programmes so that people can pay directly for what they view in much the way that they buy or subscribe to a newspaper or magazine. In short, it is now possible to remodel broadcasting along the competitive, unregulated lines of the press.

This argument has created, however, considerable dissension within the ranks of neo-liberals. At the heart of the split between traditional and social market liberals on the right is the fact that conventional market rules do not apply in broadcasting. Television can put on extra 'sales' in terms of ratings at negligible additional cost. Consequently, advertising funded channels have an enormous financial incentive to concentrate on common denominator programmes which attract high ratings and a large advertising yield. A TV system based on advertising tends therefore to narrow consumer choice by ignoring minorities. On the other hand, pay-TV potentially generates a much wider choice because audiences have the opportunity to pay for the programmes that they particularly want. But pay-TV runs into public good problems because some viewers (and in particular low-income viewers) are excluded who could be catered for at little extra cost. Pay-channels (i.e. subscription-based channels) do not provide the answer either. They are less sensitive to intensities of consumer preference than pay-TV but have the same public good defects. The solution, argue most neo-liberals, is to construct a broadcasting system which is based on a plural system of funding: advertising, pay-TV, and pay-channels. This allegedly overcomes the drawbacks inherent in each individual system of payment.

But this is easier said than achieved. At the heart of the neo-liberal dream is a vision, articulated with notable eloquence by Peter Jay, of 'electronic publishing' based on the nation-wide installation of fibre-optic cable. This would enable every household to have pay-TV sets with infinite channel capacity. The cable grid would be a two-way 'common carrier' permitting television producers to transmit any programme they wanted on payment of a transmission fee and enabling viewers to summon up any programme they wanted on payment of a programme charge. But although technically feasible, this would involve an enormous financial investment. For a time, many neo-liberals were under the illusion that this was a realistic prospect because they thought that British Telecom would install an extensive fibre-optic grid in the process of modernizing the copper wiring of household phones.[1] But as this prospect receded, so too did the dream of a perfect broadcasting market in which pay-TV would be a central feature.

The failure of cable television to take off in Britain further set back neo-liberal hopes. It was fondly believed that private sector capital would help finance the installation of fibre-optic cable by developing a network of multi-channel cable television stations. But the anticipated boom in cable television never took place in Britain due to lack of demand. In early 1990, only 1.5 million homes had been passed by cable (including old as well as new systems) and of these homes only 19 per cent subscribed to cable television. In a desperate bid to boost flagging investment in cable television, the government relaxed in 1990 its restrictions on major holdings in cable television by companies outside the EC.[2] But many commentators now believe that cable television has missed its historic opportunity to become established as a major force in Britain before the advent of direct broadcasting satellites.

The new generation of high- and medium-powered satellites is capable of transmitting television channels direct to peoples' homes over a large area, and requires only relatively inexpensive, small receiving dishes. On them increasingly rests the neo-liberals' hope for creating a competitive market. In 1988, Sky Television launched its new four-channel satellite package for the UK market. This became a five-channel service when it merged in 1990 with ailing BSB satellite TV. In addition, the government announced a significant expansion of over-the-air broadcasting: three new national radio channels, the proliferation of new, local radio stations on vacant frequencies, and the introduction of a fifth television channel capable of being received by the majority of households in Britain. In addition, some argue that MVDS (the cheap relaying of television channels in local areas by a low-powered transmitter) provides further potential for extending market competition.

Neo-liberals are divided, however, over whether the competitive market has matured to the point when broadcasting can be deregulated. The Adam Smith Institute led the way in 1984 by calling for the BBC to be broken up into 'an association of independent and separately financed stations', funded partly by advertising. Many neo-liberals now want to go much further and press the detonator button destroying all agencies regulating programme content. Cento Veljanovski, research director of the influential Institute of Economic Affairs, writes: 'Broadcasters must operate within the legal framework which governs taste and decency and the protection of privacy. But beyond the minimum constraints the market should decide.' The government, he adds, should simply 'sell franchises and then allow them to be traded among potential broadcasters'.[3] Even tough anti-monopoly controls (something that neo-liberals generally favour) can be set aside, in the view of some, in order to promote investment in new television outlets and greater choice. As Rupert Murdoch argued in an eloquent lecture, 'cross-ownership of the media is a force for diversity'.[4]

But there are aspects of the present situation that make even some convinced neo-liberals uneasy. The finite size of the advertising cake, and the lack of a developed pay-TV sector, make it potentially hazardous in their view to abandon all broadcasting controls. Premature deregulation now, they argue, could lower standards and reduce choice. They are the reformists who, when the crunch came, sided with the public service 'enemy' against free market revolutionaries. Their most notable monument is the social market Peacock Report (1986) on financing broadcasting.

## Social market approach

Reformers in the social market tradition broadly endorse the core assumptions of the free market approach. Where they differ from traditional neo-liberals is in stressing that public intervention is needed to offset market distortions. The more interventionist among them also argue that a policy of *laissez-faire* is inherently incapable of producing the range of choice that free market theory promises, and consequently they favour public intervention to enlarge choice. This is usually justified with reference to the wider political or cultural role of the media in society.

This social market approach led the Peacock Committee to justify in the short term extensive public regulation of broadcasting. Its central thesis was that the best way of mimicking a fully competitive market in a situation where spectrum shortage limited competition was to make broadcasting organizations provide a mixed diet of programmes, and rely on different sources of revenue. 'Collective provision and regulation of programmes', concluded the Committee, 'does provide *a better simulation of a market* designed to reflect consumer preferences than a policy of laissez-faire' (emphasis supplied). This conclusion was influenced by two things: evidence suggesting that there was not sufficient advertising expenditure to fund a high level of programme investment in both the BBC and ITV; and research undertaken from the Leeds University Centre for TV Research which indicated that intense competition in the market-based TV system in the US restricted the diversity of peak-time programmes.

Instead, the Committee argued for a phased-in introduction of a market system. In the first phase, the government should expand the broadcasting system, privatize a bit of it, promote independent production, and initiate the first steps towards deregulation. In the second phase (the 'later 90s'), the BBC should be funded by individual subscriptions. In the third and final phase, broadcasting regulation should be abolished. However, even in this final phase, the Committee suggested that there should continue to be a Public Service Broadcasting Council (PSBC) which would foster 'programmes of a more demanding kind with a high content of knowledge, culture, education and experiment (including entertainment)' because not enough of these programmes would be generated by a market-driven system. The PSBC would give grants to broadcasting organizations for the production of specific programmes, and would be financed by general taxation or rental payments for airwave frequencies.

The government's 1990 Broadcasting Act largely followed the logic of this gradualist approach. It expanded the number of broadcasting outlets through more efficient spectrum management. It initiated some deregulation by announcing that ITV franchises would be put out to competitive tender, and that the Independent Broadcasting Authority (IBA) would be replaced by the 'light touch' Independent Television Commission (ITC). Satellite television and licensed commercial radio would also be subject to less public service requirements than the rest of the broadcasting system. And all television channels, including the BBC, would be required to commission 25 per cent of their programmes (with exemptions) from independent production companies.

But in fact a public service regime still remained at the heart of the broadcasting system under this reorganization. The BBC survived intact, without being obliged to accept advertising. Although Channel 4 will be compelled to sell its own advertising, it will also be assured a safety net income from television franchise companies if it makes a loss. This will enable Channel 4 to continue to be oriented towards minorities rather than a mass audience. Some public service safeguards were also built into a bidding system for ITV (renamed Channel 3) franchises, ensuring that the top bidder will not automatically win. The 'light touch' new regulatory authority, ITC, has been given an arsenal of new powers – including the power to fine, and to shorten franchises – with which to police Channel 3. And even the new Radio Authority has a remit to promote mixed programming and extend the range of local radio services in order to avoid back-to-back, mainstream pop music.

Whether these good intentions will be translated into practice remains to be seen. But the 1990 Broadcasting Act produced an angry response from the neo-liberal lobby, and indeed some criticism from social market neo-liberals on the Peacock Committee who complained angrily that their more radical proposals such as the privatization of BBC Radios 1 and 2, the auctioning of radio franchises, and the establishment of a Public Service Broadcasting Council had been ignored. In the event, social market reformism paved the way for the preservation of public service broadcasting by a new right government.

But the social market challenge to public service broadcasting remains, and it has adherents on the left as well as the right. Typical of the left-wing variant is a plan for reorganizing radio services, advanced by Geof Mulgan and Peter Jenner from the libertarian new left of the Labour Party. Their starting point is that 'the BBC model of a large public bureaucracy has little to do with a modern idea of socialism'. It stifles risk and challenge, and is too closely linked to the state. More generally, they argue, the model of planned diversity through public regulation is insensitive to public demand. It 'implicitly assumes that radio should provide what people need rather than what they want . . . regulation is used to impose its own idea of what is valuable', which in the case of the BBC means that the great majority of radio resources should be devoted to minority middle-class audiences. On the other hand, a policy of *laissez-faire* would encourage common denominator programming, concentration of ownership, and underfunding of the system. The answer, they suggest, is a third route in which a public agency would act as an enterprise board intervening in the market economy rather than acting as a conventional regulator. Funded by receipts from spectrum fees or auctions, as well as public finance, its role would be to promote diversity in the ownership and output of the radio system. This would include new and innovative forms of ownership and control: employee ownership, subscribers with voting rights, consumer co-ops, and stations linked to institutions.

Similar embryonic schemes have been proposed from the left in relation to television. They generally entail five elements: the defence of Channel 4; the promotion of an independent sector through a requirement on national networks to commission independently produced programmes; strict monopoly controls to prevent the growth of concentration in the independent sector; public subsidy for the development of a fibre-optic cable TV system which would provide a new delivery system for independently made programmes; and a revision of franchising arrangements for commercial television in a way that would encourage new forms of ownership and control. In addition, social market advocates on the left usually favour public intervention in the European television economy – something that we will review later since this has become a coalition position supported by, among others, public service traditionalists.

The social market position in relation to broadcasting is still in the state of evolution, largely because discussion about broadcasting has been until recently defined by a public service consensus. Social market prescriptions are more developed in relation to the press where discussion has been grounded generally on acceptance of the market system. They boil down to three things: legislation to curb chain ownership; measures designed to assist the survival of weak publications; and public finance to assist the launch of new publications.

Press anti-monopoly legislation was first introduced in 1965, requiring large press groups to secure government permission before being allowed to buy new titles. Between 1965 and early 1990, 125 press acquisitions fell under the terms of this legislation. Yet permission for a take-over was refused in only five instances, none of which involved a major national title.[5] Because the Fair Trading Act has proved to be so ineffective, some reformers argue that it should be strengthened. It should place the onus, it has been suggested, on large press groups to demonstrate that their acquisition is in the public interest rather than the other way round. The Act should also be extended to include the smaller regional chains, and the criteria for referring cases to the Monopolies Commission should be made more stringent.

Other reformers argue that the situation has been allowed to deteriorate so badly that a policy of active divestment of the major press groups should be pursued. This could take the form of a set limit on the market share that any one group should be allowed to control in specified sectors of the press or a limit on the number of titles that any one group can control. Thus if press groups were restricted to owning no more than one national daily and one Sunday paper, ten local dailies and fifty local weeklies (paid-for and freesheet), it would result in Murdoch having to sell three national titles, Stevens and Maxwell each having to sell one national paper, the Thomson Corporation shedding three local dailies, and seven major groups having to sell between them over two hundred local weekly papers.

Critics point out, however, that this divestment approach has considerable problems. Press chains could offload marginal or loss-making publications. Cut off from a corporate cross-subsidy, these publications could go under unless there was a public agency established to offer relaunch finance. Some local weeklies are also only viable if they obtain group editorial support. Furthermore the net effect of unscrambling a large number of titles might be merely to initiate a game of musical chairs in which divested papers were bought by conglomerates like Lonrho, which were able to buy under the new monopoly rules.

One way of circumventing these difficulties is to restrict divestment to the profitable powerhouse of the press – national papers. Labour's shadow media and arts minister, Mark Fisher, has also mooted the possibility of establishing a statutory option period in which sales of divested papers would be restricted to management–worker buy-outs or to independent consortia with no press interests. This could be organized in the form of an auction, with an independent market valuation establishing a reserve price. Bidders would be able to raise most of the money from private sources but could also apply for public venture capital. In this way, it is argued, anti-monopoly legislation would modify the capitalist character of the press and allow genuinely new voices to be heard.

It has also been suggested that joint *control* of television, radio, and newspapers should be prohibited by law as a way of promoting media diversity. The most notable effect of this legislation would be to force Murdoch to choose between Sky Television and his British press group.

Another anti-monopoly proposal, advocated by Bruce Page, is for the ownership of the Press Association to be divorced from the press chains. This would inject, he maintains, new variety into the press by encouraging a much-used news service to develop more autonomous news values.

The second, much-canvassed social market approach is to promote competition through the public funding of new ventures. This has been proposed in various forms: a National Print Corporation which would make available modern plant facilities, at subsidized prices, to under-resourced groups; or a Launch Fund which would aid the setting up of new publications with development grants, low interest loans, and management advice; or, more ambitiously, a Media Enterprise Board which would assist new companies and projects in both the press and broadcasting industries.

The rationale for these proposals is that high market entry costs need to be offset if under-represented groups, with limited funds, are to gain a voice in the press. This will make the press more diverse and representative, and promote political debate essential to the healthy functioning of a democracy. An example of this policy working in practice is provided by the Press Subsidies Board in Sweden which helped to finance seventeen new papers between 1976 and 1984. The large majority of these papers survived, and their establishment helped to reverse the long-term trend towards increased market domination by a few, powerful press chains.

Objections have been raised to public funding of new media ventures principally on the grounds that they could lead to a waste of public money in failed projects, and could be misused to help friends of the government or powerful media interests who do not need public subsidies. Advocates of a Media Enterprise Board (MEB) have sought to meet these objections in the way they have framed their proposal. The MEB would be required to support only those projects which appear, on the basis of professional assessment, to have a reasonable chance of success. It would also support only consortia 1) without extensive media interests, 2) with a demonstrable need for public venture capital, and 3) whose projects would extend the cultural or political diversity of the media. To avoid politically partisan awards, the supervisory board of the MEB would be composed of representatives from different political parties, media industry organizations (including both employers and unions), and relevant independent organizations like the Consumers' Association. The MEB would be an enabling organization, not a regulator. It could be funded by a levy on all media advertising, which if set at a flat rate of 2 per cent would yield a gross annual income of over £100 million.

The other principal social market strategy in relation to the press is to promote competition through public grants. In some European countries, this has taken the form of blanket industrial subsidies such as postal or VAT tax concessions. These have the disadvantage of affording the greatest help to the strongest publications and so do little to offset the unequal competitive relationship between strong and weak papers. Advocates of this approach argue that a non-discriminatory approach avoids the danger of government control, and provides a subsidy cushion to an industry that has an especially important role in liberal democracies.

The alternative approach entails the giving of selective aid to weak publications. This is justified on the grounds that small circulation papers benefit less from economies of scale than their larger circulation rivals, and tend to have lower advertising revenues per reader. The purpose of the subsidy is to equalize the competitive relationship between strong and weak papers, and thereby sustain a high level of competition. The most elaborate version of this approach is that in operation in Sweden: subsidies are awarded to 'secondary' papers (i.e. non-market leaders) in relation to their circulation and volume of editorial newsprint, funded by a tax on all advertising. The danger of government manipulation is mitigated by organizing, as far as possible, the allocation of subsidies according to impersonal, automatic criteria. This has prevented a partisan allocation of subsidies to the government's friends in the press: indeed, the largest subsidy has long gone to a consistent right-wing critic of successive Social Democratic governments, *Svenska Dagbladet*.

Left-wing critics of this subsidy system in Sweden complain that it fails to compensate down-market papers for the lower advertising generated by working-class readers. Various schemes have been advocated in Britain which indirectly confront this problem by seeking to redistribute advertising revenue from strong to weak advertising papers, although all ambitious schemes so far advocated have technical difficulties. In a few instances, they might damage those papers which the redistributive scheme was designed to assist. This is because some strong advertising media would seek to offset an advertising levy by raising their rates, which could result in advertisers cutting out weaker papers in order to pay the increased rate charges.

This possibility has prompted some reformers to advocate a narrowly targeted strategy geared to a limited objective: making middle- or down-market papers viable with a circulation as small as that of the *Independent* or *Sunday Telegraph*. One proposal, adapted from a scheme already in operation in France, would award a cash bounty to national newspapers which receive less than 40 per cent of their revenue from advertising but devote over 25 per cent of their editorial content to public affairs. The grant would be allocated on a rising scale linked to circulation, until a ceiling of 750,000 was reached after which the grant would start to taper off. No British paper would currently qualify for this grant but it would encourage the launch and survival of new, non-élite minority papers.

Another proposal, also adapted from a French precedent, is to implement the press equivalent of a broadcasting 'common carrier' policy. A legal obligation could be imposed on wholesalers and newsagents to handle and display lawful publications wherever they were requested to do so by publishers. The commercial interests of distributors could be protected, it is claimed, if a regulated administration charge were imposed on unsold copies and legal privilege was granted in relation to defamation cases. This would ensure, argue reformers, that minority publications gain as much access to the market in Britain as they do in France.

Underlying discussion of these various forms of public intervention is a wider strategic debate. The main impetus behind their implementation in other European countries has been a desire to preserve the political press in the face of competition from more entertainment-oriented papers. But in Britain, the non-élite political press has largely disappeared: the rationale for a conservationist policy sustaining a political press in the name of editorial diversity has thus been partly overtaken by events. Times have changed, according to this argument, and public intervention designed to maintain the media as an arena of open public debate should concentrate on broadcasting.

The counter-argument asserts that an aim of public policy should be to re-establish editorial diversity in the press. Priority should be given to assisting the birth of new publications through a public agency like the proposed MEB. But if the new public agency is not to become an incubator for lame ducks, the ground rules of publishing also need to be modified to give new papers a fair chance of making their way. One reason why the Swedish Press Subsidy Board has been a successful midwife of new ventures is because it has also adopted a 'level playing field' policy that has given all minority papers a better prospect of survival. As for the wider contention that the press is not worth bothering about, interventionists argue that the press still performs a political function in liberal democracies and that its reform should be seen as part of a wider strategy for improving the media, for which there is growing support. Indeed, the proposal for a Media Enterprise Board, originating from the social market left of the Labour Party, has a clear resemblance to the Public Service Broadcasting Council, proposed by the social market right on the Peacock Committee.

## Public service approach

Although the public service approach has been discussed already in this book, it may be helpful to summarize its main arguments here. Its central credo is that broadcasting should be publicly owned or regulated so that it serves the public good rather than private gain. Only in this way, it is argued, can broadcasting be prevented from becoming subservient to the commercial forces that make for low quality, cultural uniformity, and right-wing bias.

Traditionalists argue that the ideals of public service broadcasting were successfully realized by the British broadcasting system in the late 1980s. Although the BBC competed with ITV for viewers, it did not compete for the same source of revenue. This produced, in their view, a creative balance of pressures encouraging both cultural purpose and audience responsiveness. The BBC had to attract viewers and listeners from the commercial system in order to justify the licence fee: it was thus under pressure to shed some of its Reithian paternalism. At the same time, the standards of ITV were raised through the active intervention of the IBA and by being forced to compete in quality against the BBC.

As a consequence we enjoyed in the late 1980s, according to conservationists, by far the best broadcasting system in the world. This was manifested in various ways: high-quality programmes for both minorities and mass audiences; balanced and unsensational news coverage in marked contrast to the bingo-jingo press; broadcasting provision that reflected the diversity of British society rather than a bland transatlantic culture; and a cheap, universally available service that did not discriminate against inaccessible areas or the poor.

This celebration of British broadcasting is based on certain judgements about the role it should perform in society. In the view of traditional public service exponents, broadcasting should not be organized solely in order to maximize the gratification of consumer demand. Rather, it should seek to educate public taste by making accessible the best products of our cultural heritage, by sponsoring innovation and experiment, and by making available a wide diversity of programmes; it should also inform the electorate so that people are equipped to participate in a popular democracy; and it should entertain but within a publicly accountable framework that is sensitive to conventions of public decency and taste. Broadcasting, some traditionalists add, should also promote social cohesion at a time of increasing individualism and fragmentation.

Public service supporters have attacked the Conservative government's broadcasting reforms on several counts. They claim that its 'greedy' fiscal policy of imposing a 'double tax' on commercial television in the form of an auction payment and a TV levy will result in less money for programmes and lower quality. They predict that the auctioning of the ITV franchises will lead inevitably to increasing commercialization – with more formula-based programmes – and that this will depress, in turn, the quality of the BBC. Some also argue that the independent production quota is a way of undermining the core institutions of public service broadcasting.

These arguments have given rise to a programme of restoration, which would undo the controversial features of the 1990 Broadcasting Act. Some traditionalists have come round to the view, however, that certain positive changes are needed in order to conserve the excellence of British broadcasting. Their first concern is that the public licence fee funding of the BBC – in their view, the cornerstone of the Corporation's political independence and public service commitment – may eventually be abolished in response to the combined clamour of left- and right-wing critics. These have argued variously that the fee makes the BBC vulnerable to political manipulation by governments, which alone have the power to authorize increases; that it has resulted in a

growing gap between the funding of public and commercial broadcasting (with commercial television spending an estimated 62 per
cent more on television services than the BBC in 1985); that it is
inherently objectionable because it is a flat rate, regressive tax;
and that it is too high due to the embargo on BBC advertising.
The Conservative government's decision to peg the licence fee to
the retail price index for three years from 1988 further underlined
the need to rethink the funding of the BBC. Its effect was, in the
words of the then Home Secretary, Douglas Hurd, to impose 'in
practice a substantial financial squeeze' since the inflation of
broadcasting costs has long exceeded rises in the retail price
index.

Still more disturbing for traditionalists, the government indicated
that it favoured replacing the licence fee in due course with a
voluntary, private subscription. The possible implications of this
were spelt out in the 1987 Jonscher Report which suggested, on
the basis of a small market research sample, that there was no
level of subscription fee which would finance the current level of
funding of BBC1 and BBC2.[6] Some people would opt out of
paying the licence fee if it were made an optional charge for BBC
services: this would necessitate an offsetting increase of the fee,
which would deter further subscribers. A private subscription-
based BBC would thus be a very different organization from what
we have now.

This has prompted conservationists to press for changes in
the licence fee system as a way of answering critics and securing
the long-term future of the BBC's public funding. The regressive
nature of the licence fee could be mitigated, they suggest, if old-
age pensioners and those on long-term benefit were exempted
from payment, with the money made up by a Treasury grant. The
BBC could also be insulated from political pressure through the
establishment of an independent review body to advise the government about licence fee increases. Alternatively, the licence fee
could be linked to increases in national earnings, which would
remove the fee from the political sphere and guarantee the BBC a
secure and rising income.

Traditionalists' second main concern has been that satellite and
cable television may undermine the public service tradition of
broadcasting. Their response has been to press for the regulation
of the new television industries so that they are an extension of
the public service broadcasting system. They have met with only
limited success. British satellite broadcasting has no statutory

duty to provide high quality or mixed programming but following a late amendment to the 1990 Broadcasting Act, became subject to conventional impartiality rules.

Public regulation of high-powered satellite television is made more difficult by the fact that it can be received by countries which have no jurisdiction over it. Traditional public service adherents argue, therefore, that there needs to be European-wide agreement to regulate satellite television in accordance with public service precepts. Each national government should be responsible for ensuring that these are adhered to by all broadcasting organizations that employ a satellite link-up within their jurisdiction or use satellite capacities or frequencies allocated to their state. In this way, the new 'space invaders' can be 'controlled'.

The two agencies for negotiating such an agreement are the Council of Europe and the European Commission. The Council has a wider membership (currently 22 countries) but the 'conventions' it issues carry less force than the directives of the European Commission which are in principle binding on all members of the EC and require, where appropriate, changes in national legislation.[7] But while the machinery for securing an international public service framework is available, the political will is not. Europe has different broadcasting traditions, and there is no unanimity in favour of a restrictive public service regime.

In the event, the two broadcasting agreements negotiated at the Council of Europe and the European Commission in 1989 imposed no requirements for balanced news coverage, mixed programming, or programme quality. Partly at the insistence of the British government, provision was made to curb pornography and undue violence. But in the more important of the two agreements – the directive of the European Commission – the prohibition took the qualified form of an injunction against 'programmes which might seriously impair the . . . development of minors'.[8] The implication is that pornographic or violent programmes which are transmitted late at night or which can be screened from children through technical means are perhaps not covered by the Commission's directive.

There is another focus of concern which extends beyond the ranks of public service traditionalists to include a wider constituency: the fear that satellite and cable television will in the long run destabilize the economy of British broadcasting. British public service television has flourished partly because it has been heavily protected. Its cornerstone is a restrictive quota that allows only 14 per cent of transmission time (with some minor exceptions) to be taken up with programmes made outside the EC. But satellite television is not subject to this restriction, and draws heavily on US television programmes because these can be bought at a fraction of the price of making new programmes (and, indeed, at only a small proportion of their original cost in the USA). The fear in essence is that cheap imported programmes, priced for international sale and transmitted across frontiers by satellite, will undermine the economy for making necessarily expensive programmes for a national market.

The related concern is the effect that satellite broadcasting will have in the long term on the central institutions of public service broadcasting. If satellite television succeeds in building a significant audience, this will make it more difficult for the BBC to justify licence fee increases, and could reduce the advertising revenue of over-the-air commercial television. This could result in less programme investment and lower quality. The combination of a contracting audience and a squeeze on revenues could also affect the policies of public service broadcasting organizations. They might cut back on minority programmes. They could also make more programmes for the common denominator of the global market rather than for the varied interests and experiences of the domestic audience – more series instead of single plays, more costume drama instead of contemporary fiction, more nature films instead of documentaries.

Some have urged, therefore, the retention of some kind of protectionism. In particular social market radicals on the left have generally argued for two things: a limit on the proportion of non-EC programmes that are transmitted on satellite and cable television in order to sustain domestic television production, and a restriction on satellite and cable television advertising in order to protect the revenue base of publicly regulated commercial television. This has been strongly opposed by neo-liberals (including many social market radicals on the right) on the grounds that protectionism distorts the processes of the free market. In the event, the Council of Europe and the European Commission opted for an almost identical compromise in 1989. Advertising on all television channels was restricted to 15 per cent of daily transmission time, and a maximum of 20 per cent in any one hour – far more than regulators had been demanding. And only a permissive programme quota was agreed in which member states were required 'where practicable' to ensure that 51 per cent of television fiction and documentaries originated from the EC. This was a considerable dilution of what had originally been proposed in response to strong opposition from the British government and US television industry.

In addition, some reformers have urged public service broadcasting organizations in Europe to work closely together by, for example, initiating more co-productions and selling to each other at a discounted price as a way of emulating the economies of scale of the US television industry. In particular, the European Commission should play a much more active role, they maintain, in preparing European television public service institutions to withstand open competition from the world's television superpower in the era of cross-frontier television. However, in 1989 the total budget of the Commission's 'Media '92' policy – which includes support for television productions using advanced technology, and the dubbing or subtitling of programmes – amounted to only £4.5 million.

Just as right-wing reformers have argued that broadcasting should be remodelled on the press, so some left-wing reformers have advanced the same logic in reverse. Thus, Tony Benn has suggested that *The Times* should be established as a public corporation on the model of the BBC, while the former Labour MP Stuart Holland has argued that a publicly owned press distribution agency should be established in much the way that broadcasting transmitters were publicly owned. This would assist, in his view, the proper distribution of minority magazines which sometimes encounter censorship from newsagents and wholesalers.

But the public service approach most favoured by a number of left-wing politicians is the regulation of franchised newspapers along the lines of commercial television. Labour MP Michael Meacher has proposed an Independent Press Authority, modelled on the IBA, which would franchise existing newspapers and require them to adhere to an ethical code of conduct and maintain 'a reasonable balance' in the presentation of news and opinion. These franchises would be subject to periodical review, and could be revoked.

A more radical version of this scheme has been advanced by another Labour MP, Chris Mullin. Under his plan, the Independent Press Authority would franchise profitable groups rather than individual newspapers. Preference in the allocation of franchises would be given to staff consortia, companies with staff representation, or companies without major commercial interests, all of which should be able, according to Mullin, to raise the necessary finance from the City due to the high earnings of the franchises. While the Authority would be required to ensure pluralism of viewpoints in its allocation of franchises, the newspapers concerned would not be obliged to provide balanced news coverage. Another variant of this approach has been advocated that would require papers reaching a specified circulation to allocate a set amount of editorial space to certain categories of content (such as public affairs coverage). This is in effect a press equivalent of the mixed programming duty imposed on ITV by the IBA.

Underlying this approach is the belief that British broadcasting is superior to the press. However, the two media are very different and some surgery is needed before a transplant will 'take'. For Meacher's scheme to work, for instance, a substitute would have to be found for the corporate cross-subsidies that keep alive some loss-making newspapers. Otherwise, a revocation of their franchise could result in their closure. And although the monopoly position of some local papers effectively precludes the establishment of new rivals, the press is not physically constrained, like over-the-air broadcasting, by the availability of spectrum frequencies. This weakens the political justification for all press franchising schemes, particularly in relation to new papers. Franchising proposals which involve a wholesale change of ownership also invite the accusation that they are disenfranchising consumers.

An alternative approach, preferred by some in the public service tradition, is to reform the press by taking 'skin grafts' from the broadcasting system and applying them to 'infected areas'. Successive Broadcasting Acts (including the 1990 Act) have restricted the acquisition of broadcasting franchises to individuals and companies in Britain or other EC countries. Since becoming leader of the Labour Party, Neil Kinnock has suggested that the same stipulation should apply to the ownership of newspapers on the grounds that the current trend towards global concentration of media power is unhealthy, and that press controllers should be accountable to the communities they serve. This would have the effect of impaling Murdoch on the legislative equivalent of Morton's fork. Murdoch changed his nationality from Australian to American in the 1980s in order to circumvent the Federal Communications Commission's prohibition of foreign ownership of US television stations. Kinnock's proposal would thus force him to choose between his American television and British press interests. But it would also have other far-reaching consequences. The Canadian controllers of the Telegraph and Thomson groups would have to sell their British interests, while Maxwell would have to reorganize his empire currently controlled by a holding company registered in Liechtenstein. This perhaps explains why Kinnock's original proposal was watered down in Labour's 1987 general election manifesto to a commitment to 'ensure that ownership and control of the press and broadcasting are *retained* by citizens of Britain' (emphasis supplied). By implication, a citizenship requirement would apply only to future press acquisitions.

Another skin graft proposal is for the Press Complaints Commission to be reconstituted along the lines of the Broadcasting Complaints Commission, first established by the 1981 Broadcasting Act. This would transform a voluntary organization, funded by the press industry, into a statutory body with teeth. It would have the legal authority to call for evidence and require publication of its judgements in offending publications.

A more ambitious and innovative approach, rooted in the public service tradition, seeks to elevate editors into trustees of the public interest by reinforcing their autonomy and authority. Tom Baistow has argued that editors should be legally protected from improper pressure from proprietors, advertisers, and trade unions. Under his plan, editors could only be appointed or dismissed with the agreement of independent directors. This proposal leaves unclear, however, how independent directors would be appointed – whether by parliament, boards of directors, staff, elected readers' representatives, or a combination of these. It also allows considerable scope, in practice, for proprietors to exercise 'proper' control over editors through the allocation of editorial budgets. His scheme could also be criticized for championing the integrity of editors but not that of others employed on newspapers. However, a conscience clause could be inserted into journalists' and production workers' contracts of employment which would entitle them to appeal against unfair dismissal if they refused to act in a way that was contrary to the Press Complaints Commission's code of conduct.

## Radical public service

There is a heterogeneous group of reformers which broadly accepts the core assumptions of the public service approach but which thinks that the ideals of public service cannot be equated with the flawed institutions of British broadcasting.

Some reformers complain that the BBC and commercial television provide news and current affairs coverage from a narrow
range of perspectives roughly corresponding to those of the leadership of the parliamentary parties. They point to broadcasting
reporting of Northern Ireland which, they claim, has tended to
define the crisis as being essentially one of maintaining law and
order against criminals and terrorists, to the exclusion of other
interpretations. This is merely an extreme instance, they maintain,
of the way in which broadcasting generally reflects the ethos of
the establishment.

Another (though partly overlapping) group of critics advances
broadly the same argument in 'cultural' terms. Although public
service rhetoric sometimes stresses innovation and experiment, in
practice British broadcasting provides, they allege, mainly safe
and formulaic programmes. They argue that ITV is in reality a
highly centralized network, geared to satisfying the lowest common
denominator of mass viewing, while the BBC has largely abandoned
its public service commitment in favour of a shallow professionalism defined by market values. The BBC is also often criticized
for being steeped in the culture of London and the Home Counties.

While there is no unifying body of theory that informs the
radical public service approach, the emphasis is on the role of
broadcasting as a public sphere. This sees broadcasting as primarily
an open arena of argument and debate, a public space in which
different interests are negotiated and in which democratic pressure
is exerted on government through the formation and expression of
public opinion. Although this view of broadcasting usually refers
to news and current affairs programmes, it can be extended to
television drama which also provides a way of 'talking together
about the processes of our common life'. Much of television
fiction is, in a sense, a running commentary on the nature of
prevailing social relationships. It provides a means for society to
commune with itself, and for people to gain insight into the lives,
circumstances, and needs of others.

This conception of broadcasting is rooted in a view of society
that stresses social association and mutual obligation, and tacitly
rejects the neo-liberal view of society as an aggregation of
contracting and exchanging individuals.[9] Television is seen not
simply as a source of individual gratification but as an agency
linking together different class, ethnic, and regional cultures. A
central objective of broadcasting policy is therefore to ensure that
television gives adequate expression to cultural diversity and

political dissensus: that it is truly an institution of the public rather than of dominant power groups.

This orientation has given rise to two broad strategies of reform: one, ameliorative and reformist, working with existing institutions and modifying them; and the other, a fundamentalist approach of reconstructing media institutions on the basis of entirely new blueprints. Each will be reviewed in turn.

One reformist concern has been to try to reshape the formal control of broadcasting organizations so that it is more representative of society and more fully independent of government. This arises from two things. First, evidence that members of broadcasting authorities tend to be drawn from a narrow constituency. Thus, in early 1985, seven out of twelve BBC governors had been educated in Oxbridge. Nine out of twelve IBA members were also higher education graduates and, of the remaining non-graduates, one was a university Vice-Chancellor.

Second, members of broadcasting authorities are all appointed by government and there are signs that this system is beginning to be abused. Increasing numbers of appointees are known friends of the government. Indeed the present Chairman of the BBC, Marmaduke Hussey, is a brother-in-law of a government minister, while his immediate predecessor, Stuart Young, was the brother of one.

Concern about the political packing of broadcasting authorities has been reinforced by government attempts to chip away at the independence of television. The BBC board of governors tried to suppress in 1985 a controversial *Real Lives* programme about Northern Ireland in response to pressure from the Home Secretary, and relented only after an unprecedented strike by the BBC staff. It also emerged in 1985 that the state security service, MI5, had long been routinely involved in vetting recruits to the BBC (though this practice was subsequently restricted to a small number of appointments). In 1988 the government banned the direct transmission of political statements by members of named organizations in Northern Ireland (including elected politicians) as well as utterances supportive of these organizations. In a variety of direct and indirect ways, the Thatcher government also sought (as its predecessors had done) to generate pressure within broadcasting organizations for political self-censorship.

Reformers have tried therefore to devise a better way of appointing people to broadcast authorities than direct, unmediated patronage by the government of the day. Three alternatives have been suggested: the appointment of an independent review body to advise the government, direct elections, and nominations by representative national organizations and broadcasting staff. The superficially most attractive of these proposals – direct elections – is not without problems. Political parties are the only organizations really geared to mobilizing large numbers of people to vote. Direct elections may result therefore in the party in office gaining control of broadcasting authorities, which would frustrate the purpose of the reform – distancing public service broadcasting from the state. An alternative approach is to reconstitute broadcasting authorities along corporatist lines: with central and local government appointees, nominees from organizations representative of the plurality of interests in British society, and members elected by broadcasting staffs.

Another preoccupation of reformers has been to find ways of extending the ideological range and cultural diversity of the broadcasting system through the adoption of new structures and guidelines. Campaigners in the radical public service tradition played a key role in persuading the Conservative government to establish Channel 4 in 1980. They argued that a new type of public service organization was needed – one that commissioned rather than made programmes, with a remit to innovate and appeal to minority audiences – as a way of reinvigorating the public service tradition. Channel 4 fulfilled its prospectus mainly perhaps because it was financed through subscription income by ITV companies. These had a vested interest in Channel 4 remaining a minority channel.

Some within the radical public service tradition argued also in favour of liberalizing the rules governing British broadcasting. The radical Changing Television Group claimed, for instance, that the injunction to report and interpret the news with 'due impartiality' was misconceived since there is no neutral point either side of which opposing viewpoints can be balanced. The difficulties inherent in the broadcasters' remit are resolved, according to the Group, through 'the homogeneous social, educational and economic background of the individuals who control and operate the BBC and ITV'. It would be far better, its representatives suggest, if broadcasting organizations had a public service duty to 'represent fairly and accurately the differences within society, and ... produce programmes from the different perspectives in society'. This can be best achieved, in their view, by having openly partisan, clearly authored programmes 'given always the requirement to report with accuracy'. Their views thus converge from a different direction towards those of the neo-liberal right who want to deregulate.

Some critics are in favour of going only half-way down this road. They fear that big business control of commercial broadcasting would cause it to lurch to the right in the absence of restraining guidelines; and that the personal prejudices of overwhelmingly white, male, and middle-class broadcasters would result, if given more play, in the ideological range of broadcasting contracting still further. They argue, therefore, that broadcasting rules should be liberalized but not fundamentally changed: the obligation to maintain an overall balance should apply not to individual series of TV programmes, as required under the 1990 Broadcasting Act, but to the full spectrum of programmes put out by any one channel.

Some radicals in the public service tradition also pressed for a general relaxation of regulation. In particular, they argued that the IBA should be stripped of its pre-transmission censorship powers which were being used, they complained, to compress television's current affairs coverage into a consensual straitjacket. Again critics on the left echoed deregulators on the right, contributing to a climate of opinion in which the IBA was replaced by a 'light touch' authority.

A variety of schemes have also been advanced from a radical public service perspective for reorganizing the BBC principally on the grounds that it is over-large (with over 20,000 employees), hierarchical, and bureaucratic. Among them are proposals that BBC2 should be established as an independent, regionally based channel, funded by a set proportion of the licence fee in order to avoid head-on competition with BBC1; that BBC television should be separated from BBC radio, with the latter funded by a radio licence; and that the BBC should lose responsibility for developing public service local radio.

The alternative, fundamentalist approach takes the form of blueprints for a new media system that bears little relationship to what we have now but which is held up as an ideal to aim for. The proposal is for the leasing of publicly owned media facilities to the principal corporate interests in society or to dispersed, decentralized, and democratically run units. One example of the corporatist approach is a plan for reorganizing the British media advanced by the Militant Tendency, a Trotskyist group within the Labour Party. It proposes that *editorial* control of both newspapers and broadcasting should be vested in political parties in proportion to the votes that they win at general elections, and that specialist publications should be controlled by scientific, technical, and professional groups and organizations. This scheme significantly omits how the important women's press should be organized. It is also only a quasi-pluralist plan since fascist political parties and specialist organizations without democratic structures would be excluded from having a stake in the media.

A more pluralist version of the same model is afforded by the Dutch broadcasting system. This allocates both airtime and publicly owned production facilities, with technical staff, to different groups on the basis of their membership, linked to the sale of their programme guides. As a result, a variety of organizations from the commercial enterprise TROS, to political-cultural groupings like VARA (with close links to the Labour Party) and NCRV (a conservative, protestant organization) all provide a comprehensive package of services, with smaller organizations also being responsible for a limited quota of broadcasting hours each year. However, this system has encountered consumer resistance, reflected in the rapid development of cable television channels carrying a heavy diet of US programmes.

An alternative approach is based on an evolutionary model in which pluralism is built into the media system through the development of a varied pattern of ownership including public trusts, self-managing collectives, public corporations with elected authorities, joint stock companies, and consortia launched with the help of public grants. This model is implicit in some of the radical social market and public service reforms that have been outlined. Lurking behind them is the hope that they will evolve over time into a media system in which all important groups and interests will have a voice.

One common theme that runs through radical proposals for reorganizing the media is a debate about how much control should be exercised by media workers. There is a basic split between those who favour media workers' control, on the one hand, and those who argue that outside interests should be represented since media workers are unrepresentative of society as a whole. There is a further dispute as to whether media workers should be differentiated in terms of the spheres of operation that they should control or influence. One school of thought holds that journalists should shape editorial policy, while production workers should oversee the operation of production. Opinion also differs about what form co-determination or internal democracy

should take. The basic options in an ascending order of significance are: the right to be consulted about major decisions;
participation in senior appointments; the election of senior personnel at regular intervals; representation on decision-making
committees (editorial committees, boards of management, supervisory boards, etc.); and democratic control of all decision-
making bodies.

Reformers also differ in terms of how they propose the demo-
cratizing measures should be implemented. Some advocate a
gradualist approach in which the terms of reference of franchise-
and grant-giving bodies are changed to favour applications from
organizations with democratic structures. Others argue that industrial democracy should be pioneered in publicly owned media,
notably the BBC. A further group contends that workers should be
given rights of representation by statute in all enterprises (including
media organizations) where the majority of workers vote in favour
of acquiring them.

## Paternalism vs. libertarianism

Overlaying the different approaches to media reform that have
been outlined is a conflict between paternalism and libertarianism.
This does not correspond to a simple dichotomy between free
market and public service philosophies (although some in the
neo-liberal tradition claim misleadingly that it does). There are
free market paternalists as well as libertarians, just as there are
public service paternalists as well as libertarians.

Those in the libertarian tradition want to minimize restraints on
freedom of expression. Liberty, as George Orwell once powerfully
put it, means allowing people freely to say things that one does
not want to hear. It is a definition of freedom which many
libertarians believe should be a foundation stone in our media
system.

The most prominent group among libertarians is made up of
those who have campaigned for changes in the law. Their central
argument is that greater weight should be given to the public's
right to know the basis upon which all decisions affecting the
common good are made, and to the fundamental right of freedom
of expression, at the expense of other rights and interests which
are overprotected by law. Many of them now argue that the right
to freedom of expression should given special protection, whether
in the form of a bill of rights, the incorporation of Article 10 of

the European Convention on Human Rights into British law, or something more akin to the First Amendment to the American Constitution.

They have also argued for the revision of a whole range of laws in a way that would extend the freedom of the media. Their principal target is the 1989 Official Secrets Act, which outlaws the unauthorized disclosure of information over a wide area not directly connected with national security. For example Sarah Tisdall, jailed in 1984 for leaking to the *Guardian* how the government proposed to manage public opinion when the first US Cruise missile was sited in England, would still be liable for prosecution under the new Act even though her crime was to embarrass the government rather than endanger the country's defence. Another offensive feature of the Act, argue its critics, is that it fails to provide a public interest defence for those who reveal protected information.

Some libertarians argue that the Official Secrets Act should be revised so that it applies only to the betrayal of secrets to a national enemy. They also argue that this reform should be accompanied by the introduction of a Freedom of Information Act which would give a legal right of access to documents in all government departments, with a High Court judge determining government claims to privilege. In their view, this reform would improve government by making it more accountable. They also claim that the arguments based on cost and efficiency that have been advanced against a freedom of information law are refuted by the experience of countries like Australia, Canada, and the USA where such a law has already been introduced.

Libertarians also call for the abolition of a number of ancient and restrictive laws, most notably the law of blasphemy and the Incitement of Disaffection Act which makes it an offence to encourage members of the armed forces or the police to disobey orders. Under its provision, Pat Arrowsmith was jailed in 1975 for distributing a leaflet to soldiers calling upon them not to serve in Ulster.

A powerful case has also been made that laws which make investigative journalism difficult in Britain should be modified. The contention is that the laws of confidence and copyright are being manipulated to turn information into a restrictive property right; that defamation law deters critical probing of the powerful while failing to provide adequate protection for the general public (since freedom from unjustified defamation is the only important civil right not covered by legal aid); and that the law of contempt prevents the publication of some information which should be in the public domain.

A number of libertarian lawyers argue therefore that greater weight needs to be given in the courts to public interest justifications for breaching copyright and confidence laws. Contempt law needs to be abolished, some would urge, in cases not tried by juries since judges should be capable of reaching proper judgements uninfluenced by media reporting. Some reformers also contend that most libel cases (other than criminal libel) should be handled by a media ombudsman with the power to authorize retractions and award damages. This would diminish the lottery penalties of investigation, and make public remedy more widely available by making it much cheaper to initiate proceedings for redress.

A similar reasoning is deployed in relation to invasions of privacy. Many libertarians are opposed to the introduction of a privacy law on the grounds that it would discourage the exposure of wrongdoing by powerful individuals. They argue that unjustified intrusions of privacy and other excesses of tabloid journalism are best curbed by a voluntary code of conduct, whether upheld by readers' representatives on individual papers or by the Press Complaints Commission. Ultimately, this system of self-regulation depends on sanctions taken by employers against individual journalists.

An alternative, beefed-up version of this approach is provided by the system of self-regulation in Sweden, where a code of conduct is negotiated between the publishers' organization and journalists' union. Journalists have the right to refuse to write a story that transgresses the code of conduct: the collective organization of journalists thus underwrites the exercise of individual responsibility by its members. In addition, members of the public can appeal to the Press Ombudsman for redress. Where the alleged offence is a serious one, the case is referred to the Press Council which is vested by publishers with the power to fine and order publication of its judgements. This model thus seeks to establish an effective system of self-regulation without resorting to state-sanctioned, legal control.

Some lawyers argue also that the exercise of prior restraint is also an often unjustified limitation on media freedom. A major obstacle to investigative reporting is, they maintain, the readiness with which High Court judges issue injunctions if it is suggested that a forthcoming programme or article will infringe the law. The granting of injunctions can amount, in their view, to a form of pre-censorship since it can result in delays causing the report to become out of date and unusable. It also makes for bad journalism since it discourages journalists from cross-checking their stories for fear of provoking a gagging injunction. Some lawyers argue, therefore, that there should be no prior restraint by court injunction except in relation to information which damages the national interest or prejudices criminal proceedings. The only remedy for breach of confidence or copyright (other than patents) would be money damages assessed after publication or transmission. Alternatively, it has been suggested that no injunction banning publication of material should be granted without the judge first hearing both sides argue their case.

Some libertarians also argue that obscenity and indecency laws should be modified. Their views influenced the Williams Committee (1979) which recommended that legal restraint should be formally lifted from all explicit writing in publications where there is no offensive illustration. However, it also advocated that forms of pornography, 'whose unrestricted availability is offensive to reasonable people', should not be sold to persons under the age of 18, and that pictorial pornography featuring under-age or sadistic sex should remain subject to specific prohibition. The Committee's recommendations, which would have led to a significant liberalizing of the law, were rejected.

Critics have also attacked the Video Recordings Act (1984), complaining that it has resulted in a massive apparatus of censorship involving the inspection of all videos featuring sex or violence (with minor exemptions). This has led, they maintain, to an unnecessarily restrictive policy. 'Video nasties' – the target of the Act – could be better dealt with, in their view, by empowering the British Board of Film Classification to respond to complaints from the police and public about specific videos and, where desirable, prohibit their sale.

Libertarians usually oppose the suggestion frequently mooted by public service radicals that broadcasters should be subject to a duty to 'combat racism, sexism and class bias'. They argue that laws already lay down the acceptable levels of racial intolerance, obscenity, and defamation, and that to impose a more restrictive code on broadcasting is an unacceptable limitation on freedom of expression. They also argue that it sets a precedent that could become the basis for a widening gyre of censorship extending for example to communism and other forms of political thinking judged to be anti-social.

The conventional libertarian argument is usually constructed in terms of securing the maximum legal freedom of expression *of* the media compatible with the public interest. But essentially the same argument has been recast by some libertarians in a differently inflected form: securing the maximum freedom of expression *through* the media. It currently costs up to £2 million to establish a local commercial radio station; over £15 million to establish a new national daily; about £30 million to develop a cable television station; and well over £500 million to establish a new, multi-channel satellite service. These high costs explain, according to some libertarians, why it is necessary to lower the barriers to media ownership through public intervention if wider interests are to be represented and true diversity of expression is to be secured.

A similar argument is sometimes articulated in terms of extending access to the media through a legal right of reply. The former Labour MP Frank Allaun proposed a celebrated private members' bill in 1981 which would have extended readers' freedom of expression in the press by giving them the right, enforceable in the courts, to secure counter-statements to 'distortions'. Others have since argued for a more circumscribed right of reply to factual misrepresentations in newspapers enforced either by the courts or by a press ombudsman. The legal right of reply exists in many European countries, and is notionally available in the case of British television and radio through the Broadcasting Complaints Commission, set up in 1981.

Finally, libertarian arguments are sometimes deployed in support of internal democracy within the media. The case for extending the freedom *of* the media is recast to justify extending freedom *within* the media. A small flick of the wrist, so to speak, changes the trajectory of the argument. The freedom of proprietors – the locus of media freedom in conventional liberal rhetoric – is redefined as a constraint, limiting the freedom of expression of journalists.

Whereas libertarians stress the benefits of freedom, paternalists stress the harm that may result from licence. Certain individual rights – the right to privacy, a good reputation, a fair trial, security, and property – should override freedom of expression unless an overwhelming case can be made to the contrary. In the paternalist approach, these rights are also broadly defined to ensure adequate protection. For example, the right to security covers not only the protection of defence secrets and other matters relating to national security but also the maintenance of law and order, support for discipline in the armed forces, the protection of minors, and the prohibition of incitement to group hatred.

Some paternalists also argue that the freedom of the media should be curtailed so that it conforms to the moral consensus of the nation or, at least, does not violate the sensibilities of reasonable people. As the Broadcasting Standards Council argued in its 1989 code of practice: 'The assumption of freedom in broadcasting still requires some expression of a responsible understanding between audience and broadcasters on how and when it is to be expressed.'[10] This implicitly goes beyond the case for limited censorship – the prohibition of communications which do manifest and unjustified harm to others – to a plea for a broader measure of control in the name of social responsibility.

This can become the basis for censorship over quite a wide area: for example, bad language that may cause offence; displays of indecency which offend a sense of sexual modesty; and portrayals of violence that cause distress. The protection of sensibilities can override, according to this logic, the disclosure of information with a strong public interest justification. Thus, it has long been customary to sanitize the reporting of wars by editing out pictures that may upset people even though these pictures may have the effect of encouraging aversion to unjustified violence.

Public harm is also invoked as a justification for suppressing communications which are still widely available – namely displays of pornography and gratuitous violence. It is claimed (with little empirical justification)[11] that the depiction of violence encourages imitative acts of violence, while pornography leads to sex crimes. A more sophisticated version of this argument postulates a more indirect causal relationship: namely that certain forms of pornography promote indirectly male violence against women by reinforcing misogynistic elements within male culture, while television violence (particularly when portrayed in a positive light) feeds violence in real life by fostering aggressive elements in popular culture.

Censorship is also advocated as an instrument of social engineering. Pornography expresses anti-social attitudes, it is argued, that should be suppressed. It is inherently oppressive: it demeans with its constant suggestion of women's availability, and it fosters through the expression of scorn and contempt values that give rise to discriminatory acts against women. A parallel is sometimes made between pornography and incitement to racial hatred on the grounds that both detract from the status of the victim. But in fact, incitement to racial hatred is only usually prosecuted in Britain when public disorder is likely to be the outcome – a criterion that excludes most racist communications.

The gathering impetus towards moral censorship in the 1980s gave rise to changes in media regulation. The Broadcasting Standards Council was established in 1988 to provide a focus for public concern about sex, violence, and standards of taste and decency in broadcasting. Its remit was to monitor the performance of broadcasting, respond to public complaints, and draw up and maintain a moral code of conduct for broadcasting. The Council was strengthened in 1990 by being put on a statutory footing with the power to compel publication of its indictments by offending channels, although it does not have the authority to enforce its moral code. However, the 1990 Broadcasting Act requires licensed broadcasters not to transmit programmes offensive to public feeling, and charges all broadcasters to 'reflect the general effect' of the Council's code. Broadcasting was also made subject for the first time in 1990 to the Obscene Publications Act.

Paternalism in a broad sense has been the guiding philosophy underpinning the organization of broadcasting since its inception, and the demand for increased moral regulation can be accommodated through existing structures of control. But demands for increased moral and ethical regulation of the press – prompted in part by a backlash against the excesses of tabloid journalism – can only be realized through the adoption of new measures. The two most strongly canvassed proposals in the late 1980s were the introduction of a restrictive privacy law, and the establishment of the Press Council as a statutory body able to exact fines and compel publication of its indictments.

## Map of media politics

The simple dichotomy of left and right does not adequately describe the politics of the media. In broad terms, those on the right are still more inclined to support a free market policy than those on the left. But this difference is overlaid by a cleavage between paternalism and libertarianism that does not correspond to a left–right split. This has resulted in strange convergencies. The radical community radio movement and the right-wing Adam Smith Institute have both pressed for the deregulation of broadcasting: similarly, some left-wing feminists like Clare Short have joined conservative traditionalists like Mary Whitehouse in calling for greater moral regulation of the media (for a summary guide, see Table 10). Indeed, both the Conservative Party and the Labour Party are split over media policy. While these splits are not coterminous, there are striking points of similarity.

Table 10    *Politics of the media*

*Paternalism*

| Thatcherite | Reithian |
|---|---|
| Mary Whitehouse | Puritan feminists |
| New legal controls | Franchising newspapers |
| Conservative policy on broadcasting | Labour policy on broadcasting |

*Free market* ———————————————— *Regulated market*

| Conservative policy on press | Labour policy on press |
|---|---|
| Adam Smith Institute | Libertarian New Left |

*Libertarianism*

One powerful group of radicals in the Conservative Party, epitomized by Margaret Thatcher, are neo-liberal paternalists who favour both a free market regime for the media and extensive moral and national security controls. They pressed for more privatization and commercialization, including the introduction of advertising on the BBC. But they also urged the setting up of the Broadcasting Standards Council to check the permissiveness of television, pressed for concerted European regulation of pornography on television, and backed the television ban on Sinn Fein.

There is another radical group within the Conservative Party, represented by the nominally non-aligned Adam Smith Institute and the Institute of Economic Affairs, who favour the relaxation of both content and economic controls over broadcasting. Believing in both the free market and libertarian reform, they increasingly clashed with their right-wing allies, accusing them of 'new-style authoritarianism'. As Samuel Brittan, an influential figure on the libertarian new right and a former member of the Peacock Committee, put it:

> In putting forward the idea of a free broadcasting market without censorship, Peacock exposed many of the contradictions in the Thatcherite espousal of market forces. In principle, Mrs Thatcher and her supporters are all in favour of deregulation, competition and consumer choice. But they are also even more distrustful than traditionalist Tories of policies that allow people to listen to and watch what they like, subject only to the law of the land. They espouse the market system but dislike the libertarian value-judgements involved in its operation.[12]

But the main body of opinion in the Conservative Party still falls within the neo-Reithian tradition that is committed to a regulated broadcasting system dedicated to informing, educating, and entertaining. It includes traditionalists who attach importance to defending standards of excellence and maintaining British cultural standards as well as some revisionists, influenced by neo-liberals, who feel that some modification in favour of the market-place is desirable. This centrist tendency, epitomized by Douglas Hurd, who as Home Secretary presided over the 1990 broadcasting reorganization, favoured a compromise: expanding the broadcasting system, liberalizing it a little in economic rather than in moral terms, but leaving it fundamentally unchanged. These Conservatives (with a small as well as a large 'c') were the dominant influence shaping the 1990 Broadcasting Act.

There is also a dominant, centrist bloc within the Labour Party, flanked on either side by strongly paternalistic and libertarian wings.

On the paternalistic left there is a dwindling group of old-fashioned Reithians, morally affronted by commercial advertising, who at heart favour a public service monopoly informed by the belief that 'few know what they want and fewer still know what they need'. There is also another, growing group, who are in a sense the modern heirs of Reithian paternalism. They want to restore a sense of mission to broadcasting – but as a force against sexism and racism. Some of them favour controls over sex on television not far removed from those advocated by the moral regulators of the traditional right.

On the libertarian left there are a number of groups. One idealistic group with limited influence would like to go back to the drawing board and create a new broadcasting system based on autonomous, local units. Another more significant group, represented by GLC veterans like Geoff Mulgan, are committed to the liberalization of programme controls within the framework of a social market economy for broadcasting. Their views on broadcasting policy are more closely aligned, in practice, to those of the libertarian new right than to paternalists on their own side.

However, the dominant tendency within the Labour Party wants to slap a preservation order on the broadcasting system as it was in about 1989, and is fearful that the development of a new greenfield site in the form of satellite television may in due course undermine the listed buildings of Britain's historic past. As represented by Roy Hattersley, their views on broadcasting policy are remarkably similar to those of traditional Conservatives like Douglas Hurd. They believe in a publicly regulated mixed economy of broadcasting, informed by a commitment to inform, educate, and entertain. Their only significant difference from their Tory counterparts is that they are more opposed to gradual economic liberalization (in particular, the auctioning of franchises), and are more inclined to favour economic regulation of satellite television. In conjunction with the dominant bloc in the Conservative Party, they represent the consensual, middle ground of broadcasting politics.

There are also parallel lines of cleavage within the Conservative and Labour Parties over press policy. However, internal differences over press policy are less pronounced than they are over broadcasting because the press is judged to be less controversial. They are also less symmetrical.

A sizeable bloc within the parliamentary Labour Party – once a majority but now probably a minority – wants no real change in press policy. This bloc is flanked, on the one hand by public service regulators who want to franchise newspapers and, on the other hand, by social market radicals who want to promote newspaper competition and diversity. The Labour Party is also divided between those who want to curb the excesses of tabloid journalism through new legal controls, and those who want to liberalize media law (with some quixotically wanting to do both). A new consensus appears to be emerging, however, within the parliamentary Labour Party in favour of 'doing something about the press'. This is likely to result in an official commitment to social market reform within a libertarian framework: new anti-monopoly controls, accompanied by a freedom of information law and liberalization of the Official Secrets Act.

The majority of the Conservative Party wants no change in press policy. But it too has competing libertarian and paternalist wings – one favouring a liberalized Official Secrets Act, and the other pressing for tougher legislative controls, including a privacy law. While there is no right-wing equivalent to left-wing socialists who want public service regulation of franchised newspapers, there are some on the neo-liberal right who are as committed to curbing the growth of media monopoly as radicals on the left.

In short, the real battle lines in the debate about media reform do not correspond to the dragooned confrontations between 'whipped' MPs in the Commons. Even within the two major parties, there are groups which have more affinity with their opponents over media policy than they have with people on their own side. Adding to the fluidity of the situation is the dynamic created by rapid change in the technology of the media. In this unpredictable situation, it is just possible to hope that a modified media system may emerge over time: one with power *and* responsibility – but to the public rather than to proprietors and governments.

## Notes

1. This is a central flaw at the heart of the Peacock Committee Report [*Report of the Committee on Financing the BBC* (London, HMSO, 1986)].
2. However, this restriction had been evaded with the connivance of the Cable TV Authority through the creation of trust companies registered in the Channel Islands. It is unlikely, therefore, that the relaxation of this restriction will make much difference.
3. Cento Veljanovski, 'Competition in broadcasting' in C. Veljanovski (ed.), *Freedom in Broadcasting* (London, Institute of Economic Affairs, 1989), p. 24.
4. Rupert Murdoch, 'Freedom in broadcasting', *MacTaggart Lecture 1989* (London, News International, 1989), p. 9.

5. Derived from *Royal Commission on the Press 1974–7 Final Report* (London, HMSO) pp. 131–2; written answers from the Department of Trade and Industry to Austin Mitchell MP (19 December 1980) and Mark Fisher MP (29 January 1990).

6. *Subscription Television: A Study for the Home Office* (London, HMSO, 1987).

7. For a useful discussion of European broadcasting politics, see in particular Vincent Porter, 'The Janus character of television broadcasting' in Gareth Locksley (ed.), *Integration: The Single European Market and the Information Communication Technologies* (London, Pinter, 1990).

8. Council Directive (3 October 1989), *Official Journal of the European Communities*, No. L 298/23, Article 22. A more restrictive formulation is contained in *European Convention on Transfrontier Television*, Council of Europe (text adopted 15 March 1989), Article 7.

9. For example, see Richard Sparks and Ian Taylor, 'Mass communications' in Philip Brown and Richard Sparks (eds), *Beyond Thatcherism* (Milton Keynes, Open University Press, 1989).

10. British Standards Council, *Annual Report 1988–9 and Code of Practice* (London: British Standards Council, 1989), p. 9.

11. See Guy Cumberbatch and Denis Howitt, *A Measure of Uncertainty: The Effects of the Mass Media* (London, Libbey, 1989).

12. Samuel Brittan, 'The case for the consumer market' in C. Veljanovski (ed.), op. cit., 1989, p. 40.

# Bibliography

## Public reports and papers

### Broadcasting

*Broadcasting Committee: Report* (Sykes Report, 1923) [Cmd 1951].

*Report of the Broadcasting Committee* (Crawford Report, 1926) [Cmd 2599].

*Report of the Television Committee* (Selsdon Report, 1935) [Cmd 3703].

*Report of the Broadcasting Committee* (Ullswater Report, 1936) [Cmd 5091].

*Report of the Television Committee* (Hankey Report, 1944) (Privy Council Office).

*Broadcasting Policy* (1946) [Cmd 6852].

*Report of the Broadcasting Committee* (Beveridge Report, 1951) [Cmd 8116].

*Report of the Broadcasting Committee 1949* (1951/2) [Cmd 8117].

*Broadcasting, Memorandum on the Report of the Broadcasting Committee* (1951) [Cmd 8291].

*Broadcasting, Memorandum on the Report of the Broadcasting Committee, 1949* (1952) [Cmd 8550].

*The Television Act 1954*, 2 & 3 Eliz. II, c. 55.

*Report of the Committee on Broadcasting* (Pilkington Report, 1962) [Cmnd 1753].

*The Television Act 1964*, 12 & 13 Eliz. II, c. 21.

*The University of the Air* (1966) [Cmnd 2992].

*An Alternative Service of Radio Broadcasting* (1971) [Cmnd 4636].

*Sound Broadcasting Act 1972*, 19 & 20 Eliz. II, c. 31.

*Session 1971–2 Independent Broadcasting Authority*, Sub-Committee B, House of Commons Paper 465 (1972).

*Observations on the Second Report of the Select Committee of the Nationalized Industries* (1973) [Cmnd 5244].

*Report of the Committee on the Future of Broadcasting* (Annan Report, 1977) [Cmnd 6753].

*Radio Choices and Opportunities* (1982) [Cm 92].

*Broadcasting without Frontiers*, EEC paper, No. 9 (1984).

*Report of the Committee on Financing the BBC* (Peacock Report, 1986) [Cmnd 9824].

*Subscription Television: A Study for the Home Office* (London, HMSO, 1987).

*Radio: Choices and Opportunities* (1987) [Cm 92].

*Broadcasting in the '90s: Competition, Choice and Quality* (1987) [Cm 517].

*The Future of Broadcasting*, Home Affairs Committee (1988).

*Broadcasting Bill*, House of Commons (1989).

## The press

Monopolies Commission (1965–6), *The Times Newspaper and Sunday Times* (London, HMSO, 1966).

Monopolies Commission (1967–8), *Thomson Newspapers and Crusha and Son Ltd*, House of Commons Paper 66 (London, HMSO, 1968).

Monopolies Commission (1969–70), *George Outram and Company Ltd and Hamilton Advertiser Ltd and Baird and Hamilton Ltd*, House of Commons Paper 76 (London, HMSO, 1970).

Monopolies Commission (1971–2), *The Berrows Organisation Ltd and the County Express Group*, House of Commons Paper 224 (London, HMSO, 1972).

Monopolies Commission (1972–3), *Westminster Press Ltd and Kentish Times Ltd, Gravesend and Dartford Reporter Ltd and F. J. Parsons Ltd, Subsidiaries of Morgan-Grampian Ltd*, House of Commons Paper 460 (London, HMSO, 1973).

Monopolies Commission (1973–4), *Courier Printing and Publishing Company Ltd and Associated Newspapers Group Ltd*, House of Commons Paper 108 (London, HMSO, 1974).

Monopolies Commission (1974–5), *G. and A. N. Scott Ltd and The Guardian and Manchester Evening News Ltd*, House of Commons Paper 349 (London, HMSO, 1975).

Monopolies and Mergers Commission, *The Observer and George Outram* (London, HMSO, 1981).

Monopolies and Mergers Commission, *Wholesaling of Newspapers and Periodicals* (London, HMSO, 1978).

National Board for Prices and Incomes, *Wages, Costs and Prices in the Printing Industry* (1965) [Cmnd 2750].

National Board for Prices and Incomes, *Costs and Revenue of National Daily Newspapers* (1967) [Cmnd 3435].

National Board for Prices and Incomes, *Journalists' Pay* (1969) [Cmnd 4077].

National Board for Prices and Incomes, *Costs and Revenue of National Newspapers* (1970) [Cmnd 4277].

*Report of the Committee on Contempt of Court* (1975) [Cmnd 5794].

*Report of the Committee on Data Protection* (Lindop Committee, 1978) [Cmnd 7341].

*Report of the Committee on Defamation* (Faulks Committee, 1975) [Cmnd 5571].

*Report of the Committee on the Official Secrets Act* (1972) [Cmnd 7140].

*Report of a Court of Inquiry into the Problems Caused by the Introduction of Web-offset Machines* (1967) [Cmnd 3184].

*Royal Commission on the Press 1947–9 Report* (1949) [Cmnd 7700].

*Royal Commission on the Press 1961–2 Report* (1962) [Cmnd 1811].

*Royal Commission on the Press Interim Report* (1976) [Cmnd 6553].

*Royal Commission on the Press 1974–7 Final Report* (1977) [Cmnd 6810].

*Royal Commission on the Press Final Report Appendices* (1977) [Cmnd 6810–1–6].

Select Committee of the House of Commons on Newspaper Stamps, *Parliamentary Papers, xvii* (1851).

## *Film*

*Cinematograph Films Act* (1927) [Cmnd 2053].

*Report of the Committee appointed by the Board of Trade* (Moyne Report, 1936) [Cmnd 2053].

*Report on Tendencies to Monopoly in the Cinematograph Film Industry* (Palache Report, 1944) [Cmnd 4059].

*Report of the Working Party on Film Production Costs* (Gater Report, 1949) [Cmnd 7837].

*Report of the Committee on the Distribution and Exhibition of Cinematograph Films* (Plant Report, 1949) [Cmnd 7837].

*Cinematograph Films Council, Distribution and Exhibition of Cinematograph Films* (London, HMSO, Board of Trade, 1950).

*Cinematograph Films Bill 1960*, 8 & 9 Eliz. II.

*The Films Act*, House of Commons Paper 206 (1960).

*Board of Trade Review of Films Legislation* (1968) [Cmnd 3584].

*The Prime Minister's Working Party on the Future of the Film Industry* (Wilson Report, 1976) [Cmnd 6372].

## *Miscellaneous public reports referred to in the book*

*Machinery of Government Report* (1918) [Cmnd 9230].

Board of Education, *Inspectors' Report* (1932) [Cmnd 4068].

*Board of Education Consultative Committee on Secondary Education* (Spens Report, 1938), 10/119.

*Report of the Department Committee on Curriculum and Examinations in Secondary Schools* (Norwood Report, 1943).

*The Nation's Schools: their Plans and Purposes*, Ministry of Education Pamphlet 1 (London, HMSO, 1945).

*Royal Commission on Local Government* (1969) (Redcliffe Maud Report), Research Paper 9, *Community Attitudes Survey* [Cmnd 3409].

*Report of the Committee on Privacy* (1972) [Cmnd 5012].

*Royal Commission on the Distribution of Income and Wealth, Report 4* (1976) [Cmnd 6626].

*Report of the Committee on Film Finance* (1985) [Cmnd 7610].

## The press

### General historical perspectives

R. D. Altick, *The English Common Reader* (Chicago, Ill., University of Chicago Press, 1957; London, Phoenix, 1963).

A. Andrews, *History of British Journalism*, 2 vols (London, Richard Bentley, 1859).

G. Boyce, 'The fourth estate: the reappraisal of a concept' in G. Boyce, J. Curran, and P. Wingate (eds), *Newspaper History* (London, Constable, 1978).

P. Brendon, *The Life and Death of the Press Barons* (London, Secker & Warburg, 1982).

C. J. Bundock, *The National Union of Journalists: A Jubilee History, 1907–1957* (London, Oxford University Press, 1957).

D. Chaney, *Processes of Mass Communication* (London, Macmillan, 1972).

G. A. Cranfield, *The Press and Society* (Harlow, Longman, 1978).

J. Curran, 'Capitalism and control of the press 1800–1975' in J. Curran, M. Gurevitch, and J. Woollacott (eds), *Mass Communication and Society* (London, Edward Arnold/Open University, 1977).

——'The press as an agency of social control: an historical perspective' in G. Boyce, J. Curran, and P. Wingate (eds), *Newspaper History* (London, Constable, 1978).

——'Communications, power and social order' in T. Bennett, J. Curran, M. Gurevitch, and J. Woollacott (eds), *Culture, Media and Society* (London, Methuen, 1981).

H. R. Fox Bourne, *English Newspapers* (London, Chatto & Windus, 1887; London, Russell & Russell 1966).

J. Grant, *The Newspaper Press*, 3 vols (London, Tinsley Brothers, 1871–2).

M. Harris and A. Lee (eds), *The Press in English Society from the*

*Seventeenth to Nineteenth Centuries* (London and Toronto, Associated University Presses, 1986).

R. Harrison, G. Woolven, and R. Duncan, *The Warwick Guide to British Labour Periodicals 1790–1970* (Brighton, Harvester, 1977).

S. Harrison, *Poor Men's Guardians: A Record of the Struggles for a Democratic Newspaper Press 1763–1973* (London, Lawrence & Wishart, 1974).

H. Herd, *The March of Journalism* (London, Allen & Unwin, 1952).

F. Knight Hunt, *The Fourth Estate* (London, David Bogue, 1850).

P. Knightley, *The First Casualty: The War Correspondent as Hero, Propagandist and Myth Maker from the Crimea to Vietnam* (London, Deutsch, 1975).

S. Koss, *The Rise and Fall of the Political Press in Britain*, vols 1–2 (London, Hamish Hamilton, 1981 and 1984).

A. Marshall, *Changing the Word: The Printing Industry in Transition* (London, Comedia, 1983).

M. Milne, *Newspapers of Northumberland and Durham* (Newcastle, Frank Graham, 1972).

S. Morison, *The English Newspaper* (Cambridge, Cambridge University Press, 1932).

A. E. Musson, *The Typographical Association: Origins and History up to 1949* (London, Oxford University Press, 1954).

C. Pebody, *English Journalism* (London, Cassell, Petter & Galpin, 1882).

G. Scott, *Reporters Anonymous: The Story of the Press Association* (London, Hutchinson, 1968).

F. S. Siebert, T. Peterson, and W. Schramm, *Four Theories of the Press* (Urbana, Ill., University of Illinois Press, 1956; New York, Books for Libraries Press, 1973).

A. Smith, *The Newspaper: An International History* (London, Thames & Hudson, 1979).

—— 'Technology and control: the interactive dimensions of journalism' in J. Curran, M. Gurevitch, and J. Woollacott (eds), *Mass Communication and Society* (London, Edward Arnold/Open University, 1977).

G. Storey, *Reuter's Century 1851–1951* (London, Parrish, 1951).

K. von Stutterheim, *The Press in England* (London, Allen & Unwin, 1934).

H. A. Taylor, *The British Press* (London, Arthur Barker, 1961).

J. Tunstall, 'Editorial sovereignty in the British press: its past and present' in *Studies on the Press*, Royal Commission on the Press 1974–7 Working Paper 3 (London, HMSO, 1977).

A. P. Wadsworth, 'Newspaper circulations 1800–1954', *Transactions of the Manchester Statistical Society*, iv (1955).

C. White, *Women's Magazines, 1693–1968* (London, Michael Joseph, 1970).

F. Williams, *Dangerous Estate* (Harlow, Longman Green, 1959; London, Arrow, 1959).

R. Williams, *The Long Revolution* (London, Chatto & Windus, 1961). ——'The press and popular culture: an historical perspective' in G. Boyce, J. Curran, and P. Wingate (eds), *Newspaper History* (London, Constable, 1978).

C. Wilson, *First with the News: The History of W. H. Smith 1792–1972* (London, Cape, 1985).

## Newspaper histories

Anon, *The History of the Times*, vols 1–5 (1935–58).

D. Ayerst, *The Guardian: Biography of a Newspaper* (London, Collins, 1971).

Lord Burnham, *Peterborough Court: Story of the Daily Telegraph* (London, Cassell, 1955).

P. Chippendale and C. Horrie, *Disaster! The Rise and Fall of the News on Sunday* (London, Sphere, 1988).

A. Christiansen, *Headlines All My Life* (London, Heinemann, 1961).

P. Cockburn, *The Years of the Week* (Harmondsworth, Penguin, 1971).

H. Cudlipp, *Publish and be Damned* (London, Andrew Dakers, 1953).

M. Edelman, *The Mirror – A Political History* (London, Hamish Hamilton, 1966).

W. Fienburgh, *25 Momentous Years: A 25th Anniversary in the History of the Daily Herald* (London, Odhams, 1955).

G. Fraser and K. Peters, *The Northern Lights* (London, Hamish Hamilton, 1978).

M. A. Gibb and F. Beckwith, *The Yorkshire Post: Two Centuries* (Leeds, Yorkshire Conservative Newspaper Co., 1954).

P. M. Handover, *History of the London Gazette, 1665–1965* (London, HMSO, 1965).

A. Hetherington, *Guardian Years* (London, Chatto & Windus, 1981).

D. Hill, *Tribune 40* (London, Quartet, 1977).

W. Hindle, *The Morning Post, 1772–1937* (London, Routledge & Kegan Paul, 1937).

H. Hobson, P. Knightley, and L. Russell, *The Pearl of Days: An Intimate Memoir of the Sunday Times, 1822–1972* (London, Hamish Hamilton, 1972).

L. Lamb, *Sunrise* (London, Macmillan, 1989).

R. J. Lucas, *Lord Glenesk and the Morning Post* (London, Alston Rivers, 1910).

I. McDonald, *History of the Times 1939–66*, vol. 5 (London, Times Books, 1984).

R. McKay and B. Barr, *The Story of the Scottish Daily News* (Edinburgh, Canongate, 1976).

J. W. Robertson Scott, *The Story of the Pall Mall Gazette* (London, Oxford University Press, 1950).

H. R. G. Whates, *The Birmingham Post, 1857–1957* (Birmingham Post and Mail, 1957).

O. Woods and J. Bishop, *The Story of the Times* (London, Michael Joseph, 1983).

## *Nineteenth-century press history*

W. E. Adams, *Memoirs of a Social Atom*, 2 vols (London, Hutchinson, 1903).

Anon, *Guide to Advertisers* (London, 1851).

A. Aspinall, 'Statistical accounts of London newspapers 1800–36', *English Historical Review*, lxv (1950).

——*Politics and the Press, 1780–1850* (London, Home & Van Thal, 1949; Brighton, Harvester, 1973).

I. Asquith, 'Advertising and the press in the late eighteenth and early nineteenth centuries: James Perry and the *Morning Chronicle*, 1790–1821', *Historical Journal*, xvii (1975).

P. Bailey, *Leisure and Class in Victorian England* (London, Routledge & Kegan Paul, 1978).

V. Berridge, 'Popular Sunday papers and mid-Victorian society' in G. Boyce, J. Curran, and P. Wingate (eds), *Newspaper History* (London, Constable, 1978).

T. Boyle, *Black Swine in the Sewers of Hampstead* (London, Hodder & Stoughton, 1989).

L. Brown, *Victorian News and Newspapers* (Oxford, Clarendon, 1985).

T. Catling, *My Life's Pilgrimage* (London, John Murray, 1911).

I. R. Christie, 'British newspapers in the late Georgian age' in *Myth and Reality in Late 18th Century British Politics* (London, Macmillan, 1970).

C. D. Collet, *History of the Taxes on Knowledge* (London, T. Fisher Unwin, 1899).

S. Coltham, 'The *Bee-Hive* newspaper: its origins and early struggle' in A. Briggs and J. Saville (eds), *Essays in Labour History* (London, Macmillan, 1960).

——'The British working-class press in 1867', *Bulletin for the Society for the Study of Labour History* (autumn 1967).

F. Dilnot, *Adventures of a Newspaper Man* (London, Smith, Elder, 1913).

J. A. Epstein, 'Feargus O'Connor and the *Morning Star*', *International Review of Social History*, xxi (1976).

T. H. S. Escott, *Masters of English Journalism* (London, T. Fisher Unwin, 1911).

J. Foster, *Class Struggle and the Industrial Revolution: Early Industrial Capitalism in Three English Towns* (London, Weidenfeld & Nicolson, 1974).

M. D. George, *English Political Caricature, 1792–1832* (London, Oxford University Press, 1959).

E. Glasgow, 'The establishment of the *Northern Star* newspaper', *History*, xxxix (1954).

B. Harrison, 'A world of which we had no conception: liberalism and the temperance press, 1830–1872', *Victorian Studies*, xiii (December 1969).

J. Hatton, *Journalistic London* (London, Sampson, Low, 1882).

A. F. Havighurst, *Radical Journalist: H. W. Massingham* (Cambridge, Cambridge University Press, 1974).

P. Hollis, *The Pauper Press* (London, Oxford University Press, 1970).

D. Hopkin, 'The socialist press in Britain 1890–1910' in G. Boyce, J. Curran, and P. Wingate (eds), *Newspaper History* (London, Constable, 1978).

D. Hudson, *Thomas Barnes of the Times* (Cambridge, Cambridge University Press, 1943).

L. James (ed.), *Print and the People, 1819–1851* (London, Allen Lane, 1976).

E. E. Kellett, 'The press' in G. M. Young (ed.), *Early Victorian England* (London, Oxford University Press, 1934).

C. Kent, 'Higher journalism and the mid-Victorian clerisy', *Victorian Studies*, xiii (December 1969).

S. Koss, *Fleet Street Radical: A. G. Gardiner and the Daily News* (London, Allen Lane, 1973).

A. J. Lee, 'The management of a Victorian local newspaper: the *Manchester City News*, 1864–1900', *Business History*, xv (1973).

——'The radical press' in A. Morris (ed.), *Edwardian Radicalism, 1900–1914* (London, Routledge & Kegan Paul, 1974).

——*The Origins of the Popular Press, 1855–1914* (London, Croom Helm, 1976).

J. R. McCulloch, *Dictionary of Commerce and Commercial Navigation* (London, Longman, Brown, & Green, 1854).

*Mitchell's Newspaper Press Directory* (Mitchell).

P. Mountjoy, 'The working-class press and working-class conservatism' in G. Boyce, J. Curran, and P. Wingate (eds), *Newspaper History* (London, Constable, 1978).

A. E. Musson, 'Newspaper printing in the Industrial Revolution', *Economic History Review*, x, 2nd series (1957–8).

V. Neuberg, 'The literature of the streets' in H. J. Dyos and M. Wolff (eds), *The Victorian City* (London, Routledge & Kegan Paul, 1973).

T. Nevett, 'Advertising and editorial integrity in the nineteenth century' in M. Harris and A. Lee, *The Press in English Society from the Seventeenth to Nineteenth Centuries* (London and Toronto, associated University Presses, 1986).

L. O'Boyle, 'The image of the journalist in England, France and Germany, 1815–1848', *Comparative Studies in Society and History*, x (1968).

P. O'Malley, 'Capital accumulation and press freedom, 1800–1850', *Media, Culture and Society*, 3, 1 (1981).

H. J. Perkin, 'The origins of the popular press', *History Today*, vii (1957).

R. Pound and G. Harmsworth, *Northcliffe* (London, Cassell, 1959).

R. Price, *An Imperial War and the British Working Class: Working-class Attitudes and Reactions to the Boer War 1899–1902* (London, Routledge & Kegan Paul, 1972).

D. Read, *Press and People 1790–1850* (London, Edward Arnold, 1961).

J. Roach, 'Education and public opinion' in C. Crawley (ed.), *War and Peace in an Age of Upheaval* (Cambridge, Cambridge University Press, 1965).

F. G. Salmon, 'What the working class read', *Nineteenth Century*, cxiii (1886).

M. Sanderson, 'Literacy and social mobility in the Industrial Revolution', *Past and Present*, 5, 6 (1972).

A. R. Schoyen, *The Chartist Challenge: A Portrait of George Julian Harney* (London, Heinemann, 1956).

J. Shattock and M. Wolff (eds), *The Victorian Periodical Press: Samplings and Soundings* (Leicester, University of Leicester Press, 1982).

H. Simonis, *The Street of Ink* (London, Cassell, 1917).

J. A. Spender, *Life, Journalism and Politics*, 2 vols (London, Cassell, 1927).

J. F. Stephen, 'Journalism', *Cornhill Magazine*, 6 (1862).

L. Stone, 'Literacy and education in England 1640–1900', *Past and Present*, 42 (1969).

J. D. Symon, *The Press and its Story* (London, Seeley Service, 1914).

T. Tholfsen, *Working-Class Radicalism in Mid-Victorian Britain* (London, Croom Helm, 1976).

D. Thompson, *The Chartists* (London, Maurice Temple Smith, 1984).

E. P. Thompson, *The Making of the English Working Class* (London, Gollancz, 1963).

R. K. Webb, *The British Working-Class Reader, 1790–1848* (London, Allen & Unwin, 1955).

W. H. Wickwar, *The Struggle for the Freedom of the Press, 1819–1832* (London, Allen & Unwin, 1928).

J. H. Wiener, *The War of the Unstamped* (New York, Cornell University Press, 1969).

## Twentieth-century press history

R. Adams, *Media Planning* (London, Business Books, 1971).

A. Angell, *The Press and the Organisation of Society* (London, Labour Publishing Co., 1922).

D. Ayerst, *Garvin of the Observer* (London, Croom Helm, 1985).

Lord Beaverbrook, *Men and Power* (London, Hutchinson, 1956).

W. Belson, *The British Press* (London, London Press Exchange, 1959).

T. Bower, *Maxwell: The Outsider* (London, Aurum, 1989).

O. Boyd-Barrett, C. Seymour-Ure, and J. Tunstall, *Studies on the Press*, Royal Commission on the Press, Working Paper 3 (London, HMSO, 1977).

R. Braddon, *Roy Thomson* (London, Fontana, 1968).

P. Brendon, *Eminent Edwardians* (London, Secker & Warburg, 1979).

T. B. Browne, *Advertisers' ABC* (Browne).

A. Calder, *The People's War* (London, Panther, 1971).

S. Chibnall, *Law-and-Order News* (London, Tavistock, 1977).

C. Chisholm, *Marketing and Merchandising* (London, Modern Business Institute, 1924).

H. Christian (ed.), *The Sociology of Journalism and the Press*, Sociological Review Monograph 29 (Keele, University of Keele, 1980).

A Christiansen, *Headlines All My Life* (London, Harper, 1961).

T. Clarke, *My Northcliffe Diary* (London, Gollancz, 1931).

——*Northcliffe in History* (London, Hutchinson, 1950).

G. Cleverley, *The Fleet Street Disaster* (London, Constable, 1976).

C. Cockburn, *Brothers: Male Dominance and Technological Change* (London, Pluto, 1983).

M. Cockerell, P. Hennessy, and D. Walker, *Sources Close to the Prime Minister* (London, Macmillan, 1984).

R. Cockett, *Twilight of Truth* (London, Weidenfeld & Nicolson, 1989).

S. Cohen and J. Young, *The Manufacture of News* (London, Constable, 1973).

H. Cox and D. Morgan, *City Politics and the Press* (Cambridge, Cambridge University Press, 1973).

R. A. Critchley, *UK Advertising Statistics* (London, Advertising Association, nd).

H. Cudlipp, *At Your Peril* (London, Weidenfeld & Nicolson, 1962).

——*Walking on the Water* (London, Bodley Head, 1976).

J. Curran, 'The impact of TV on the audience for national newspapers, 1945–68' in J. Tunstall (ed.), *Media Sociology* (London, Constable, 1970).

——(ed.), *The British Press: A Manifesto* (London, Macmillan, 1978).

——'Advertising and the press' in J. Curran (ed.), *The British Press: A Manifesto* (London, Macmillan, 1978).

T. Driberg, *Beaverbrook* (London, Weidenfeld & Nicolson, 1956).

H. W. Eley, *Advertising Media* (London, Butterworth, 1932).

H. Evans, *Good Times, Bad Times* (London, Weidenfeld & Nicolson, 1983).

B. Falk, *He Laughed in Fleet Street* (London, Hutchinson, 1933).

M. Ferguson, *Forever Feminine* (London, Heinemann Educational, 1983).

P. Ferris, *The House of Northcliffe* (London, Weidenfeld & Nicolson, 1971).

C. Freer, *The Inner Side of Advertising: A Practical Handbook for Advertisers* (London, Library Press, 1921).

H. Fyfe, *Sixty Years of Fleet Street* (London, W. H. Allen, 1949).

F. R. Gannon, *The British Press and Germany, 1936–1939* (London, Oxford University Press, 1971).

J. E. Gerald, *The British Press under Government Economic Controls* (Minneapolis, University of Minnesota Press, 1956).

P. Gibbs, *Adventures in Journalism* (London, Harper, 1923).

F. Giles, *Sundry Times* (London, Murray, 1986).

G. Glenton and William Pattinson, *The Last Chronicle of Bouverie Street* (London, Allen & Unwin, 1963).

P. Golding and S. Middleton, *Images of Welfare* (Oxford, Martin Robertson, 1982).

D. Goodhart and P. Wintour, *Eddie Shah and the Newspaper Revolution* (London, Coronet, 1986).

J. Haines, *Maxwell* (London, Macdonald, 1989).

S. Hall, 'The social eye of *Picture Post*', *Cultural Studies*, ii (1971).

——'Deviancy, politics and the media' in M. McIntosh and P. Rock (eds), *Deviancy and Social Control* (London, Tavistock, 1973).

S. Hall, C. Critcher, T. Jefferson, J. Clarke, and B. Roberts, *Policing the Crisis: Mugging, the State, and Law and Order* (London, Macmillan, 1978).

J. Halloran, P. Elliott, and G. Murdock (eds), *Demonstrations and Communication* (Harmondsworth, Penguin, 1970).

D. Hamilton, *Who is to Own the British Press?* (London, Birkbeck College, 1976).

R. Harris, *Gotcha: The Media, The Government and The Falklands War* (London, Faber, 1983).

W. Harris, *J. A. Spender* (London, Cassell, 1946).

G. Harrison and F. C. Mitchell, *The Home Market: A Handbook of Statistics* (London, Allen & Unwin, 1936).

N. Hartley, P. Gudgeon, and R. Crafts, *Concentration of Ownership in the Provincial Press*, Royal Commission on the Press 1974–7, Research Series 5 (London, HMSO, 1977).

P. Hartmann, 'Industrial relations in the news media', *Industrial Relations Journal*, 6, 4 (London, HMSO, 1977).

——'News and public perceptions of industrial relations', *Media, Culture and Society*, 1, 3 (1979).

P. Hartmann and C. Husband, *Racism and the Mass Media* (London, Davis-Poynter, 1974).

J. Harvey (ed.), *The War Diaries of Oliver Harvey 1941–5* (London, Collins, 1978).

H. Henry (ed.), *Behind the Headlines* (London, Associated Business Press, 1978).

——*The Dynamics of the British Press 1961–1984* (London, Advertising Association, 1986).

A. Hetherington, *News, Newspapers and Television* (London, Macmillan, 1985).

C. Higham, *Advertising* (London, Williams & Norgate, 1925).

F. Hirsch and D. Gordon, *Newspaper Money: Fleet Street and the Search for the Affluent Reader* (London, Hutchinson, 1975).

P. Hoch, *The Newspaper Game* (London, Calder & Boyars, 1974).

R. Hoggart (ed.), *Your Sunday Paper* (London, University of London Press, 1967).

M. Hollingsworth, *The Press and Political Dissent* (London, Pluto, 1986).

D. Hubback, *No Ordinary Press Baron* (London, Weidenfeld & Nicolson, 1985).

*Hulton Readership Surveys* (London, Hulton, 1947–55).

N. Hunter, *Advertising Through the Press* (London, Pitman, 1925).

Institute of Incorporated Practitioners in Advertising, *An Analysis of Press Circulations 1934* (London, IIPA, 1934).

——*Survey of Press Readership* (London, IIPA, 1939).

——*National Readership Surveys* (London, IIPA, 1956–67).

——*Joint Industry Committee for National Readership Surveys* (London, IIPA, 1968–84).

S. Inwood, 'The press in the First World War, 1914–1916', unpublished PhD thesis (University of Oxford, 1971).

I. Jackson, *The Provincial Press and the Community* (Manchester, Manchester University Press, 1971).

S. Jenkins, *Market for Glory* (London, Faber, 1986).

N. Kaldor and R. Silverman, *A Statistical Analysis of Advertising Expenditure and of the Revenue of the Press* (Cambridge, Cambridge University Press, 1948).

P. Kimble, *Newspaper Reading in the Third Year of the War* (London, Allen & Unwin, 1942).

C. King, *The Future of the Press* (London, MacGibbon & Kee, 1967).

——*Strictly Personal* (London, Weidenfeld & Nicolson, 1969).

——*With Malice Towards None: A War Diary* (ed. W. Armstrong) (London, Sidgwick & Jackson, 1970).

——*Without Fear or Favour* (London, Sidgwick & Jackson, 1971).

——*The Cecil King Diary 1965–70* (London, Cape, 1972).

S. Koss, *Fleet Street Radical: A. G. Gardiner and the Daily News* (London, Allen Lane, 1973).

G. Lansbury, *The Miracle of Fleet Street* (London, Victoria House, 1925).

M. Leapman, *Barefaced Cheek* (London, Hodder & Stoughton, 1983).

H. P. Levy, *The Press Council* (London, Macmillan, 1967).

London Research Bureau, *Press Circulations Analysed 1928* (London Research Bureau, 1928).

A. G. Lyall, *Market Research: A Practical Handbook* (London Research Bureau 1933).

D. McLachlan, *In the Chair, Barrington-Ward of The Times, 1927–48* (London, Weidenfeld & Nicolson, 1971).

I. McLaine, *Ministry of Morale* (London, Allen & Unwin, 1979).

D. McQuail, *Analysis of Newspaper Content*, Royal Commission on the Press 1974–7, Research Series 4 (London, HMSO, 1977).

Mass Observation, *The Press and its Readers* (London, Art & Technics, 1949).

T. S. Mathews, *The Sugar Pill: An Essay on Newspapers* (London, Gollancz, 1957).

R. J. Minney, *Viscount Southwood* (London, Odhams, 1954).

S. Mulvern, *The End of the Street* (London, Methuen, 1986).

G. Munster, *Rupert Murdoch* (Victoria, Viking, 1985).

G. Murdock, 'Class, power and the press: problems of conceptualisation and evidence' in H. Christian (ed.), *The Sociology of Journalism and the Press*, Sociological Review Monograph 29 (Keele, University of Keele, 1981).

D. Murphy, *The Silent Watchdog: the Press in Local Politics* (London, Constable, 1976).

*News Chronicle, A Survey of Reader Interest* (1934).

H. Nicolson, *Diaries and Letters* (London, Collins, 1967).

Lord Northcliffe, *Newspapers and their Millionaires* (London, Associated Newspapers, 1922).

L. Owen, *Northcliffe: The Facts* (privately published, 1931).

*Periodicals and the Alternative Press*, Royal Commission on the Press 1974–7, Research Series 6 (London, HMSO, 1977).

W. Parsons, *The Power of the Financial Press* (Aldershot, Elgar, 1989).

F. Pethick-Lawrence, *Fate Has Been Kind* (London, Hutchinson, 1943).

H. Porter, *Lies, Damned Lies and Some Exclusives* (London, Chatto & Windus, 1984).

R. Pound and G. Harmsworth, *Northcliffe* (London, Cassell, 1959).

A. Rappaport, *The British Press and Wilsonian Neutrality* (London, Oxford University Press, 1951).

*Report on the British Press* (London, Political & Economic Planning, 1938).

G. Robertson, *People Against the Press* (London, Quartet, 1983).

T. Russell, *Commercial Advertising* (London, Putnam, 1919).

A. P. Ryan, *Lord Northcliffe* (London, Collins, 1953).

C. Seymour-Ure, *The Press, Politics and the Public* (London, Methuen, 1968).

——'Policy-making in the press', *Government and Opposition*, iv, 4 (1969).

——*The Political Impact of the Mass Media* (London, Constable, 1974).

——'The press and the party system between the wars' in G. Peele and C. Cook (eds), *The Politics of Reappraisal, 1918–1939* (London, Macmillan, 1976).

A. Sharf, *The British Press and Jews Under Nazi Rule* (London, Oxford University Press, 1964).

K. Sisson, *Industrial Relations in Fleet Street* (Oxford, Blackwell, 1975).

A. Smith, *The British Press Since the War* (Newton Abbot, David & Charles, 1974).

A. C. H. Smith, E. Immirzi, and T. Blackwell, *Paper Voices: The Popular Press and Social Change, 1933–1965* (London, Chatto & Windus, 1975).

Social and Community Planning, *Attitudes to the Press*, Royal Commission on the Press 1974–7, Research Series 3 (London, HMSO, 1977).

J. A. Spender, *Life, Journalism and Politics* (London, Cassell, 1927).

R. Stannard, *With the Dictators of Fleet Street* (London, Hutchinson, 1934).

*Survey of the National Newspaper Industry* (London, Economist Intelligence Unit, 1965).

A. J. P. Taylor, *English History 1914–1945* (Harmondsworth, Pelican, 1970).

——*Beaverbrook* (London, Hamish Hamilton, 1972).

——(ed.), *Off the Record: W. P. Crozier, Political Interviews, 1933–1943* (London, Hutchinson, 1973).

Lord Thomson of Fleet, *After I Was Sixty* (London, Hamish Hamilton, 1975).

*The Times, The History of The Times, iv: The 150th Anniversary and Beyond, 1912–1948*, 2 vols (London, The Times Publishing Co., 1952).

J. Tunstall, *The Westminster Lobby Correspondents* (London, Routledge & Kegan Paul, 1970).

——*Journalists at Work* (London, Constable, 1971).

——'The problem of industrial relations news in the press' in *Studies on the Press*, Royal Commission on the Press 1974–7, Working Paper 3 (London, HMSO, 1977).

——*The Media in Britain* (London, Constable, 1983).

J. Whale, *Journalism and Government* (London, Macmillan, 1972).

C. White, *The Women's Periodical Press in Britain 1946–1976*, Royal Commission on the Press, Working Paper 4 (London, HMSO, 1977).

H. Wickham Steed, *The Press* (Harmondsworth, Penguin, 1938).

T. Wilson (ed.), *The Political Diaries of C. P. Scott* (London, Collins, 1970).

R. Winsbury, *New Technology and the Press*, Royal Commission on the Press and Acton Society Press Group (London, HMSO, 1975).

C. Wintour, *Pressures on the Press: An Editor looks at Fleet Street* (London, Deutsch, 1972).

J. E. Wrench, *Geoffrey Dawson and our Times* (London, Hutchinson, 1955).

## Broadcasting

### *Memoirs and biographies*

R. Baker, *Here is the News* (London, Leslie Frewin, 1966).

G. Beadle, *Television, A Critical Review* (London, Allen & Unwin, 1963).

A. Boyle, *Only the Wind Will Listen: Reith of the BBC* (London, Hutchinson, 1972).

C. Brewer, *The Spice of Variety* (London, Muller, 1948).

D. G. Bridson, *Prospero and Ariel: The Rise and Fall of Radio* (London, Gollancz, 1971).

H. Brittain, *The ABC of the BBC* (London, Pearson, 1932).

J. C. Cassell, *In Town Tonight* (London Harrap, 1935).

S. Chesmore, *Behind the Microphone* (London, Nelson, 1935).

Sir Kenneth Clark, *The Other Half: A Self-Portrait* (London, Murray, 1977).

Sir Alfred D. Cooper, *Old Men Forget* (London, Hart-Davis, 1953).

N. Davenport, *Memoirs of a City Radical* (London, Methuen, 1959).

R. Day, *Television – A Personal Report* (London, Hutchinson, 1961).

——*Day by Day* (London, William Kimber, 1975).

B. Deane, *Seven Ages, An Autobiography, 1927–72* (London, Hutchinson, 1973).

J. Dimbleby, *Richard Dimbleby: A Biography* (London, Hodder & Stoughton, 1975).

R. Dimbleby, *The Waiting Year* (London, Hodder & Stoughton, 1944).

P. P. Eckersley, *The Power Behind the Microphone* (London, Cape, 1941).

R. Eckersley, *The BBC and All That* (London, Sampson, Low, Marston, 1946).

L. Fielden, *The Natural Bent* (London, Deutsch, 1960).

V. Gielgud, *Years of the Locust* (London, Nicholson & Watson, 1947).

G. W. Goldie, *Facing the Nation: Television and Politics, 1936–76* (London, Bodley Head, 1977).

M. Gorham, *Sound and Fury* (London, Percival-Maskell, 1948).

F. Grisewood, *The World Goes By* (London, Secker & Warburg, 1952).

——*Years in the Mirror* (London, Gollancz, 1967).

H. Grisewood, *One Thing at a Time* (London, Hutchinson, 1968).

H. Hall, *Here's to the Next Time* (London, Deutsch, 1935).

L. Henry, *My Laugh Story* (Edinburgh, Simon Paul, 1937).

A. S. Hibberd, *This is London* (Plymouth, Macdonald & Evans, 1950).

Lord Hill of Luton (C. Hill), *Both Sides of the Hill* (London, Heinemann, 1967).

——*Behind the Screen* (London, Sidgwick & Jackson, 1974).

J. Hilton, *This and That* (London, Allen & Unwin, 1938).

J. Isaacs, *Storm over Four: A Personal Account* (London, Weidenfeld & Nicolson, 1989).

P. J. Kavanagh, *The Itma Years* (London, Heinemann, 1974).

T. Kavanagh. *Tommy Handley* (London, Hodder & Stoughton, 1949).

L. Kennedy, *Ludo: A Life* (London, Macmillan, 1989).

R. S. Lambert, *Ariel and All his Quality* (London, Gollancz, 1940).

C. A. Lewis, *Broadcasting from Within* (London, George Newnes, 1924).

E. Maschwitz, *No Chip on My Shoulder* (London, Jenkins, 1957).

S. A. Mosely, *Broadcasting in my Time* (London, Rich & Cowan, 1935).

——*Private Diaries* (London, Parrish, 1960).

E. Nixon, *John Hilton* (London, Allen & Unwin, 1946).

J. Payne, *This is Jack Payne* (London, Marston, 1932).

——*Signature Tune* (Edinburgh, Simon Paul, 1947).

W. Pickles, *Between You and Me* (London, Heinemann, 1949).

J. B. Priestley, *Margin Released* (London, Mercury, 1966).

J. C. W. Reith, *Into the Wind* (London, Hodder & Stoughton, 1949).

R. Silvey, *Who's Listening?* (London, Allen & Unwin, 1974).

C. Stuart, *The Reith Diaries* (London, Collins, 1975).

Sir Stephen Tallents, *Man and Boy* (London, Faber, 1943).

H. Thomas, *With an Independent Air* (London, Weidenfeld & Nicolson, 1977).

M. Tracey, *A Variety of Lives: A Biography of Sir Hugh Greene* (London, Bodley Head, 1982).

M. Whitehouse, *Who Does She Think She Is?* (London, New English Library, 1971).


## The history of broadcasting

M. Abrams, *Granada Viewership Survey* (1959).

R. Alston, *Taking the Air* (London, Hodder & Stoughton, 1951).

G. L. Archer, *A History of Broadcasting to 1926* (London, Allen & Unwin, 1938).

J. Bakewell and N. Garnham, *The New Priesthood: British Television Today* (Harmondsworth, Allen Lane, 1970).

E. Barnouw, *A Tower in Babel: The History of Broadcasting in the United States* (London, Oxford University Press, 1966).

*BBC Handbook* (London, BBC, annually).

BBC, 'Comparative European programming', *BBC Handbook* (London, BBC, 1934).

——*The Third Programme: Plans for October–December 1944* (London, BBC, 1944).

——*The Public and their Programmes* (London, BBC, 1959).

J. Bennett, *British Broadcasting and the Danish Resistance Movement 1940–1945* (Cambridge, Cambridge University Press, 1965).

P. Black, *The Biggest Aspidistra in the World* (London, BBC, 1972).

——*The Mirror in the Corner* (London, Hutchinson, 1972).

P. Bloomfield, *BBC* (London, Eyre & Spottiswoode, 1941).

A. Briggs, *The History of Broadcasting in the United Kingdom*: vol. I, The Birth of Broadcasting; vol. II, *The Golden Age of Wireless*; vol. III, *The War of Words*; vol. IV, *Sound and Vision* (London, Oxford University Press, 1961, 1965, 1970, and 1979).

——'The rise of the mass entertainment industry' (Fisher Lecture, 1961).

——*The BBC Governors* (London, BBC, 1979).

——*The BBC: The First Fifty Years* (Oxford, Oxford University Press, 1985).

P. J. Brown, 'Broadcasting in Britain', *London Quarterly Review*, 145, 1 (January 1926).

A. R. Burrows, *The Story of Broadcasting* (London, Cassell, 1924).

Sir Cyril Burt, 'The psychology of listeners', *BBC Quarterly*, iv, 2 (April 1949).

H. L. Childs and J. B. Whitton (eds), *Propaganda by Shortwave* (London, Oxford University Press, 1943).

J. A Cole, *Lord Haw Haw – and William Joyce* (London, Collins, 1964).

C. A. R. Crosland, 'The mass media', *Encounter* (November 1962).

R. H. S. Crossman, 'The politics of viewing', *New Statesman* (25 October 1968).

——'The BBC, Labour and the public', *New Statesman* (17 July 1971).

C. Curran, *Code or Conscience* (London, BBC, 1970).

——*A Maturing Democracy* (London, BBC, 1973).

——*The Seamless Robe* (London, Bodley Head, 1979).

R. Day, 'Troubled reflections of a TV journalist', *Encounter* (May 1970).

B. Deane, *The Theatre At War* (London, Harrap, 1956).

S. Delmer, *Black Boomerang* (London, Secker & Warburg, 1962).

D. Docherty, D. E. Morrison, and M. Tracey, *Keeping Faith? Channel Four and its Audience* (London, Libbey, 1988).

L. W. Doob, 'Goebbels' principles of propaganda', *Public Opinion Quarterly*, 21, 2 (1950).

P. P. Eckersley, *Captain Eckersley Explains* (London, Hodder & Stoughton, 1924).

——*All About your Microphone* (London, BBC Broadcast Library, 1925).

——*The Power Behind the Microphone* (London, Cape, 1941).

H. Fairlie 'TV, idiot box', *Encounter* (August 1959).

——'The BBC' in H. S. Thomas (ed.), *The Establishment: A Symposium* (London, New English Library, 1962).

Sir Robert Fraser, *The Coming of Independent Television* (London, Hutchinson, 1955).

——*ITA Notes* (October 1970).

V. Gielgud, *British Radio Drama 1922–1956* (London, Harrap, 1957).

G. W. Goldie, 'The new attraction', *Listener* (26 December 1940).

——'TV report', *Listener* (23 October 1968).

——*Facing the Nation: Television and Politics 1936–1976* (London, Bodley Head, 1977).

M. Gorham, *Broadcasting and Television Since 1900* (London, Collins, 1952).

T. Green, *The Universal Eye: World Television in the Seventies* (London, Bodley Head, 1972).

——'The future of broadcasting in Britain', Granada Guildhall Lecture (1972).

H. C. Greene, 'The BBC since 1958', *BBC Handbook* (1969).

——*The Third Floor Front: A View of Broadcasting in the Sixties* (London, Bodley Head, 1969).

T. Harrisson, 'War books', *Horizon* (December 1941).

D. Hawkins and D. Boyd (eds), *BBC War Report* (London, Oxford University Press, 1946).

Sir William Hayley, *The Central Problem of Broadcasting* (London, BBC, 1948).

IBA, *Annual Reports*.

ITV, *The Annan Report: An ITV View* (London, ITV, 1977).

E. T. Lean, *Voices in the Darkness* (London, Allen & Unwin, 1943).

M. Leapman, *The Last Days of the Beeb* (London, Coronet, 1987).

D. McLachlan, *Room 39* (London, Weidenfeld & Nicolson, 1968).

Mass Observation, *The War Begins at Home* (London, Chatto & Windus, 1940).

H. Matheson, *Broadcasting* (London, Butterworth, 1933).

——'Listener research in broadcasting', *Sociological Review*, xxvii, 3 (1935).

A. Mitchell, 'The decline of current affairs television', *Political Quarterly*, 44, 1 (1973).

H. Nicolson, *The Third Programme: A Symposium of Opinions and Plans* (London, BBC, 1947).

S. Orwell and I. Angus (eds), *The Collected Essays, Letters and Journalism of George Orwell* (Harmondsworth, Penguin, 1971).

B. Paulu, *British Broadcasting: Radio and Television in the United Kingdom* (Oxford, Oxford University Press, 1957).

G. Pedrich, *Battledress Broadcasters* (London, Marston, 1964).

R. Postgate, *What to Do with the BBC?* (London, Hogarth, 1935).

J. B. Priestley, *Postscripts* (London, Heinemann, 1940).

J. C. W. Reith, *Broadcast over Britain* (London, Hodder & Stoughton, 1924).

N. Riley, *999* (London, Gollancz, 1943).

C. J. Rolo, *Radio Goes to War* (London, Hutchinson, 1943).

G. Ross, *T.V. Jubilee* (London, W. H. Allen, 1961).

P. Rotha (ed.), *Television in the Making* (London, Bodley Head, 1956).

P. Scannell, 'The social eye of television, 1946–1955', *Media, Culture, and Society*, 1, 1 (1979).

P. Scannell and D. Cardiff, 'The social foundations of British broadcasting' in J. Curran, M. Gurevitch, and J. Woollacott (eds), *Mass Communication and Society* (London, Edward Arnold/Open University, 1977).

J. Seaton, 'The BBC and the Holocaust', *European Journal of Communication*, vol. 2, 1 (1987).

——'Reporting atrocities' in J. Seaton and B. Pimlott, *The Media in British Politics* (Aldershot, Gower, 1987).

G. Seldes, *The Great Audience* (London, Oxford University Press, 1950).

R. Silvey, 'Some recent trends in listening', *BBC Handbook* (London, BBC, 1946).

——'TV viewing in Britain', *Public Opinion Quarterly*, 25, 2 (1950).

——*Whose Listening?* (London, Bodley Head, 1974).

Lord Simon of Wythenshawe, *The BBC from Within* (London, Gollancz, 1953).

A. Smith, *The Shadow in the Cave* (London, Allen & Unwin 1973).

——*British Broadcasting* (Newton Abbot, David & Charles, 1974).
S. W. Smithers, *Broadcasting from Within* (London, Pitmans, 1938).
N. Swallow, *Factual Television* (London, Focal, 1966).
J. Swift, *Adventures in Vision* (London, Lehmann, 1950).
I. Thomas, *Warfare By Words* (London, Gollancz, 1942).
*The Times*, special broadcasting number (14 August 1934).
P. Todd, 'Scarcity of TV time', *Campaign* (26 January 1979).
M. Tracey, *Whitehouse* (London, Constable, 1979).
R. West, *The Meaning of Treason* (London, Macmillan, 1948).
H. Wheldon, 'Competition in television', Address to the Royal Society of Arts (1971).
——*Tastes and Standards in BBC Programmes* (London, BBC, 1973).
H. H. Wilson, *Pressure Group* (London, Secker & Warburg, 1961).
F. Worsley, *ITMA* (London, Collins, 1948).

## The background to broadcasting

M. Abrams, 'Advertising', *Listener* (15 December 1956).
——'Motivation research', *Advertising Quarterly* (November 1959).
P. Addison, *The Road to 1945* (London, Cape,1975).
K. Allsop, *The Angry Decade* (London, Owen, 1958).
N. Annan, 'Love among the moralists', *Encounter* (February 1960).
D. Bell, 'Advertising: is it worth it?', *Listener* (13 December 1956).
W. H. Beveridge, *Unemployment: A Problem of Industry* (London, Longman Green, 1910).
——*Public Service in War and Peace* (London, Constable, 1920).
——*Constructive Democracy* (London, Allen & Unwin, 1937).
——*Power and Influence* (London, Hodder & Stoughton, 1953).
V. Bogdanor and R. Skidelsky, *The Age of Affluence* (Harmondsworth, Penguin, 1970).
E. Bowen, *The Heart of the Matter* (London, Faber, 1944).
V. Brittain, *Testament of Friendship* (London, Macmillan, 1940)
G. Bruntz, *Allied Propaganda and the Collapse of the German Empire in 1918* (Stanford, Calif., Stanford University Press, 1938).
Sir Cyril Burt, *The Distribution and Relations of Educational Abilities* (London, London County Council, 1917).
——'The measurement of mental capacities', Henderson Trust Lecture 7, Edinburgh (1927).
——(ed.), *How The Mind Works* (London, Allen & Unwin, 1933).
——*Intelligence and Fertility* (London, Cassell, 1952).
D. Butler and R. Rose, *The British General Election of 1959* (London, Macmillan, 1960).
Lord Butler, *The Education Act of 1944 and After,* First Noel Buxton Lecture, University of Essex (Harlow, Longman, 1965).
——*The Art of the Possible* (London, Hamish Hamilton, 1971).

A. Calder, *The People's War: Britain 1939–45* (London, Cape, 1969).

H. Cantril, *Public Opinion 1935–46* (Princeton, NJ, Princeton University Press, 1951).

C. Cockburn, *I Claud* (Harmondsworth, Penguin, 1967).

C. A. R. Crosland, *The Future of Socialism* (London, Cape, 1956).

R. H. S. Crossman, 'Psychological warfare', *Journal of the Royal United Services Institution* (August 1952).

——'The lessons of 1945' in P. Anderson and R. Blackburn (eds), *Towards Socialism* (London, Fontana, 1965).

H. Dalton, 'The "popular front"', *Political Quarterly*, 4, 7 (1936).

M. E. Dimmock, *British Public Utilities and National Development* (London, Allen & Unwin, 1933).

C. H. Dobinson (ed.), *Education in a Changing World* (Oxford, Oxford University Press, 1951).

T. Driberg, *The Best of Both Worlds* (Phoenix House, 1958).

M. R. D. Foot, *Resistance: An Analysis of European Resistance to Fascism* (London, Methuen, 1976).

P. Foot, *The Politics of Harold Wilson* (Harmondsworth, Penguin, 1968).

Fougasse (pseud. C. K. Bird), *The Changing Face of Britain* (London, Methuen, 1950).

M. Gilbert, *Churchill*, vol. 5 (London, Heinemann, 1976).

M. Gilbert and R. Gott, *The Appeasers* (London, Weidenfeld & Nicolson, 1963).

D. Gordan, 'Ten points about the crisis in the British film industry', *Sight and Sound*, 43, 2 (1974).

L. Gorden, *The Public Corporation in Great Britain* (Oxford, Oxford University Press, 1938).

P. H. J. H. Gosden, *Education in the Second World War* (London, Methuen, 1972).

J. Harris, *William Beveridge* (Oxford, Clarendon, 1977).

N. Harris, *Competition and the Corporate State* (London, Methuen, 1972).

R. Harris, *Politics Without Prejudice* (Tonbridge, Staples, 1956).

T. Harrisson, 'Who'll win?', *Political Quarterly*, 15, 4 (1944).

——*Living Through the Blitz* (Harmondsworth, Penguin, 1978).

J. A. Hodson, *Somewhere in France. . . . B.E.F.* (London, Whithey Grove, 1940).

——*War Diary* (London, Gollancz, 1941).

——*The Home Front* (London, Gollancz, 1944).

L. J. Kamin, *The Science and Politics of IQ* (Harmondsworth, Penguin, 1977).

Labour Party, *Twelve Wasted Years* (London, Labour Party, 1963).

D. Low, *Low's Autobiography* (London, Michael Joseph, 1956).

R. Low, *The History of the British Film*, vol. 1 (London, Allen & Unwin, 1948).

I. McLaine, 'The Ministry of Information', unpublished DPhil thesis (University of Oxford, 1976).

——*The Ministry of Morale* (London, Allen & Unwin, 1978).

F. Marquis (ed.), *The Memoirs of the Rt Hon. the Earl of Woolton* (London, Cassell, 1959).

A. Marwick, 'Middle opinion in the thirties', *English Historical Review*, lxxix, 2 (1964).

Mass Observation, *The War Begins at Home* (London, Chatto & Windus, 1940).

——*Home Propaganda* (London, Chatto & Windus, 1941).

——*War Factory* (London, Gollancz, 1943).

——*The Journey Home* (London, Murray, 1944).

——*The Press and Its Readers* (London, Art & Technics, 1949).

Ministry of Pensions, *Neuroses in War Time* (London, HMSO, 1940).

J. Montgomery, *The Fifties* (London, Collins, 1965).

H. Morrison, *Socialization and Transport* (London, Constable, 1933).

H. Nicolson, *Diaries and Letters* (London, Collins, 1967).

T. H. O'Brien, *British Experiments in Public Ownership and Control* (London, Allen & Unwin, 1937).

F. Owen, 'This war', *Horizon* (February 1940).

V. Packard, *The Hidden Persuaders* (London, Longman, 1957).

H. Pelling, *Britain and the Second World War* (London, Collins, 1970).

B. Pimlott, *Labour and the Left in the 1930s* (Cambridge, Cambridge University Press, 1977).

——*Hugh Dalton* (London, Cape, 1985).

J. W. C. Reith, *Personality and Career* (London, George Newnes, 1925).

——*Winning Spurs* (London, Hutchinson, 1966).

P. Renshaw, *The General Strike* (London, Methuen, 1975).

W. A. Robson, *Public Enterprise* (London, New Fabian Research Bureau, 1937).

——*Nationalized Industry and Public Ownership* (London, Allen & Unwin, 1960).

R. J. W. Selleck, 'The scientific educationalist', *British Journal of Educational Studies*, xv, 3 (June 1967).

B. Simon, *Education and the Labour Movement, 1870–1920* (London, Lawrence & Wishart, 1965).

——*The Politics of Educational Reform, 1920–1940* (London, Lawrence & Wishart, 1971).

——*Intelligence, Psychology and Education* (London, Lawrence & Wishart, 1978).

P. Sissons and R. French (eds), *The Age of Austerity* (Harmondsworth, Penguin, 1962).

R. Skidelsky, *Politicians and the Slump* (London, Macmillan, 1967).
——'Keynes and the reconstruction of liberalism', *Encounter* (April 1979).
J. Strachey, *Post D* (London, Gollancz, 1940).
B. Sweet-Escott, *Baker Street Irregular* (London, Collins, 1966).
J. Symons, *The General Strike* (London, Cressett, 1957).
S. Tallents, *The Projection of England* (London, Empire Marketing Board, 1932).
A. J. P. Taylor, *English History 1914–1945* (London, Allen & Unwin, 1965).
——*Beaverbrook* (London, Hamish Hamilton, 1972).
R. Titmuss, *Problems of Social Policy* (London, Longman/HMSO, 1950).
Sir Robert Vansittart, *Black Record: Germans Past and Present* (London, Hamish Hamilton, 1941).
P. E. Vernon and J. B. Barry, *Personnel Selection in the British Forces* (London, University of London Press, 1949).
*Beatrice Webb's Diaries, 1924–32*, ed. M. Cole (London, Longman Green, 1956).
N. S. Wilson, *Education in the Forces, 1939–1946: The Civilian Contribution* (London, Allen & Unwin, 1949).
S. W. L. Woodward, *British Foreign Policy in the Second World War* (London, HMSO, 1970/1).

## Sociology

T. W. Adorno, *Prisms* (Sudbury, Spearman, 1967).
——*The Jargon of Authenticity* (London, Routledge & Kegan Paul, 1973).
T. W. Adorno, E. F. Brunswick, D. J. Levinson, and R. N. Sandford, *The Authoritarian Personality* (London, Harper & Row, 1950).
M. Alvarado and E. Buscombe, *Hazell: The Making of a Television Series* (London, British Film Institute, 1978).
H. Arendt, *The Burden of Our Time* (London, Secker & Warburg, 1950).
——*The Life of the Mind*, vol. 2, *Thinking* (London, Secker & Warburg, 1978).
P. Becker and M. McCombs, 'The development of political cognition' in S. H. Chaffee (ed.), *Political Communication: Issues and Strategies* (Beverly Hills, Calif., Sage, 1975).
B. Berelson, 'The state of communication research', *Public Opinion Quarterly*, 31, 2 (1959).
S. Blanchard, *What's This Channel Four?* (London, Comedia, 1983).
J. G. Blumler, 'The audience', in *The Political Effects of Mass Communication* (Milton Keynes, Open University Press, DE 353, 1977).

——'The intervention of television in British politics', *Report of the Committee on the Future of Broadcasting* (Annan Report) (1977) [Cmnd 6753, Appendix E].

——'An overview of recent research into the impact of broadcasting in democratic politics' in M. J. Clark (ed.), *Politics and the Media* (Oxford, Pergamon, 1979).

J. G. Blumler and M. Gurevitch, 'Towards a comparative framework for political communication' in S. H. Chaffee (ed.), *Political Communication: Issues and Strategies* (London, Sage, 1975).

J. G. Blumler and D. McQuail, *Television in Politics: Its Uses and Influences* (London, Faber, 1968).

J. G. Blumler and J. Madge, *Citizenship and Television* (London, Political & Economic Planning, 1965).

D. Boorstin, *The Image, Or What Happened to the American Dream* (Harmondsworth, Penguin, 1963).

P. Bourdieu, *Outline of a Theory of Practice* (Cambridge, Cambridge University Press, 1977).

O. Boyd-Barrett, D. Seymour-Ure, and J. Tunstall, *Studies on the Press*, Royal Commission on the Press 1974–7, Working Paper 3 (London, HMSO, 1977).

B. Brown, 'An interview with the film censor', *Screen*, 23, 5 (1982).

——'Pornography: some modest proposals', *M/F* (January 1982).

S. Bryant, *The Television Heritage* (London, British Film Institute, 1990).

M. Bulmer, *Working-Class Images of Society* (London, Routledge & Kegan Paul, 1975).

T. Burns, *The BBC, Public Institutions and Private World* (London, Macmillan, 1977).

H. Cantril, *The Invasion From Mars: A Study in the Psychology of Panic* (Princeton, NJ, Princeton University Press, 1940).

D. Chaney, *Processes of Mass Communication* (London, Macmillan, 1972).

M. Cockerell, P. Hennessy, and D. Walker, *Sources Close to the Prime Minister* (London, Macmillan, 1984).

S. Cohen, *Images of Deviance* (Harmondsworth, Penguin, 1971).

S. Cohen and J. Young (eds), *The Manufacture of News* (London, Constable, 1973).

Conference of Socialist Economics Microelectronics Group, *Microelectronics: Capitalist Technology and the Working Class* (CSE Books, 1980).

I. Connell, 'Commercial broadcasting and the British left', *Screen*, 24, 6 (1983).

G. Cumberbatch and D. Howitt, *A Measure of Uncertainty: The Effects of the Mass Media* (London, Libbey, 1989).

J. Curran, 'The boomerang effect: the press and the battle for London

1981–6' in J. Curran and A. Smith (eds), *Impacts and Influences* (London, Methuen, 1986).

——'Culturalist perspectives of news organizations: a reappraisal and a case study' in M. Ferguson (ed.), *Public Communication* (London, Sage, 1990).

——'The new revisionism in mass communication research: a reappraisal', *European Journal of Communications*, 5, 2–3, (1990).

R. Dyer, *Light Entertainment*, BFI Television Monograph 2 (London, British Film Institute, 1973).

M. Edelmann, *The Symbolic Uses of Politics* (Urbana, Ill., University of Illinois Press, 1964).

P. Elliot, *The Making of a Television Series* (London, Constable, 1972).

——'Intellectuals and "The information society" and the disappearance of the public sphere', *Media, Culture and Society*, 6, 4 (1982).

P. Elliot, G. Murdoch, and P. Schlesinger, 'Terrorism and the state: a case study in the discourse of television', *Media, Culture and Society*, 5, 2 (1983).

——*Televising Terrorism* (London, Comedia, 1984).

J. Ellis, *Visible Fiction: Cinema, TV, Video* (London, Routledge & Kegan Paul, 1982).

E. J. Epstein, *News from Nowhere* (New York, Random House, 1973).

R. Ericson, P. Baranec, and J. Chan, *Visualizing Deviance* (Milton Keynes, Open University Press, 1987).

J. Fiske, *Television Culture* (London, Methuen, 1987).

S. Frith, *The Sociology of Rock* (London, Constable, 1979).

P. Fussell, *The Great War in Modern Memory* (London, Oxford University Press, 1975).

N. Garnham, *Structures of Television*, BFI Television Monograph 1 (London, British Film Institute, 1973).

——'Contribution to a political economy of mass communications', *Media, Culture and Society*, 1, 2 (April 1979).

——'Public service versus the market', *Screen*, 24, 1 (1983).

T. Gitlin, 'Prime time ideology: the hegemonic process in television entertainment', *Social Problems*, 25, 3 (1979).

——*The Whole World is Watching* (Berkeley, Calif., University of California Press, 1982).

Glasgow University Media Group, *Bad News* (London, Routledge & Kegan Paul, 1976).

——*More Bad News* (London, Routledge & Kegan Paul, 1980).

P. Golding, *The Mass Media* (Harlow, Longman, 1974).

P. Golding and P. Elliot, *Making the News* (Harlow, Longman, 1979).

P. Golding and S. Middleton, *Images of Welfare* (London, Macmillan, 1980).

J. H. Goldthorpe and D. Lockwood, *The Affluent Worker: Political Attitudes and Behaviour* (Cambridge, Cambridge University Press, 1968).

S. Hall, 'The external/internal dialectic on broadcasting', *4th Symposium on British Broadcasting Policy*, February 1972.

——'The determination of news photographs' in S. Cohen and J. Young (eds), *The Manufacture of News* (London, Constable, 1973).

——'The hinterland of science: ideology' in Centre for Contemporary Cultural Studies, *On Ideology* (London, Hutchinson, 1977).

——'Culture, the media, and the ideological effect' in J. Curran, M. Gurevitch, and J. Woollacott (eds), *Mass Communication and Society* (London, Edward Arnold/Open University, 1977).

——'Newspapers, parties and classes', in J. Curran (ed.), *The British Press: A Manifesto* (London, Macmillan, 1978).

S. Hall, C. Critcher, T. Jefferson, J. Clarke, and B. Roberts, *Policing the Crisis: Mugging, the State, and Law and Order* (London, Macmillan, 1978).

S. Hall, C. Curtis, and I. Connell, 'The unity of current events TV' in Centre for Contemporary Cultural Studies, *Working Papers in Cultural Studies*, 9, (Spring 1976).

J. D. Halloran and G. Murdoch, *Demonstrations and Communications* (Harmondsworth, Penguin, 1970).

P. Halmos (ed.), *Sociology of Mass Media Communicators*, Sociological Review Monograph 13 (Keele, University of Keele, 1969).

R. Harris, *Gotcha! The Media and the Falklands War* (London, Faber, 1983).

M. Harrop, 'Voters and the media' in J. Seaton and B. Pimlott (eds), *The Media in British Politics* (Aldershot, Gower, 1987).

M. Harrop and R. Worcester (eds), *Political Communication: The 1979 General Election* (London, Macmillan, 1981).

P. Hartmann and C. Husband, *Racism and the Mass Media* (London, Davis-Poynter, 1973).

F. Hayek, *The Road to Serfdom* (London, Routledge & Kegan Paul, 1944).

C. Heller, *Broadcasters and Accountability*, BFI Television Monograph 3 (London, British Film Institute, 1978).

E. Herman and N. Chomsky, *Manufacturing Consent* (New York, Pantheon, 1988).

P. M. Hirsch, 'Processing fads and fashions', *American Journal of Sociology*, xxlvi, 1 (1977).

D. Hobson, *Crossroads* (London, Methuen, 1983).

P. Hoch, *The Newspaper Game* (London, Calder & Boyars, 1974).

R. Hoggart, *The Uses of Literacy* (London, Chatto & Windus, 1957).

A. Hooper, *The Military and the Media* (London, Routledge & Kegan Paul, 1981).

M. Horkheimer, *The Eclipse of Reason* (Oxford, Oxford University Press, 1947).

C. I. Hovland, *Experiments in Mass Communication* (Princeton, NJ, Princeton University Press, 1949).

——'Reconciling conflicting results derived from experimental and survey studies of attitude change', *American Psychologist*, 14, 3 (1959).

J. Howkins, *New Technologies, New Policies* (London, British Film Institute, 1982).

G. A. Huaco, *The Sociology of Film Art* (New York, Basic Books, 1965).

C. Husband (ed.), *White Media and Black Britain* (London, Routledge & Kegan Paul, 1962).

B. Jackson and D. Marsden, *Education and the Working Class* (London, Routledge & Kegan Paul, 1962).

M. Jay, *The Dialectical Imagination* (London, Heinemann, 1973).

E. Katz and P. Lazarsfeld, *Personal Influence: The Part Played by People in the Flow of Mass Communication* (West Drayton, Free Press, 1955).

T. Klapper, *The Effects of Mass Communication* (West Drayton, Free Press, 1960).

F. G. Kline and P. J. Tichenor, *Current Perspectives in Mass Communications Research* (London, Sage, 1972).

W. Kornhauser, *The Politics of Mass Society* (London, Routledge & Kegan Paul, 1959).

R. Kuhn, 'Government broadcasting in the 1980s: cross channel perspective', *Political Quarterly*, 53, 4 (1982).

——'Ballot box', *Stills* (May–June 1983).

K. Kumar, 'Holding the middle ground: the BBC, the public, and the professional broadcaster' in J. Curran, M. Gurevitch, and J. Woollacott (eds), *Mass Communication and Society* (London, Edward Arnold/Open University, 1977).

——*Policy and Progress* (Harmondsworth, Penguin, 1978).

S. Lambert, *Channel 4* (London, British Film Institute, 1982).

K. Lang, 'Images of society, media research in Germany', *Public Opinion Quarterly,* xxii, 3 (1974).

K. Lang and G. Lang, *Politics and Television* (New York, Quadrangle, 1968).

——*The Battle For Public Opinion: Watergate and the Media* (Westport, Conn., Greenwood, 1982).

H. D. Lasswell, *Psychopathology and Politics* (Chicago, Ill., University of Chicago Press, 1930).

——'The garrison state', *American Journal of Sociology*, 46, 2 (1941).

P. Lazarsfeld, B. Berelson, and H. Gaudet, *The People's Choice* (New York, Columbia University Press, 1944).

P. Lazarsfeld and R. Merton, 'Mass communication, popular taste and organised social action' in B. Rosenberg and D. White (eds), *Mass Culture* (West Drayton, Free Press, 1957).

P. Lazarsfeld and F. Stanton, *Radio Research 1942–3* (Boston, Mass., Duell Sloan Pearce, 1944).

M. Leapman, *Treachery? The Power Struggle at TUAH* (London, Allen & Unwin, 1984).

F. R. Leavis, *Mass Civilisation and Minority Culture* (London, Minority Press, 1930).

——*The Common Pursuit* (London, Chatto & Windus, 1952).

——*Scrutiny: A Retrospect* (Cambridge, Cambridge University Press, 1962).

——*A Selection From Scrutiny*, 2 vols (Cambridge, Cambridge University Press, 1968).

F. R. Leavis and D. Thompson, *Culture and Environment* (London, Chatto & Windus, 1933).

Q. D. Leavis, *Fiction and the Reading Public* (London, Chatto & Windus, 1932).

T. Lovell, 'Sociology of aesthetic structures' in D. McQuail (ed.), *Sociology of Mass Communications* (Harmondsworth, Penguin, 1972).

L. Lowenthal, *Prophets of Deceit* (New York, Harper & Row, 1949).

R. S. Lynd and H. M. Lynd, *Middletown: A Study on Contemporary American Culture* (London, Constable, 1929).

——*Middletown: In Transition* (London, Constable, 1935).

A. McBarnett, 'The North Sea oil story', *Scottish Journal of Sociology*, 3, 1 (1977).

D. McQuail, *Towards a Sociology of Mass Communication* (West Drayton, Collier Macmillan, 1969).

——*Sociology of Mass Communications* (Harmondsworth, Penguin, 1972).

——'Review of sociological writings on the press', Royal Commission on the Press 1974–7 Working Paper 2 (London, HMSO, 1977).

——*Mass Communication Theory: An Introduction*, second edition (London, Sage, 1987).

H. Marcuse, *'The End of Utopia', Five Lectures* (Harmondsworth, Allen Lane, 1970).

——*One Dimensional Man* (London, Routledge & Kegan Paul, 1974).

M. Mendelsohn and I. Crespi, *Polls, Television and the New Politics* (New York, Harper & Row, 1970).

R. K. Merton, *Social Theory and Social Structure* (West Drayton, Free Press, 1957).

F. Mulhearn, *The Moment of Scrutiny* (London, New Left Books, 1979).

T. Pateman, *Language, Truth and Politics* (Brighton, Southern Books, 1974).

——*Television and the February 1974 General Election* (London, British Film Institute, 1976).

J. A. R. Pimlott, *Public Relations and American Democracy* (Princeton, NJ, Princeton University Press, 1951; repr. 1974).

A. Ray and K. Rowan (eds), *Inside Information: British Government and the Media* (London, Constable, 1982).

D. Reisman, *The Lonely Crowd* (New Haven, Conn., Yale University Press, 1950).

J. P. Robinson, 'The press as king-maker', *Journalism Quarterly*, 41, 4 (1974).

B. Rosenberg and D. White (eds), *Mass Culture* (West Drayton, Free Press, 1957).

P. Schlesinger, *Putting 'Reality' Together* (London, Constable, 1974).

——'Rethinking the sociology of journalism: source strategies and the limits of media-centrism' in M. Ferguson (eds), *Public Communication* (London, Sage, 1990).

J. Seaton, 'The image of trade unions in the media' in B. Pimlott and C. Cook (eds), *Trade Unions in British Politics* (Harlow, Longman, 1982).

——'The media and the politics of unemployment' in S. Allen, S. Waton, and S. Wood (eds), *Unemployment* (London, Macmillan, 1985).

——'Politics and the media in Britain', *Journal of Western European Politics*, special broadcasting issue (London, summer 1985).

J. Seaton and B. Pimlott, 'The role of the media in the Portuguese Revolution' in A. Smith (ed.), *Newspapers and Democracy* (Cambridge, Mass, MIT Press, 1980).

——'The Portuguese media in transition' in K. Maxwell (ed.), *The Press and the Rebirth of Iberian Democracy* (Westport, Conn., Greenwood, 1983).

——'Political power and the Portuguese media' in L. Graham (ed.), *In Search of Modern Portugal: The Revolution and its Consequences* (Wisconsin, University of Wisconsin Press, 1983).

C. Seymour-Ure, *The Press, Politics and Public* (London, Methuen, 1968).

——*The Political Impact of the Mass Media* (London, Constable, 1974).

——*The American President: Power and Communication* (London, Macmillan, 1982).

——'The SDP and the media', *Political Quarterly*, 53, 4 (1982).

E. Shils, *The Intellectuals and the Powers* (Chicago, Ill., University of Chicago Press, 1972).

E. Shils and M. Janowitz, 'Cohesion and disintegration in the Wehrmacht in World War II', *Public Opinion Quarterly*, xii, 3 (London, 1948).

P. Siegelhart (ed.), *Chips with Everything* (London, Comedia, 1982).

P. Slater, *The Origin and Significance of the Frankfurt School* (London, Routledge & Kegan Paul, 1977).

A. Smith, *The Politics of Information* (London, Macmillan, 1968).

——*The Shadow in the Cave* (London, Allen & Unwin, 1973).

——(ed.), *Television and Political Life* (London, Macmillan, 1979).

——'The fading of the industrial age', *Political Quarterly*, 53, 3 (June 1983).

B. L. Smith, H. D. Lasswell, and R. Casey, *Propaganda Communication and Public Opinion* (Princeton, NJ, Princeton University Press, 1946).

A. Swingewood, *The Myth of Mass Culture* (London, Macmillan, 1977).

M. Tracey, *The Production of Political Television* (London, Routledge & Kegan Paul, 1978).

J. Trenaman, *Communications and Comprehension* (London, Collins, 1967).

J. Trenaman and D. McQuail, *Television and the Political Image* (London, Methuen, 1961).

G. Tuchman, 'Making news by doing work', *American Journal of Sociology*, 79, 1 (1973).

——(ed.), *The TV Establishment* (New York, Random House, 1975).

J. Tunstall, *Advertising Man* (London, Constable, 1969).

——*The Westminster Lobby Correspondents* (London, Routledge & Kegan Paul, 1970).

——*Journalists at Work* (London, Constable, 1971).

——*The Media in Britain* (London, Constable, 1983).

E. G. Wedell, *Broadcasting and Public Policy* (London, Michael Joseph, 1968).

——*Structures of Broadcasting* (Manchester, Manchester University Press, 1970).

J. Whale, *The Half Shut Eye* (London, Macmillan, 1969).

——*The Politics of the Media* (London, Fontana, 1977).

R. Williams, *The Long Revolution* (Harmondsworth, Pelican, 1965).

——*Communications* (London, Chatto & Windus, 1966).

——*Television: Technology and Cultural Form* (London, Fontana, 1974).

——*Drama from Ibsen to Brecht* (Harmondsworth, Penguin, 1976).

——*Keywords* (London, Fontana, 1976).

——*Marxism and Literature* (Oxford, Oxford University Press, 1977).

——*Politics and Letters: Interviews with the New Left Review* (London, New Left Books, 1979).

J. Willis and T. Wollen (eds), *The Neglected Audience* (London, British Film Institute, 1990).

P. Willis, *Learning to Labour* (Farnborough, Saxon House, 1977).

——*Sacred and Profane Culture* (London, Routledge & Kegan Paul, 1978).

P. Willmott and M. D. Young, *Family and Class in a London Suburb* (London, Routledge & Kegan Paul, 1960).

——*The Symmetrical Family* (London, Routledge & Kegan Paul, 1973).


## *Mass communications readers*

S. Ball-Rokeach and M. Cantor (eds), *Media, Audience and Social Structure* (Beverly Hills, Calif., Sage, 1986).

R. Collins, J. Curran, N. Gamham, P. Scannell, P. Schlesinger, and C. Sparks (eds), *Media, Culture and Society: A Critical Reader* (London, Sage, 1986).

J. Curran, M. Gurevitch, and J. Woollacott (eds), *Mass Communication and Society* (London, Edward Arnold/Open University, 1977).

J. Curran and A. Smith (eds), *Impacts and Influences* (London, Methuen, 1987).

L. F. Dexter and D. M. White, *People, Society and Mass Communications* (Glencoe, Free Press, 1964).

P. Drummond and R. Paterson (eds), *Television in Transition* (London, British Film Institute, 1986).

M. Ferguson (ed.), *Public Communication* (London, Sage, 1990).

M. Gurevitch, T. Bennett, J. Curran, and J. Woollacott (eds), *Culture, Society and the Media* (London, Methuen, 1982).

P. Halmos (ed.), *Sociology of Mass Media Communicators*, Sociological Review Monograph 13 (Keele, University of Keele, 1969).

D. McQuail (ed.), *Sociology of Mass Communication: Selected Reading* (Harmondsworth, Penguin, 1972).

R. Manoff and M. Schudson, *Reading the News* (New York, Pantheon, 1987).

B. Rosenberg and D. M. White, *Mass Culture and the Popular Arts in America* (Glencoe, Free Press, 1956).

W. Schramm and D. Roberts, *The Process and Effects of Mass Communication* (Urbana, Ill., University of Illinois, 1971).

E. Seiter, H. Borchers, G. Kreutzner, and E.-M. Warth (eds), *Remote Control* (London, Routledge, 1989).

G. Tuchman, *The TV Establishment* (Englewood Cliffs, NJ, Prentice Hall, 1974).


## Economic approaches to the media

T. P. Barwise, A. S. C. Ehrenberg, and G. J. Goodhart, 'Audience appreciation and audience size', *Journal of the Market Research Society*, 21, 4 (October 1979).

O. Boyd-Barrett, *Mass Communications in Cross Cultural Contexts: The Case of the Third World*, Mass Communications and Society DE 353, Unit 5 (Milton Keynes, Open University, 1977).

L. Brown, *Television: The Business Behind the Box* (New York, Harcourt Brace Jovanovich, 1971).

M. Cave, 'The conduct of auctions for broadcasting franchises', *Fiscal Studies*, 10, 1 (February 1989).

R. H. Coase, *British Broadcasting: A Study in Monopoly* (London, Longman Green, 1950).

——'The market for goods and the market for ideas', *American Economic Review* (1974), p. 384.

R. Collins, N. Garnham, G. Locksley, *The Economics of Television: The UK Case* (London, Sage, 1987).

——*The Economics of Television* (London, Sage, 1988).

J. Curran, 'Advertising and the press' in J. Curran (ed.), *The British Press: A Manifesto* (London, Macmillan, 1978).

——'Press freedom as a property right', *Media, Culture and Society*, 1, 1 (1979).

——'Advertising as a patronage system', *Sociological Review Monograph* 29 (1980).

——'The impact of advertising on the British mass media' in R. Collins *et al.* (eds), *Media Culture and Society: A Critical Reader* (London, Sage, 1986).

J. Curran, A. Douglas, and G. Whannel, 'The political economy of the human interest story' in A. Smith (ed.), *Newspapers and Democracy* (Cambridge, Mass., MIT Press, 1981).

R. Darlington, 'Telecoms: the broadband revolution', *Information Technology and Public Policy*, 8, 1 (winter 1989).

E. Epstein, *Broadcast Journalism. The Ratings Game* (Vintage, 1975).

J. E. Gerald, *The British Press under Government Economic Controls* (Minneapolis, University of Minnesota Press, 1956).

T. Gitlin, *Inside Prime Time* (New York, Pantheon, 1983).

G. J. Goodhart, A. S. C. Ehrenberg, and M. A. Collins, *The Television Audience: Patterns of Viewing* (Farnborough, Saxon House, 1975).

T. H. Gubach, *The International Film Industry* (Indiana, University of Indiana Press, 1971).

A. Henney, 'Regulating public and privatized monopolies: a radical approach', *Policy Journal for the Public Finance Corporation* (February 1986).

F. Hirsch and D. Gordan, *Newspaper Money* (London, Hutchinson, 1975).

P. M. Hirsch, 'Processing fads and fashions', *American Journal of Sociology*, 77 (1972).

S. Hoyer, S. Hadenius, and I. Weibull, *The Politics and Economics of the Press: A Developmental Perspective* (Beverly Hills, Calif., Sage, 1975).

R. E. Jackson, 'Satellite business systems and the concept of the dispersed enterprise', *Media, Culture and Society*, 1, 3 (1979).

F. D. Klingender and S. Legg, *Money behind the Screen* (London, Lawrence & Wishart, 1937).

M. Matson, 'Telecoms: the broadband revolution', Parliamentary Information Technology Committee 2 (22 November 1989).

A. Mattelart (trans. M. Chanon), *Multinational Corporations and the Control of Culture* (Brighton, Harvester, 1979).

K. Morgan and A. Sayer, *Microcircuits of Capital: Sunrise Industry and Uneven Development* (London, Polity Press, 1987).

V. Mosca, *The Political Economy of Information* (Madison, Wisconsin University Press, 1988).

G. Mulgan, *The Economics of the Media* (London, Polity Press, 1990).

G. Murdock, 'Redrawing the map of the communications industries: concentration and ownership in the era of privatization' in M. Ferguson (ed.), *Public Communication* (London, Sage, 1990).

G. Murdock and P. Golding, 'For a political economy of mass communication' in J. Saville and R. Milliband (eds), *The Socialist Register 1973* (London, Merlin, 1974).

——'Capitalism, communication and class relations' in J. Curran, M. Gurevitch, and J. Woollacott (eds), *Mass Communication and Society* (London, Edward Arnold/Open University, 1977).

Political and Economic Planning, *The British Press* (London, Political & Economic Planning, 1938).

——*The Factual Film* (London, Arts Enquiry, PEP, 1947).

——*The British Film Industry* (London, PEP, 1952).

K. Robins and F. Webster, 'Mass communications and information technology' in R. Milliband and J. Saville (eds), *The Socialist Register 1979* (London, Merlin, 1979).

H. Schiller, *Who Knows: Information in the Age of Fortune 500* (New Jersey, Ablex, 1981).

M. Sharp (ed.), *Europe and New Technologies* (London, Pinter, 1989).

A. Smith, 'Subsidies and the press in Europe', *Political and Economic Planning*, xliii, 569 (1977).

——*The Geopolitics of Information* (London, Faber, 1980).

——*Goodbye Gutenburg: The Newspaper Revolution of the 1980s* (London, Oxford University Press, 1980).

S. G. Sturmey, *The Economic Development of Radio* (London, Duckworth, 1958).

J. Taylor, 'The broadband revolution: implications for major networks', *Information Technology and Public Policy*, 8, 1 (winter 1990).

J. Tunstall, *The Media are American* (London, Constable, 1977).

T. Varis, 'The international flow of television programmes', *Journal of Communication*, 34 (1984).

F. Wolf, *Television Programming for News and Current Affairs* (New York, Praeger, 1972).

## Politics of British mass media

Adam Smith Institute, *Omega Report: Communications Policy* (London, Adam Smith Institute, 1984).

——*Funding the BBC* (London, Adam Smith Institute, 1985).

N. Ascherson, 'Newspapers and internal democracy' in J. Curran (ed.), *The British Press: A Manifesto* (London, Macmillan, 1978).

T. Baistow, *Fourth-Rate Estate* (London, Comedia, 1985).

D. Berry, L. Cooper, and C. Landry, *Where is the Other News?* (London, Comedia, 1980).

S. Brittan, 'The fight for freedom in broadcasting', *Political Quarterly*, 58 (1987).

——'The case for the consumer market' in C. Veljanovski (ed.), *Freedom in Broadcasting* (London, Institute of Economic Affairs, 1989).

Broadcasting Research Unit, *The Public Service Idea* (London, Broadcasting Research Unit, 1985).

M. Cockerell, *Prime Ministers and Television* (London, Macmillan, 1989).

R. Collins, 'Broadband Black Death cuts queues: the information society and the UK' in R. Collins *et al.*, *Media, Culture and Society: A Critical Reader* (London, Sage, 1986).

L. Cooper, C. Landry, and D. Berry, *The Other Secret Service* (London, Comedia, 1980).

J. Curran (ed.), *The British Press: A Manifesto* (London, Macmillan, 1978).

——'Reconstructing the mass media' in J. Curran (ed.), *The Future of the Left* (London, Polity, 1984).

J. Curran, J. Ecclestone, G. Oakley, and A. Richardson (eds), *Bending Reality: The State of the Media* (London, Pluto, 1986).

C. Dunkley, *Television Today and Tomorrow* (Harmondsworth, Penguin, 1985).

M. Ferguson (ed.), *New Communication Technologies and the Public Interest* (London, Sage, 1986).

C. Gardiner and J. Sheppard, 'Transforming TV: the limits of left policy', *Screen*, 25, 2 (1984).

N. Garnham, 'Public service versus the market', *Screen*, 24, 1 (1983).

——'Telecommunications policy in the United Kingdom', *Media, Culture and Society,* 7, 1 (1985).

Glasgow University Media Group, *Really Bad News* (London, Writers & Readers, 1982).

P. Golding and G. Murdock, 'Confronting the market: public intervention and press diversity' in J. Curran (ed.), *The British Press: A Manifesto* (London, Macmillan, 1978).

——'The new communications revolution' in J. Curran, J. Ecclestone, G. Oakley, and A. Richardson (eds), *Bending Reality: The State of the Media* (London, Pluto, 1986).

S. Hearst, 'The development of cable systems and services', *Political Quarterly*, 54, 3 (1983).

P. Hennessy, D. Walker, and M. Cockerell, *Sources Close to the Prime Minister* (London, Macmillan, 1985).

S. Holland, 'Countervailing press power' in J. Curran (ed.), *The British Press: A Manifesto* (London, Macmillan, 1978).

Labour Party, *People and the Media* (London, Labour Party, 1974).

S. Hood and G. O'Leary, *Questions of Broadcasting* (London, Methuen, 1990).

C. Landry, D. Morley, R. Southwood, and P. Write, *What a Way to Run a Railroad* (London, Comedia, 1985).

C. MacCabe and Olivia Stewart (eds), *The BBC and Public Service Broadcasting* (Manchester, Manchester University Press, 1986).

D. McQuail and K. Siane (eds), *New Media Politics* (London, Sage, 1986).

T. Madge, *Beyond the BBC* (London, Macmillan, 1989).

W. Melody, 'Communication policy in the global information economy: whither the public interest' in M. Ferguson (ed.), *Public Communication* (London, Sage, 1990).

Militant, *What We Stand For* (London, Militant, 1985).

E. Moonman (ed.), *The Press: A Case for Commitment* (London, Fabian Society Trust, 391, 1969).

G. Mulgan and K. Worpole, *Saturday Night or Sunday Morning* (London, Comedia, 1986).

R. Murdoch, 'Freedom in broadcasting', *MacTaggart Lecture 1989* (London, News International, 1989).

V. Porter, 'The Janus character of television' in G. Locksley (ed.), *Integration: The Single European Market and the Information Communication Technologies* (London, Pinter, 1990).

G. Robertson, *People Against the Press* (London, Quartet, 1983).

G. Robertson and A. Nicol, *Media Law* (London, Sage, 1985).

P. Schlesinger, 'From public service to commodity: the political economy of teletext in the UK', *Media, Culture and Society*, 7, 4 (1984).

J. Seaton, 'Government policy and the mass media' in J. Curran (ed.), *The British Press: A Manifesto* (London, Macmillan, 1978).

——'Broadcasting and politics in Britain' in R. Kuhn (ed.), *Broadcasting and Politics in Western Europe* (London, Sage, 1985).

——'The media and politics in Britain', *Journal of Western European Politics*, 6, 3 (June 1985).

——'Pornography annoys' in J. Curran (ed.), *Bending Reality: The State of the Media* (London, Pluto, 1986).

——'The media and the politics of unemployment' in S. Allen (ed.), *The Experience of Unemployment*, (London, Macmillan, 1986).

——'Atrocities and the media', *European Journal of Communications*, 2, 1 (January 1987).

——'The Holocaust: a case study of atrocities and the media' in J. Seaton and B. Pimlott (eds), *The Media in British Politics* (Aldershot, Gower, 1987).

——'Down with Aunt Tabitha: a modest media proposal' in B. Pimlott and T. Wright (eds), *The Alternative: Politics for a Change* (London, W. H. Allen, 1990).

J. Seaton and B. Pimlott, 'The struggle for balance: the BBC and the politicians 1926–1945' in J. Seaton and B. Pimlott (eds), *The Media in British Politics* (Aldershot, Gower, 1987).

C. Seymour-Ure, 'Leaders and the media' in J. Seaton and B. Pimlott (eds), *The Media in British Politics* (Aldershot, Gower, 1987).

A. Smith, *Subsidies and the Press in Europe* (London, Political & Economic Planning, 1977).

R. Sparks and I. Taylor, 'Mass communications' in P. Brown and R. Sparks (eds), *Beyond Thatcherism* (Milton Keynes, Open University Press, 1989).

C. Veljanovski (ed.), *Freedom in Broadcasting* (London, Institute of Economic Affairs, 1989).

J. Whale, *The Politics of the Media* (London, Fontana, 1980).

P. Whitehead, 'Reconstructing broadcasting' in J. Curran, J. Ecclestone, G. Oakley, and A. Richardson (eds), *Bending Reality: The State of the Media* (London, Pluto, 1986).

# Index

Note: Sub-entries are arranged in chronological order where significant: all others are in alphabetical order.

Abrams, Mark 207
accountability 362; broadcasting 4, 301–3, 322; market 278
ACCT Report 303
Adam Smith Institute 340, 367, 368–9
Adams, Mary 147
Addison, P. 187
Adorno, T. W. 250–5 *passim*
advertisers (pressures) 219–28
advertising 7–8, 298, 324, 340; and circulation 58–9, 64–5, 346, 347; commercial television 107, 123, 190, 193, 195, 206–8, 210, 219–28, 329–33, 338, 342, 352; growth 11–12; increased competition 322, 331; post-war 111, 172; press 38–44, 330–1, 346–7; press conglomerate 106–11, 114–18, 122; radical press 18–19, 64, 106–10, 321; radio 133; system 109–11; wartime 81; women consumers 109, 116, 222
*Advertising Quarterly* 212
agenda setting 262–3
Aitken, Ian 120
Aitken, Sir Max 85
Al Fayed brothers 99
Allaun, Frank 365
Alvarado, E. 267
Amalgamated Press 51
Anderson, Sir John 72, 74, 77, 80
Andrews, Alexander 28

Annan, N. 205
Annan Report (1977) 286, 296–8, 301–3, 305–6, 317–18, 322–3, 327, 330–1
Annand (editor) 56
announcers: BBC 170–2; ITN 200
anti-monopoly measures 285–6, 340, 343–5, 371
anti-Semitism 63
Anti-Waste League 59
appeasement, BBC and 149
appointments (to broadcasting authority) 357–8
Arendt, Hannah 251, 254, 255
*Ariel* (BBC staff magazine) 195–6
Arnold, M. 180, 323
Arrowsmith, Pat 362
art movies 318
Articles of Association 88, 102
Arts, Communications and Entertainments (Ministry proposal) 333
Arts Council 320
Askew, Barry 87
Asquith, Herbert H. 40, 59, 61
Asquith, Ivor 7–8
Associated Newspapers 90, 96
Associated Rediffusion 225
Association for the Promotion of the Repeal of the Taxes on Knowledge 29
Astor, D. 85
Astor, Lord J. J. 52
Atlantic Richfield 100–1
Attlee, Clement 74, 82, 147, 171

*ATV Showbook* 195, 199
audience: active 260–1;
    discovering (BBC) 131–3;
    knowledge 261–3; mass media
    3, 256–61, 267; television
    195–7, 203–32, 304, 328, 338,
    352; *see also* listeners
Audience Appreciation Index 223
audience creation 212; advertisers
    and 219–28; Channel 4 230–2;
    franchises/owners 217–18; IBA
    213–15; ownership/control
    218–19; public regulations and
    public interest 228–9; regions
    and 215–16; 1960s/1970s 229
Audience Research Department
    156
Audit Bureau of Circulation 64
austerity (BBC) 189–92
Austin, Sir Herbert 146
autonomy: broadcasting 269, 273,
    281, 309–10; commercial
    television 218; editors 355; *see
    also* independence
    (broadcasting)

Baistow, Tom 355
Baldwin, Stanley 49, 60–1, 67, 291
Bambridge, Anthony 104
Barnett, A. 270
barons, press (era of) 49–68, 315;
    empire creation 50–2;
    proprietorial control 52–6;
    profits and politics 56–8; rise of
    fourth estate 58–60; social
    order 61–3; modified economic
    controls 63–8
Barry (psychologist) 183
Bartholomew (editor) 66
Battle of Britain 157, 164, 175
BBC: accountability 299–300;
    advertising 368; expansion in
    1960s 201–2; finance 8, 341;
    news 153–4, 161, 170–5, 177,
    268, 329; public policy 317,
    321–5, 327, 329–30, 331;
    public service ideal 297–8, 303;
    radio separate from television

359; social reforms 178–88;
    television 189, 192–202, 212,
    217, 224, 229, 230–1; *see also*
    BBC (fall); BBC (origins and
    growth); BBC reforms;
    programmes (BBC); World
    War II (BBC in)
BBC (fall) 189–202; austerity
    189–92; commercial television
    and 192–202; monopoly ends
    201–2; *see also* BBC; BBC
    (origins and growth); BBC
    reform (alternative approaches)
BBC (origins and growth)
    131–50; audience 131–3; first
    Director General *see* Reith,
    John; as public corporation
    134–9; political independence
    139–41, 150; General Strike
    141–3, 168; and government in
    1930s 143–5; society and
    programmes 145–8; and
    journalism 148; and
    appeasement 149; end of
    decade 150; *see also* BBC;
    BBC (fall); BBC reforms;
    World War II (BBC in)
BBC reforms (alternative
    approaches) 340–2, 348–50,
    356–7, 359, 361, 368
Beadle, Gerald 193
Beavan, John 109
Beaverbrook, Lord W. M. A. 37,
    49, 51–6, 58–60, 74, 85
Becker, P. 259, 262
Beckett-Denison, E. 44
*Beehive* 37
Bell, Daniel 207, 235
Bellenger, Frederick 78, 80
Benjamin, W. 255
Benn, A. W. 353
Bennett, T. 172
Berelson, B. 259
Bernstein, Sidney 232
Berridge, Virginia 33–4, 35
Berry, Don 104
Berry brothers 51, 52, 85
Beveridge, W. 134, 135, 138–9,

198, 303
Beveridge Report (1942) 82
Beveridge Report (1951) 189–92, 297, 322
Bevin, Anthony 105
Bevin, Ernest 72, 76, 77, 164
bias 309, 321
bingo 113
Bird, C. K. (Fougasse) 206
Black, Conrad 90
Black, Peter 194, 195, 197, 199
Blackwood (journalist) 54
blasphemy laws 362
blitz, broadcasting and 151–77
Blum, Leon 174
Blumler, J. 261, 268
Blunden, E. 154
Board of Education 181
Board of Trade 326, 328
Boer War 47
*Bolton Evening News* 44
Boorstin, D. 266
Bourdieu, P. 273
Bowen, Elizabeth 173
Bracken, Brendan 76, 78, 165, 171
'brain washing' advertisements 206–8
Brains Trust 160, 162, 163, 165
Braverman, Henry 235
breakfast television 222
Bridson, D. G. 145, 147
Briggs, Asa 134, 175, 198
British Aerospace 99
British Board of Film Censors 244–5, 364
British Broadcasting Corporation *see* BBC
British Bureau of Market Research 226
*British Gazette* 141, 142
British Institute of Public Opinion 82, 154
*British Journalism Review* 292
British Satellite Broadcasting 239, 339, 350–1
British Standards Council 366, 367, 368–9
British Telecom 339

British Union of Fascists 60
Brittain, Vera 151
Brittan, Samuel 298–9, 316, 337, 369
broadcasters: announcers 170–2, 200; duties 358–9
broadcasting: accountability 301–3; appointments 357–8; control of 2–3; influence of 1–4; power of 1, 249–56; public policy 315–18, 320–9, 331–2; public service theory 295–310; reform (alternative approaches) 335–43, 348–53, 355–61, 364–70; state and 299–301
Broadcasting Act (1981) 286, 327, 355
Broadcasting Act (1990) 230, 296, 316, 327, 341–2, 349, 354, 359, 367, 369
Broadcasting Bill (1989) 304
Broadcasting Complaints Commission 355, 365
broadcasting history: influence 1–4; Reith/denial of politics 131–50; World War II 151–77; social revolution 178–88; fall of BBC 189–202; class, taste and profit 203–10; audience creation 212–32; information society 234–45; public service theory 295–310; *see also* BBC; media
Brown, F. J. 136
Brown, George 112
Brown, Lucy 33, 55
Bruntz, G. 152
Buckle, G. E. 54
Burnett, Leo 226
Burns, T. 193, 195, 198, 304
Burt, Cyril 181, 182–3
Buscombe, E. 267
Butler, R. A. 181, 184, 204

Cabinet Office 333
cable television: audience 228; conglomerates 95; free market

approach 338–9; information society 234, 236–9; media reform 338–9, 343, 350–2, 360, 365; public policy 234–5, 331, 332; public service theory 295–310

Cadbury, G. and family 52, 58

Calcutt Report (1990) 287, 316, 317

Calder, A. 156, 187

*Campaign* 216, 221

Campaign for Press and Broadcasting Freedom 292

Campbell, Commander 162, 163

Campbell, Lord 12

Camrose, Lord W. E. 51, 52, 85

Canada 324

capital: freedom of 35–8; *see also* costs (broadcasting); costs (film-making); costs (newspaper running/ setting up)

capitalism 19, 204, 252–4, 271–2, 274, 303, 344

capitalist: class blocs 100, 125; free press 7, 344; press expansion 26–7

Cardiff, D. 137–8, 199

Carnegie, A. 50

Cassandra (Connor) 79

Cassell, John 38

Castlereagh, Lord 13

censorship 8, 9, 146–7, 298, 319–20, 329–30, 353, 359, 363–4, 366–7; in information society 244–5

censorship (wartime): BBC 162–3, 165, 167, 169; communist press 72–3; defeat of 79–80; left press 73–9; resistance 71–2

Centre for Contemporary Cultural Studies 269

chains, press 50–2, 94, 99, 279–80, 283–5, 343, 344, 345

Chamberlain, Austen 61, 149

Chamberlain, Joseph 6

Chamberlain, Neville 60, 71

Chaney, David 7

Changing Television Group 358

Channel 3 (ITV) 341, 342, 348–9, 358

Channel 4 230–2, 241, 243, 295, 298, 318, 320, 323, 342, 343, 358

Channel 5 239, 305, 333, 339

character formation 178–9, 180–1

Charles, Prince of Wales 116

Chartists 18, 20–1, 32, 41, 45, 47

choice 307–9; consumer 281–5, 337–8, 349, 369; curtailment 118–19

Churchill, Winston S. 71, 73–8, 80, 132, 141–2, 149, 157, 163–6, 168, 191

Cinematograph Act (1927) 326

circulation, press: advertising and 58–9, 64–5, 346–7; increased 36–7, 42–3, 279–80; press barons and 50–1, 56–7; radical 15–16, 19, 20, 107–8, 111–12, 122–3

Citrine, Walter 144

*Clarion* 64

Clark, Sir K. 195, 196, 214

class 187, 359; and capitalist blocs 100, 125; conflict 22–3, 45; coverage and 109, 110; mass media and 269–71; radical press and 19–23; structure 117–18; taste and profit 203–10; *see also* middle class; working class

Cleave (publisher) 17, 34

closures, newspaper 72–3, 107–8, 281–2, 283, 354

coalition government 59, 60, 71, 73, 78

Coase, R. H. 131

Cobbett, William 12, 15, 19, 22

Cobden, R. 27

Cole, G. D. H. 140

Collet, C. D. 26

Collins, Norman 191, 192, 195

Collins, Richard 235

Colman (manufacturer) 44

comedy 176, 229

commercial: broadcasting 189,

213; controls (freedom from)
80–3; radio 341, 365
commercial television 189–202;
advertising *see* advertising;
audience 195–7, 215–16,
219–28; BBC fall and 189–202;
BBC as model 197–8; Channel
Four 230–2, 241, 243, 295,
298, 318, 320, 323, 342, 343,
358; competition 194–5, 212,
230, 242, 244; finance 198;
IBA 213–15, 220, 223, 228–9,
286, 298, 300, 302, 327–8, 341,
348, 353–4, 357, 359; ITV
(Channel 3) 341, 342, 348–9,
358; new programmes and
styles 198–201; news 199–200,
264; ownership 93–4, 217–19;
programmes 198–201, 213,
229; public policy 320, 323,
325, 327–8, 331; public
preference 208–10; public
regulation 228–9; public
service theory 295–8, 300, 302,
305; reforms (alternative
approach) 342–3, 348–9;
regions and franchises 212,
215–18, 343
'commercialization': of popular
press 9, 33; television 349
'common carrier' policy 347
*Commonweal* 35
communication revolution 335–71
communications policy 320, 327,
330, 333–4, 366
communism 207, 364
Communist Party 61, 62, 63, 72–3
communist press 72–3, 78–9
community radio 367
competition 27, 341; advertising
322, 331; commercial
television 194–5, 212, 230,
242, 244; industrial (for BBC)
134–7; media reform 340; press
56, 112–13, 281–5, 345, 346
complaints 355, 365
computers 235, 236, 333
confidence laws 362, 363, 364

conglomerates (press in age of)
84–126, 280–1; advertising system
109–11; choice curtailment
118–19; compliance and
resistance 102–6; market control
85–90, 106–7; mass market
111–16; media concentration
91–4, 95–8; ownership and
ideologies 123–6; popular press
117–18; profit/politics 94,
99–102; proprietors 85–94;
quality press 117–18; radical
press 107–8, 113, 116, 124;
technology (impact) 119–23;
*see also* multinationals
Connor (Cassandra) 79
Conrad (*Telegraph* proprietor) 105
Conservative Party 75, 204, 231,
237, 308, 323–4; BBC (fall)
189–92; conglomerates 87, 90,
101, 108, 110–12, 124–5;
media reform 349, 368–71;
press barons 58–60, 62; press
freedom 279, 286
conservative press *see* right,
political consumer choice
281–5, 337–8, 349, 369
Consumers' Association 346
contempt laws 363
control 136–7; of broadcasting
2–3, 357; financial assistance
and 317–18, 323; political 7–9,
11–12, 329; social 137–8, 269,
273–4; of television 218–19
Cook (editor) 56
Cooper, Duff 60, 155
Co-operative movement 73, 79,
124
copyright 362–3, 364
Corn Law 28
corporations: and commercial
television 217–18; and press
280–1; *see also* conglomerates
corruption, entertainment as 253
costs (broadcasting) 195, 198,
244, 365
costs (film-making) 317–18, 320,
326–8

costs (newspaper running/setting
up) 279, 283–4, 319, 345, 365;
early days 16–17, 35–7; rise of
37, 50–2, 63–4; fall in wartime
81–2; post- war 101, 113,
119–23
Coulton, D. C. 36
Council of Europe 351, 352
*Country Life* 164
Court of Star Chamber 7
Cowdray, Lord 36
Cowdray family 97, 101
Cox (news director) 200
Crawford Report (1926) 133, 297,
299, 321, 322
criticism of government (press)
73–9
Cromwell, Oliver 244
Crosland, C. A. R. 204, 209
Crossman, Richard 172, 173, 174
Cudlipp, Hugh 52–3, 67, 112
cultural: diversity of society
230–1, 356–7; force (BBC as)
131, 138–9, 154–5;
homogeneity 178–81, 187–8,
202, 204–6; pessimistic view
235, 245; standards 323, 328–9,
332, 369; television standards
208–9, 215, 221, 243
culture, mass 250, 254–5
current affairs 200–1, 268, 329–30

*Daily Chronicle* 36, 50, 58
*Daily Citizen* 37–8
*Daily Express* 32, 37, 160;
conglomerates 86, 108, 110,
114, 116; press barons 52–6
*Daily Graphic* 58
*Daily Herald* (later *Sun*) 8, 36–8;
conglomerates 85–6, 108–11,
113–14, 116, 124; press barons
56–8, 63–5; public regulation
73, 82
*Daily Mail* 32, 35, 46, 132, 194,
199, 292; conglomerates 86,
105, 108, 110, 114, 116; press
barons 50, 53–7, 60–4; public
regulation 86

*Daily Mirror* 32; conglomerates
85–6, 90, 110–13, 115; press
barons 50, 52, 60–1, 66–7;
public regulation 73–82
*Daily News* 39–40, 58
daily newspapers 42–3, 50–2,
91–3, 101, 279–80, 282–3, 344;
*see also individual papers*
*Daily Record* 50, 95
*Daily Sketch* 86, 108
*Daily Star* 89–90, 116, 119
*Daily Telegraph* 56, 57;
conglomerates 86, 90, 94, 105,
108, 110, 115, 117
*Daily Worker* 52, 63; public
regulation 72–3, 78–9, 80
Dalton, Hugh 138, 140, 144
Dalziel, J. H. 42, 52, 58
Day, Sir Robin 200
Deane, Basil 154
Delane, J. T. 55
democracy, industrial 360–1
Department of Education and
Science 334
Department of Trade and Industry
334
depoliticization of press 113, 116,
124
deregulation 324, 337–8, 340,
341, 359, 367, 368, 369
determinism (class/market) 269–74
Diana, Princess of Wales 116
Dicks family 42
direct elections 358
direct satellite broadcasting 339
*Dispatch* 20
Disraeli, Benjamin 36
diversification policies 94, 99–102
diversity: free market 278; mass
media (threats to) 337
documentaries 135, 199, 201, 214,
224
Donald (editor) 56
Driberg, Tom 54, 199, 208
Dunkirk 156–7, 164
Durkheim, Emile 251
Dyer, R. 267

Eady levy 326, 327, 328
Eaton (acquittal of) 12
Eckersley, Peter 132, 147, 148, 154
Eckersley, Roger 154
economic controls 319–20; modified 63–8
Economic and Social Research Council 320
economic structure (radical press) 16–19
Economic Warfare, Ministry of 167
*Economist* 64, 198
editorial content 113–16
editors 85–90, 99–100, 289, 359–60; autonomy 355; *see also* journalists education: advancement 44–5; by broadcasting 178; social control 273–4; social revolution 181–4
Education Act (1944) 181–4
EEC 124, 327, 351–3, 354, 362; *see also* Europe; European Commission; Europeans (attitudes to USA)
Eerie County Survey 256, 259
efficiency 317–18
election campaigns 200, 204, 257, 259, 261–2; *see also* political/ politics
electronic publishing 338–9
Elliot, P. 264
*Empire News* 108
empires, press (creation) 50–2
Empson, W. 154
*Encounter* 138, 193
ENSA 154
Ensor, Sir Robert 55
entertainment: BBC radio 180, 184–6; mass media 3, 253, 266–7; politics of 329–30; television 194–6, 198, 205–6, 209–10, 215, 223–4
Epstein, J. A. 16
Europe 318, 343, 353; *see also* EEC
European Commission 351–3

Europeans (attitude to USA) 250
Evans, Harold 85, 88–9
*Evening Echo* 42
*Evening News* 60
evening newspapers 42, 51, 280, 283; *see also individual papers*
*Evening Standard* 52, 89
evolutionary model (media reform) 360
experience, class, culture and 270–1
experimental psychology 259–60

Fair Trading Act 343–4
Fairlie, Henry 191
Falk, Bernard 54
Falklands War 302
fascism: emergence 60, 251–2; fear of 151–2, 166, 174–5
Federal Communications Commission 354
Ferrie, William 146–7
*Field* 164
Fielden, L. 21
films 136; censorship 298; Eady levy 326, 327, 328; finances 317–18, 320, 326–8; legislation 326–8; on television 201, 318
finances *see* costs
financial assistance: control and 317–18, 323–4; film industry 327–8; media reform 319–21, 327, 345–8 *passim*
*Financial Times* 97
Finn, D. 270
Food, Ministry of 159, 162, 176
Foot, M. R. D. 173
Foot, Michael 55
foreign: broadcasts (wartime) 172–4; commercial radio 194; imports on television 347, 352–3; investment 327–8; ownership of USA television 354
Foreign Office 143–5, 167
Fougasse (Bird) 206
fourth estate 8, 305; proprietorship 280–1; rise of

58–60
Fox, C. J. 7, 12
Fox TV 93
France 305, 319
franchises 212, 217–18, 320,
 340–3, 349, 353–4, 370, 371
Frankfurt School 249–56
Fraser, Sir Robert 214, 215, 219
Fraser Stores Group 99
free broadcasting 303–5
free market approach (media
 reform) 326, 335–6, 337–40;
 social market approach 335–7,
 340–8
free press 316, 337–40; struggle
 for 11–23; symbol of
 democracy 80; theory of 277–93
free trade debate (press) 60
freedom: of capital 35–8;
 expression 361–5; information
 333, 362; to publish 278–9; of
 speech 333; *see also* free press
Freedom of Information Act 362
freesheets 92, 120, 282–3, 344
Frith, S. 272
fundamentalist approach (reform)
 357, 359–60

Gardiner (editor) 56
Garnham, Nick 235, 271, 304
Gater Report (1949) 317
Gaudet, H. 259
General Forces Network 185, 194
General Strike (1842) 23
General Strike (1926) 62, 141–3,
 168
George V 146
Germany 238; Frankfurt School
 249–56
Gielgud, Val 161
Gilbert, Martin 142, 149
Giles (cartoonist) 160
Giles, Frank 88
Gitlin, T. 266
Gladstone, H. G. J. 27, 29
*Glasgow Evening News* 50
*Globe* 58, 77
Goebbels, J. 71, 175

Goldie, G. W. 185, 193, 200, 201
Golding, P. 264
Goodhardt, G. J. 225, 226–7
Gorden, Lincoln 134
Gordon, D. 268
Gorham, Maurice 148, 170
Gott, R. 149
government: and BBC (1930s)
 143–5; criticism of (press)
 73–9; *see also* state
Grade, Sir Lew 199, 217
Graham, Willie 143
grammar schools 180, 182, 187
Grant, P. 270
grants (media reform) 346, 347,
 350
Graves, G. (BBC Deputy
 Director) 144, 161
Greene, Sir Hugh 202, 203, 210,
 229
Greenham Common protest 104
Greenwood (editor) 56
Gresham, Sir T. 252
Grimsditch. Peter 89–90
Grisewood, H. 153
Grote, Q. 26
*Guardian* 86, 120, 362; *see also
 Manchester Guardian*

Haley, Sir W. 186, 192, 198, 217
Halifax, Lord 144
Hall, Stuart 269–70, 272–3
Hamilton, Sir D. 108
*Handbooks* (BBC) 133, 139, 156,
 174, 179, 198
Handley, T. 159–60
Hankey, Lord 183
Hardy (acquittal of) 12
Harmsworth, Sir Lester 51
Harmsworth brothers *see*
 Northcliffe; Rothermere
Harper and Row 94
Harper Collins 94
Harris, Ralph 181
Harrison, Tom 157, 161
Harrop, Martin 262
Hartwell, Lord 100
Hastings, Max 105

Hattersley (machine-maker) 35
Hattersley, Roy 370
'Haw Haw, Lord' 155–6
Hay, Ian 184
Hayek, F. 252
Healey, Denis 124
Heath, Edward 103
Hebdige, D. 272
Heller, C. 302
Hetherington (publisher) 16, 17, 19
Hetherington, Alastair 90
'Hi Gang' 176
Hibberd, Stuart 170
Hickson, W. 29
Higham, Sir Charles 40
Hill, William 17
Hilton, Isobel 104
Hilton, John 160
Hirsch, F. 268
Hitler, A. 63, 75, 154, 249, 255
Hobson, J. 17, 151–2
Hodson, C. A. 176
Hoggart, Richard 204–5, 206
Holland 360
Holland, Stuart 353
Hollinger 98
Hollis, P. 16
Home Intelligence Report 76
Home Morale Emergency Committee 70, 171
Home Office 151, 333
Home Security, Minsitry of 71
Home Service 161, 169, 185, 187, 193, 196
homogeneity, cultural 178–81, 187–8, 202, 204–6
Hone (acquittal of) 12
Hood, Stuart 200, 229
Hoover, H. G. 136
*Horizon* 159, 161
Horkheimer, M. 251, 252
House of Fraser 99
Hovland, C. I. 259–60
Howard, Anthony 99
Howkins, John 235
Hulton group 51
human interest 109, 113–16

*passim*, 126
humour 176, 229
Hunt Report 296, 298, 331
Hurd, Douglas 350, 369, 370
Hussey, Marmaduke 357
Huxley, Julian 138, 162

IBA 213–15, 220, 223, 228–9, 286, 298, 300, 302, 327–8, 341, 348, 353–4, 357, 359
ideology: mass media and 269–70; press ownership and 123–6
impartiality 358; of BBC 200
imperialism 46
Incitement to Disaffection Act 362
indecency laws 364
independence (broadcasting) 303–7, 357–8; *see also* autonomy
*Independent* 89, 105, 121, 122, 123
*Independent on Sunday* 123
Independent Press Authority 353–4
independent television *see* commercial television
Independent Television Commission 220–1, 341, 342
Independent Television Companies Association 213
individualism (loss) 251–2
industrial democracy 360–1
industrial relations 125; *see also* strikes; trade unions
industrialization, leisure and 253–4
industrialization of the press 32–47; advertising 38–44; freedom of capital 35–8; impact 44–7
influence (personal) 256–61
information: control 361–5; politics of 329–30; technology *see* information society; understanding and 259–60
Information, Ministry of 70, 72, 78–80, 82, 149, 151, 154–5,

165–9, 171
information society 234–45;
  censorship 244–5, 366; politics
  and new technology 242–4;
  public service broadcasting
  (end of) 239–42
Information Technology Advisory
  Panel 237
Institute of Economic Affairs 340,
  369
Institute of Practitioners in
  Advertising 107
institutional pluralists 267–9
integrated approach (policy) 332–3
intelligence testing 182–4
International Publishing
  Corporation 96, 110
International Thomson
  Organization 94, 97, 344
intervention policies 318–26; *see
  also*, media reform (alternative
  approaches)
interventionist proprietors 85–90
Inveresk chain 58
investigative journalism 281,
  362–3
investment 340; foreign 327–8
IPC 96, 110
*Ipswich Express* 44
ITMA 159–60, 176
ITN 199–200
ITV 341, 342, 348–9, 358

Jackson, B. 205
Jacob, Sir Ian 195–6
Japan 238, 319
Jarrow March 63
Jay, Peter 338
Jenkins, Simon 89
Jenner, Peter 342
Jennings, Humphrey 154
Joad, C. E. M. 162
*John Bull* 42, 65
Jonscher Report (1987) 350
journalism 148, 355; investigative
  281, 362–3
journalists: editorial role 360;
  education 288, 290; importance

86, 88–9, 124; independence
  303–5, 317; mass media 264–5;
  resistance 102–6; self-
  regulation 363; unfair dismissal
  355; union 119, 287, 289
Joyce, W. (Lord Haw Haw) 155–6
*Justice* 35

Katz, Emmanuel 173, 258, 261
Kemsley, Lord 51, 52, 85
Keynes, John Maynard 138
King, Cecil 66, 67, 74, 78, 82, 85,
  100, 112
Kinnock, Neil 124, 292, 354–5
Kipling, Rudyard 49
Koss, S. 9, 84–5, 86–7, 89
Kumar, Krishan 235, 304

labour movement *see* trade unions
Labour Party 137, 231; BBC (fall)
  189–90; class (taste and profit)
  203–4, 208; conglomerates 85,
  87, 89–90, 108–12, 124–5;
  media reform 342, 348,
  359–60, 368–71; press barons
  era 60–1, 66; press
  industrialization 33, 43; public
  regulation 73, 78–9, 82
Labour Party Study Group 292
Lamb, Sir Larry 88
Lambert, R. S. 139, 147
lame ducks, state and 326–7
Lansbury, George 42–3
Laski, Harold 144
Lasswell, H. D. 152, 252, 254
Launch Fund proposal 345, 371
Lawrence, D. H. 205
laws *see* legislation
Lawson, Edward 56
Lazarsfeld, P. 253–4, 257–9
  *passim*
Leavis, F. R. 205, 207, 250
Lee, A. J. 9
*Leeds Intelligence* 18
*Leeds Mercury* 18, 45
Leeds University Centre for TV
  Research 341
left *see* communism; Communist

Party; communist press; radical/
left press
legal freedom of expression 361–5
legal right of reply 365
legislation: education 181–4; films
326–8; freedom of expression
361–5; libel 7, 12, 363;
monopoly 285, 286, 343–5;
television 213, 215, 217
Leigh, David 99
leisure 93–4, 132, 205–6, 253–4,
333–4
Lewis, Sir George 29
libel laws 7, 12, 363
Liberal Party 32, 45, 61–2, 78
liberal pluralism 296
liberal theory (press freedom)
277; competition in 281–5;
freedom to publish 278–9;
functionalist view 290–1;
labour market 291–2;
proprietors 279–81, 291–3;
reforms 285–8; reworked
theory 288–90
liberalism: failure 251–2; neo-
338–40, 342, 352, 359, 368–9,
371
*Liberator* 17
libertarianism/paternalism
(conflict) 335, 361–7, 369–70,
371
licence fees 7, 133, 145, 195–7,
202, 322, 324, 348–50, 352, 359
Liddell, A. 170
*Life in London* 15
light entertainment *see*
entertainment
Light Programme 185, 187, 191,
196, 198
*Listener* 147, 160, 161, 163, 168,
173, 176, 185, 201, 207
listener, BBC 131–3; cultural
homogeneity 178–80, 187–8,
202; model of 180; wartime
151–3, 156, 161–6; *see also*
audience
literacy levels 44
'live' viewing hours 240

Lloyd, Edward 36, 50, 52, 56
Lloyd, Selwyn 190
Lloyd George, David 58, 59, 61,
71, 75, 144
*Lloyds Weekly* 15, 34, 50
local newspapers 43, 46–7, 280,
282–4, 331, 333
local radio 327, 339, 342, 359
Local Radio Authority 342
London Business School 232
*London Daily News* 121
London Dispatch 16, 17, 18, 19,
34
*London Evening News* 50
Long, Gerald 88
Lonrho 98, 99, 102, 103, 122, 344
Lorymer (editor) 17
Luxembourg radio 194
Lynd, R. and H. 250
Lynn, Vera 161
Lytton, E. G. B. 26

McBarnett, A. 266
McCombs, M. 259, 262
MacDonald, Ramsay 60, 142
McGregor Report (1977) 319
Macintyre, Donald 103–4
McKay, M. 116
MacLaine, Ian 168
MacLeod, Joseph 171
Macleod, Lewis 54
Macmillan 94
Macmillan, Harold 137
McQuail, Denis 125, 242, 257, 260
magazines 42, 51, 57, 279, 330,
331, 333, 353
Maguire (politician) 25
*Mail on Sunday* 119
*Manchester Guardian* (later
*Guardian*) 55, 82, 217
Marcuse, Herbert 250–5 *passim*
market: access 117–18; approach
(free) 326, 335–40; approach
(social) 335–7, 340–8; controls
106–7; mass media and 3, 269,
271–2; pluralism free 271–2;
press barons and 50; *see also*

mass markets
market research 82; BBC 154,
   156, 167, 169–70; mass media
   effect 256–9; press barons 57,
   64–5; press conglomerates 109,
   110, 117; television 190–1,
   196, 207, 222–6, 231
Marsden, D. 205
Marsh, Richard 112
Martin, Kingsley 152
Marwick, A. 138, 187
Marx, Karl 42
Marxists 61
mass culture 250, 254–5
mass markets 219–28 *passim*;
   consensual pull 111–16
mass media *see* media
Mass Observation 154, 157, 167,
   169, 175; *see also* market
   research
mass society 255–6
Massingham (editor) 56
Matheson, Hilda 134, 141, 148,
   180
Matthews (publisher) 89, 90
Maxwell, Robert 90, 91, 94–5,
   112, 344, 355
Mayhew, Christopher 191, 200
Meacher, Michael 353, 354
media: influence/objectives 1–4;
   ombudsman 363; organization
   263–9; ownership 91–4, 286;
   politics (map) 367–71; power
   3–4, 206–8, 255–7; press
   conglomerates and 91–102;
   public policy 315–34;
   sociology of 249–75
Media Enterprise Board
   (proposed) 345–6, 348, 371
media reform (alternative
   approaches): free market
   approach 337–40; media
   politics 367–71; paternalism/
   libertarianism (conflict) 361–7;
   polarizations 335–7; public
   service approach 348–55;
   radical public service 355–61;
   social market approach 340–8

'Media Show' 231–2
Melba, Dame Nellie 132
Merton, R. 254
MI5 357
middle class 254, 342; BBC and
   138; press 15, 41–5, 81,
   109–10, 117–18, 347; tastes
   203–6 *passim*, 226, 323; *see
   also* class
Militant Tendency 359
Milner-Gibson, T. 29
Ministry of Arts, Communications
   and Entertainment 333
Ministry of Economic Warfare 167
Ministry of Food 159, 162, 176
Ministry of Home Security 71
Mi/nistry of Information 70, 72,
   78–80, 82, 149, 151, 154–5,
   165–9, 171
minority media 213, 214, 227–8,
   230–2, 318, 342, 347, 348, 352
mixed programming 179, 186,
   342, 351, 354
modern schools 182, 187
Monopolies Commission 285,
   286, 344
monopoly: anti- (measures)
   285–6, 340, 343–5, 371; BBC
   189–92, 201–2; laws 285, 286,
   343–5; local press 280, 281
'Mopp, Mrs' 160–1
moral regulation 366, 367, 368
morale, wartime 151–3, 156, 160,
   259–60
More, Hannah 44
*Morning Advertiser* 18
*Morning Chronicle* 18
*Morning Post* 18, 58
morning press *see* daily
   newspapers
Morrison, H. 74, 78, 135, 140
Mosley, O. 143
Moyne Report (1936) 317
Mugabe, Robert 102
Mulgan, Geoff 342, 370
Mullin, Chris 353–4
multinationals 333; *see also*
   conglomerates

Murdoch, Rupert 84, 87–91, 93, 95, 99, 102–3, 110, 120–3, 239, 273, 286, 340, 344–5, 354
Murdock, Graham 100
Murray, Gilbert 163
Murrow, E. R. 165
music publishing 330
MVDS 339

Napoleonic Wars 13, 22, 164
'narcotyzing dysfunction' of mass media 253
National Coal Board 103
National Film Finance Corporation 320, 326, 327, 328
National Graphical Association 120
National Health Service 162–3
national newspapers 43–4, 50–1, 86, 90, 101, 107–8, 111–16, 278–84 *passim*, 344; *see also individual papers*
National Print Corporation 345
national security 362, 365–6, 368
National Television Council 191
National Union of Journalists 119, 287, 289
National Union of the Working Classes 18, 20–1
nationalism 45–7, 151–2
Nazism 63, 75, 249–50, 252, 255
NCVR 360
Neild, A. 88, 103–4
neo-liberalism 338–40, 342, 352, 359, 368, 369, 371
neophiliac view (information society) 235, 245
neutrality (free market) 200, 277
New Deal 265
New Fabian Research Bureau 137
*New Outlook, The* 137
*New Statesman* 152–3, 160, 165, 199, 208
new technology *see* information society; technology
news: making 264–5; mass media 268; media reform 345, 351, 353–4; press 345; pseudo-

events 265–6; radio 153–4, 161, 166–8, 170–5, 177; television 199–200, 215, 268, 320, 358; values and power 272–3
*News Chronicle* 57, 82, 86, 108, 109, 124
News Corporation 95
*News of the World* 34, 35, 87, 116
*News on Sunday* 107, 121, 122
Newspaper Emergency Council 79
Newspaper Proprietors' Association 73, 74, 289–90
newspapers *see* press
newsprint rationing 81–2, 106, 113, 331
Next Five Years Group 137, 138
Nicholson, H. 70, 166, 171, 176, 186
Nkomo, Joshua 102
Northcliffe, Lord A. C. W. 35, 49–56, 59, 61, 86, 132
*Northern Daily Express* 44
*Northern Echo* 97
Northern Ireland 356, 357, 369
*Northern Leader* 44
*Northern Star* 15–18, 21, 36, 41, 45
Northumberland, Duke of 58
Norwood Report 182

O'Brien, C. C. 17
obscenity laws 364, 367
*Observer* 11; conglomerates 85, 90, 99, 102–3, 115, 117, 120; press barons 58, 62
O'Connor, F. 20, 21
Odhams group 58, 63–4, 65, 110
Official Secrets Act 362, 371
Ogilvie (BBC Director General) 144, 153, 184
ombudsman, media 363, 365
Open Broadcasting Authority (proposed) 317–18, 323
opinion leaders 170, 258–9
opinion polls *see* market research
ORTF 305
Orwell, George 154, 307, 361

outside broadcasts 145, 169–70
Owen, Frank 159
owners, franchises and 217–18
ownership: commercial television
    93–4, 217–19; ideologies and
    123–6; media (concentration)
    91–4; media (control) 343–4,
    360; media (joint) 286; press
    11–13, 16–19, 279–81; *see also*
    barons, press (era of);
    conglomerates (press in age of)

Page, Bruce 345
Palache Report (1944) 328
*Pall Mall Gazette* 39, 58
Palmerston, H. J. T. 27
pamphleteering 9
paper shortages 81–2, 106, 113,
    331
'paranoid theory of change' 251
Parnell, Val 199
paternalism 348; and
    libertarianism (conflict) 335,
    361–7, 369-70, 371
patriotism 63, 156–61
pay television 324–5, 338–9, 340
Payne, Jack 154
Peacock Committee 8, 298–9,
    317–18, 323–5, 329, 331,
    340–2, 348, 369
Pearson, Sir C. A. 58, 97
Pearson group 51, 52, 93, 101
Pelham, C. 13
Pelling, H. 187
Penguin 93
people *see* audience; listener,
    BBC; public; readers of press
*People* 52, 115, 116
*People's Paper* 42
PEP 137
Pergamon 94, 95
personal influence (role) 256–61
personality: BBC employees
    154–5; press barons 85, 87–90;
    Reith 132–3, 137, 139–40
pessimism, cultural 235, 245
Philimore, Dr 21–2
Pickles, Wilfred 171

*Picture Post* 82, 168
Pilkington Report (1962) 203,
    206, 208–10, 213, 229, 297,
    300, 303, 322–3, 330
Pimlott, B. 138
Pimlott, J. A. R. 265
pirate radio 210
Place, Francis 26
pluralism 297, 303, 309, 360;
    audience knowledge 261–3;
    free market 271–2, 296; mass
    media and 267–9; personal
    influence and audience 256–61,
    274–5
policy: contradictions 315–34;
    goals 327–9; pressure groups
    and 330–2; unified (for
    communications) 333–4
political/politics: affiliation of
    press 43, 45; bi-partisanship
    86; Channel 4 230–2;
    consensus 62, 200; control 7–9,
    11–12, 85–6, 100–1, 329;
    coverage (changed) 57, 66–7,
    111–12; denial of (BBC)
    124–30; depoliticization (press)
    113, 116, 124; elections 200,
    204, 257, 259, 261–2; of
    entertainment 329–30;
    information disclosure 361–5;
    left- wing *see* radical/left press;
    mass media 249–52, 254,
    257–63, 265–6, 267–8, 270–1;
    media (map) 367–71; media
    reform 347, 359–60, 367–71;
    new technology and 242–4;
    power 84, 86–7, 106–7;
    prejudice 39–40, 73–9; press
    barons and 49, 58–60; profits
    and 56–8, 94, 99–102; public
    service theory 295–310 *passim*;
    right-wing 32, 45, 87, 120,
    123–4, 321; television 200–2,
    203–4, 216, 228, 242–4, 261–2;
    *see also* state
Political and Economic Planning
    137
Political Intelligence Department

167
*Political Quarterly* 151–2
*Political Register* 19, 20, 22
Pollitt, Harry 143
Poole, I. 143
*Poor Man's Guardian* 17, 18, 20, 23
pop music 272, 342
popular press 111–18
popularization of press 33–4, 56–8
pornography 351, 364, 366, 369
Portugal 263
Post Office 131, 132, 133, 134, 135
'Postscripts' 164–5
post-war period *see* conglomerates (press in age of)
Powell, E. 263
power (media) 3–4, 206–8, 255–7, 272–3
press: advertising 38–44, 330–1, 346–7; barons *see* barons, press (era of); BBC and 168–9; chains 50–2, 94, 99, 279, 283–5, 343–5; costs *see* costs (newspaper running/ setting up); empires (creation) 50–2; franchises 370, 371; freedom 3, 7, 277–93; influence 1–4; ombudsman 363; power of 1, 249–56; profits 7–8, 16–17, 19, 81, 94, 99–102, 125, 331; public policy 315–17, 319–21, 323, 326–31, 333; quality 107, 113, 117–18, 331; reform 25–30, 285–8, 336, 343–8, 353–5, 363–4, 367–8, 370–1; stamp duty 7, 12–15, 16, 17, 19, 27–30; television competition 329, 330; *see also* free press; media; press history
Press Amalgamations Court 285
Press Association 345
Press Commissions *see* Royal Commissions on the Press
Press Council 287–8, 293, 355, 363, 367
press history: influence 1–4; Whig

press 7–9; free press struggle 11–23; reform 25–30; industrialization 32–47; press barons 49–68; public regulation 70–83; conglomerates 84–126; *see also* free press; media; press
Press Ombudsman 363, 365
Press Subsidy Board (Sweden) 345, 348
pressure groups 170, 330–2
Prices and Incomes Board 317
Priestley, J. B. 158, 161, 163–6 *passim*
print technology 35, 326
Printing and Publishing Industry Training Board 288
privacy rights 340, 363, 365, 367, 371
privatization 338, 342, 368
production workers 355
professionals (broadcasting) 303–5
profit: BBC 135–6; class and taste 203–10; commercial television 202, 209, 213, 218, 228–9; conglomerates' 94, 99–102; politics and 56–8, 94, 99–102; press 7–8, 16, 17, 19, 81, 94, 99–102, 125, 331
programme schedules 2, 219–28
programmes (BBC) 145–8, 229; media reform and 348–9, 352; social reform 178–88; wartime 153–6
programmes (commercial television) 198–201, 213, 229
promotions (and press barons) 56
propaganda 259–60, 265, 270; BBC 136, 141–2, 151–2, 154, 174–5; German 155–6, 174–5; newspaper 49, 59–61, 70–6; power of press/ broadcasting 249–56
proprietors *see* ownership
protectionism 352
provincial newspapers *see* local newspapers
pseudo-events 265–6
psychology, experimental 259–60

public: BBC attitude 151–3, 156–66; *see also* audience; listener, BBC; readers of press
public affairs 112, 114–16
public good 322–3
public interest 228–9
public opinion 187, 362; press and 33, 124, 277; *see also* market research; opinion leaders
public policy (contradictions) 315–34
public preferences 208–10
public regulation 228–9, 321–3, 341
public regulation, press under 70–83; censorship (defeat) 79–80; censorship and resistance 71–2; commercial controls 80–3; communist press 72–3; left-wing press 73–9; satellite television 351
public service: approach (traditional) 335–7, 348–55; ideal 295–7; press 290; radical 335–6, 355–61
public service broadcasting 197–8, 214, 217, 219, 228–9, 321–6; end of 239–42; theory 295–310
Public Service Broadcasting Council (proposed) 341, 342, 348
Pye Radio 190

quality press 107, 113, 117–18, 331

racism 63, 364, 366–7, 370; and press barons 63
radical/left press 353; advertising 18–19, 64, 106–10, 321; circulation *see* circulation, press; decline 32–3, 107–8, 124–5; de-politicizaiton 113; economic structure 16–19; growth (in wartime) 70–1, 79–80; harassment (in wartime) 73–9; impact 19–23; moderated to attract readers 39–40; struggle for 11–23; working class and 1, 14, 15, 17–23, 27, 30
radical public service 335–6, 355–61
radio: advertising 133; commercial 341, 365; community 367; local 327, 339, 342, 359; pirate 210; press conglomerates and 96–7, 330; privatization 342; reforms 342–3; *see also* BBC; media
Radio Authority 342
*Radio Times* 155, 160, 165, 170, 173
ratings, television 194, 195, 215, 222
Read, Herbert 154
readers of press: numbers per copy 14–16; press barons and 60–4; wartime 81–2
*Real Lives* (BBC programme) 357
record industry 330
Reed group 90, 96
reform *see* media reform (alternative approaches)
reform of press 25–30, 336–7, 343–8, 353–5, 363–4, 367–8, 370–1; Commission programme (1949–77) 285–8
regional press *see* local newspapers
regional television 215–16
Regulation 2D 78, 79
reinforcement 257–8
Reisman, D. 253
Reith, John 168, 189, 198, 301–2; denial of politics 131–50; social reform 178–80, 184, 186
Reithian paternalism 348, 368, 369–70
Renshaw, Patrick 142
repetition in media 253–4
*Republican* 12, 20
resistance (by journalists) 102–6
resistance movement 172–3
Reuters 119, 145

*Reynolds News* 15, 16, 18; co-operative takeover 64; conglomerates 85, 108, 124; industrialization 32, 34, 39, 41–2; public regulation 73, 82

Reynolds, George 41, 42

Riddell, Lord G. A. 52

right, political 32, 45, 87, 120, 123–4, 321

right of reply 365

Riley, Nigel 168

Roach, Professor 7

Robens, Alfred 112

Roberts, Wilfred 78, 80

Robson, William 134, 135, 140

Rodgers, Bill 120

Roebuck (politician) 26

Rose, R. 204

Rosenberg, D. 253, 254

Rothermere, Lord 49–52 *passim*, 56, 58–60, 66, 85, 90

Rowland, 'Tiny' 90, 98, 99, 102–3, 123

Royal Commissions on Press 94, 107, 278–93, 317, 319–21, 326–31 *passim*

royalty 116, 146

rumours, wartime 166–7

rural life 164–5

Russia *see* Soviet Union

Ryan, W. 165

sales *see* circulation, press

Sarnoff, David 131

satellite television 228, 296; conglomerates 94, 99; information society 235, 239, 241; media reform 335, 338, 341, 345, 350–2, 365, 370; public policy 325, 332, 333

Scannell, P. 137–8, 199

Schramm, W. 257

Science Research Council 320

scientific management 304

*Scotsman* 97

Scott, C. P. 55

*Scottish Daily News* 107

SDP 112, 120

secrecy, official 362, 371; *see also* censorship

security rights 365–6

self-interest 315

self-regulation 363

Selsdon Report (1935) 198

sensationalism 34

serious content (media) *see* cultural

sexism 364, 370

Seymour-Ure, C. 262–3, 305, 306–7

Shah, Eddy 120, 121–2

Shaw, B. 138

Shils, E. 153

Shirley, John 103–4

Short, Clare 367

Silvey, Robert 156, 161, 163, 196

Simon, Brian 181, 184

Simon of Wythenshawe, Lord 192

'simulcasting' 339

Sinn Fein 369

Skidelsky, Robert 138

Sky Television 94, 100, 239, 339, 345

Smith, A. C. H. 81

Smith, Anthony 141, 194, 197–8, 229, 235, 267–8, 305–6

Smith, Joan 104

Smith, W. H. 36

Snooks, W. J. 54

Snowden, Ethel 139–40

Snowden, Philip 139

social: change (wartime) 82; cohesion 125–6; control 137–8, 269, 273–4; engineering 178, 181–4, 187–8, 366; justice 163, 165, 177; order 21–3, 44, 60–3, 125–6, 164–5; pattern (readers) 16–23; reform 178–88; relations 254–5; revolution, broadcasting as 178–88; system 44–5

social market approach 335–7, 340–8

socialism 204, 342

society 145–8; media influence 1–4; social system 44–5

*Sociological Review* 180
sociology of mass media 269–75;
   determinism 269–74; Frankfurt
   School 249–56; media
   organizations 263–9; pluralism
   256–63
Somerville, Mary 148
South Africa 102
*South Shields Gazette* 44
Soviet Union: BBC and 173–4;
   press 61, 70, 79
*Spectator* 42
spectrum management 341, 343,
   354
Spens Report (1938) 180, 181
spot advertising 190, 221
Spring Rice (politician) 14
stamp duty 7, 12–17, 19;
   campaign 27–30
*Standard* 58
standards: cultural 323, 328–9,
   332, 369; television 208–9,
   215, 221, 243
state: attitude to media 315–17;
   benign 321–6; broadcasting and
   299–301, 310; efficiency
   317–18; integrated approach
   332–3; lame ducks 326–7;
   policy goals 327–9; politics of
   information and entertainment
   329–30; pressure groups 330–2;
   as threat 318–21; unified
   communications policy 333–4;
   *see also* government; political/
   politics; public regulation;
   public regulation, press under
Stephen, J. F. 29
Stevens, Lord 90, 91, 96, 344
Stevenson family 44
Stoessel, Sue 227
Stoppard, Tom 277
Strachey, John 158, 160
streaming (in schools) 182–3
strikes 125; General Strike (1842)
   23; General Strike (1926) 62,
   141–3, 168; Wapping dispute
   120–1
student readers 117

subsidies 319–21, 327, 345,
   346, 348
Summerfield, S. 87
*Sun* (earlier *Daily Herald*) 87,
   105, 109–10, 112, 114, 116,
   119, 292
*Sunday Citizen* (earlier *Reynolds
   News*) 108
*Sunday Correspondent* 121, 123
*Sunday Dispatch* 108
*Sunday Express* 36–7, 52, 64, 115
*Sunday Graphic* 108
*Sunday Mail* 50
*Sunday Mirror* 115, 116, 117
Sunday newspapers 43, 91–3, 101,
   280, 344; *see also individual
   papers*
*Sunday People* 115, 116, 117
*Sunday Pictorial* (later *Sunday
   Mirror*): conglomerates 115,
   116; press barons 50, 52, 66,
   67; public regulation 73, 74–5,
   81–2
*Sunday Sport* 122
*Sunday Telegraph* 94, 119
*Sunday Times* 15, 64;
   conglomerates 85, 87–8, 103–5,
   108, 123, 286
*Sunday Today* 121–2
*Sunday Worker* 63; *see also Daily
   Worker*
Sutcliffe, Peter 116
Sweden 319, 345, 346, 348, 363
Swingewood, A. 255
Sykes Report (1923) 133, 136,
   296–7, 299, 300
Symons, Julian 141

Tallents, Sir Stephen 135, 144
TAM 195
taste 161–6, 203–10, 349
Taverne, Richard 200
'taxes on knowledge' *see* stamp
   duty
Taylor, A. J. P. 61, 132
Taylor, Robert 120
Taylor, Vice-Admiral 59
technical schools 182, 183–4, 187

technology (new): effects 119–23, 332–3; 371; politics and 242–4; press and 281–5, 321, 337; *see also* cable television; information society; satellite television; videos
teletext 332–3
television: advertising *see* advertising; audience 195–7, 203–32; foreign imports 347, 352–3; legislation 213, 215, 217; pay 324–5, 338–9, 340; and press conglomerates 93–4, 95–8, 330; ratings 194, 195, 215, 222; reforms *see* media reform (alternative approaches); *see also* BBC; cable television; commercial television; media; satellite television; teletext; videos
Television Act (1954) 215, 219
testing, intelligence 182–4
Thatcher, Margaret 88, 90, 99, 111, 299, 357, 368, 369
Third Programme 186, 187, 196
Thomas, H. 162, 195, 199
Thomas Nationwide Transport 120
Thompson, E. P. 270
Thompson, J. W. 66, 190
Thompson, Lord R. H. 85, 101, 117, 215–16
Thomson Organization 94, 97, 344
Tillotson family 44
*Times, The* 11, 18, 27, 152, 156, 191, 217, 353; conglomerates 85–8, 94, 99–101, 105, 108, 117, 286; press barons 50, 52, 54–5, 62, 65
Tisdall, Sarah 362
Titmuss, R. 153, 160, 175
*Today* 87, 121–2
Tomalin, Claire 103
Tooke (acquittal of) 12
topicality (BBC) 159, 169–70; *see also* news
Topping, Sir Robert 59
totalitarianism *see* fascism
Touraine, Alain 235

Tracey, Michael 229, 266, 267, 303
trade unions: BBC and 146–7; press and 16–18, 26, 32–3, 62, 119–21, 124–5, 265, 289, 291–2, 337; press barons 62; radical press and 19–23, 26, 32; wartime censorship and 79–80; *see also* TUC
*Trades Newspaper* 17
traditional public service approach (media reform) 335–6, 348–55
Trafalgar House 101
Trelford, Donald 102–3
Trenaman, J. 257
Trevelyan, Sir Charles 136, 152, 299
Triangle 94
*Tribune* 36
TROS 360
TUC 33, 43, 58, 73, 79, 109, 118, 124, 142, 144
Tuchman, G. 264
Tunstall, J. 86, 106
Twentieth-Century Fox 93
'twinning' (BBC and ITV) 224
*Twopenny Trash* 15, 20

Ullswater Report (1936) 147, 297, 300, 322
understanding, information and 259–60
Unemployed Workers' Movement 62
unfair dismissal 355
unified policy (communication) 333–4
United Empire party 59
United Newspapers 96, 101
United States 333; attitudes to UK in wartime 173; broadcasting 249, 322; cable television 239–41, 324, 360; distaste for 250; film industry 326–7, 328; imported programmes from 353; news and public opinion 265; television 191, 193, 213,

215, 218–19, 341, 352–4
USSR *see also* Soviet Union
'V' campaign 172–3
Vansittart, R. G. 145
VARA 360
Veljanovski, Cento 340
Vernon (psychologist) 183
Victoria, Queen 46
Video Recordings Act 364
videos 93, 223, 234, 239–40, 241,
    243, 298, 332, 364
violent programmes 351, 364,
    366, 367
*Voice of the People* 17
*Voice of West Riding* 17
Volunteer Force 32

wages 11, 44, 113, 121, 195
wants, real and false 208–10
Wapping dispute 120–1
war *see* Falklands War; World
    War I; World War II (BBC in)
Watson (publisher) 17, 56
Waugh, E. 53, 162
Webb, B. 138, 139, 140, 141
Webb, S. 138, 140
*Week* 72
*Weekend* 96
*Weekly Dispatch* (later *Sunday
    Dispatch*) 15, 50, 53
weekly newspapers 13, 43, 50–1,
    92, 279–80, 282–3, 344; *see
    also individual newspapers*
*Weekly Police Gazette* 15, 20, 34
Wells, H. G. 138
West, R. 155
*Westminster Gazette* 36, 46–7, 58
Westminster Press 93
Whale, John 8, 84–5, 277
Whicker, Alan 215
Whig press history 7–9
White Papers: on broadcasting
    186; on cable television 240,
    296, 298
Whitehouse, Mary 368
Wilby, Peter 103
Williams, Francis 8
Williams, Raymond 9, 206, 270

Williams Committee 364
Willis, P. 271, 273
Wilmott, P. 205, 206
Wilson, H. H. 191, 192
Wolf, F. 218
women 366; advertising aimed at
    109, 116, 222; in BBC 148;
    opinion leaders 258–9; press
    360; working class 160–1
Wooler (acquittal of) 12
Woolf, Leonard 101
Woolton, Lord 191
worker participation 360–1
'Workers' Playtime' 176
working class: conglomerates and
    106–7, 109–11, 123–5; mass
    media and 255, 271–2, 274;
    myth of disappearance 203–6;
    press and 37, 81, 346; press
    barons and 61–2, 67–8; radical
    press and 1, 14–15, 17–23, 27,
    30; television 195, 202, 209,
    210, 229; women 160–1; *see
    also* class
working hours 44
Working Party on the Film
    Industry 330–1
Works Ministry 159
World War I 134, 141
World War II (BBC in) 149–50;
    first months 153–5; news
    166–8, 170–5, 177; patriotism
    156–61; people (morale)
    151–3; people (serious attitude)
    161–6; press and 168–9;
    programme changes 155–6;
    propaganda 174–7; social
    reform 178, 181–8; topicality
    159, 169–70; *see also*
    propaganda; public regulation
Worsley, Frank 160
Wright, Basil 154
Wyatt (politician) 200

XYZ club 137

*Yearbook* (BBC) 179
*Yearbook* (ITV) 192

*Yorkshire Post* 44
Yorkshire Television 93
Young, M. D. 205, 206
Young, Stuart 357

Zec (cartoonist) 76
Zimbabwe 102
Zinoviev letter 61